PUBLICATIONS OF
THE WELLCOME INSTITUTE FOR THE HISTORY OF MEDICINE
Catalogue Series Amer. 1 (1983)

Medical

AMERICANA

in the Wellcome Institute Library

Frontispiece. BARRIOS, Juan de. *Verdadera medicina, cirugia, y astrologia.* Mexico: F. Balli. 1607. **(M.9)**

An Annotated Catalogue of

Medical
AMERICANA

in the Library of the Wellcome Institute for the
History of Medicine

by
ROBIN PRICE
Deputy Librarian

*Books and printed documents 1557–1821 from Latin America and the
Caribbean Islands and Manuscripts from the Americas 1575–1927*

LONDON
THE WELLCOME INSTITUTE FOR THE HISTORY OF MEDICINE

1983

The Wellcome Institute for the History of Medicine
183 Euston Road
London NW1 2BP

First published 1983

ISBN 0 85484 040 0

Composed in APS 4 Bembo and printed
in Great Britain by Spottiswoode Ballantyne Ltd
Colchester and London

CONTENTS

1. LIST OF FIGURES

2. PREFACE

The Latin American Collection, which forms part of a larger collection on medicine in the Americas as a whole, is an amalgam of three important collections in Latin American medicine. The collection made by Sir Henry Wellcome [1853–1936] resulted from his manufacturing and commercial activity which early focused his attention on the history of therapeutically active plants native to the Americas. Wellcome's continued interest led him in 1927 to purchase the third collection of Dr. Nicolás León [1859–1929], the Mexican obstetrician, historian of medicine, bibliophile, bibliographer, and sometime Director of the Museo Nacional de México.

Finally, the Wellcome Trustees acquired in 1962 the collection of Dr. Francisco Guerra [b. 1916], bibliophile, bibliographer, and historian of Latin American medicine, whose remarkable knowledge of the bibliography of Latin American colonial medicine brought the collection as a whole to fruition. For a number of years after its acquisition and during the tenure of a Wellcome Fellowship, Dr. Guerra worked on the arrangement of the collection and on the documentation of a card and printed catalogue to it. Without Dr. Guerra's enthusiasm and devotion this collection, and therefore of course the present catalogue by Mr. Robin Price, would not exist.

PETER O. WILLIAMS
Director

3. INTRODUCTION

I. *The Books and Printed Documents (1557–1821)*

(a) *Definition and comments*

The 1,200 printed items from colonial Latin America and the Caribbean which appear in this catalogue comprise a small but important part of the 6,000 volumes of the specially housed American collection.

Place. The catalogue includes books and printed documents relating to medicine and surgery published in the Americas south of the Rio Grande in pre-1822 colonial territories as diverse as the Spanish Viceroyalties of New Spain (Mexico), New Granada (Colombia and Venezuela), Peru, and La Plata (Argentina), the Captaincy-General of Guatemala, and the Portuguese Viceroyalty of Brazil; it also includes similar material from the Caribbean islands, whether Spanish, French, or English speaking. Cuba, Guadeloupe, Martinique, Saint-Domingue (Haïti), and Jamaica, all therefore appear in this category.

Date. The catalogue of printed work is confined to the years 1557 to 1821, as an approximation both to the colonial facts and to the nature of the collection. The first date is the year of publication of the *Phisica, speculatio* of Alonso de la Vera Cruz by Juan Pablos in the City of Mexico, of which the library holds a fine copy, and with which scientific publishing in the New World can reasonably be said to have been instituted. By 1821 most of the newly independent colonies of the Hispanic Empire had begun to take their modern shape, and, by a fortunate but perhaps not altogether fortuitous occurrence, this date is within a year of the date set by Robert B. Austin in his most useful *Early American medical imprints; a guide to works printed in the United States 1668–1820*, Washington, D.C., Public Health Service, 1961. Since in due course a parallel but unannotated catalogue is envisaged for the North American part of the Institute's American Collection, the choice of the year 1821 as the term for the present catalogue was regarded as particularly appropriate.

The choice of 1821 inevitably means that some anomalies result. Medical imprints after 1821 from such long-remaining colonies as Cuba (1898) are for instance excluded; the same applies to Jamaica (1962); and to a substantial group of 160 books, pamphlets, and documents published in the newly-named country of Mexico between 1822 and 1833, where the Establecimiento de Ciencias Médicas took the place of the ancient Real

Tribunal del Protomedicato already abolished in 1831. The familiar and insoluble question of formal versus psychological dependence is, however, always likely to remain open. This apart, it was decided that the advantage for reference purposes of one final date for the whole catalogue of printed items far outweighed the more scholarly precision of strict adherence to the formal dates of secession for each of the eleven political units of the American colonial period represented in this collection. Medical works in the Institute published in those countries which remained under colonial domination after 1821 are easily retrievable either through the card catalogues housed with the collection, or in some cases on the shelves, since many of the works are arranged in chronological order of publication within their country of origin.

In passing, it should be noted that where national independence brought about a change to a name now more familiar to us (e.g. the change from New Spain to Mexico), the colonial name is given in parenthesis in the contents list together with the dates during which it existed under the status relevant to this catalogue. Users needing to establish political status of a colony at any particular date will find a ready and reliable guide in Henige (1970); but they should be warned that detailed knowledge of the often surprisingly complex changes of political master and status (particularly in the Caribbean) is impossible to make clear within the confines of a handlist and requires careful search in a wider range of literature.

The manuscripts (1575–1927) of the collection, whose scope in place and time is necessarily different from that of the printed items, are introduced separately in Section II below.

The sources of the collection have already been described in the Preface to this catalogue; it is here sufficient to add that the items which it contains are often of unusual rarity and interest and are found housed together only in the Wellcome Institute. These works, with the rich background collection of contemporary European imprints relating to the impact of American materia medica on European medicine (also from the original Wellcome collections); with the national histories of medicine and works on regional materia medica (primarily collected by Dr. Guerra); with the diverse array of modern secondary literature still in course of collection; with the many specialist and uncommon bibliographies; with the collection of rare and important colonial and post-colonial periodical titles (including the *Gazeta de Mexico* 1728–39, the *Gazetas de Mexico* 1784–1809, the *Mercurio volante* 1772–73 (the first medical periodical published in the Americas); and with the complete set of the *Gaceta médica de México* from 1864; together make the collection a uniquely rich source of material for the study of the development of medicine in Latin America and the Caribbean.

It should be added that the collection includes 303 Mexican theses, brief studies, and reprints (1862–1950) primarily on indigenous materia medica; about 2,000 reprints (separately catalogued and subject-indexed) from the collection of Dr. Nicolás León; and a recently re-classified and re-catalogued collection of 19th and early 20th century American travel literature, including much of classic ethnographical importance on the American Indians of North, Central, and South America, and their medical concepts and healing practices. All this interesting material falls outside the categories of date and origin laid down for this catalogue. Of considerable marginal interest, but for reasons of expense and time deliberately omitted from the present catalogue, are: (i) the small pamphlet invocations to saints in times of pestilence published primarily in the City of Mexico, of which there are 76 in the collection published from 1702 to 1821, and a further 28 items from 1822 to 1850; (ii) the 66 colonial imprints on hospitaller orders and Provincial Councils of the Church, which have some bearing on the practice of colonial medicine; and (iii) the 424 broadside theses of medical interest presented before the Royal and Pontifical University of Mexico from 1598 to 1820, all of which already appear in Francisco Guerra, *Iconografía médica mexicana*, Mexico, Imprenta del Diario Español, 1955. On the other hand it was thought appropriate in so specialized a catalogue to include, without format statement or bibliographical or other comment, brief entries for the 113 facsimiles of printed works deriving from the region, since the original material, particularly that from Saint Domingue (Haïti), is rare or otherwise difficult of access.

(b)   *Entries*
The cataloguing procedures follow those originally described in the first volume of the *Catalogue of printed books in the Wellcome Historical Medical Library* (1962) and reprinted with modifications appropriate to the later period in the introduction of Volume III (1976) of the same series. Further minor modifications were necessary for the present specialized catalogue. In transcribing titles for instance, the original spelling, punctuation, and accentuation (or lack of it) have been preserved, as far as possible, beyond the year 1800 (laid down as the limit for this particular method of transcription in the introduction to Volume III (1976) of the catalogue series) to 1821, the term of the catalogue; as much of the title has been transcribed as will indicate clearly the contents of the work. Circumflexes in the original text have been ignored and *grave* accents where they appear in the original text have been transcribed as the modern acute accent. An '&c.' is frequently inserted, particularly for the transcription of official documents whose title has often had to be used as the text of the entry. Items under the same entry have been placed in date order, as more meaningful for the purposes of this catalogue than the more usual alphabetical order of title. Family names remain in their original form; Christian names have been modernised and accented according to present usage.

(c)   *Annotations*
The annotations provide bibliographical citations, bibliographical comments,

biographical notes, and notes on the contents of the item where that is not already covered by the entry itself. Fuller annotations have been adopted for the few 16th century imprints in the catalogue, which are regarded as 'American incunables', and which survive in a limited number of copies, often in a highly defective state. Few annotations have been provided for theses, almanacs, or for items whose entry is self-explanatory, unless they include material of exceptional interest. The author entry, the title transcription, and the annotations are intended to act as a single condensed source of information and reference.

(i) *Bibliographical citations* are more numerous for the earlier period, where interest has in the past tended to concentrate. All available specialized and reasonably sound bibliographical sources have been listed for early items including even the unreliable J.M. Beristáin de Souza (except where he is more than usually inaccurate) since his errors and guesses tend to reappear in Nicolás León, *Bibliografía mexicana del siglo XVIII*, 7 vols., Mexico, F. Díaz de León [&c.], 1902–1945, and on occasion in other bibliographies. To minimize complication in bibliographical citation, entry numbers are referred to wherever possible; but since Beristáin's system in the 1883 edition of his *Biblioteca hispano-americana septentrional*, Mexico, Ediciones Fuente Cultural, used for this catalogue, is particularly complex, it was thought best to refer to the volume and page number where the entry begins. Sabin, as a general American bibliography not at all inclusive within the field of this catalogue, and to a great extent superseded in the Hispano-American area by Palau, has not been listed.

(ii) *Bibliographical comments* have been made for the most part in abbreviated form, but in a rather more expanded form with regard to the few American incunables and early 17th century works in the collection, where it was thought that complexity, peculiarity, or rarity warranted it. Detailed bibliographical descriptions have not been thought appropriate even for the 'incunable' period in a catalogue which includes material of later and more diverse interest. A full list of bibliographical references is provided at the end of the catalogue.

(iii) *Biographical notes* incorporate details principally of medical interest; much that is generally known is therefore omitted as available, if required, from common sources. Where the details given are generally available from encyclopaedias or medical and biographical dictionaries, or from the full text of the title-page of the item under consideration, no reference to source has been made. Where the sources disagree, or where the source is obscure, or where substantial research has been carried out, the reference is given. A full list of such general citations is provided at the end of the catalogue. Dates of birth and death are provided as part of the author heading wherever possible.

(iv) *Notes on contents* are intended only to amplify the information already implicit in the transcription of the title-page where it seemed necessary, or to add such information where it is wanting. Such information is frequently an essential aid to the rapid assimilation, for instance, of the contents and relative importance of late 18th century official documents and pamphlets from New Spain, in which this collection fortunately abounds. Additional comment has been inserted only when it seemed strictly necessary. Translation from the Spanish has been avoided wherever possible despite the risk of littering the English annotations with the italicised names of Spanish institutions, offices, words of connotation peculiarly Hispanic. *Cátedra de prima de medicina* and *Protomédico* are, for instance, untranslatable into English institutional formulae, and for the purposes of this specialized catalogue need not be attempted. The English meanings of Hispanic academic titles and phrases are conveniently defined for the unspecialized reader by John Tate Lanning, *The University in the Kingdom of Guatemala*, Cornell University Press, 1955, at pages vi–ix.

(d) *Periodicals*

The medical and non-medical periodicals whose first number was issued before 1822 form a separate alphabetical sequence at the end of the main sequence of entries for printed books. Many Latin American periodicals exist in the American Collection (129 titles in all), and form part of the full roster of some 2,670 periodical titles, both historical and modern, available in the Wellcome Institute Library. Many of the colonial periodicals are of some rarity.

II. *The Manuscripts (1575–1927)*

(a) *Definition and comments*

This section includes all those manuscripts of American interest in the Wellcome Institute of whatever date, whether of Latin American, Caribbean, or British provenance, which were intentionally omitted from S.A.J. Moorat's 3-volume catalogue of Wellcome Manuscripts. Like the printed items they too derive from the Wellcome, León, and Guerra collections, and they are of unusually mixed provenance. Some are of great interest. Among the more notable are: an *expediente* relating to the ill-health of Melchor Antonio de la Cadena y Sotomayor [1539–1607], Dean of Tlaxcala; the *Pojha Ñaña*, a text on indigenous materia medica written *c.* 1730 by the priest Marcos Villodas, S.J., in Old Guaraní; a summary of both the well-known *Pars prima physiologica* of Marcos José Salgado [1671–1740] published in Mexico in 1727, and of the second part (containing tractates on pathology and fermentation), seemingly unpublished, and apart from this manuscript, otherwise unknown; and an order in the hand of George Washington [1732–99], first President of the United States, to his English suppliers, for household and plantation supplies including medicinal, culinary, and veterinary items.

(b)   *Entries and annotations*

The primary purpose of the catalogue of the manuscripts has been to establish authorship, date, and provenance; to provide the date of acquisition whenever known; to provide compendious notes on contents either by transcribing existing titles or by abbreviated notes; and to provide notes on the author wherever possible. The references are incorporated in the general citations at the end of the catalogue. Critical comments have been added where it seemed necessary. When no author has been traced the manuscript has been entered under the first word of the title; where the author may be regarded as a government department or as an institution, the manuscript has been entered under the appropriate contemporary name of the Viceroyalty, Captaincy-General, region, or city, followed by the name of the department or institution, in the manner usual for printed books. As to the date of acquisition, it may be assumed that items from the León Collection were purchased by Sir Henry Wellcome in 1927 and that the items from the Guerra Collection were purchased by the Wellcome Trustees for the Institute in 1962. The remainder were acquired singly or with other similar material on diverse occasions.

III.   *The Catalogue: comments and acknowledgments*

(a)   *Bibliographies and indexes*

A list of bibliographical references and another of general references appear at the end of the catalogue; these cover both the printed and the manuscript items. Where general references are particularly obscure or where they relate only to the one item under examination they are quoted in full in the entry and omitted from the list of references.

A name index also appears at the end. A subject index, notoriously artificial for the changing concepts of medicine, particularly over a period of nearly 400 years, has not been attempted.

(b)   *Latin American Studies*

The implementation of the Report of the Parry Committee of the University Grants Committee of 1965 resulted in a renewed interest in Latin American studies in the United Kingdom which this specialized catalogue may do something to further. The place of the collection within the study of history as a whole must of course be sought not only within the extensive medical and general historical material available within the American Collection and the larger reference collections of the Wellcome Institute Library, but also within the social, economic, and political material available in the more general academic libraries which specialize in Latin American studies. The catalogue is intended for use by both the medical historian and the regional specialist, and is intended, with its bibliographical and general references, to act as a guide through a maze of often conflicting and sometimes not wholly satisfactory reference material. It is hoped that the annotations err neither on the side of over-specialism, nor on the side of over-generality.

(c) *Acknowledgments*

It has been a privilege to have been so closely involved with this unique collection, and I hope that this preparatory work will be of use to future workers in the growing area of Latin American, colonial, and historical medical studies. My thanks are due to all my colleagues past and present but I would like to record my especial gratitude to the late Dr. Nöel Poynter, former Director of the Institute who originally allotted me this fascinating task; to Eric Gaskell, formerly Librarian of the Institute, for his original enthusiasm and for his lively encouragement of the project; to my colleague Eric Freeman, Deputy Director and Librarian of the Institute, for his unfailing kindness and patience, and for his interest and assistance in matters of presentation of this catalogue; to Mr. H.R. Denham, formerly Chief Cataloguer to the Institute Library, whose early advice on the minutiae of cataloguing style for the project was greatly appreciated and to a large extent adopted, and whose index completes this catalogue; and to Mrs Christine English who had the unenviable task of double-checking the proofs. Any errors, or deviations from the usual Wellcome cataloguing style, are of course my sole responsibility. I hope that in bringing this project to a conclusion I return to my colleagues both here and in the Americas at least a part of that debt which is always due to other workers in the field.

ROBIN PRICE

4. ABBREVIATIONS

Used in bibliographical enumerations.

Argentina	A.1–9
Brazil	B.1–13
Columbia	C.1–3
Cuba	Cu.1–6
Guadeloupe	G.1–3
Guatemala	Gt.1–17
Haïti	H.1–56
Jamaica	J.1–6
Martinique	Ma.1–4
Mexico	M.1–221
Peru	P.1–34
Periodicals	Per.1–19
Manuscripts	WMS. Amer. 1–149 (ADAMS-ZACATECAS)

5. THE CATALOGUE

A. Printed Materials 1557–1821

ARGENTINA

1780–1813

A.1 **ARAUJO, José Joaquín de**

Guia de forasteros del Vireynato de Buenos-Ayres para el año de 1803. Dispuesta con permiso del Superior Gobierno. *tables (2 fldg.)*. 2 ll., pp. 180 (=182), 3 ll. (last 2 bl.).

8vo. [Buenos Aires:] Real Imprenta de los Niños Expósitos. [1803].

Furlong 675.
Medina (Buenos Aires) 253.

This copy wants the subsidiary title-page *Estado político del Vireynato del Rio de la Plata . . . . Para . . . 1803* at Sig. D3 [i.e. pp. 37–38] and Sig. O1 [i.e. pp. 113–114 of the text]. A *Nota* of one leaf has been inserted between Sig. X3 and X4 [i.e. pp. 174 & 175], not included in the pagination. The final blank leaf of the last gathering has been removed.

The almanack, produced by the *Visitador general* of the Real Hacienda, includes historical and financial details as well as full lists of public appointments in Buenos Aires and the Intendancies, in the civil, ecclesiastical and military departments. It is the fullest contemporary account of the state of the Viceroyalty before its disappearance. A final note refers to a corrected edition for 1804 which did not in fact appear.

Though the name of the *Visitador general* of the Real Hacienda, Diego de la Vega, appears on the title-page, the compiler was observed by Medina to have been the third Clerk of the Contaduría [see p. 46 of the *Guia*], a native of Buenos Aires who became *Ministro general de las cajas* after the revolution. Earlier but briefer *Guías de forasteros* for the Viceroyalty had appeared in Buenos Aires in 1781, 1782, 1792–95, and 1797.

A.2   **GORMAN, Miguel [1736/49–1819]**

Instrucciones para la inoculacion vacuna. pp. 20.

4to. Buenos Aires: Imprenta de Niños Expósitos. 1813.

Furlong 2938.
Medina (Buenos Aires) 289.
Molinari (1941) 11 (pp. 66–70).
Molinari (1943) p. 37.

This second edition of a terse and factual pamphlet originally published at the same press in 1805 describes the local symptoms following vaccination, the distinguishing signs of unsuccessful vaccination and its probable causes, the methods of collecting and preserving the fluid, and the several methods of vaccination. It also describes the constitutional symptoms in normal cases, and the topical remedies occasionally required in cases of difficulty; it advises re-vaccination whenever doubt arises.

Gorman, the most distinguished physician of his day in Río de la Plata, was born in Ireland and studied in Rheims and Paris where he qualified as physician. In 1770–71 he studied inoculation in England, and in 1777 arrived in Río de la Plata with the expedition against the Portuguese in South America, headed by Pedro de Ceballos Cortés y Calderón [first Viceroy 1776–78]; at the time of his appointment as *Protomédico* in 1779 [see A.7] he was Director-General of the military hospitals of Montevideo and Buenos Aires. He remained as *Protomédico* until 1816. [See Cantón 1921, *i*, pp. 319–359; Furlong (1947), pp. 160–164; and Molinari (1959), pp. 257–287].

A.3   **HERMANDAD DE LA STA. CARIDAD**

Reglamento acordado por la Junta de gobierno de la Hermandad de la Sta. Caridad [&c.]. 2 ll.

4to. Buenos Aires: [Real Imprenta de los Niños Expósitos]. 1798.

Furlong 536.
Medina (Buenos Aires) 216.
Molinari (1941) 6.

This by-law circulated to the charitable ladies of the city forbids the contribution of elaborate bed-linen and limits expenditure on this and on the supply of a day's food to the women patients in the Hospital de Mujeres. Copies are dated January [ ] 1798; the copy used by Medina and another illustrated by Molinari (1941) have the date [i.e. 20] January inserted in MS at the end, and [14] January inserted as the date of the meeting of the *Cabildo* at the beginning.

The Hospital de Mujeres is said to have been founded in 1766 or 1767, but the founder of the Hermandad de N.S. Jesucristo, Juan Guillermo Gutiérrez González y Aragón, had already established a room for poor women patients by 1743. By the 1780s it had become a large and well-regulated body [see Molinari (1937), pp. 83–91].

A.4　**HERMANDAD DE LA STA. CARIDAD**

[Begins:] La Hermandad de la Sta. Caridad, que anhela con el mayor empeño al servicio de las pobres enfermas del Hospital de su cargo, se propuso proporcionarles la mas comoda habitacion que le fue dable [&c.]. 2 ll. (2nd bl.).

fol. Buenos Aires: [Real Imprenta de los Niños Expósitos]. 1798.

Furlong 528.
Molinari (1941) 7.

This circular letter directed to the ladies of the city seeks their assistance in supplying changes of bedding or a day's food each month for the patients in the Hospital de Mujeres. Plenary indulgences are offered in return. Copies are dated January [ ] 1798; the copy illustrated by Molinari (1941, fig. 12) has the date [i.e. 20] January inserted in MS. The letter may therefore have accompanied the *Reglamento* of the same date [see entry above].

A.5　**HERMANDAD DE LA STA. CARIDAD**

[Begins:] Señoras que caritativamente se han hecho cargo de proveer de camas á los cincuenta y un canceles destinados para pobres enfermas [&c.]. 2 ll.

fol. Buenos Aires: [Real Imprenta de los Niños Expósitos]. 1798.

Furlong 537.
Molinari (1941) 8.

This circular sets out the names of the 50 ladies against the numbered list of 51 beds in the Hospital de Mujeres to which they have been assigned; it reminds them of the rules against elaborate bed-linen. Dated June [ ] 1798.

A.6   **HERMANDAD DE LA STA. CARIDAD**

[Begins:] Numero 2. Señoras que caritativamente alimentan á las pobres enfermas del Hospital de mugeres en varios dias del año [&c.]. 1 l.

broadside. [Buenos Aires: Real Imprenta de los Niños Expósitos. 1798].

Furlong 532.
Molinari (1941) 9.

The second part of the preceding circular listing the names of 27 ladies who regularly contributed 5 pesos towards the care of poor patients.

A.7   **RIO DE LA PLATA. Laws, statutes, &c.**

[Begins:] Ynformado del desarreglo, y ábusos con que se exercita la medicina, cirujia, y la pharmacia, y phlebotomía á ellas anexa, con especialídad en las províncias distantes de esta, capital, he resuelto por áhora establecer, y crear en ella un Tribunal de Proto-medícato, como lo hay en las Ciudades de Lima, y Mexico [&c.]. 2 ll. (2nd bl.).

fol. Buenos Aires: [Real Imprenta de los Niños Expósitos]. 1780.

Furlong 2.
Medina (Buenos Aires) 4.
Molinari (1941) [1].

This circular and its variants, illustrated and commented on by Molinari *et al* (1965), are dated variously in MS 17 August or 16 November of the same year. The present copy, neither signed nor dated in MS, is identical to that illustrated at fig. 4 of the paper cited; unhappily, however, the printer of that paper has transposed figs. 3 and 4 so that the text no longer relates to the figures as numbered. All variants bear the printed date 1780, the first year of printing at Buenos Aires on the press formerly belonging to the Jesuits brought at the command of the Viceroy from Córdoba (de Tucumán).

The circular sets out the decision of Juan José de Vértiz y Salcedo [Viceroy 1778–84] to establish the Protomedicato and to appoint Miguel Gorman as *Protomédico* [see A.2]. He requests the decision to be made known in all areas, and forbids future practice by the medical professions unless they have qualified by examination. Those then practising as physicians, surgeons, blood-letters and apothecaries are to submit their qualifications to their local justices for forwarding to the Protomedicato; those not submitting their qualifications will be forbidden to practise.

The Protomedicato was officially inaugurated on 17 August 1780 [see WMS. Amer. 78 (GORMAN)] and was established as a teaching body by a Real Orden of 19 July 1798. [See Canton (1921), *i*, pp. 201–234.]

Figure 1.

✠

YNFORMADO del desarreglo, y ábusos con que se exercita la Medicina, Cirujia, y la Pharmacia, y Phlebotomia à ellas anexa, con especialidad en las Provincias distantes de esta, Capital, he resuelto por àhora establecer, y crear en ella un Tribunal de Proto-medicato, como lo hay en las Ciudades de Lima, y Mexico, con las mismas facultades, prerrogativas, y exempciones, para que por este medio, que tanto se conforma con las Leyes, se corrija, y extirpe el desorden: y he venido en elegir, y nombrar al Doctor Don Miguel Gorman, en quien concurren las partes, y Calidades necesarias por Proto-Medico, y Alcalde mayor de todos los respectivos Profesores à efecto de que desde luego proceda, y providencie lo conveniente al expresado fin, que consulta à la salud publica.

Y como no seria àsequible, si à sus mandamientos no seles diese en los Pueblos, y distritos de estas Provincias el cumplimiento, que à toda Carta de Justicia es necesario, he dispuesto consiguientemente, participarlo à V. para que en esta inteligencia haga reconocer en todas las Ciudades, Villas, y Pueblos de su jurisdiccion, y V. reconosca al mencionado Don Miguel de Gorman por Proto-Medico del Tribunal Real del Proto-medicato nuevamente establecido, y creado en esta Capital embiando à sus Cabildos, y respectivos Gefes Copia de esta mi orden para que teniendolo todos entendido, igualmente den en lo subcesivo el fomento, auxilio, y ayuda, que necesiten las Providencias de dicho Proto-Medico relativas al expresado fin; siendo por ahora lo que mas deve llamar la atencion de todos, y con especialidad la de V. no permitir desde el recivo de esta en adelante en ningun Pueblo de Españoles de essa Provincia el que alguno entre à exercer de nuevo la Medicina, Cirujia, Pharmacia, y Phlebotomia, sin que primero conste por recaudos bastantes, y en debida forma haver sido examinado por el Real Proto-medicato de essa Ciudad, merecido la aprovacion de sus examinadores, y hallarse en su consequencia autorizado para exercerlas; haciendo al mismo tiempo, que todos los que al presente pasan plaza de Medicos, Cirujanos, Sangradores, y Boticarios presenten dentro de un breve termino sus titulos ante las justicias de los respetivos Pueblos, de los quales se sacarà una Copia, y los Originales se remitiran al Tribunal del Real Proto-medicato, para que vistos, y examinados en èl se provea lo conveniente àcerca de su uso, y à los que no los presentasen dentro de el termino referido se les prohivirà bajo las penas establecidas por Leyes este exercicio, no permitiendoseles en adelante sin que primero hagan los estudios, y practica necesaria, y ocurran à examinarse, y solicitar la competente aprovacion, y licencia; dandome V. aviso en primera oportunidad de haverlo asi cumplido en todo, y de pronto efecto de esta.

Dios guarde à V. m. a. Buenos-ayres. de de 1780.

Figure 1. RIO DE LA PLATA. Laws, statutes, &c. *Ynformado del desarreglo, y ábusos con que se exercita la medicina* [&c.]. Buenos Aires: [Real Imprenta de las Niños Expósitos]. 1780. **(A.7)**

A.8   **RIO DE LA PLATA. Laws, statutes, &c.**

Arancel general de los derechos de los oficiales de esta Real Audiencia, de los jueces ordinarios, abogados, y escribanos publicos, y reales de provincia, medidores y tasadores, y de las visitas y examenes del Proto-medicato de este distrito. 1 l., pp. 58.

fol. Buenos Aires: Real Imprenta de los Niños Expósitos. [1787].

Furlong 279.
Medina (Buenos Aires) 96.
Molinari (1941) 5.
Palau 14764.

Sig. K1 (i.e. p. 39) to end is from another copy.

Rúbrica and addressee in MS on the title-page, and MS certification on the last page.

The fees due to the Protomedicato and its officials for the examination of physicians, surgeons, apothecaries, oculists, blood-letters and barbers, midwives, and for official visits to the shops of apothecaries are set out on pp. 56–57. The *Auto* dated 17 March 1787 under which these scales of fees were issued is printed at the end; five hundred printed copies were required for distribution. As Medina notes, the *Arancel* was based on another published in Lima in 1779 [see P. 22]; apart from certain local adjustments the texts and the fees are the same.

A.9   **RIO DE LA PLATA. Laws, statutes, &c.**

Modo de hacer la operacion cesarea despues de muerta la madre. 4 ll.

fol. [Buenos Aires: Real Imprenta de los Niños Expósitos. 1805].

Furlong 733.
Medina (Buenos Aires) 290.
Molinari (1941) 12.

The *Real Cédula* dated 13 April 1804 printed at the end of this *Instrucción* and promulgated by Rafael de Sobremonte, Marqués de Sobremonte [Viceroy 1805–07] on 30 January 1805, records that it was drawn up by the Colegio de Cirugía de San Carlos of Madrid on 25 October 1803 and approved by the *Proto-cirujanato*. Sufficient copies were ordered to be printed for official distribution throughout the Viceroyalty.

BRAZIL
1808–1820

B.1 **ALMANACK**

Almanack da Corte do Rio de Janeiro para o anno de 1811. *tables.* pp.v, 7–255 (=355), 2 bl. ll.

24mo. Rio de Janeiro: Impressão Regia. 1810.

This first almanack issued after the arrival of the Regent in Brazil in 1808 contains, among much else, a full list of members of official bodies including the hospitals, the *Provedoria môr da saude* set up in 1809 in place of the Proto-medicato, and the royal physicians and surgeons.

Figure 2.

B.2 **BOMTEMPO, José Maria [1774–1843]**

Compendios de medicina pratica feitos por Ordem de Sua Alteza Real. *table.* pp.xx, 293, 1 l.

4to. Rio de Janeiro: Regia Officina Typografica. 1815.

Blake v p.39.
Guerra (Brasil.) 33.
Pires de Lima 587.
Silva v p.23.

A highly elaborated nosological treatise (systematic table at pp. 245–293), based upon the *Nosographie philosophique* of Philippe Pinel [1745–1826] first published in Paris in 1798, providing a succinct conspectus of early 19th century medicine. The headings are supplied where appropriate with descriptions and with brief notes on predisposition and causes, symptoms, and treatment.

After graduating in medicine and philosophy from Coimbra, Bomtempo spent seven years in Angola where he was appointed *Physico-mór* (1798) and *Juiz commissário da junta do proto medicato.* Arriving in Brazil with the Regent in 1808 he became *Delegado do physico-mór* (1808–21), *Médico da câmara*, and *Lente de medecina* in the Hospital Real Militar. In 1809 he was appointed lecturer in materia medica and pharmacy in the Escola de Anatomia e Cirurgia, and in 1820 became acting Director of the Academia Medico-Cirurgica which succeeded it. He published

ALMANACK
D A
CORTE
D O
RIO DE JANEIRO
P A R A   O   A N N O
D E
1 8 1 1.

RIO DE JANEIRO
N A   I M P R E S S Ã O   R E G I A.
1 8 1 0.
Com Licença de S. A. R.

Figure 2. ALMANACK. *Almanack da Corte do Rio de Janeiro para . . . 1811.* Rio de Janeiro: Impressão Regia.
1810. **(B.1)**

Compendios de materia medica, Rio de Janeiro, Regia Officina Typografica, 1814; also *Trabalhos medicos*, Rio de Janeiro, Typographia Nacional, [1825], a copy of which is in the Wellcome Institute Library; and two other works are listed by Blake. His life is outlined, with a further reference, by Guerra (Brasil.) 29, and by Vasconcellos (1960; 1961); some further details appear in the Almanack listed in the previous entry.

B.3 **BRAZIL. Laws, statutes, &c.**

Alvará, pelo qual Vossa Alteza Real ha por bem ordenar, que se executem os Regimentos do Fysico Mór, e Cirurgião Mór, e mais Ordens Regias; e Regular a Jurisdicção delles, e dos seus Delegados [&c.]. 2 ll.

fol. Rio de Janeiro: Impressão Regia. 1808.

The order lays down the area of competence of the two officials and makes provision for appeal if they exceed it. Dated 23 November 1808.

B.4 **BRAZIL. Laws, statutes, &c.**

Alvará com força de Lei, pelo qual Vossa Alteza Real Ha por bem abolir a Real Junta do Proto-Medicato, e Ordenar, que o Fysico Mór, e Cirurgião Mór do Reino, Estados, e Dominios Ultra-Marinos exercitem a competente Jurisdicção nos Reinos de Portugal, e Algarve por meio de seus Delegados [&c.]. 1 l.

fol. Rio de Janeiro: Impressão Regia. 1809.

Having appointed Manoel Vieira da Silva as *Fysico-mór* and José Correia Picanço as *Cirurgião mór* on 27 February 1808, the Proto-medicato has become obsolete and is therefore abolished. Dated 7 January 1809.

B.5 **BRAZIL. Laws, statutes, &c.**

Alvará, pelo qual Vossa Alteza Real Ha por bem ... Ordenar que o Sallario nelle estabelecido para as Visitas das Boticas, e Lojas de Drogas seja a quantia de seis mil e quatrocentos reis ... e o dobro quando os Boticarios forem tambem Droguistas [&c.]. 1 l.

fol. Rio de Janeiro: Impressão Regia. 1811.

The increase in fees takes into account the economic difficulties of the time. Dated 30 January 1811.

B.6   **BRAZIL. Laws, statutes, &c.**

Regimento dos preços dos medicamentos simplices, preparados e compostos, assim como se descrevem na Farmacopea Geral do Reino, feito, e publicado por Ordem de Sua Magestade El-Rei Nosso Senhor para governo dos boticarios no Reino de Portugal, e Algarves. [pp. 50].

Rio de Janeiro: Impressão Regia. 1818.

Facsimile.

B.7   **GOMES, Luiz de Sant' Anna [*c.* 1770–1840]**

Methodo novo de curar segura e promptamente o antraz ou carbunculo, e a pustula maligna. pp. 32.

8vo. Rio de Janeiro: Impressão Regia. 1811.

Blake v p.463.
Fac. Med. Lisb. Bib. p. 137.
Guerra (Brasil.) 13.
Silva v p.210.

In discussing the nature and treatment of anthrax, the author quotes A. Ferreira, L. Heister, A.B. Richerand, G.L. Bayle, and the essay by J. Enaux and F. Chaussier, *Méthode de traiter les morsures des animaux enragés, et de la vipère; suivie d'un précis sur la pustule maligne*, Dijon, A.M. Defay, 1785. He is particularly interested in the success achieved by the physician Ducros of Ste. Tulle (evidently one of the earlier members of that able medical family of the Basses Alpes), by the use of plasters and cataplasms of opium; a method which he also tried with outstanding success and for which he quotes cases. In urging other physicians to experiment similarly with opium and to publish their cases he quotes the prolific veterinarian writer and teacher Philibert Chabert [1737–1814], *Description et traitement du charbon dans les animaux*, Paris, Imprimerie Royale, 1780, (1 ed.) which ran into 7 editions in 11 years, and which is now recognised as containing the first important clinical description of anthrax. Gomes was, *inter alia*, surgeon to the Hospital da Misericórdia of Rio de Janeiro and a member of the Academia Imperial de Medicina of the same city. According to Blake, he published four other medical texts in Rio de Janeiro in 1820 and 1821.

B.8 **MIRANDA, João Cardoso de [d. 1773]**

Prodigiosa lagôa, descoberta nas congonhas das Minas do Sabará, que tem curado a várias pessoas dos achaques, que nesta relaçam se expõem. Lisboa. Na officina de Miguel Manescal da Costa, Impressor do Santo Officio. Anno de 1749. pp. 38, 1 l.

4to. Rio de Janeiro: Impressam Regia. 1820.

Borba de Moraes ii p.65.
Guerra (Brasil.) 51.

Few copies of the well-known original of this imprint of early Brazilian medical interest survive; the reprint itself is rare, and it lacks the map of the lake as originally published. The reprint was itself reprinted in Coimbra, Imprensa da Universidade, 1925, with a biographical and bibliographical study by Augusto da Silva Carvalho, a copy of which exists in the Wellcome Institute Library.

It recounts 107 cures of diverse infirmities following regular bathing in this lake situated six leagues to the north of Sabará in the Captaincy of Minas Geraes; according to the publisher's note on the final leaf it was reprinted from the collection made by Diogo Barbosa Machado [now in the national collections in Rio de Janeiro], in the hope that further investigations would be made. The text suggests that religious fervour played a part in the cures.

The author, a Portuguese surgeon qualified in 1722, lived and worked in Bahia and in the Minas area. He also wrote *Relaçao cirurgica, e medica, . . . para curar a infecçao escorbutica*, Lisbon, M. Soares, [1747], and a tract in its defence.

B.9 **PEIXOTO, Domingos Ribeiro Guimaraens [1790–1846]**

Memoria sobre o encephalo-cele, acompanhada da observação de hum hidro-encephalo-cele curado no Hospital Real Militar da Corte do Rio de Janeiro. [pp. 42].

Rio de Janeiro: Impressam Regia. 1811.

Facsimile.

B.10 **REICH, Gottfried Christian [1769–1848]**

Da febre e da sua curação em geral, ou novo e seguro methodo de curar facilmente, por meio dos acidos mineraes, todas as especies de febre; . . . Traduzido do Alemão em Francez pelo Doutor Marc, tirado em linguagem, e ampliado com annotações por M.J.H. de P[aiva]. [pp. 130].

Bahia: M.A. da Silva Serva. 1813.

Facsimile.

B.11   **RICHERAND, Anthelme Balthasar,** *Baron* **[1779–1840]**

Tratado de inflammação, feridas, e ulceras extrahido da nosographia cirurgica de Anthelmo Richerand ... por Joaquim da Rocha Mazarem. 2 ll., pp. 212.

8vo. Rio de Janeiro: Impressão Regia. 1810.

Fac. Med. Lisb. Bib. p. 183.
Guerra (Brasil.) 11.
Silva iv p. 150.

This is a translation of extracts from Richerand's *Nosographie chirurgicale*, first published in Paris in 1805; the expanded second edition, the first volume of which coincides exactly with this translation, was published in 4 volumes in Paris in 1808. Mazarem adds some footnotes of substance to his original.

Richerand, a daring and highly successful surgeon, was chief surgeon to the Hôpital Saint-Louis and taught at the École de Médecine, where his influence on the future generation of French surgeons was profound; he was created Baron in 1829. His *Nouveaux élémens de physiologie*, first published in Paris in 1801, also ran into many editions and translations.

Joaquim de Rocha Mazarém [1775–1849] sailed for Brazil with the royal family in 1807, where he held senior civil and military appointments in medicine and surgery. The dedication of the present work to the Regent, João, records the necessity for him as holder of one of the chairs of medicine and surgery in the royal military hospital to provide material in the vernacular for students. He returned to Lisbon in 1822 where from 1825 he became professor of obstetrics in the Escola Médico-cirurgica; he published several works on obstetrics, and among other marks of distinction became a corresponding member of the Academia das Ciências.

B.12   **WEIKARD, Melchior Adam [1742–1803]**

Prospecto de hum systema simplicissimo de medicina; ou illustração e confirmação da nova doutrina medica de Brown .... Traduzido do Alemaõ em Italiano pelo Dr.

José Frank. Terceira impressão com os accrescentamentos da segunda impressão Alemãe, e com as novas annotações do Dr. Luiz Frank. Tirado em linguagem desta nova impressão, e ampliado com outras annotações por Manoel Joaquim Henriques de Paiva. 2 vols.

8vo. Bahia: M.A. da Silva Serva. 1816.

Fac. Med. Lisb. Bib. p.231.
Guerra (Brasil.) 42.
Silva vi pp.12–18.

As the title-page indicates, the translation follows fairly closely the third edition of M.A. Weikard, *Prospetto di un sistema piú semplice di medicina*, 2 vols., Venice, G.A. Pezzana, 1802, translated into Italian by J. Frank; there are a few minor differences. Much of the text is ultimately a translation of extracts from J. Brown, *Elementa medicinae*, Edinburgh, C. Elliot, 1780. The notes by J. Frank, son of the well-known Johann Peter Frank, L. Frank (his cousin), and Paiva have been gathered at the end of both volumes of the present edition.

This well-known attempt by John Brown [1735–88], first a protegé and later a critic of W. Cullen in Edinburgh, to systematise medicine and medical treatment enjoyed its widest success throughout Europe for only a few years. During this time translations, adaptations, and commentaries and polemical essays on the Brunonian system were issued, and interest in the system was naturally transferred to all the American colonies.

Weikard, after filling many official medical positions in the towns of Germany, was appointed court physician to the Empress Catherine of Russia and later to the Tsar Paul I; he wrote several tracts in support of the Brunonian system, but is remembered primarily for his treatise on the philosophy of medicine.

M.J.H. de Paiva [1752–1829], doctor of medicine of Coimbra, was professor of philosophy there with occupancy of the chair of pharmacy in Lisbon, *Médico da real cámara*, deputy of the Real Junta do Proto-Medicato, and member of the Academia das Ciências of Lisbon and many other learned bodies. In 1809, suspected of Jacobinism, he was stripped of his appointments and banished. He retired to Bahia where he remained until his death. Restored to his honours in 1818, he was appointed in 1824 to the chairs of pharmacy, materia medica and therapeutics in Bahia. Among his many printed works he published the *Farmacopéa lisbonense*, Lisbon, F. da Silva e Azevedo, 1780; many translations principally from J.J. von Plenck, S.A.A.D. Tissot, W. Buchan, and Weikard, and on the Brunonian system; and original treatises on such varied topics as the symptoms of poisoning by therapeutic substances (e.g. snakeroot, lead and mercury), the raising of children, resuscitation, naval medicine, pharmacy, and papers on the applied sciences read before the Academia das Ciências.

B.13   **WEIKARD, Melchior Adam [1742–1803]**

Manual de medicina e cirurgia practica fundada sobre o systema de Brown . . . . Traducção livre da segunda edição Alemãe, em Italiano: enrequecida de discursos preliminares e de commentarios pelo Dr. Valeriano Luiz Brera. Tirado em linguagem, e ampliado dos additamentos da terceira impressão Alemãe, e de annotações por Manoel Joaquim Henriques de Paiva. 4 vols. in 2.

8vo. Bahia: M.A. da Silva Serva, & Widow of Serva, & Carvalho. 1818–19.

Fac. Med. Lisb. Bib. pp.231.
Guerra (Brasil.) 46.
Silva vi pp.12–18.

The translation follows fairly closely the second edition of Weikard, *Elementi di medicina pratica*, 6 vols., Venice, G. Pasquali, 1801–03 (the first 4 vols. only) translated into Italian by Valeriano Luigi Brera [1772–1840], who was appointed first physician to Venice in 1809 after occupying medical and surgical chairs at Pavia, Bologna and Padua; he was an ardent Brunonian. [See entry above].

COLOMBIA
[?1779]–1797

C.1   **GIL DE TEXADA, Vicente**

Memoria sobre las causas, naturaleza, y curacion de los cotos en Santafé. 1 l., pp.19.

4to. Santa Fé de Bogotá: [s.n. 1797].

Medina (Bogotá) 16.

No signatures. The first leaf is a singleton.

This appears to have been the last, unnumbered and separately paginated, special issue of the *Papel periodico de Santafe de Bogota*; the previous issue in the British Museum set is no. 265 of 6 January 1797. The special issue is not reprinted in the facsimile edition of the journal issued by the Banco de la República, Bogotá, in 7 vols. in 1978.

The author, priest and member of the Franciscan Observants or Friars Minor, discusses the endemic goitre of the Santa Fé region in the light of contemporary theory, and concludes that relative cold is its cause. He advises a dietary and purging regimen to balance the system, accompanied by specific internal and topical treatments. His aetiology, derived from European sources, which discusses the place of climate, water and mountains in the condition comes close to modern knowledge of the rôle of iodine deficiency in the disease.

The first paper on goitre in this area was published by José Celestino Mutis, in the same periodical, 1794 (no. 137), pp. 669–676.

C.2   **LOPEZ RUIZ, Sebastián José**

Modo de sacar cortezas de los arboles de quina, para que sea apreciable por su virtud, y eficacia medicinal; la que se pagará á tres pesos cada arroba, estando perfectamente seca al sol [&c.]. 1 l.

fol. [Santa Fé de Bogotá: ?Imprenta Real de A. Espinosa de los Monteros. ?1779].

Rúbrica and signature of the author on the verso, at whose establishment the bark was dried and sold.

His *Relación de los méritos y servicios*, Madrid, 1794, a copy of which is in the Wellcome Institute Library, refers to his *Instrucción muy sencilla y lacónica*, perhaps the present item, which he printed at his own cost [probably in 1779] to distribute free to householders and inhabitants of the areas where the trees were to be found.

López Ruiz, the eccentric son of an upper-class family of the City of Panamá, acquired wide learning in philosophy and the humanities in that university, and in jurisprudence and the natural sciences in the University of San Marcos of Lima. His claim to have discovered cinchona near Bogotá in 1774 initiated a quarrel with Mutis over the priority of discovery. The subject is fully covered by Steele (1964), pp. 198–203.

C.3   **MUTIS, José Celestino [1732–1808]**

Prospecto de los nombres y propiedades de las quinas oficinales. 1 l.

4to. [Santa Fé de Bogotá: s.n. 1793].

This schema setting out the varieties and medical properties of cinchona was originally printed as p. 465 of "El arcano de la quina revelado a beneficio de la humanidad" by Mutis, the first parts of which appeared in the *Papel periodico de Santafe de Bogota*, 1793–4 (nos. 89–128), pp. 285–600 (10 May 1793–7 February 1794). It is here issued separately with a note on the verso indicating its source and recommending the hitherto unknown *Quina blanca*.

The later part on the non-medical aspects of cinchona does not seem to have appeared separately as promised in the note in no. 129 (14 February 1794) of the same periodical. These first parts were however edited by the botanist Manuel Hernández de Gregorio and published with additional medical material as *El arcano de la quina; discurso que contiene la parte médica de las cuatro especies de quinas oficinales, sus virtudes eminentes y su legítima preparacion*, Madrid, Ibarra, 1828.

Physician, mathematician, mineralogist, natural scientist and priest, Mutis was born in Cádiz and arrived in Santa Fé de Bogotá with the incoming Viceroy in 1761. In 1783 he was appointed *Primer botánico y astrónomo* to the *Expedición botánica de la América septentrional*. He published little during his lifetime, and his enormous collections for a flora of Nueva Granada are only now being published by the Ediciones Cultura Hispánica. His life is well covered by Hoyos Sainz (1949) and his work by Steele (1964).

CUBA
1787–1814

Cu.1   **BOLDO, Baltasar Manuel [d. 1799]**

Balthasar Emmanuel Boldo, Bot. Reg. Caesaraug. in insulam Cubensem nunc legatus, D.D. Thomae Villanova, Bot. Prof. Valent. S.P.D. pp.7.

4to. Havana: Typographia Curiae Episcopalis. [1798].

Palau 31721.
Trelles i p.334.

Format uncertain.

Rúbrica and gift inscriptions by the author to Ignacio Maria Luzuri[aga].

Boldó, a native of Zaragoza and well-known as physician and field-botanist in Spain, was appointed a member of the expedition [1797–1800] directed by the Conde de Mopox y Jaruco [1769–1807]. [See Wilson (1962), pp. 228–262].

This pamphlet, addressed to the learned and immensely productive Tomás Manuel de Villanova Muñoz y Poyano [1737–1802], professor of botany at Valencia, is concerned with the proper description and classification of the genus Villanova (Compositae). Boldo's *Plantarum cubensium historia*, written between 1796 and 1798, to which he refers, remained in MS until Trelles' day. He published widely during his life-time on medicine, botany and the analysis of mineral waters.

Cu.2   **CORDOBA, Francisco Xavier de**

Tratado teorico-pratico del typhus á calórico comunmente dicho vómito-prieto, ó fiebre amarilla. 2 ll., pp. xvii, 227.

8vo. Havana: E.J. Boloña. [*c.*1790].

Palau 61858.
Trelles ii pp. 193–194.

The pagination of the blank page at sig. N3ᵛ has been omitted, which places the even page numbers on the recto of each succeeding leaf.

This copy lacks the five-page list of subscribers noted by Trelles.

This freshly-perceived and vigorous account covers the predisposition to the disease, its symptoms, causes, prognosis, and method of treatment. In the appendix [pp. 154–197] Córdoba sets out his reasons for believing the disease not to be infectious. In the final section [pp. 198–227] he describes two case histories which demonstrate his successful use of laudanum.

Among his many official appointments recorded on the title-page, Córdoba is described as *Profesor de medicina*, *Primer ayudante de cirujía* of the Royal Armies, *Cirujano mayor* to the King, and *Catedrático de anatomía y cirujía* of the Royal Military Hospital of the army garrison of Havana. According to Trelles, he was of Spanish origin, received his doctorate from the Colegio de Barcelona, and died before 1816.

Cu.3   **OYARVIDE Y SAMARTIN, Roque José de**

Discurso apologético, que convense clarissimamente con observaciones, y experiencias, la qualidad contagiosa de la enfermedad mortifera vulgarmente llamada vómito negro, fiebre amarilla, ó mal de Siam [&c.]. 2 ll., pp. 76, 1 bl. l.

4to. Havana: M.J. [de Boloña?]. 1801.

Palau 207856.

Part of the imprint is missing, but the press is likely to have been owned by one of the descendants of Esteban José de Boloña who began printing in Havana in 1787. [See Thompson (1962), p. 97].

No signatures.

The pagination of the blank page at sig. $\pi4^v$ has been omitted, which places the even page numbers on the recto of each succeeding leaf.

MS notes on the verso of p. 76 and the recto of the final blank leaf.

The main discourse [pp. 4–43], illustrated by the author's cases, confirms his belief in the ancient miasmatic theory. The supplement [pp. 44–70] deals with the yellow fever diathesis, methods of preventing its spread, and means of treating patients; from his basic theory he concludes, *inter alia*, that damp and marshy places should be filled in, that cemeteries should be provided and that large numbers of patients should be prevented from congregating in private houses. A separate dissertation [pp. 70–75] concludes that *vómito negro*, yellow fever, and *mal de Siam* are the same entity. The whole is addressed to Don T[omás?] R[omay?]. [See Cu.5].

Oyarvide is described on the title-page as *Ex-Catedrático de método curativo* in the University of S. Gerónimo, a member of the Real Sociedad Patriotica, and *Protomédico juez alcalde mayor* of the Protomedicato of Havana.

Cu.4   PARRA, Antonio

Descripcion de diferentes piezas de historia natural, las mas del ramo maritimo, representadas en setenta y cinco laminas. *75 plates (2 fldg.)*. 1 l., pp.4, 1 bl. l., pp.195, 3 ll.

4to. Havana: Imprenta de la Capitanía General. 1787.

Palau 213307.
Trelles i pp.261.

Trelles records that Parra was born in Tavira, Portugal, and that he arrived in Havana in 1766. In 1781 he was already gathering examples of minerals and of animal and plant life. His son, Manuel Antonio Parra, the artist and engraver of the plates in this work, was born in Havana in 1768.

The last page and a half of text describe a large hydrocele, and the last three plates illustrate it.

Cu.5 **ROMAY, Tomás [1764–1849]**

Disertacion sobre la fiebre maligna llamada vulgarmente vómito negro, enfermedad epidemica en las Indias occidentales, leida en junta de Sociedad Patriotica de La Havana, el dia 5 de abril de 1797. [2 ll., pp.49].

Havana: Imprenta de la Capitanía General. 1797.

Facsimile.

Cu.6 **SANCHEZ RUBIO, Marcos**

Tratado sobre la fiebre biliosa y otras enfermedades. *tables.* 2 ll., pp.360, 2 ll (2nd bl.).

8vo. Havana: Imprenta del Comercio. 1814.

Palau 296192.
Trelles ii p.211.

This individual and poorly organised attempt to meet a questionnaire on yellow fever [pp. 5–9] sent out by the metropolitan government on 10 November 1813 includes meteorological figures for a variety of years between 1806 and 1814.

The author is described on the title-page as formerly *Catedrático del método de curar* of the University of Havana, doctor of medicine and surgery, and member of the Real Cuerpo Patriótico of Havana. Evidently highly regarded by the Protomedicato, he published other works in Havana, on tetanus (1815), on the waters of San Diego [&c.] (1817), and on vaccination (1822). He claims in the present work [p. 336] to have personally vaccinated more than 20,000 people.

GUADELOUPE
1775–*c*.1790

G.1 **B. de S.**

Mémoire sur la Guadeloupe, ses isles dépendentes, son sol, ses productions & généralement sur toutes les parties, tant militaires que d'administration. [pp.iv, 44].

Isles du Vent: [s.n. *c*.1790].

Facsimile.

G.2 **BERTIN**

Memoire sur les maladies de la Guadeloupe et ce qui peut y avoir rapport. 2 pts.

Guadeloupe: J. Benard. 1778–80.

Facsimile.

G.3 **LAVERGNE**

Exposition faite à MM. les Général & Intendant des Isles du Vent . . . concernant les moyens curatifs . . . relativement à l'epizootie éprouvée en cette colonie pendant le cours de l'année dernière. [pp.9].

Basse-Terre, Guadeloupe: [s.n.]. 1775.

Facsimile.

GUATEMALA
1697–1818

Gt.1 **ARRESE, Pedro José de [d. 1795]**

Rudimentos fisico-canonico-morales. O glosa al edicto del Ylustrisimo Señor Don Cayetano Francos, y Monroy Dignisimo Arzobispo de Guatemala, publicado en veinte y dos de diciembre del año de 1785. Sobre el bautismo de fetos abortivos, y operacion cesarea en las mugeres, que mueren embarazadas. 10 ll., pp.58.

4to. Nueva Guatemala: Widow of S. de Arévalo. 1786.

Beristáin i p.174 no.273.
Medina (Guatemala) 541.
Palau 17409.
Villacorta 106.

Signatures of 2 leaves only; the last leaf is a singleton.

Following the Archbishop's edict which is here reprinted, the text urges in catechetic form the necessity for (1) the baptism of the aborted foetus and for (2) caesarean operation on the dead mother by a surgeon or, in his absence, the parish priest, to ensure the baptism and salvation of the child. The operation is separately described.

The Creole author was born in Guatemala, was ordained priest, and served as *Promotor fiscal* of the archbishopric and as secretary to two Archbishops. [See Medina, *loc.cit.*]

Gt.2   **ARRESE, Pedro José de [d. 1795]**

Rudimentos fisico-canonico-morales, o glosa al edicto del Ylustrisimo Señor Don Cayetano Francos, y Monroy Dignisimo Arzobispo de Guatemala, publicado en veinte y dos de diciembre del año de [1785]. Sobre e! [*sic*] bautismo de fetos abortivos, y operacion cesarea en las mugeres, que mueren embarazadas. 8 ll., pp.52.

4to. Nueva Guatemala: M.J. Arévalo. 1807.

Medina (Guatemala) 1474.
Palau 17409.
Villacorta 269.

Signatures of 2 leaves only.

The reprint of the first edition of 1786.

Gt.3   **BETETA, Ignacio [c. 1757–1827]**

Kalendario y guia de forasteros de Guatemala y sus provincias. Para el año de 1803. *tables.* 1 l., pp.165 (=168), 1 bl. l.

12mo. [Nueva Guatemala:] I. Beteta. 1803.

Medina (Guatemala) 1232.
Palau 28780.

The title-page *Estado militar del Reyno de Guatemala* of 1 leaf is inserted between sigs. F and G, and is not included in the pagination. This is the variant with printed, not engraved title-pages, as noted by Medina.

These almanacks, published from 1792 to at least 1805, and the *Gazeta de Guatemala* (1797–1816), constitute Beteta'a major achievement as printer and publisher. This issue lists official appointments.

Gt.4   **ESPARRAGOSA Y GALLARDO, Narciso [1759–1819]**

Metodo sencillo y facil para el conocimiento y curacion de las viruelas asi de las que se presentan generalmente con un caracter inflamatorio como de las malignas . . . . Tambien sobre el modo de precaver las poblaciones de esta plaga desoladora [&c.]. [pp. 17].

Nueva Guatemala: I. Beteta. 1815.

Facsimile.

Gt.5   **FLORES, José Felipe [1751–1824]**

Instruccion sobre el modo de practicar la inoculacion de las viruelas, y metodo para curar esta enfermedad, acomodado a la naturaleza, y modo de vivir de los indios, del Reyno de Guatemala. [pp. 17].

Nueva Guatemala: I. Beteta. 1794.

Facsimile.

Gt.6   **FUENTES, Francisco de**

Assertationes philosophiae mentis, et sensuum mechanicae, ad usus physicos accommodatae: atque aliae physico-theologicae juxta mentem recentiorum propugnandae in hac Regia, ac Pontificia D. Caroli Guathemalana Academia. [Thesis.] *front.* 1 bl. l., 3 ll., pp. 16, 1 bl. l.

4to. [Nueva Guatemala:] Widow of S. de Arévalo. 1788.

Medina (Guatemala) 591.

Contemporary MS note on recto of 1st blank leaf recording the time and date of the disputation.

Medina (Guatemala) 576 records an identical thesis under the name of the candidate Francisco Arrevillaga.

Gt.7 **GUATEMALA. Bishop**

[Begins:] Nos el M.D. Fray Andres de las Navas, y Quevedo . . . . A todos los vecinos, y moradores estantes, y avitantes en esta Ciudad de Guathemala . . . . Innocencio Papa XI. Ad perpetuam rei memoriam. Presediendo por la inefable abundancia de la divina bondad [&c.].

broadside. Guatemala: [A. de Pineda Ibarra?]. 1697.

A broadside in two sheets joined horizontally. A filing endorsement appears on the verso in a contemporary hand. The date of the edict, 17 July 1697, is inserted in MS.

The Bishop orders the publication of the Spanish translation of the apostolic brief of 26 March 1687 which confirmed, at the request of the *Procurator-general* Rodrigo de la Cruz, the new constitutions of the Bethlehemites. The brief had been detained in the Council of the Indies until given passage on 17 March 1696, perhaps pending the result of the case brought by his fellow-Bethlehemites against the appointment of Rodrigo de la Cruz as Prefect General [see M.32] on condition that the Crown acted as patron of the hospitals of the order, having the right to appoint physicians, surgeons, apothecaries and chaplains, to provide any shortfall between income from alms and expenditure, and to forbid the ownership of property to the Order. These conditions effectively curtailed the activity of its hospitals [see Muriel (1956–60), 2, pp. 92–107].

Beristáin and Medina (Guatemala) agree that Andrés de las Navas y Quevedo [1622?–1702] was consecrated Bishop of Nicaragua in 1668 and was translated to Guatemala in 1682; neither records this edict.

Gt.8 **GUATEMALA. Junta de Salud**

Instruccion que da la Junta de Salud Publica de esta Ciudad, para la curacion de la tos epidemica de los niños. [2 ll.].

Guatemala: Arévalo. 1814.

Facsimile.

Gt.9   **GUATEMALA. Laws, statutes, &c.**

Metodo, que se ha de observar en la curacion de sarampion, y viruelas, formado de Orden del Superior Govierno .... A que acompaña el despacho dirigido a su observancia. [4 ll.].

[Guatemala:] J. de Arévalo. 1769.

Facsimile.

Gt.10   **GUATEMALA. Laws, statutes, &c.**

[Begins:] El Excelentisimo Señor D. José Antonio Caballero, Secretario de Estado, y del Despacho Universal de Gracia y Justicia, con fecha 1. de Septiembre proximo pasado me comunicó la Real Orden .... "Deseando el Rey ocurrir á los estragos que causan en sus dominios de Indias las epidemias freqüentes de viruelas .... se ha servido resolver ... que se propague á ambas Americas ... la inoculacion de la vacuna [&c.]." [pp. 5, 1 l.].

Guatemala: [s.n.]. 1804.

Facsimile.

Gt.11   **GUATEMALA. Laws, statutes, &c.**

Reglamento para la propagacion y estabilidad de la vacuna en el Reyno de Guatemala. Dispuesto, de Orden de S.M., por el Superior Gobierno del mismo reyno. 4 ll. (1st bl.), pp. 29, 2 ll. (2nd bl.).

fol. Nueva Guatemala: I. Beteta. 1805.

Medina (Guatemala) 1383.
Villacorta 158.

Rúbrica and MS filing endorsement on the verso of the final blank leaf.

The *Reglamento*, issued by authority of the Real Orden dated Aranjuez 20 May 1804 and here reprinted, was intended to provide rapid protection against a largely defenceless population, to maintain the vaccine and to stimulate the discovery of indigenous cowpox and its maintenance. The elaborate regulations set up a *Junta central* and *Juntas provinciales*, regulated the means of propagating the vaccine, provided for its conservation, laid down the place of parish priests and justices as agents of the scheme, and prescribed the duties of the physicians and vaccinators. The last two regulations provided for vaccination in the ports and frontier-posts in the event of an epidemic. The *Junta central* lasted until 1817. The *Reglamento* is described in Martínez Durán (1964), pp. 493–495.

Medina (Guatemala) 1436 records an *Adiciones al Reglamento* of 3 pages dated 10 April 1806 [see entry below].

Figure 3.

REGLAMENTO

PARA LA PROPAGACION Y ESTABILIDAD

DE LA VACUNA

EN EL REYNO DE GUATEMALA

Dispuesto, de Orden de S. M.,

por el Superior Gobierno del mismo reyno.

NUEVA GUATEMALA.
1805.

Por D. Ignacio Beteta.

Figure 3. GUATEMALA. Laws, statutes, &c. *Reglamento para la propagacion y estabilidad de la vacuna.* Nueva Guatemala: I. Beteta. 1805. **(Gt.11)**

Gt.12   **GUATEMALA. Laws, statutes, &c.**

Adiciones al Reglamento aprovado por S.M. para la propagacion y conservacion de la vacuna en el Reyno de Guatemala. [2 ll.].

Guatemala: [s.n.]. 1806.

Facsimile.

Gt.13   **LA CONDAMINE, Charles Marie de [1701–74]**

Methodo de la inoculacion de las viruelas que refiere M. de la Condaminé en su celebre memoria, sobre dicha inoculacion (1) leida en la Asamblea publica de la Academia Real de las Ciencias de Paris el 24 de Abril de 1754. (2) traducida del idioma frances al castellano por Don Manuel Gonzales de Batres [&c.]. pp. 8.

4to. Nueva Guatemala: A. Sanchez Cubillas. 1780.

Medina (Guatemala) 446.
Villacorta 76.

The description of the method is translated directly from pp. 631–634 of La Condamine (1759). The five questions and their answers at the end of the tract are extracted variously from the same *Mémoire sur l'inoculation* and its second part in La Condamine (1763).

A printed note dated 'Nueva Guatemala Agosto 22 de 1780' on pp. 4–5 of the tract describes the local method of inoculation first developed by José de Flores.

Gt.14   **LEON, José Eustaquio de**

Virtudes de la essencia tinturada de el balsamo virgen. [2 ll.].

Guatemala: J. de Arévalo. 1756.

Facsimile. [See entry below].

Gt.15   **LEON, José Eustaquio de**

Virtudes de la essencia tinturada de el balsamo virgen. 2 ll.

fol. Guatemala: [s.n.]. 1769.

Beristáin iii p.118 no.1670 [1756, and 1768].
Medina (Guatemala) 356.
Palau 135181.

2nd ed.

Palau 135180 and Medina (Guatemala) 257, like Beristáin, note the 1st edition of 1756. Medina (Guatemala) 829 and Villacorta 123 record the 3rd edition. A variant of this 2nd edition is recorded [see WMS. Amer. 63 (LEON, J.E. DE)].

The author describes the manifold uses and methods of administering the tincture created by him more than twelve years since, all of which he had tested. He warns against the inactive imitations on the market and directs buyers to the apothecary's shop of Francisco Sanches. His recommendation is given licence by the physician and *Protomédico* Cristóbal de Hincapié [1689–1772] [see WMS. Amer. 79 (HINCAPIE)], the physician Francisco Azetuno [*c.* 1730–1774], and the *Protocirujano* Manuel Artiaga y Carranza. [See Martínez Durán (1964)].

The author is described in the title as priest of the Archbishopric of Mexico and Director and Founder of the Royal Mint of Guatemala.

Following Ramírez (1902) and *Nueva Farmacopea Mexicana* (1904) pp. 53–55, 282, the tincture is likely to have been made from the fruits of *Myroxylon pereirae* (Balsam of Peru).

Gt.16 **QUIÑONES, Francisco**

Illustrissimo principi D.D.D. Jos. Antonio de la Huerta Casso singulari dei munere antistiti meritissimo Nicaraguensis. [Thesis].

broadside. [Nueva Guatemala:] Widow of S. Arévalo. 1799.

The date '29 Januarii' is completed in MS; and the date and time of the act are printed on the verso.

The candidate, who obtained his doctorate, was one of the disciples of José de Flores. Six months before taking his bacchalaureate at the end of 1795 [see Medina (Guatemala) 834] he had been appointed one of the three interns to serve in the Hospital de San Juan de Dios in Guatemala under the general reforms of that Order's hospitals [see Martínez Durán (1964), pp. 406–407]. In 1811 he had been teaching both medicine and surgery in León in the province of Nicaragua [see Lanning (1956), pp. 299–300].

Gt.17 **RIVA, Juan Antonio de la**

Bautismo de los fetos abortivos, y extraidos por la operacion cesarea. pp. 12.

4to. Nueva Guatemala: M. Arévalo. 1818.

Medina (Guatemala) 2222.

Palau 269794 records another edition of 1818 published in Valencia; the present edition is taken from the edition published in Murcia by M. Bellido in 1817.

A theologian advances reasons for the prompt baptism of aborted fetuses and for the performance of cesarean operations on dead women to save the soul of the child. The operation and the forms of baptism are described, and the argument is supported by reference to F.E. Cangiamila [see M.93, M.184], G. Florentini [?], P. Zacchia, and Hippocrates, as well as to the *Pragmática* [of 1749] issued by Charles III as King of Naples [i.e. as Charles IV, 1734–59] which commanded the operation to be performed on the death of all pregnant women.

HAÏTI
1765–1803

H.1   ALMANACH

Almanach historique et chronologique de Saint-Domingue, pour l'année commune 1779 [&c.]. [pp. 120].

Cap-François: Dufour de Rians. [1779].

Facsimile.

H.2   ANNUAIRE

Annuaire français, ou manuel du colon, a l'usage de Saint-Domingue, pour l'an X [i.e. 1801–1802] de la République Française .... Mis en ordre, par P.M.D. [pp. 108].

Port-Républicain: Gauchet, Lagrange & Co. [1802].

Facsimile.

H.3   ARTHAUD, Charles

Mémoire sur l'inoculation de la petite vérole. [pp. 17].

Cap-François: Donnet. 1774.

Facsimile.

H.4   **ARTHAUD, Charles**

Traité des pians. [pp. 15].

Cap-François: Dufour de Rians. 1776.

Facsimiles (2 copies).

H.5   **ARTHAUD, Charles**

Dissertation et observations sur le tétanos, publiées par le Cercle des Philadelphes au Cap-François. [pp. 104].

Cap-François: Dufour de Rians. 1786.

Facsimile.

H.6   **ARTHAUD, Charles**

Précis historique sur Monsieur le Chevalier Lefebvre-Deshayes, lu dans la séance publique du Cercle des Philadelphes, du Cap-François, le 20 juin 1786. [pp. 12].

Cap-François: Imprimerie Royale. 1786.

Facsimile.

H.7   **ARTHAUD, Charles**

Recherches sur la constitution des naturels du pays, sur leurs arts, leur industrie, et les moyens de leur subsistance. 1 bl. l., pp. 13.

4to. Cap-François: Imprimerie Royale. 1786.

The blank leaf and B3 [i.e. the final leaf] are conjugate.

An eloquent and well-informed attack on notions of the laziness of the Indians of Haïti as expressed by the Jesuit traveller P.F.X. Charlevoix [1682–1761]. The author's acquaintance with the nature, social behaviour, and artefacts of the Indians is both full and remarkable. He promises a further paper on the constitution of the Creoles and Europeans, and on the precautions the latter should take to avoid disease.

After qualifying at Nancy in 1770 Arthaud left for Cap-François where he remained until *c.*1792. There he became head of the military hospital, president and later secretary of the influential Cercle des Philadelphes which he founded in 1784, and was nominated physician to the King.

A facsimile from another copy is in the Wellcome Institute Library.

H.8   ARTHAUD, Charles

Mémoire a consulter, pour M. Arthaud, médecin du Roi au Cap . . . sur la plainte formée contre lui par quelques apothicaires. [pp. 32].

Cap-François: Imprimerie Royale. 1790.

Facsimile.

H.9   ARTHAUD, Charles

Observation sur le septième chef d'accusation contre M. le comte de la Luzerne, inséré dans Feuille du Port-au-Prince, numéro 57. [pp. 3].

Cap-François: Imprimerie Royale. 1790.

Facsimile.

H.10   ARTHAUD, Charles

Réfutation de la pièce justificative du septième chef de la première dénonciation solennelle d'un Ministre, faite à l'Assemblée nationale, en la personne du comte de la Luzerne, ministre d'État, de la Marine & des Colonies; par M. le comte de Gouy, député de Saint-Domingue [&c.]. [pp. 16].

Cap-Français: Imprimerie Royale. [*c.* 1790].

Facsimile.

H.11   ARTHAUD, Charles

Observations sur les lois, concernant la médecine et la chirurgie dans la colonie de St-Domingue, avec des vues de réglement, adressées au Comité de Salubrité de l'Assemblée nationale et à l'Assemblée coloniale. [1 l., pp. 104].

Cap-Français: Dufour de Rians. 1791.

Facsimile.

H.12 ARTHAUD, Charles

Description de l'Hôpital Général du Cap. [&c.]. [pp. 14].

Cap-François: [s.n.]. 1792.

Facsimile.

H.13 ARTHAUD, Charles, and others

Supplément au mémoire pour la femme Bordes, contre le sieur Donzac. [pp. 12].

Cap-François: Imprimerie Royale. 1775.

Facsimile.

H.14 BARADAT

Avis au public. Nouvelle méthode d'administrer la salsepareille & d'en faire usage en substance, ses vertus, & quelles maladies elle attaque sous cette forme avec succès. [broadside].

[Cap-François: s.n. 1784].

Facsimile.

H.15 BAUDRY DES LOZIERES, Louis Narcisse [1751–1841]

Notices adressées a MM. les habitants. Fragment de l'ouvrage intitulé: Essais théoriques sur l'acriculture [*sic*] de Saint-Domingue. [pp. 140].

Cap-François: Imprimerie Royale. 1788.

Facsimile.

H.16 BERARD

Manière de faire usage de l'élixir anti-syphillitique [*sic*]. [broadside].

[Port-au-Prince: s.n. *c.* 1785].

Facsimile.

H.17   **BERTIN[?]**

Des moyens de conserver la santé des blancs et des nègres, aux Antilles ou climats chauds et humides de l'Amérique. [&c.]. [2 ll., pp. 126].

Saint-Domingue: [s.n.]; Paris: Méquignon l'aîné. 1786.

Facsimile.

H.18   **BRUN**

Pommade américaine. Vertus de la pommade vulnéraire & sarcotique. [broadside].

[Cap-François: ?Imprimerie Royale. 1765].

Facsimiles (2 copies).

H.19   **BRUN**

Traité sur le sucre. [pp. 87].

Cap-Français: Imprimerie Royale. 1769.

Facsimile.

H.20   **BRUN**

Prospectus sur l'utilité de café employé en médecine. [1 l.].

Cap-François: Guillot. 1773.

Facsimile.

H.21   **CASTILLON**

Lettre de M. Castillon . . . en réponse à la lettre que lui a écrit M. Loubeau, Maître en Chirurgie, datée du Quartier-Morin du 10 janvier dernier. [pp. 16].

Cap-François: Imprimerie Royale. 1775.

Facsimile.

H.22 **CASTILLON**

Réponse de M. Castillon … a la deuxieme lettre de M. Loubeau, Maître en Chirurgie, datée du Quartier-Morin le 22 février dernier. [pp. 19].

Cap-François: Imprimerie Royale. 1775.

Facsimile.

H.23 **CASTILLON**

Observations pratiques sur les effets de la poudre antiscorbutique, restaurante, & de l'élixir aussi antiscorbutique, propres à guérir radicalement le scorbut. [pp. 48].

[Cap-François: s.n. 1778].

Facsimiles (2 copies).

H.24 **CASTILLON**

Observations pratiques sur les effets de la poudre antiscorbutique restaurante, et de l'élixir aussi antiscorbutique, propres à guérir radicalement le scorbut. pp. 118.

8vo. Cap-François: Dufour de Rians. 1781 [i.e. *c.*1783].

Sig. E is of 4 leaves only.

The author, Surgeon-Major-Consultant to the King in St. Domingue, describes the symptoms of scurvy and prints letters, opinions, and 105 cases in favour of his remedies, which remain secret. They were available at Port-au-Prince and St. Marc, and by mail.

A facsimile from another copy is in the Wellcome Institute Library.

H.25 **CERCLE DES PHILADELPHES. Cap-François**

Prospectus du Cercle des Philadelphes, établi au Cap. [pp. 4].

Cap-François: Imprimerie Royale. [*c.*1785].

Facsimile.

H.26   CERCLE DES PHILADELPHES. Cap-François

Statuts du Cercle des Philadelphes. [pp.21].

Cap-François: Imprimerie Royale. 1785.

Facsimile.

H.27   CERCLE DES PHILADELPHES. Cap-François

Questions relatives à l'agriculture de Saint-Domingue. [pp.19].

Cap-François: Imprimerie Royale. 1787.

Facsimile.

H.28   CERCLE DES PHILADELPHES. Cap-François

Tableau du Cercle des Philadelphes, établi au Cap-François avec l'approbation du Roi, le 15 août 1784. [pp.4].

Cap-François: Imprimerie Royale. 1787.

Facsimile.

H.29   CERCLE DES PHILADELPHES. Cap-François

Notice sur la seance publique du Cercle des Philadelphes, tenue le 15 Août 1788. [broadside].

[Port-au-Prince: Imprimerie de Mozard]. 1788.

Facsimiles (2 copies).

H.30   CERCLE DES PHILADELPHES. Cap-François

Programme des prix proposés par le Cercle des Philadelphes. [2 ll.].

Port-au-Prince: Imprimerie de Mozard. 1788.

Facsimile.

H.31 **CERCLE DES PHILADELPHES. Cap-François**

Recherches, mémoires et observations sur les maladies épizootiques de Saint-Domingue. [2 ll., pp. 141 only].

Cap-François: Imprimerie Royale. 1788.

Facsimile [incomplete].

H.32 **CERCLE DES PHILADELPHES. Cap-François**

Prospectus des travaux que la Société Royale des Sciences et des Arts du Cap-François se proposoit de présenter dans la séance publique, qui devoit avoir lieu le 17 août 1790. [pp. 8].

Cap-François: Imprimerie Royale. 1790.

Facsimile.

H.33 **CHABERT, Philibert [1737–1814]**

École Royale Vétérinaire de Paris. [2 ll.].

Cap-François: Imprimerie Royale. 1778.

Facsimile.

H.34 **CHERVAIN**

Prospectus sur l'eau minérale du Sieur Chervain. [pp. 2].

[?Cap-François: s.n. 1769].

Facsimile.

H.35 **CHERVAIN**

Recette pour la composition de l'eau minérale du Sr. Chervain. [pp. 8].

[?Cap-François: s.n. 1769].

Facsimile.

H.36   CHERVAIN

Avis au public [sur l'eau minérale]. [1 l.].

[?Cap-François: s.n. *c.*1770].

Facsimile.

H.37   CHERVAIN

[Begins:] Avis. L'eau minérale est à la connoissance de tous MM. les Habitans de la Colonie depuis 1769 que le Sieur Chervain en a publié la recette. [&c.].

Cap-François: Guillot. 1773.

Facsimile.

H.38   COSME DANGERVILLE, Jean [d. 1787]

Réflexions sur la gastrotomie, ou l'ouverture du bas ventre dans le volvulus, ce que le vulgaire appelle les intestins noués. [broadside].

[Cap-François: s.n. *c.*1785].

Facsimile.

H.39   DECOUT

Apperçu sur les maladies de Saint-Domingue, avec les remèdes qu'il faut y appliquer. [pp.7, 70].

Cayes: Imprimerie de Lemery. An 6 [i.e. 1797].

Facsimile; wanting pp.25–26, 35–36.

H.40   DE LA HAYE, L'abbé

Prospectus d'un ouvrage ayant pour titre: Florindie, ou histoire phisico-économique des végétaux de la torride. [pp.4].

Cap-François: Imprimerie Royale. 1788.

Facsimile.

H.41 DONZAC, Pierre Césaire

Mémoire pour le sieur P.-C. Donzac . . . intimé en appel de sentence rendue au siege royal du Fort-Dauphin, le 6 mars 1775 : contre Catherine Plantion, femme de Pierre Bordes. [&c.]. [pp.41].

Cap-François : Imprimerie Royale. 1776.

Facsimiles (2 copies).

H.42 FRANCE, Armée de Saint-Domingue

[11 "Ordres du Jour", 28 Germinal, an X, *to* 26 Thermidor, an XI (i.e. 1802–1803)]; [Followed by :] Analyse chronologique et alphabétique des Ordres du Jour de l'Armée de St-Domingue. [26 Brumaire, an X, *to* 24 Fructidor, an X (i.e. 1801–1802)]. [16 ll.; pp.17, 2 ll.].

Cap-Français, [&c.] : Imprimerie du Gouvernement, [&c.]. [1801–1803].

Facsimile.

H.43 JOUBERT DE LA MOTTE, René Nicolas [d. 1787]

Avis intéressant pour MM. les habitans de Saint-Domingue [sur l'onguent vert]. [broadside].

[Port-au-Prince : s.n. 1786].

Facsimile.

H.44 JOUBERT DE LA MOTTE, René Nicolas [d. 1787]

Effets merveilleux de l'onguent vert, du Sieur Chanson. [broadside].

[Port-au-Prince : Imprimerie Royale. 1788].

Facsimile.

H.45 LALIBERT

Mémoire pour Catherine Plantion, femme de Pierre Bordes . . . réprésentée en cette colonie par le sieur Lalibert, Maître en Chirurgie . . . appellante de sentence rendue au siege royal du Fort-Dauphin le 6 mars 1775. Contre le sieur Pierre Césaire-Donzac. [&c.]. [pp.73].

Cap-François: Imprimerie Royale. 1775.

Facsimile.

H.46   LAPOLE, Jean Lompagieu

Observations relatives a la santé des animaux, ou essai sur leurs maladies. [*front.* (*port.*) to pt. 1; *4 plates* at end of pt. 2]. 2 pts.

Paris: Serviere; Cap-François: the Author. 1788.

Facsimile.

H.47   LOUBEAU

Lettre a Monsieur Castillon ... par M. L., Maître en Chirurgie, datée du Quartier-Morin le 10 janvier. [2 ll.].

Cap-François: Imprimerie Royale. 1775.

Facsimile.

H.48   MOREAU DE SAINT-MERY, Méderic Louis Élie [1750–1819]

Loix et constitutions des colonies françoises de l'Amérique sous le Vent.

Paris, [&c.]: the Author, [&c.]; Cap-François: Baudry des Lozieres. 1784–90.

Facsimiles of selected passages from the 6 vols. of this work.

H.49   MOREAU DE SAINT-MERY, Méderic Louis Élie [1750–1819]

Fragment sur les moeurs de Saint-Domingue. [pp. 14].

[?Port-au-Prince: s.n. *c.* 1788].

Facsimiles (2 copies).

H.50 **NOTICE**

Notice sur la ville du Port-au-Prince. [pp. 8].

[?Port-au-Prince: ?Imprimerie de Mozard. 1788].

Facsimile.

H.51 **POLONY, Jean Louis,** *and* **CHATARD, Pierre François**

Procès-verbal de l'analyse des eaux minérales du Port-à-Piment. [pp. 25].

Cap-François: Guillot. 1772.

Facsimile.

H.52 **SAINT-DOMINGUE. Laws, statutes, &c.**

Règlement concernant l'ordre & le service des troupes & milices en campagne & la police militaire dans les quartiers de la colonie. [pp. 72].

Cap-François: Imprimerie Royale. 1780.

Facsimile.

H.53 **SAINT-DOMINGUE. Laws, statutes, &c.**

Lettres patentes pour la confirmation de l'établissement d'une Maison de Providence au Port-au-Prince. [broadside].

Port-au-Prince: Bourdon. 1789.

Facsimile.

H.54 **SAINT-DOMINGUE. Laws, statutes, &c.**

Lois de la colonie française de Saint-Domingue. [pp. 104].

Cap-François: P. Roux. [1801].

Facsimile.

SOCIÉTÉ ROYALE DE SCIENCES ET DES ARTS. Cap-François. *See*
CERCLE DES PHILADELPHES. Cap-François.

H.55   **TARDIF DELABORDERIE**

Traité particulier de l'indigo marron, ou indigo batard, et de sa manipulation [&c.].
[1 l., pp.40].

Cap-Français: Martin. 1792.

Facsimile.

H.56   **THIERY de MENONVILLE, Nicolas Joseph [1739–1780]**

Traité de la culture du nopal, et de l'éducation de la cochenille dans les colonies
françaises de l'Amérique; précédé d'un voyage a Guaxaca. *2 col. fldg. plates* (at end of
vol. 2). 2 vols.

8vo. Cap-Français: the Widow Herbault. 1787.

According to Moreau de Saint-Méry (1958), ii, 1019 (footnote), this work was
printed in Bordeaux.

Loose MS notes on the nopal in a contemporary hand in vol. 1.

The plates depict the female and male cochineal ['Cochenille sylvestre'] on the nopal
['Nopal cochenillifere'].

The author of this classic and graphic work on the culture of the cochineal beetle
risked great personal danger in travelling to Oaxaca ("Guaxaca") in New Spain
during 1777 to unravel the methods of cultivation and to gather living specimens of
both the cochineal and the nopal. As an important article of export its cultivation
had long been held secret. Owing to Thiery's efforts its cultivation was successfully
transferred, with that of other plants of commercial and medical value, to the Jardin
Royal des Plantes at Port au Prince. His efforts earned for him the title of botanist to
the King and a corresponding membership of the Académie Royale des Sciences.

His account of the journey throws much light on the state of the Spanish Empire and
on Thiery's own robust and determined character. Further experiments on cochineal
cultivation are described in the Preface to the present work by C. Arthaud at pp.
lxxxiv–xcviii who adds an *éloge* at pp. xcix–cxviii on the author, originally read to
the Cercle des Philadelphes in 1785 at whose direction this posthumous work was
published.

The history of cochineal is well covered by Donkin (1977).

JAMAICA
1781–1820

J.1   **BARHAM, Henry [1670?–1726]**

Hortus americanus: containing an account of the trees, shrubs, and other vegetable productions, of South-America and the West-India Islands, and particularly of the island of Jamaica; interspersed with many curious and useful observations, respecting their uses in medicine, diet, and mechanics. pp.7, 212, 18 ll.

8vo. Kingston, Jamaica: A. Aikman. 1794.

Cundall 426.

The fly-leaf is inscribed 'To the Hon. William Mitchell' from the editor.

This is an alphabetical list of useful plants with a commentary on each. One index converts vernacular names into the Linnaean nomenclature, while others provide a key to diseases, medicinal qualities of the plants, and the substitutes for better-known remedies. Printed over 80 years after its completion in MS, it clearly reflects the change in scientific presentation during the period.

The author was elected to the Royal Society in 1717 having practised early in life as surgeon's mate in the Navy, and later as surgeon-major to the forces in Jamaica. Sir Hans Sloane (1707–25), *2*, Introduction, acknowledges his assistance and refers warmly (pp. viii–ix) to the usefulness of his *Hortus americanus*.

J.2   **DANCER, Thomas [*c.* 1750–1811]**

A brief history of the late expedition against Fort San Juan, so far as it relates to the diseases of the troops: together with some observations on climate, infection and contagion; and several of the endemial complaints of the West-Indies. pp.63.

fol. Kingston: Printed and sold by D. Douglass & W. Aikman [&c.]. 1781.

Inscribed on title-page: 'Lieut. Franc[i]s. Pyne.'

Early in 1780 a small army of 500 troops sailed from Jamaica "upon a secret expedition against some part of the Spanish territories in South America", taking Dancer as physician. Though it succeeded in capturing the fort the army was partly destroyed by fevers, wounds, and exposure: but most of all by infections caused by the filthy living conditions at the fort.

Horatio Nelson was senior naval officer on the expedition.

Pp. 25–63: 'Observations on climate, infection, and contagion'.

For notes on Dancer's life see entry below.

Medical Society of London deposit; also Tract 496.5.

J.3   **DANCER, Thomas [*c.* 1750–1811]**

The medical assistant; or Jamaica practice of physic: designed chiefly for the use of families and plantations. 2 ll., pp. vi, 1 l., pp. 384, 5 ll.

4to. Kingston, Jamaica: A. Aikman. 1801.

Cundall 466.

The last 5 ll., containing *Corrections and additions to the medical assistant, &c.*, were possibly separately published.

With its general introductory essay on medicine, its descriptions and treatments of the diseases common to Jamaica and the West Indies among both planters and slaves, and two formularies listing the drugs recommended in the text, this is a remarkably full and up to date compendium of contemporary tropical practice. The subsequent editions of 1809 and 1819 aimed to keep the material up to date. All editions contain the posological table, the list of medicines requisite for a family or for a plantation containing one hundred negroes, and the list of Jamaica simples.

The little that is known of Dancer is drawn from the autobiographical sketch and note in the London and Kingston edition of this work, 3 ed., 1819, referred to by Cundall, *loc cit.*, and quoted in *Academy Bookman*, 1975, *28*(1), pp. 10–11; and from other confirmatory sources. The son of a farmer, he matriculated at Edinburgh in 1768 where he read medicine until 1771. He spent a year in the London hospitals, settled in the Haymarket in 1772, and obtained his doctorate from Marischal College, Aberdeen, by recommendation in 1773. Passing in the same year to Jamaica he settled in Spanish Town in 1776, and, following his attachment as physician to the expedition of 1780, he published his well-observed *Brief history of the late expedition against Fort San Juan* [*de Nicaragua*], Kingston, D. Douglass & W. Aikman, 1781 [see J.2]. As physician to the Jamaican Bath from 1781 he published *A short dissertation on the Jamaica Bath waters*, Kingston, A. Aikman, 1784; and, as Island Botanist (officially appointed in 1797), he published two tracts in 1792 and 1804 on the Jamaica Botanical Garden founded *c.* 1775. The last of his tracts on diverse topics appeared with the imprint St. Jago de la Vega (i.e. Spanish Town) in 1809.

THE

MEDICAL ASSISTANT,

OR

JAMAICA PRACTICE OF PHYSIC.

DESIGNED CHIEFLY FOR THE USE OF

FAMILIES AND PLANTATIONS.

BY THOMAS DANCER, M. D.

LATE PHYSICIAN TO THE BATH, AND ISLAND BOTANIST.

THE SECOND EDITION.

NAM MULTUM EGERUNT QUI ANTE NOS FUERINT, SED NON PEREGERUNT; MULTUM ADHUC RESTAT
OPERÆ; MULTUM RESTABIT, NEQUI ULLI NATO POST MILLE SECULA PRÆCIDETUR OCCASIO
ALIQUID ADHUC ADJICIENDI.
SENECA.

St. JAGO DE LA VEGA:

PRINTED BY JOHN LUNAN,

PRINTER TO THE HONOURABLE THE COUNCIL.

1809.

Figure 4. DANCER, Thomas. *The medical assistant, or Jamaica practice of physic*. St. Jago de la Vega: J. Lunan. 1809.
(J.4)

J.4   **DANCER, Thomas [*c.* 1750–1811]**

The medical assistant, or Jamaica practice of physic. Designed chiefly for the use of families and plantations. *front (port.).* 2 ed. pp.xii, 2 ll., pp.434, 1 bl. l.

4to. St. Jago de la Vega: J. Lunan. 1809.

Cundall 466.

1 leaf of critical notices of the 1st edition of 1801 is inserted after sig. a2.

The text is revised from the 1st edition. A list of the mineral waters of Jamaica [pp. 399–400] and an *Additamenta* [pp. 404–407] which includes a list of the diseases of patients admitted to Kingston Hospital from 1 November 1807 to 31 October 1808, are added. The author also adds *Quackery exposed, in a set of extracts from the Medical Observer, 1808* [pp. 417–434] which quotes vigorously critical descriptions of current nostrums. The *Addenda to yellow fever* [pp. 381–384] in the 1st edition is not incorporated into the text.

Figure 4.

J.5   **DANCER, Thomas [*c.* 1750–1811]**

The medical assistant, or Jamaica practice of physic, designed chiefly for the use of families and plantations. 3 ed. pp.ii, ix, 355.

4to. [Kingston], Jamaica: A. Aikman, Jun. 1819.

This is the Kingston (or "American") 3rd ed., and not the London and Kingston 3rd ed. listed by Cundall (1902) 466 as the "3rd ed. corrected by himself, with much additional matter" and carrying the imprint "London: Printed by R. Gilbert, St. John's Square, Clerkenwell; for Smith and Kinnear, Kingston, Jamaica. 1819." The copy of the London and Kingston 3rd ed. in the New York Academy of Medicine includes a biographical footnote at p. xx, and an autobiographical sketch at pp. xv–xix [see J.3], neither of which are included in the Kingston edition.

One leaf of critical notices of the 1st edition of 1801 precedes the title-page with which it is conjugate.

The text is generally taken from the 2nd edition, with a number of minor additions and omissions. The *Additamenta* of the 2nd ed., 1809 are incorporated, except for the list of diseases of patients admitted to the Kingston Hospital in 1807–08. *Quackery exposed*, which appeared at the end of the 2nd ed., is here reprinted together with a new note by an anonymous author on fever, vaccination, the yaws, mercury, and the trismus of infants.

J.6 **THOMSON, James**

A treatise on the diseases of negroes as they occur in the island of Jamaica with observations on the country remedies. pp. viii, 168.

4to. [Kingston], Jamaica: A. Aikman, Jun. 1820.

Cundall 469.

Wanting: 1st (blank?) leaf of the preliminaries, and the last 4 leaves of the text containing the formulary, the lists of indigenous medicines and the medicines to be imported.

This, apparently the only work published by this otherwise unknown physician, is an unusually humane and closely-observed account of disease and its treatment among plantation slaves. Apart from its obviously humanitarian motives, this work must have been partly stimulated by the comparative scarcity of new stock following the *Abolition of Slave Trade Act, 1807*, and by the drastically declining birth rate among the slaves.

Following internal evidence, the author read medicine at the University of Edinburgh where he came under the influence of the well-known William Wright, formerly a physician in Jamaica. In London he examined the bodies of those who died as a result of burns received at the "dreadful conflagration" of Drury Lane Theatre, probably that of 24 February 1809. The section, *Some observations and experiments on the medicinal plants of Jamaica* [pp. 144–156] reflects an unusually radical and practical approach to the study of the therapeutic value of little-known indigenous plants, inspired by similar experiments by himself and his fellow-students at Edinburgh.

MARTINIQUE
1774–1788

Ma.1 **BOUFFER**

Mémoire contenant la description & usage de ruches fourmillieres pour la destruction des fourmis, adressé à Messieurs les habitans de l'Isle de la Martinique & autres Isles Françoises du Vent. [pp. viii, 23].

Saint-Pierre (Martinique): P. Richard. 1774.

Facsimile.

Ma.2   **CHEVALIER**

Mémoire pour Chevalier Chirurgien-major, au Régiment de la Martinique, et Apothicaire en la Ville du Fort Royal . . .; contre M. Bagour, Ecrivain Principal des Colonies faisant Fo[n]ction de Contrôleur. [1 l., pp. 42].

[Saint-Pierre (Martinique): s.n.]. 1788.

Facsimile.

Ma.3   **L'ESTRADE**

Mémoire sur la maniere dont se forment les pierres dans le corps humain, et sur les moyens de les dissoudre. [pp. 15].

Saint-Pierre (Martinique): P. Richard. [c. 1780].

Facsimile.

Ma.4   **ROUX, L'ESTRADE, GABRIE**

Analyse des eaux minérales de la Martinique et de Sainte-Lucie [&c.]. [pp. 52].

Saint-Pierre (Martinique): P. Richard. 1787.

Facsimile.

MEXICO
1557–1821

M.1   **ALEMAN Y TRUXILLO, Didacus Josephus**

[Begins:] Cæleste ut hominum saluti consuleret . . . . De rebus naturalibus. [&c.]. [Thesis]. *woodcut.*

broadside. Mexico: Heirs of the Widow of F.R. Lupercio. 1729.

Guerra (Icon.) 247.

M.2   **ALTOLAGUIRRE, Francisco Ignacio**

Relacion del milagro, que obró Dios por intercession de San Luis Gonzaga á primero de Marzo de 1765 en Sor Maria Josepha Ramona de San Fermia Perez de Eulate. 4 ll.

4to. Mexico: Colegio Real de San Ildefonso. 1765.

Guerra (Icon.) 359.
León (Mex.) i 77.

Palau [259619] records the original edition published in Pamplona in 1765 [presumably after 31 July, the date of the licence to print], and notes briefly that it was reprinted at various times. The present edition, reprinted from the Madrid edition of the same year, demonstrates the speed at which the Jesuit press worked to distribute the latest religious information. The Order was banished from New Spain in 1767.

M.3   **ALZATE Y RAMIREZ, José Antonio de [1737–99]**

Consejos utiles para socorrer á la necesidad en tiempo que escasean los comestibles . . . . Continuacion del papel [&c.] . . . . Suplemento al papel [&c.]. 3 pts.

4to. Mexico: F. de Zúñiga y Ontiveros. 1786.

Beristáin i p.135 no.175.
Guerra (Icon.) 447.
León (Mex.) i 85 [Pt. 1 only].
Medina (Mex.) vi 7603.
Palau 10133; 10134.

These papers recommend little-used vegetable and animal foods and ways of preparing them; they were issued with official approval following the poor harvest of 1785.

This well-known figure of the Enlightenment in New Spain was priest, mathematician, and natural scientist. His journals [see Per. 1] did much to spread a new attitude to ideas and the useful arts.

M.4   **ARANDA SIDRON, Bartolomé [d. 1708]**

Informe en derecho, por la justicia que assiste á los medicos de esta ciudad en el pleyto, que les han movido los mayordomos, y mandatarios de las Hermandades. 1 l., ff. 17.
fol. [Mexico: s.n. 1686].

Beristáin i p.156 no.222.
Guerra (Icon.) 128.
León (1915) 33.
Medina (Mex.) iii 1811.

Osores (1908), who outlines the life of this wellknown Mexican advocate, gives 1686 as the date of publication of his seven-point brief in favour of the physicians' concerted refusal to treat members of certain recently introduced *cofradías*.

M.5 **ARECHEDERRETA Y ESCALADA, Juan Bautista [1771–1835]**

Catálogo de los Colegiales . . . de Santa María de Todos Santos, que . . . Francisco Rodriguez Santos . . . fundó en México á 15 de Agosto de 1573 años, con una breve noticia del orígen y fundacion del Colegio, y de los empleos honoríficos que cada uno de sus individuos ha obtenido hasta la presente. *table.* 1l., pp.iv, 46.

fol. Mexico: M.J. de Zúñiga y Ontiveros. 1796.

Beristáin i p.161 no.235.
León (Mex.) i 392.
Medina (Mex.) vii 8575.
Palau 15828.

Son by an earlier marriage of the same mother as Lucas Alamán the historian and politician, and chaplain of honour and close friend of Iturbide, Arechederreta filled a prominent place in colonial and post-colonial Mexico. He was *Rector* of the Colegio de Santa María de Todos Santos at the time he published this useful list of its collegians distinguished in learning and religion.

Figure 5.

M.6 **AVENDAÑO SUAREZ DE SOUSSA, Pedro de [1654–1703?]**

Sermon de . . . San Pedro . . . . Predicado en su Hospital Real de la Ciudad de los Angeles á 4 de Julio de 1694. *woodcut coat of arms.* 6 ll., ff.[10].

4to. Mexico: J.J. Guillena Carrascoso. 1694.

Andrade 995.
Beristáin i p.183 no.304.
Medina (Mex.) iii 1559
Palau 20149.

A sermon on the text *Beatus es Simon Bar-Iona-tibi dabo Claves regni Cælorum*, Matt. 16. The preacher was a Jesuit famed for his sermons, many of which were published in the City of Mexico during his lifetime. His popularity is said to have continued when he was expelled from his Order and reduced to the secular priesthood *c.*1690.

CATÁLOGO
DE LOS COLEGIALES
DEL INSIGNE, VIEJO Y MAYOR
DE SANTA MARÍA DE TODOS SANTOS,

QUE

EL ILLMÔ. SEÑOR DR. DON FRANCISCO RODRIGUEZ SANTOS Colegial en el Mayor de Santa Cruz de Valladolid, Canónigo de los primitivos y Tesorero de México, Provisor y Gobernador de su Arzobispado, Ordinario del Santo Oficio de la Inquisicion, Rector de la Real y Pontificia Universidad, del Consejo de S. M., Obispo de Guadalaxara en la Nueva Galicia, fundó en México á 15 de Agosto de 1573 años,

Con una breve noticia del orígen y fundacion del Colegio, y de los empleos honoríficos que cada uno de sus Individuos ha obtenido hasta la presente.

HECHA EN EL AÑO DE 1796.

CON LAS LICENCIAS NECESARIAS.

EN MÉXICO:
Por Don Mariano Joseph de Zúñiga y Ontiveros, calle del Espíritu Santo, en dicho año.

Figure 5. ARECHEDERRETA Y ESCALADA, Juan Bautista. *Catálogo de los Colegiales . . . de Santa María de Todos Santos.* Mexico: M.J. de Zúñiga y Ontiveros. 1796. **(M.5)**

M.7   **BAEZA, Juan Manuel de [d. 1756]**

[Begins:] Señor. El doctor . . . Cathedratico proprietario de Visperas de Medicina en Vuestra Real Universidad de Mexico [&c.]. [*Entering his protest to the King against Dr. Joseph Dumont's appointment as physician to the Hospital Real de Indios in his place*]. pp. 11.

fol. [Mexico: s.n. *c.*1750].

Born in Puebla, Baeza took his baccalaureate in medicine in 1707 and his doctorate in 1734 in the University of Mexico; he later held the Chairs of *Método* and *Vísperas* and was physician to the Hospital del Amor de Dios [see Fernández de Recas (1960), pp. 49, 74; Flores (1886–88), *2*, 108 *et passim*; Porrua (1964–66)].

The document declares that Baeza was physician to the Hospital Real de Indios from 1737 until 1740 when he was removed by the Duque de la Conquista [Viceroy 1740–41] in favour of José Dumont later appointed *Protomédico de gracia* [see Porrua (1964–66)]. The dispute continued into the reign of the Conde de Revillagigedo [Viceroy 1746–55], the first Viceroy of that title.

M.8   **BAPTISTA, Juan [1555–before 1613]**

Advertencias para los confessores de los naturales. *woodcuts on t.ps.* 2 vols.

8vo. Mexico: M. Ocharte. 1600–[1601].

Beristáin i p.230 no.391.
Icazbalceta 179 (115).
Medina (Mex.) i 163.
Palau 23463.
Valton 69, 71.
Wagner 115, 115a.

Imperfect. This copy includes the first 8 leaves of the preliminaries in each part, though in the second part they are rearranged and exhibit the typographical corrections quoted by Wagner (115a). Neither part includes the further 4 preliminary leaves beginning with the licence issued by Alonso de Ecija, noted by Icazbalceta, Medina, Valton and Wagner as occurring in some copies; but 2 of the 4 leaves of *Indulgencias concedidas* added later and noted by the same bibliographers, are bound at the end of the *Tabla* in Pt. 1.

Pt. 1 lacks ff.41–49 [i.e. G, H1], and the last 7 leaves [i.e. G2-8 of the second sequence of signatures]; the second f. 14 is a singleton.

This notoriously complex work is further confused by a mis-binding of Pt.2, so that in this copy the Index (ff.1–104) precedes the text.

Wagner's careful analysis of the bibliographical problems raised by this work suggests that this set was not one of those bound with Baptista's *Confessionario en lengua mexicana y castellana*, Mexico, M. Ocharte, 1599, since (as noted above) the 8 leaves of preliminaries are present in both parts.

Born in New Spain, Baptista (or Bautista) took the habit in the great Franciscan convent of the City of Mexico. He taught philosophy and theology, and had as pupil Juan de Torquemada, the author of *Monarquia indiana*, Seville, 1615. As Father Guardian, Baptista was deeply involved in the work of the Colegio de Santa Cruz in Tlatelolco for the education of the sons of Indian nobles. He learned Náhuatl as an adult, and was a prolific writer on devotional topics and matters of Catholic practice in both Spanish and Náhuatl.

The present work provides valuable incidental material on the clash of cultures, and on the customs and sexual mores of the Indians.

M.9   **BARRIOS, Juan de [b. 1563]**

Verdadera medicina, cirugia, y astrologia, en tres libros dividida. *woodcut port.* 3 pts.

fol. Mexico: F. Balli. 1607.

Beristáin i p.224 no.379.
Guerra (Icon.) 12.
Icazbalceta pp.238–241.
León (1915) 12.
Medina (Mex.) ii 232.
Palau 24830.

Autograph of Lic. Juan Ponce de Leon, 1609, and other MS annotations on verso of the last leaf; annotations throughout in an early hand.

This copy, once in the León Collection, appears to be one of four recorded copies. An incomplete copy, incorrectly described in León (1915) 12, was then in his collection. It seems likely therefore that the present repaired but apparently integral copy was acquired by him after his description had been published. The preliminaries are as described by Icazbalceta (1954), pp. 238–239 (footnote), and not as described by León or Medina.

The editor of the second edition of Icazbalceta, followed by the editor of Hernández

IESVS. MARIA.

VERDADERAME
DICINA, CIRVGIA,
Y ASTROLOGIA, EN
TRES LIBROS DIVIDIDA,
POR EL DOCTOR IHOAN
DE BARRIOS NATVRAL
De Colmenar Viejo.

¶ EN EL LIBRO PRIMERO SE TRATA DELA ANOTO=
mia del cuerpo humano; y de las heridas de cabeça, pecho, y vientre: y neruios, y co=
mo se an de curar, y contra lo que a escrito el D. Hidalgo de Seuilla, y vn recetario
de las medicinas que conuienen para estas heridas tratase de las complexiones, y tē=
peramentos de cada enfermo, y de que se a de comer, y a que hora: y que cosas son
buenas, o malas. Y que astrologia an menester saber los medicos para sangrar: y pur
gar, y si ay dias electiuos: o no contra lo que an escrito algunos Astrologos, Tratase
tambien de todas las enfermedades que ay en el cuerpo humano, como se llaman, de
que se hazen, con que señales se conoceran, y que pronosticos tienen, y como se an
de curar con todas las dificultades, hasta oy dichas, y como en sus casas pueden ha=
zer los enfermos los jaraues: purgas. &c. sin que se a menester yr a las Boticas.

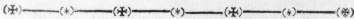

¶ EL LIBRO SEGVNDO TRATA DE QVE SEA CALENTVRA, Y DE
todas las calenturas en particular, y de que se hazen, como se conoceran, sus pronosticos. Tratase de Bubas,
de Erispela, y Viruelas, y de todas las yerbas que descubrio el Doctor Francisco Hernandez por man=
dado de su Magestad, en esta Nueua España, aplicadas a las enfermedades de el cuerpo huma
no, como despues lo hizo el Doctor Nardo Reco por mandado de su Magestad, diziendo
el nombre de la rayz, o yerba en Mexicano, o en Otomi, &c. Y luego en Roman=
ce, para que es buena, y que cantidad se a de dar, y en que la an de tomar
Tambien se trata de que agua es la mejor, y el orden que yo
di a su Excelencia el Marques de Montes Cla=
ros que es el modo como oy se
trae a esta Ciudad.

EN EL LIB. TERCERO SE TRATA DE LA ANOTOMIA
de la madre de la formacion de la criatura de los males de las pre=
ñadas, paridas, y de los niños: y de que an de saber las co=
madres, y en que consiste la virginidad, y vn
tractado de afeytes.

Con Licencia y priuilegio ympreso en MEXICO.
Por Fernando Balli.
Año 1607.

Figure 6. BARRIOS, Juan de. *Verdadera medicina, cirugia, y astrologia.* Mexico: F. Balli. 1607. **(M.9)**

(1960), pp. 404–405 (footnote), mistakenly ascribed this Wellcome Institute copy to the British Museum, which has in fact no copy of this work. The other recorded copies are therefore:

Biblioteca Agreda [see Medina, *loc. cit.*]; this copy is now in the Latin American collection of the University of Texas Library, Austin.
Biblioteca Palafoxiana de Puebla [see Icazbalceta, *loc. cit.*].
National Library of Medicine, Bethesda, Md., U.S.A. [see Surgeon-General (1896–1916), *2*, p. 115.].

These three copies are incomplete. One of the two further copies, also incomplete, in private hands in Mexico City and Lima, may be the incomplete copy formerly in the possession of León.

Most of the little we know of Barrios derives from this work. Born in Colmenar Viejo, Castile, he studied medicine at Alcalá under Pedro García Carrero, later *Médico de cámara* to Philip III and Philip IV. After practising in Valladolid he moved to New Spain between 1586 and 1596. The ascription of one of the first works on chocolate (1609) to Barrios by Medina (Mex.), ii, 245 is confirmed by his contemporary F. Ximenez [see M.207], and by the researches of León, *op. cit.*, 13.

Cast in the form of a dialogue, Barrios' remarkable treatise is a lively account of most aspects of contemporary medicine. Besides the more usual topics, he includes sections on childbirth, cosmetics and beauty, the necessity and means of supplying pure water to the City of Mexico, and the first (and much abbreviated) printed version of Francisco Hernández's work on the medicinal plants of New Spain.

Frontispiece & Figure 6

M.10   **BARTOLACHE Y DIAZ POSADAS, José Ignacio [1739–90]**

Noticia plausible para sanos y enfermos. 1 l.

4to. [Mexico: s.n.]. 1774.

Guerra (Icon.) 393.

Bartolache publishes his success in making iron pills, and gives credit to J. Gibelli, *Sobre las ventajas que trae el uso del fierro en la medicina*, Genoa, 1767, i.e. Giacinto Gibelli, *Due dissertazioni sopra li vantaggi, che si ottengono in medicina dall' uso del ferro per guarire molte infermità*, Genoa, P. Scionico, 1767 [see Surgeon-General (1896–1916), *6*, pp. 203–204].

A note at the end of Bartolache's statement records that he provided an *Instruccion sucinta*, and a corresponding set of instructions *en idioma mexicano* to be issued with the pills, doubtless the following two items.

José Ignacio Bartolache y Díaz Posadas [1739–90] was a typical son of the Enlightenment. Born of poor parents, his intelligence early attracted a patron and a good education at the Jesuit Colegio Real de San Ildefonso. After attending the University of Mexico he received his doctorate in medicine in 1772. Always a controversial and energetic figure, he published the first medical journal printed in the Americas [see Per. 14], devised the present method of administering iron orally, and published a pamphlet on suitable treatment for victims of smallpox [see M.13]. He is variously said to have held temporary chairs in subjects as far apart as theology, philosophy, medicine, surgery, and mathematics; his *Lecciones matematicas*, Mexico, Imprenta de la Biblioteca Mexicana, 1769, was a landmark in establishing the scientific spirit in New Spain. He spent his last 11 years as *Apartador general* of the Mint. [See Maza (1948); and J.A. Alzate y Ramírez, *Gacetas de literatura de México*, 4 vols., Puebla, Reimp. en la Oficina del Hospital de S. Pedro, 1831 (obituary in Vol. I., pp. 405–414, originally published in the *Gaceta de literatura* for 3 August 1790)].

M.11   **BARTOLACHE Y DIAZ POSADAS, José Ignacio [1739–90]**

Instruccion para el buen uso de las pastillas marciales, ó fierro sutil. 2 ll.

4to. [Mexico: s.n.]. 1774.

Guerra (Icon.) 390.
León (1915) 64.

M.12   **BARTOLACHE Y DIAZ POSADAS, José Ignacio [1739–90]**

Netemachtiliztli. 1 l.

4to. [Mexico: s.n. 1774].

Guerra (Icon.) 392.

M.13   **BARTOLACHE Y DIAZ POSADAS, José Ignacio [1739–90]**

Instruccion que puede servir para que se cure á los enfermos de las viruelas epidémicas, que ahora se padecen en México, desde fines del estio, en el año corriente de 1779. 4 ll.

4to. Mexico: F. de Zúñiga y Ontiveros. 1779.

Beristáin i p.226 no.384.
Guerra (Icon.) 426.
León (Mex.) i 193.
León (1915) 68.
Medina (Mex.) vi 7049.
Palau 25093.

A second revised edition is said to have been published during the small-pox epidemic in Mexico in 1797 [see Beristáin *loc. cit.*; Medina (Mex.) vii 8680; Cooper (1965) p. 59 (footnote)]; but no-one seems actually to have seen this edition of 1797, and it does not appear in any bibliography either under the name of Bartolache, or under the name of Luis Montaña, who is said by Cooper, *op. cit.*, p. 123, to have "composed a guide [in 1797], described as a revision of Bartolache's pamphlet of 1779, for the administration of inoculation", if that is indeed the same work. It may have disappeared, or perhaps exist in so few copies that it has not yet reached the standard bibliographies.

This first [?] edition describes with characteristic terseness and clarity a common-sense treatment based on a simple diet and few drugs.

M.14   **BAYARDI, Octavio Antonio.** *Archbishop of Tyre*

Relacion de lo sucedido al . . . Señor O.A.B. . . . que padecia un largo y obstinado mal escorbutico en las encías, de que sanó instantaneamente. 4 ll.

4to. Mexico: Heirs of Maria de Ribera. 1764.

Guerra (Icon.) 347.
Medina (Mex.) v 4882.

The Archbishop relates how a letter of the Venerable Juan de Palafox laid to his cheek cured him miraculously of an unbearable scorbutic condition of the gums. The author of the miraculous letter was the energetic political and ecclesiastical reformer Juan de Palafox y Mendoza [1600–59], Bishop of Puebla [1640–55], and Viceroy for six months in 1642.

The account was first published in Rome in 1763, and followed rapidly by another edition in Barcelona dated 2 November of the same year; copies of both earlier editions are in the Wellcome Institute Library and all three reprint the therapeutic letter.

M.15   **BEAUMONT, Pablo de la Purísima Concepción**

Tratado de la agua mineral caliente de San Bartholome. 6 ll., pp. 111.

4to. [Mexico:] J.A. de Hogal. 1772.

Beristáin i p.233 no.396.
Guerra (Icon.) 380.
León (Mex.) i 199.
León (1915) 60.
Medina (Mex.) vi 5492.
Palau 26150.

The author was son of Blas Beaumont, surgeon and anatomist to Philip V, and before he took the habit as a Franciscan was known as Juan Blas Beaumont. After graduating from Paris he went to New Spain where he became *Cirujano latino mayor* of the Hospital Real de Indios, and taught anatomy and surgery in the University of Mexico.

He wrote also *Crónica de ... Michoacán*, 5 vols., Mexico, 1873–74; & 3 vols., Mexico, 1932. Carlos María Bustamente published a poorly edited version of the first volume, *Historia del descubrimiento de la América septentrional por Cristóval Colón*, Mexico, 1826, which he attributed to Manuel de la Vega.

M.16   **BENEDICT XIII, Pope. [1649–1730]**

Declaracion autentica que hizo el ... Cardenal Ursini ... Arzobispo de Benevento (quien despues rigió ... con el nombre de Benedicto XIII) de los prodigios que ha obrado en la persona de su Eminencia el glorioso San Phelipe Neri, en ocasion de aver quedado dicho ... Cardenal sepultado en las ruínas de su palacio en el terremoto ... en 5 de Junio de 1688 años. 2 ll.

fol. Mexico: Imprenta Nueva de la Bibliotheca Mexicana. 1754.

Beristáin v (Sup.) p.452 no.1460.
Medina v 4157.

Spanish translations from the Italian original published in Naples in 1688 had been published in both Seville and Mexico in 1724 [see title and colophon of the present edition, and Medina (Mex.) iv 2771]. An earlier translation had been published in Mexico in 1689.

Piero Francesco Orsini [1649–1730], Archbishop of Benevento and Pope Benedict XIII, began his reign in 1724 as Benedict XIV but changed his title since the earlier

Benedict XIII (Pedro de Luna, [*c*.1328–1422/3]) was accounted a schismatic. As Archbishop of Benevento from 1686 Orsini took great interest in reconstructing the city after the earthquakes of 1688 and 1702. The Mexican edition of 1724 naturally gives his title as Benedict XIV. It is perhaps confusing that the present edition of this work was published in the reign [1740–58] of Pope Benedict XIV (Prospero Lorenzo Lambertini).

M.17   **BENEDICT XIV, Pope. [1675–1758]**

[Begins:] Ad futuram rei memoriam. Nuper pro parte dilectorum filiorum Didaci de Salinas ... Ordinis Eremitarum Sancti Augustini [&c.]. pp. 10.

fol. Mexico: [s.n.]. 1749.

Guerra (Icon.) 300.

MS annotations and signatures in several hands on the singleton sig. C 1^v (i.e. p. 10); and on the verso of the single blank leaf following, not part of the folio.

The Bull of Benedict XIV [1740–58] providing for the right of succession by the Augustinian Hospicio de Santo Tomás de Villa-nueva Extra-muros de la Ciudad de Mexico to a chaplaincy after the termination of a certain life interest.

M.18   **BETHLEHEMITES**

Forma de recibir el habito, y entrar al año de provacion, y noviciado en la Compañia de la Hospitalidad de convalecientes de Nuestra Señora de Belen .... [Followed by:] Forma de la profession [&c.]. 7 ll.

4to. [Mexico: s.n. *c*.1680].

Sig. A comprises the conjugate first and sixth leaves; sig. B the second and fifth leaves; sig. B2 the third and fourth leaves; and the seventh leaf is a singleton without signature, its conjugate leaf presumably blank.

Since only the Constitutions [of 1673] of Clement X (requiring only the simple vows) are referred to in these forms of reception and profession, the date of this *Forma* is likely to be *c*.1680; Innocent XI promulgated a definitive Constitution in 1687 erecting the Company into a regular Order. Internal evidence demonstrates that the *Forma* refers to the Hospital Real de Nuestra Señora de Belén y San Francisco Xavier, the only contemporary Hospital of this title in Mexico City, founded in 1675 by Fr. Payo Enríquez de Rivera [d. 1684], Archbishop of Mexico [1670–81] and Viceroy [1673–80]. [See Muriel (1956–60), *2*, pp. 92–99; and M.191].

M.19   BETHLEHEMITES

Constituciones de la Compañia Bethlemitica, approbadas y confirmadas por la santidad de Innocencio Undezimo. Ereccion en religion, y diferentes breves, concedidos en distintos tiempos à favor de dicha Compañia. 3 ll., pp.146.

4to. Puebla: J. Perez. 1707.

Medina (Puebla) 244.
Palau (1923–27) ii p.272.

Includes the Bull of Innocent XI of 1687 establishing the Bethlehemites as a full religious Order, and the Rule of St. Augustine which the Order was required to follow. In 1707 Clement XI renewed the constitutions and added further privileges.

The Order, originally founded *c.*1656 by Pedro de San José Betancourt in Guatemala at his Hospital de Nuestra Señora de Belén, was thus enabled to expand rapidly during the eighteenth century. At the suppression of the Order by the Cortes in 1820 the Province of Peru had 22 houses, and that of New Spain 10. Following the example of its founder, free schools for poor children were attached to its hospitals. [See Muriel (1956–60), *2*, pp. 92–107].

M.20   BETHLEHEMITES

Regla, y constituciones de la sagrada religion bethlemitica, fundada en las Indias occidentales por . . . Pedro de San Joseph Betancur. *engr. front.* 3 ll., pp.90.

4to. Mexico: Widow of J. B. de Hogal. 1751.

Guerra (Icon.) 301.
León (Mex.) ii (2) 533.
Medina (Mex.) v 4060.
Palau 254103.

The title-page and sig. M are singletons; the second leaves are presumably blank.

The Constitutions of the Order consolidated to the reign of Benedict XIV [1740–58] and the Rule of St. Augustine are included.

M.21   BEZERRA, Gerónimo

Estudioso discurso philosophica anothomia, y theatro ingenioso de los organos y sentidos interiores, y exteriores del hombre. *woodcut coat of arms.* 5 ll., ff.26 (=25).

4to. Mexico: A. de Santistevan y F. Rodriguez Lupercio. 1657.

Andrade 470.
Beristáin i p.236 no.400.
Guerra (Icon.) 97.
León (1915) 21.
Medina (Mex.) ii 840.
Palau 28876-II.

Beristáin provided the inaccurate material for the entries of Andrade, Medina and Palau.

Bezerra was Assayer to the Royal Mint of Mexico. The primary source of this formal academic essay is Aristotle, but Bezerra supports his thesis with references, *inter alia*, to Albertus Magnus, Averroes, Avicenna, St. Augustine, and St. Thomas Aquinas.

M.22 BEZERRA, Hernando

Tratado de la qualidad manifiesta, y virtud del azogue, llamado comunmente el mercurio, y por otro nombre el argentum vivum. [14 ll., ff.53, 1 l.].

Mexico: J. Ruiz. 1649.

Facsimile.

M.23 BLANCO, Ciprian

Estado que manifiesta el numero de vacunados y revacunados en esta ciudad y sus varrios en todo el presente año con inclusion de los publicados en los anteriores. 2 ll. (2nd bl.).

broadside. Campeche: [s.n.]. 1820.

Guerra (Icon.) 638.

The surgeon charged with vaccination in Campeche sets out a table breaking down the 871 vaccinations performed during 1820 by race and by month, and demonstrates that 30,555 vaccinations had been carried out from 1804 to 31 December 1820, the date of this paper.

His general statement on the verso urges parents not to disregard public notices announcing the weekly times of vaccination.

Blanco qualified as surgeon in 1812, and is noted as *Cirujano latino* practising in Mexico City in the *Guía de forasteros de México* for 1828.

M.24   **BRAVO, Francisco [*c.* 1530–*c.* 1594]**

The Opera medicinalia .... 1570; with a biographical and bibliographical introduction by Francisco Guerra. *plates.* 2 vols.

8vo. Folkestone & London: Dawsons of Pall Mall. 1970.

A facsimile reprint with a separate introduction volume.

Original copies of this, the first work on medicine to be printed and published in the New World, are known in the Lenox Collection in the New York Public Library (with a mutilated title-page and lacking the colophon), the library of the Hispanic Society of America, and the Library of the University of Puebla. The last two copies are said to be complete.

The work contains four occasional essays on typhus, venesection in pleurisy, the doctrine of critical days, and the nature and properties of sarsaparilla. The extremely crude woodcuts are said to be the first medical illustrations published in the Americas.

Little is known with certainty of Bravo's life. The evidence suggests that he was born in Osuna or Seville, studied medicine in the University of Osuna, practised in Seville from 1553, and arrived in New Spain at a date after 1560 [see the introduction by Dr. F. Guerra].

Another facsimile (xerox) copy without colophon is in the Wellcome Institute Library.

M.25   **BRIZUELA Y CORDERO, José Ignacio**

[Begins:] Regio Mexicanensi Senatui Salutaris Scientiae .... Rei Medicae Triumviris .... Francisco Gonzalez Avendaño &c. &c. .... De rebus naturalibus. [Theses]. *woodcut coat-of-arms & ornaments.*

broadside. Mexico: J. de Jauregui. 1771.

Guerra (Icon.) 370.
Palau 36064.

A contemporary MS note on the verso indicates the date and time of the contest.

This document is the notice of the theses briefly recorded in the prologue to the 2nd edition of Juan de Palafox y Mendoza, Bishop of Puebla, *Constituciones de la ... Universidad de Mexico*, Mexico, F. de Zúñiga y Ontiveros, 1775, at ¶3¹ᵛ [see M.129], and requoted by Medina (Mex.), vi, p. 192. Brizuela offered to demonstrate six of his twenty-four points by geometry.

The contestant may have been a member of the medical dynasty of this name.

M.26 BROTHERS HOSPITALLERS OF ST. JOHN OF GOD

Regla de ... S. Augustin .... Constituciones de la Orden, y Hospitalidad de ... S. Juan de Dios confirmadas por la Santidad de Urbano Papa VIII en 9 de Noviembre de 1640. [Followed by:] Breve noticia de los enfermos, que se han curado, y fallecido en los conventos de la religion de San Juan de Dios ... desde ... 1768 hasta ... 1773. 2 pts.

4to. [Mexico:] J. Jauregui. 1774.

Beristáin v (Sup.) p. 515 no. 5663 [pt. 1 only].
Guerra (Icon.) 394.
León (Mex.) ii (2) 537, 538.
León (1915) 264.
Medina (Mex.) vi 5663.
Palau 254045.

Sig. Ff is of two conjugate leaves only.

A table on A3ʳ [i.e. p. 1] of the second part, lists the hospitals of the Order throughout the Indies (including the Philippines) and tabulates the number of beds, patients, and deaths between 1768 and 1773.

The Order was founded by St. John of God [1495–1550], born in Portugal and canonised in 1690. After being traveller, shepherd, soldier, cattleherd, labourer and merchant, he underwent a conversion and gave himself to the care of the sick. His first hospital was founded for the sick poor of Granada, in Spain, *c*. 1540; and by the early years of the following century the hospitals of the order had spread to the Indies and to the Philippines. Pius V approved the Brothers Hospitallers as a Congregation in 1571 under the Rule of St. Augustine. The Order acquired its first hospital in the City of Mexico in 1604.

M.27   **BROWN, John [1735–88]**

Epítome de los elementos de medicina del Dr. Juan Brown traducido. 1 l., pp. 118.

8vo. Puebla: [s.n.] 1802.

Beristáin iv p. 209 no. 2594.
Guerra (Icon.) 538.
León (1915) 176.
Medina (Puebla) 1454.
Palau 36225.

Juan Antonio Riaño y Bárcena [1757–1810], the cultured and extremely able Intendant of Guanajuato (from 1792 to his death in defence of his city against the rebels) is regarded by most authorities as the translator if not the author of this work. The initials J.R. appear at the foot of the translator's note on the verso of the title-page, a note which expresses the hope that an epitome of Brown's work could be useful whilst a full edition of his works is in preparation. There is a short prologue by J.M. Mociño [see entry below]. The text is an independent summary of Brown's *Elementa* with additions.

M.28   **BROWN, John [1735–88]**

Elementos de medicina del Dr. Juan Brown . . . amplificados por D. Joseph Mariano Mociño vol. 1 [only]. *fldg. table at end.* 4 ll., pp. 82, 199, 5 ll.

4to. Mexico: M. de Zúñiga y Ontiveros. 1803.

Guerra (Icon.) 540.
León (1915) 180.
Medina (Mex.) vii 9571.

Medina's abbreviated notice is copied by Beristáin; and Palau 36224 records without details of pagination an edition of the same place, publisher, and date, as translated and enlarged by Luis Montaña, Martín de Sessé and the same J.M. Mociño, an entry which probably follows the *Prospecto de una obra medica* in *Gazeta de Mexico*, 1802, *11*, pp. 134–139 (10 September) and which certainly refers to the present work.

The text is a free translation and adaptation of Part I of John Brown's systematic *Elementa medicinae* first published in Edinburgh in 1780; versions of the remaining four parts were not published by Mociño. Brown's original preface is here translated with few additions.

The Brunonian system, appearing at a time of cataclysmic political, social and philosophical change, attracted wide popularity and criticism; and translations, paraphrases, expositions, epitomes and abridgments were published throughout Europe. In the New World, Austin (1961) lists 7 reprints and re-issues of the *Elements of medicine* published in Philadelphia alone between 1790 and 1806; in New Spain there was the epitome by J.M. Amable, Mexico, 1801 [see León (1915) 174] probably followed by a translation, now lost, by the same author [*Gazeta de Mexico*, 1802, *11*, p. 156 (8 October)], another epitome probably translated by J.A. Riaño, Puebla, 1802 [see entry above], and the present incomplete version of the whole work; while in Brazil there were at least two editions taken from Weikard's German version, published in Bahía, 2 vols., 1816; and 4 vols., 1818–19 [see B12, B13].

José Mariano Mociño Suares Losada [1757–1820], born in New Spain of poor Spanish colonial stock, became an outstanding pupil of the botanist Vicente Cervantes, and joined the Royal Botanical Expedition to New Spain [1788–1803] in 1790. After extensive and arduous travel he returned in 1799 to the City of Mexico where he spent much time observing the action of medicinal herbs on hospital patients, and where he also prepared the present translation. He departed for Spain in 1803 with the director Sessé and the remainder of the Expedition, where in spite of poverty he was twice Secretary and four times President of the Royal Academy of Medicine. One of the most remarkable scientists produced by the Spanish colonies, he was nevertheless exiled from Spain in 1812, returning from Montpellier only to die in Barcelona, probably in 1820. [See Rickett (1947)].

M.29 **CABRERA Y QUINTERO, Cayetano de [d. 1775?]**

Escudo de armas de Mexico: celestial proteccion de esta nobilissima ciudad . . . Maria Santissima, en su portentosa imagen . . . . En la angustia que ocasionó la pestilencia, que cebada con mayor rigor en los Indios, mitigó sus ardores al abrigo de tanta sombra. *engr. front., table.* 18 ll., pp. 522, 12 ll.

fol. Mexico: Widow of J.B. de Hogal. 1746.

Beristáin ii p. 9, no. 549.
Guerra (Icon.) 297.
León (Mex.) i 287.
León (1915) 45.
Medina (Mex.) v 3752.
Palau 38956.

Sigs ¶ and 7¶ are singletons, the second leaves presumably blank.

According to Medina 800 copies were printed of which 437 were published; the remainder were collected and burned at the order of the first Viceroy Revillagigedo [1746–55] owing to passages offensive to certain individuals.

This elaborate and pious recital by a literary cleric of events leading to the proclamation of Nra. Sra. de Guadalupe de México as Patroness of the City of Mexico, was written in thanksgiving for her protection during the great epidemic of *matlazahuatl* of 1736–37. It includes (pp. 124–126) a list of dates of the 26 processions (1577–1737) of her image in times of epidemic, drought, famine and national danger, and in Book IV, chapters XIII and XIV it provides details of mortality in other areas and a table (p. 511) of deaths in the City. In some localities the epidemic continued until 1739.

M.30   CADET DE GASSICOURT, Charles Louis [1769–1821]

Formulario magistral y memorial farmacéutico . . . . enriquecido de notas por Mr. Pariset . . . . Cuarta edicion. Revisada y aumentada en París año de 1818, y traducida al castellano por D. Nicolás Molero en México año de 1820. 6 ll., pp. 328, 1 l.

4to. Mexico: J.B. de Arizpe. 1821.

Guerra (Icon.) 651.
León (1915) 216.
Medina (Mex.) viii 12081.

The pages of sigs. 21 & 22 are mis-numbered 157–172.

Apart from a letter addressed by him to Vicente Cervantes [1755–1829] and his translator's preface, Molero closely follows the original, C.L. Cadet de Gassicourt, *Formulaire magistral et mémorial pharmaceutique . . . enrichi de notes par M. Pariset*, 4 ed., Paris, L. Colas, 1818. In the text Molero adds under the head *Debilidad de los organos de la generacion* a long footnote (pp. 230–236) on ginseng translated from J.C. Valmont de Bomare, *Dictionnaire raisonné universel d'histoire naturelle*, vol. 4, pp. 57–64 [3 ed., 9 vols., Lyon, J.M. Bruyset, 1776] and from J.J. Alibert, *Nouveaux élémens de therapeutique et de matière médicale*, vol. 1, pp. 100–101 [4 ed., 2 vols., Paris, Caille & Ravier, 1817]; and he adds his own footnote (pp. 236–238) under the head *Fiebre intermitente* on the use of an emetic, or of an electuary whose formula he describes with the success he has had in its use.

Cadet de Gassicourt, a member of the well-known family of Parisian apothecaries, became pharmacist to Napoleon, and filled several formative posts in the early nineteenth-century French medical establishment. A man of unusual versatility and energy, he published works on a variety of subjects. His *Formulaire magistrale á l'usage des élèves en medicine*, first published in 1812, ran into many editions.

Etienne Pariset [1770–1847], son of a poor family, gained his doctorate in Paris in 1808, and achieved distinction in the government medical service, particularly in the fields of insanity and infectious diseases. Following the Restoration, he was sent to Cadiz with A. Mazet in 1819–20, and to Barcelona with F.V. Bally and A. François in 1821–22 to study outbreaks of yellow fever. In 1828–30 he joined the government mission to Egypt and the Levant to study the plague. In 1822 he was appointed *Secrétaire perpétuel* to the Academy of Medicine; and in 1826 he transferred from the Bicêtre to the Salpêtrière where he remained in charge of the treatment of the insane [see Sussman (1971); for another translation by Molero see M.87].

M.31   CAPELLO, Juan Francisco

Compendio medicinal de marabillosos, y experimentados remedios contra la peste, assi preservativos, como curativos para beneficio universal [&c.]. [1 l., pp.47, 1 l.].

Mexico: Reprinted by J.B. de Hogal. 1737.

Facsimile.

M.32   CASTRO Y ARAUJO, José de

Discurso, que ha parecido adicionar a la defensa del hermano Rodrigo de la Cruz, Prefecto General de la Compañia Bethleemitica: sobre el punto principal del passo de los Breves. pp.7.

fol. [?Mexico: s.n. *c.*1690].

Guerra (Icon.) 258.

Palau [48875] quotes a work by this author and José Gurpegui on the same subject, *Representacion jurídica por el hermano R. de la C.* [&c.], fol., Madrid, 1693; but gives no details of pagination.

This forms part of a lawsuit following the appointment for six years of Rodrigo de la Cruz as Prefect General of the Order by Innocent XI in 1687. The appointment was contested by his fellow Bethlehemites [see Muriel (1956–60), 2, pp. 95–98; and Gt.7].

M.33   **CERVANTES, Vicente [1755–1829]**

Exercicios publicos de botánica que tendrán en la Real y Pontificia Universidad de México . . . Pedro Muñoz . . . Sebastian Gomez Moron . . . Manuel Maria Bernal . . . Francisco Peralta. 2 ll. (1st bl.), pp.7.

4to. Mexico: F. de Zúñiga y Ontiveros. 1792.

Medina (Mex.) vi 8210.

A preliminary notice of a public disputation on the system of Linnaeus, presided over by Vicente Cervantes.

Already *Boticario mayor* of the Hospital General de Madrid, Cervantes was appointed Professor of Botany in the University of Mexico by Charles III in 1786, where, with Sessé, he founded the Botanical Garden in 1788, becoming its Director about a year after Sessé's return to Spain in 1803. Originally a student of Casimiro Gómez Ortega [1740–1818], his 30 years of work in Mexico created a flourishing interest in botany, chemistry, and pharmacy. [See WMS. Amer. 81 (CERVANTES)].

León (Mex.) vi 97–101 records briefly five similar printed annual public disputations for the years 1788, 1789, 1790, 1793, 1794.

M.34   **CERVANTES, Vicente [1755–1829]**

Exercicios publicos de botánica, que tendrán en la Real y Pontificia . . . Universidad de México . . . Joseph Agustin Monroy . . . Pedro Regalado Tames . . . Ignacio Fernandez de Cordova. 1 l., pp.9.

4to. Mexico: Heirs of F. de Zúñiga y Ontiveros. [1793].

León (Mex.) vi 100.
Medina (Mex.) vi 8242.

A preliminary notice of a public disputation on the system of Linnaeus, presided over by Cervantes.

M.35   **CERVANTES, Vicente [1755–1829]**

Exercicios publicos de botánica, que tendrán en la Real y Pontificia Universidad de México . . . Joseph Fernandez Varela . . . Joseph Dionisio Larreategui . . . Ignacio Leon y Perez. 1 l., pp.10.

4to Mexico: Heirs of F. de Zúñiga y Ontiveros. 1794.

Guerra (Icon.) 480.
León (Mex.) vi 101.
Medina (Mex.) vi 8330.

A preliminary notice of a public disputation on the system of Linnaeus, presided over by Cervantes. It includes an additional note on the naming of *Castilla elástica*, a subject raised by the anonymous J.L.M. [José Longinos Martínez] in a supplement to the *Gazeta de literatura de Mexico* dated 5 November 1794, and to be combatted by two of the disputants. J.L.M. replied with another supplement to the same journal, dated 30 January 1795, and Larreategui, one of the two disputants, retorted fully with his two supplements to the *Gazeta de México* of 30 May 1795.

M.36   **CHAUSSIER, François [1746–1828]**

Origen y descubrimiento de la vacuna, traducido del francés . . . y enriquecido con varias notas por el Dr. D. Pedro Hernandez [&c.]. *engr. plate at end.* 6 ll. (i.e. pp. 97–108).

4to. [Mexico: M. de Zúñiga y Ontiveros. 1804].

Guerra (Icon.) 551.
León (1915) 190.

This tract was issued as the second supplement (no. 13) to the *Gazeta de México*, 1804, *12* (no. 12) of 26 May. In the original format the plate and its conjugate blank leaf form the centre of the gathering between pp. 102 and 103. In the present copy the blank leaf is wanting.

The text is taken with some minor alterations from P. Hernandez, *Origen y descubrimiento de la vaccina*, 2 ed., Madrid, B. García, 1801 [Palau 204091], which was in fact a translation, with additions, of François Chaussier, *Découverte de la vaccine*, (i.e. 2 engr. broadsheets), Paris, l'Auteur, An 9 [i.e. 1801]. Hernandez's additional dialogue at the end has been retained, though only his Plate IV, re-engraved with material from the remaining plates (slightly altered), has been reproduced. This plate is therefore at third remove, originally by L.P. Baltard [1764–1846] in the broadsheets published in Paris, secondly by J.T. da Fonseca [1754–1835] in the Madrid edition, and then by Rea in the present version.

Chaussier, a man of many interests, excelled as physician, researcher and teacher. He held the Chair of Anatomy and Physiology at the Ecole de Santé of Paris from 1795 until the School's closure in 1822, and published widely on many aspects of contemporary medicine.

M.37 CISNEROS, Diego

Sitio, naturaleza y propriedades, de la ciudad de Mexico. Aguas y vientos a que esta sujeta; y tiempos del año. Necessidad de su conocimiento para el exercicio de la medicina su incertidumbre y dificultad sin el de la astrologia assi para la curacion como para los prognosticos. *engr. t.p., fldg. map.* 13 ll., ff. 148 (= 150), 10 ll.

4to. Mexico: J. Blanco de Alcaçar. 1618.

Andrade 73.
Beristáin ii p. 115 no. 818.
Gallardo ii 1836.
Guerra (Icon.) 26.
León (1915) 16.
Medina (Mex.) ii 307.
Palau 54976.

Imperfect. The 5 preliminary leaves after the title-page, the 10 leaves at the end, and the folding map *Descripcion de Mexico* between the unfoliated half-title *Descripcion del Sitio de la Ciudad de Mexico* [*i.e.* Gg3 *verso*] and f. 118 [*i.e.* Gg4], are supplied in xerox copies. The portrait of the author (presumably a singleton), usually placed after the 13 leaves of the preliminaries, is wanting.

Cisneros was born in Spain, took his doctorate in medicine at Sigüenza, and went to New Spain, probably with his patrón the Viceroy, the Marqués de Guadalcázar [Diego Fernández de Córdoba [1578–1630]], in 1612; he may have accompanied him again on his transfer to the Viceroyalty of Peru in 1621. He became a member of the University of Mexico *c.* 1615.

The work is conceived within the enclosed pre-Copernican universe, and treats of the relationship of the four elements and astrology with medicine; its authorities are largely Hippocratic and Galenic. With all its conceptual limitations it may still reasonably be claimed as the first work on medical geography to be published in the Americas. The author attacks the "errors" of Enrico Martínez [see M.86] with a vigour that suggests a personal feud. An incomplete reprint was published by *El Sistema Postal*, Mexico, 1881, a copy of which is in the Wellcome Institute Library.

M.38 CORDERO GIRON, Juan

Tinturas cefálica y odontálgica ó específico medicinal para los dolores de cabeza y muelas [&c.]. *engr. seal.* 1 l.

fol. Mexico: [s.n. *c.* 1800].

MS annotation on verso.

An advertisement directing the use of the tinctures. According to the claim of the inventor, he was granted a ten year monopoly by the Viceroy (unnamed), and his invention was approved by José García Jove, President of the Protomedicato 1795–1823, and by Vicente Cervantes, Professor of the Jardín Botánico de México established in 1788. The advertisement is likely to have been issued after García Jove's appointment as President of the Protomedicato and before Cervantes' appointment as Director of the Jardín Botánico de México (*c.* 1805).

In Spain such grants of monopoly in drugs were normally made at the petition of their creator to the Protomedicato in Madrid. Statements by physicians testifying to the efficacy of the drug usually accompanied the petition [see Burke (1971), p. 51].

M.39 CORREA, Juan de

Tratado de la qualidad manifiesta, que el mercurio tiene; . . . . Añidido un discurso de una enfermedad que padeció en esta Ciudad una persona gravissima, con las particularidades que se vieron quando se embalsamó. [*2 plates*, 10 ll., pp. 56].

Mexico: H. de Ribera. 1648.

Facsimiles (2 copies).

M.40 CURVO SEMMEDO, João [1635–1719]

Virtudes de la piedra quadrada. 1 l.

fol. Mexico: J.B. de Hogal. 1730.

Guerra (Icon.) 255.
León (1915) 40.
Medina (Mex.) iv 3155.

A note printed at the end of the main text signed by Dr. Marcos José Salgado [1671–1740] and dated 2 May 1730, certified the accuracy of this extract from the end of the *Observaciones latinas* of Dr. Juan Cubo [*sic*] Semmedo. Its source has not been identified.

M.41 DEVOTI, Felix [*c.* 1760–1828]

Discurso sobre el cementerio general que se ha eregido extramuros de la Ciudad de Lima por el orden, zelo y beneficencia de su Exc.ᵐᵒ Señor Virey Don Jose Fernando de Abascal y Sousa. 2 ll., pp. 20.

4to. Guadalajara: José Fruto Romero. 1814.

Guerra (Icon.) 612.
Iguíniz 175.
Medina (Guadalajara) 82.
Palau 71466.

The first edition of 1808 is recorded by Medina (Lima) 2111, and Palau records another edition published in Havana in 1809.

Of Italian origin, Devoti arrived in Lima at the end of the eighteenth century by way of Jamaica, Nueva Granada and Quito. In 1803 he defended his bachelor's thesis on smallpox at the University of San Marcos. Though his thesis knew nothing of Jenner's discovery of vaccination he threw himself energetically into the work of vaccination from 1805. In 1808 he became *Catedrático de clínica externa* in the Real Colegio de Medicina y Cirugía de San Fernando, created in the same year; and in 1819 he was appointed *Regente* of the *Cátedra de prima de medicina* in the University of San Marcos by substitution to Unanue whose warm recommendation brought him this high university honour.

A bachelor of great energy, singular integrity in friendship and politics, and widely respected, Devoti was active as a liberal during Independence, suffered imprisonment for a short while in 1820, edited the *Gaceta del Gobierno de Lima Independiente*, 1821–22, and died a pensioner on the new state.

His full support for Abascal's establishment of a general cemetery outside Lima for reasons of public health provided first-class ammunition for similar (but unsuccessful) proposals for the City of Mexico. [See Lastres (1954) pp. 112–129; and M.98, M.188 for an earlier attempt to site cemeteries outside the City of Mexico]. Villalba (1802), 2, pp. 241–242, 245–248, points out that the movement for siting cemeteries away from populated areas for health reasons had been initiated in Spain in 1777.

M.42   **DIAZ CALVILLO, Juan Bautista**

Sermon que en el aniversario solemne de gracias a María Santísima de los Remedios, celebrado en esta Santa Iglesia Catedral el dia 30 de Octubre de 1811 por la victoria del Monte de las Cruces [&c.]. [Followed by:] Noticias para la historia de Nuestra Señora de los Remedios desde el año de 1808, hasta el corriente de 1812. *plate.* pp.269.

4to. Mexico: Imprenta de Arizpe. 1811–12.

Beristáin ii p.200 no.984.
Guerra (Icon.) 589.
Medina (Mex.) vii 10628.
Palau 72318.

The plate is inserted between sigs. 31 and 32 [i.e. between pp. 248 and 249]. Sig. 34 is of two conjugate leaves only; and the last leaf is a singleton.

Pp. 106–146 contain a pious but factual account of the campaign against Hidalgo and his capture and death.

The author was a priest of the Oratory of St. Philip Neri.

M.43   DIAZ DE GAMARRA Y DAVALOS, Juan Benito [1745–83]

Errores del entendimiento humano, con un apendice. Dalos al público D. Juan Felipe de Bendiaga. 4 ll., pp. vi, 258.

12mo. Puebla: Oficina del Real y Pontificio Seminario Palafoxiano. 1781.

Beristáin i p.249 no.422; ibid., ii p.334 no.1259.
Guerra (Icon.) 432.
León (Mex.) i 513.
Medina (Puebla) 1044.
Palau 72490.

Beristáin attributes this work to Juan Benito Díaz de Gamarra, and León observes that the pseudonym *Ben-Dia-Ga* is an anagram of that name. Gamarra was born in the diocese of Michoacán, attended the Colegio de San Ildefonso de México, and travelled to Italy and Spain. On his return to New Spain, he became *Rector, Regente de estudios*, and three times *Catedrático de filosofía* in the Colegio de San Francisco de Sales in San Miguel el Grande. He was a prolific writer on devotional and philosophical subjects.

M.44   DIAZ DE RIBERA, Jean

[Invitation to the obsequies of Dr. Joseph Díaz Brisuela]. 2 ll. (1st bl.).

[Mexico: s.n.]. 1692.

Guerra (Icon.) 164.

Addressees in several contemporary hands, and dated 19 September in MS.

Dr. José Díaz de Brisuela, member of the well-known medical dynasty, had been *Catedrático propietario de prima de medicina* since 1687; Juan Díaz de Ribera was his nephew.

M.45   ELIAS SAENZ, Antonio de

Vacuna. 6 ll. (i.e. pp. 201–212).

4to. [Mexico: M. de Zúñiga y Ontiveros. 1804].

This was issued as a supplement (no. 24) to the *Gazeta de Mexico*, 1804, *12* (no. 23) of 27 October. The first 3 pages print the formal request, dated 19 October, of the local administrator (*Subdelegado*) of Tenancingo (a small town about 50 miles to the S.W. of the City of Mexico) for a member of the Balmis expedition to vaccinate his charges; also the Viceroy's mode of compliance with his request; and further information from Veracruz on the Ayuntamiento's propagation in Mérida, Campeche, Tabasco, and Guatemala of the vaccine received from Havana before the arrival of the official expedition. The rest of the supplement is concerned with other affairs of official interest.

This vaccination supplement is probably a print of the letter quoted by Cook (1942) at p. 87; according to this account "it is entirely probable that Elias actually performed the [1,076] vaccinations himself", though the final total of 2,493 vaccinations by the beginning of 1806 quoted by Cook was probably achieved with the help of a qualified practitioner.

M.46   EMPLASTRO

Emplastro especifico de estavillo.

broadside. Mexico: [s.n. *c.* 1790].

Guerra (Icon.) 469.

An advertisement for a cure for all manner of wounds, bites, stings and sores, to be bought for 3 *reales*.

M.47   ESCOBAR, Matías [b. 1680?]

Voces de Triton sonoro, que da desde la Santa Iglesia de Valladolid de Mechoacan la incorrupta, y viva sangre del Illmo. Señor Doctor D. Juan Joseph de Escalona, y

Calatayud .... [Followed by:] Testimonio relativo ... sobre averiguar el estado de las partes intestinales, y liquidos, que se extraheron del cuerpo difunto. 2 pts.

4to. Mexico: J.B. de Hogal. 1746.

Beristáin ii p.234 no.1065.
León (Mex.) i 562.
Medina (Mex.) v 3764.
Palau 81077.

The author was an Augustinian canon, and a prolific writer on matters of piety.

M.48 **ESCOBAR SALMERON Y CASTRO, José de [d. 1684]**

Discurso cometologico, y relacion del nuevo cometa: visto en aqueste hemispherio mexicano, y generalmente en todo el mundo: el año de 1680; y extinguido en este de 81. *woodcuts (1 on t.p.)*. 4 ll., ff.24.

4to. Mexico: Widow of B. Calderon. 1681.

Andrade 749.
Beristáin ii p.232 no.1061.
Guerra (Icon.) 132.
León (1915) 28.
Medina (Mex.) ii 1224.
Palau 81248.

The author was a physician and *Catedrático de cirugía y anatomía* in the University of Mexico. His account of the progress of Halley's comet, entirely based on the old cosmology, sought to prove that it was composed of the exhalations (*espiritus*) and humours of man.

M.49 **ESQUIVEL NAVARRETE, José Manuel**

Sermon eucaristico por la felicidad que logro la Ciudad de Durango en la epidemia de viruelas del año de mil setecientos noventa y ocho. *table*. 3 ll., pp.21.

4to. Mexico: J.F. Jauregui. 1799.

Beristáin ii p.246 no.1109.
Guerra (Icon.) 526.
León (Mex.) v 333.
Medina (Mex.) vii 8882.

Sig. [D] [i.e. pp. 19–21] is of two conjugate leaves only.

A sermon on the text *de magnis periculis a deo liberati, magnifice gratias agimus ipsi,* 2 Maccabees 1.

The table on p. 19, provided by the *Intendente* of Durango, lists inoculated and uninoculated persons in the City of Durango who caught smallpox and the number of deaths in each category. Deaths among the uninoculated were far higher.

Born in the diocese of Michoacán, Esquivel took his degree in theology at the University of Mexico, filled a number of ecclesiastical offices, and ended his career as Archdeacon of the Cathedral of Durango.

M.50   ESTEYNEFFER, Juan de [1664–1716]

Florilegio medicinal de todas las enfermedades . . . . Reducido á tres libros. *woodcut ornaments.* 17 ll., pp. 522 (= 524).

4to. Mexico: Heirs of J.J. Guillena Carrascoso. 1712.

Beristáin iv p. 376 no. 2967.
Guerra (Icon.) 200.
León (1915) 36.
Medina (Mex.) iii 2317.
Palau 84235.

Both Juan José de Brisuela, *Protomédico decano* and *Catedrático de vísperas de medicina,* and Juan de Brisuela, *Catedrático propietario de prima de medicina* and President of the Protomedicato, give their official sanction to the publication of this work.

The Jesuit author, variously known as Esteyneffer, Steineffer, or Steinhöffer, came from Silesia to New Spain to serve in the missions. His work of popularisation, originally written to assist missionaries and others in remote places, enjoyed a great success; it was republished in Madrid in 1729 or 1730 and again in 1755, in Amsterdam in 1719, in Querétero in 1853, and again in Mexico in 1887.

The first two books comprise medicine and surgery, arranged by symptom, and the third is a dispensatory. A full description of its contents and of its influence in folk gynaecology appears in Kay (1974).

M.51   **FARFAN, Agustín [1531/32–1604]**

Tractado breve de anothomia y chirugia, y de algunas enfermedades, que mas comunmente suelen haver en esta Nueva España. [4 ll., ff. 274, 12 ll.].

[Mexico: A. Ricardo. 1579].

Facsimile.

M.52   **FARFAN, Agustín [1531/32–1604]**

Tractado brebe de medicina, y de todas las enfermedades. *woodcut on t.p.* 4 ll., ff. 353, 5 ll.

4to. Mexico: P. Ocharte. 1592.

Beristáin i p. 342 no. 102.
Guerra (Icon.) 6.
Icazbalceta 122 (102).
León (1915) 6.
Medina (Mex.) i 113.
Wagner 102.

Imperfect. The 1st 5 ll. [4 prelim. leaves & A1], f. 8 [A8], f. 160 [V8], & last 7 ll. [XX7, XX8, YY1 & YY3–6] are supplied in xerox copies. A copy of YY2 is wanting.

The 2nd edition of Farfán's *Tractado breve de anothomia y chirugia*, Mexico, A. Ricardo, 1579. The 3rd and 4th editions were published in Mexico in 1604 and 1610.

The 1st edition was intended for the faculty as well as for the laity, whereas the second and subsequent editions were designed largely as a source of domestic remedies for those in remote places lacking physicians and pharmacies. The first three books cover medicine generally; the fourth book deals with surgery, and the fifth with anatomy. Some American Indian remedies are included. Farfán's anatomy and physiology are Galenic.

A native of Seville, and a graduate of its university, García Farfán was appointed *Médico de cámara* to Philip II, a post which his deafness prevented him fulfilling. Arriving in New Spain in 1557 with his wife and family, he gained his doctorate at the University of Mexico in 1567. Following his wife's death, he entered the Augustinian order in 1568, where he continued to practise in the infirmary of his convent, and to take part in the affairs of the University as a member of the *claustro pleno* [see Icazbalceta, *op. cit.*, p. 236 (& footnote 76)].

A facsimile of this edition is also in the Wellcome Institute Library.

M53   FARFAN, Agustín [1531/32–1604]

Tratado breve de medicina y de todas las enfermedades. *woodcut on t.p.* 4 ll., ff.261, 5 ll.

4to. Mexico: G. Balli for C.A. Cesar. 1610.

Andrade 37.
Beristáin ii 1133.
Guerra (Icon.) 17.
Icazbalceta 122 (102).
León (1915) 14.
Medina (Mex.) ii 253.
Palau 86638.

The second leaf of the preliminaries (*recto*, the Viceroy's licence of 28 March 1609; *verso*, the medical licence of 28 April 1596 and the author's dedicatory sonnet to the Viceroy) may be a cancel, or an insertion from another copy. Both Andrade and Medina give the date of the Viceroy's licence as 28 March 1610.

The 4th edition of Farfán's *Tractado breve de anothomia y chirugia*, Mexico, A. Ricardo, 1579.

The text has many erasures and some additions in ink which suggest that this copy was used as a basis for a projected revised edition.

M.54   FERNANDEZ DE LIZARDI, José Joaquín [1776–1827]

Receta, o metodo curativo propuesto por medio del Pensador en la presente peste. pp.12.

4to. [Mexico:] María Fernández de Jáuregui. [1813].

Guerra (Icon.) 603
Radin pt. 1(1) p.61.

The author, editor of the liberal periodical *El pensador mexicano*, is also well-known as a prolific pamphleteer, novelist, poet, dramatist and translator.

Here he recommends several simple ways of administering a solution of tartar of potash and antimony, known as *Masdevall* after its Spanish populariser José Masdevall [d. 1801], in the treatment of the epidemic fevers of 1813 whose symptoms he describes. He refers to the article 'Compendio del método curativo antifebril de Masdeball', *Gazeta de México*, 1795, 7 (no. 50), (*Suplemento* to 18 September 1795), pp. 417—424; and to another amplified version in the *Diario de México* for 1810.

M.55   **FERNANDEZ SAAVEDRA, Juan Bautista**

[Begins:] Muy Señor mio: ... hé de tomar possession de la silla de segũdo proto-medico en el Real Tribunal del Proto-Medicato de esta Nueva-España.

broadside. [Mexico: s.n.]. 1764.

Guerra (Icon.) 348.

Impressed on the right hand side of the recto only. The invitation is addressed in MS to Domingo Pardo, and contemporary MS calculations in ink appear on the remainder of the recto and on some of the verso.

The writer of the invitation was a well-known physician who had received his doctorate in 1734 from the University of Mexico. He was *Catedrático sustituto de prima de medicina* 1761–63 and *Catedrático sustituto de anatomía y cirugía* 1763–67 in the same University.

M.56   **FLORES, José Felipe [1751–1824]**

Especifico nuevamente descubierto en el Reyno de Goatemala, para la curacion radical del horrible mal de cancro, y otros mas frecuentes. (Experimentado ya favorablemente en esta Capital de México). 2 ll., pp. 15.

4to. Mexico: F. de Zúñiga y Ontiveros. 1782.

Beristáin ii p. 277 no. 1171.
Guerra (Icon.) 433.
León (Mex.) i 626.
León (1915) 72.
Medina (Mex.) vi 7310.
Palau 92485.

León records an earlier issue of the same edition without the additional note of further cures on the verso of the title page.

Flores recounts how an Indian remedy of a diet of raw newts cured a Guatemalan citizen of cancer. A physician of lively curiosity, Flores won the *Cátedra de prima de medicina* in the University of Guatemala in 1781, and in 1793 was appointed *Médico de la real cámara* and *Protomédico* of Guatemala. In 1796 he left for Europe to pursue his scientific researches, where he visited Italy, France and England, and eventually settled in Madrid. This account, first published in Guatemala in 1781, was quickly republished in Mexico, Madrid (1781 or 1782) and Cadiz (1783) and published in translation in Lausanne (1784), Turin (1784) and Venice (1785). Four other pamphlets discussing this treatment as not only a cure for cancer but for a great variety of diseases appeared in the City of Mexico during 1782; two more appeared in 1783.

The fullest studies of this remarkable man are by Aznar López (1960) and by Martínez Durán (1964) pp. 359–393. Aspects of his work are discussed by Lanning (1956) whose pp. 265–266 also discuss the total of 7 pamphlets in this controversy, of which the Wellcome Institute Library possesses five [see also M.60, M.76, M.77, M.135].

M.57   FLORES, José Felipe [1751–1824]

Experimentos. Sobre la conservacion de las carnes. pp. 8.

4to. Mexico: M. Ontiveros. 1813.

Guerra (Icon.) 604.

Palau 92489 records the original edition published in Cadiz in 1811 and another published in Manila in 1812. Medina (Lima) iv 2936 records another edition of 1813 [see P.10].

Flores sets out the objections to pickling in salt and the course of his successful experiments in preserving barrelled meat and fish in aqueous solutions of alcohol of successively diminishing strengths. He describes his methods of barrelling and a cheap method of dry packing after soaking successive barrels of meat and fish in the same solution for seven days.

M.58   GALISTEO Y XIORRO, Juan

Remedio natural para precaverse de los rayos, y de sus funestos efectos. Secreto tan util, como curioso, sacado de las repetidas observaciones, . . . ha estampado en Madrid año de 1757 en su Diario Philosophico Don Juan Galisteo tom. 1. num. 6. pp. 7.

4to. Mexico: Reimpresso en la Imprenta del Colegio Real de San Ildefonso [?1758].

Guerra (Icon.) 323.
León (1915) 53.
Medina v 4465.

The author recalls the experiments of Franklin and of others in France on electricity and the lighting rod and concludes that rods are best shaped in the form of the cross to strike fear into the evil spirits of the clouds. He proposes rods of this shape for the important buildings of Puebla, a city which, as he says, suffers much from thunderstorms. A copy of J. Galisteo y Xiorro, *Diario philosophico* (Nos. 1–8), Madrid, A. Perez de Soto, 1757, is in the Wellcome Institute Library. [See WMS. Amer. 12 (GALISTEO Y XIORRO)].

M.59   GARCIA JOVE Y CAPELON, José Ignacio [d. 1823]

[Begins:] Señor. D. Jose Ignacio Garcia Jove Capelon, i Espinola, Doctor en la Facultad de Medicina, hace presentes á V.S. los egercicios literarios que tiene practicados. 4 ll.

4to. Mexico: [s.n. *c.*1785].

MS notes on the last 3 leaves; and signed and dated 9 July 1785 as a correct account of García Jove's activities by the Secretary of the University of Mexico.

Having received his doctorate in medicine from the University of Mexico in 1772, García Jove was enrolled in the Faculty of Law in 1779. He held the Chair of anatomy and surgery from 1777 to 1789, when he gained the *Cátedra de vísperas de medicina* on the death of Juan José de la Peña y Brizuela. In 1795 he became *Catedrático de prima de medicina* (from which he retired in 1797) and President of the Protomedicato of New Spain until his death. [See Flores (1886–1888), *2*, 90–91; and WMS. Amer. 34 (GARCIA JOVE Y CAPELON)].

This document is a formal application and curriculum vitae or *relación de méritos* for a university post, the title of which is not stated.

M.60   GARCIA DE LA VEGA, José Vicente

Discurso critico que sobre el uso de las lagartijas, como especifico contra muchas enfermedades [&c.]. *engr. coat of arms.* 4 ll., pp. 28.

4to. Mexico: F. de Zúñiga y Ontiveros. 1782.

Beristáin v p.105 no.3228.
Guerra (Icon.) 434.
León (Mex.) vi 318.
León (1915) 73.
Medina (Mex.) vi 7311.

Rúbricas on A2ᵛ and A3ᵛ.

This learned and sober assessment, completed by case histories, supports Flores' enthusiasm for raw newts in the cure of cancer and many other diseases. [See M.56].

According to the *Parecer* of José Giral Matienzo, *Catedrático de prima de medicina* in the University of Mexico, the author was physician to the Viceregal court.

M.61   GIL, Francisco

Extracto de la obra publicada en Madrid el año pasado de 1784 con el título de Disertacion Fisico-Médica, en la qual se prescribe un método seguro para preservar a los pueblos de viruelas. pp.12.

4to. Mexico: [s.n.]. 1788.

Guerra (Icon.) 455.

Sig. * comprises the conjugate third and fourth leaves.

Palau records the original Madrid edition of 1784, and Beristáin and Medina the unabridged Mexico edition of 1796 [see entry below] which preceded the great smallpox epidemic of 1797–98.

Rúbrica and signature on verso of the last leaf.

Among many practical precautions, this extract recommends isolation, fresh air and destruction of fomites, and may have been re-issued in New Spain as a result of the smallpox epidemic in Chile of 1787. The years 1784–87 had in any event been years of epidemics and famine in central and southern New Spain. The author was surgeon at the Escorial, and a member of the Real Academia Médica de Madrid. His work won contemporary approval [see Villalba (1802), *2*, 265–267].

M.62   GIL, Francisco

Disertacion físico-médica, en la qual se prescribe un metodo seguro para preservar a los pueblos de viruelas hasta lograr la completa extincion de ellas en todo el Reyno. 3 ll., pp.v, 92.

4to. Mexico: M. de Zúñiga y Ontiveros. 1796.

Guerra (Icon.) 491.

León (1915) 159.

Medina (Mex.) vii 8589.

The unabridged version of the preceding entry. The Marqués de Branciforte [Viceroy 1794–98] in his Order dated 6 August 1796, reprinted in the preliminaries, required 200 copies to be run off for distribution.

M.63 **GOMEZ ORTEGA, Casimiro [1740–1818]** *and* **PALAU Y VERDERA, Antonio**

Curso elemental de botanica, teorico, dispuesto para la enseñanza del Real Jardin Botanico de Madrid . . . . Parte teorica. 4 ll., pp.ix, 108, 1 l. (i.e. *fldg. table*).

4to. Mexico: F. de Zúñiga y Ontiveros. 1788.

Guerra (Icon.) 456.

Medina (Mex.) vi 7797.

Sig. Q is of 2 leaves only; Sig. R of 1 leaf only; the folding table of the sexual system of Linnaeus is inserted at the end.

The Linnaean system is followed. The first edition, published in Madrid, 2 vols., 1785 [Palau 104236], included the practice as well as the theory of botany. The second part seems not to have been published in Mexico.

Gómez Ortega was Professor of the Botanical Garden in Madrid, *Médico de cámara* and *Boticario mayor* to the king, and organiser of botanical expeditions to the Americas, one of which was the expedition directed by Martín de Sessé which began its work in Mexico in 1787. Palau was the holder of the second chair of botany in Madrid. The present work was intended as a textbook for the Jardín Botánico de México which was founded under Antonio Flores [Viceroy 1787–89] in 1788 [see Rickett (1947)].

M.64 **GONZALEZ DEL CAMPILLO, Manuel Ignacio [*c.* 1740–1813]**

Exhortacion que el Ilustrísimo Señor Don M.I.G. del C., obispo electo de la Puebla, hace á sus diocesanos para que se presten con docilidad á la importante práctica de la vacuna. 1 l., pp.27.

4to. Mexico: M.J. de Zúñiga y Ontiveros. 1804.

Beristáin ii p.28 no.602.
Guerra (Icon.) 544.
Medina (Mex.) vii 9696.

Sig. 4 [i.e. pp. 23–26] is of two conjugate leaves; the final leaf is a singleton.

The author is said by Beristáin to have become Bishop of Puebla in 1802 after serving the diocese since 1775. This active if conservative prelate published many quasi-political pastoral letters, edicts, and exhortations during his reign.

M.65   GRANADOS Y GALVEZ, José Joaquín [1734–94]

Tardes americanas: gobierno gentil y catolico: breve y particular noticia de toda la historia indiana: sucesos, casos notables, y cosas ignoradas, desde la entrada de la Gran Nacion Tulteca á esta tierra de Anahuac, hasta los presentes tiempos. *engr. plates, & coat of arms, diagr.* 36 ll., pp.540.

4to. Mexico: F. de Zúñiga y Ontiveros. 1778.

Beristáin ii p.381 no.1370.
Guerra (Icon.) 418.
León (Mex.) i 718.
Medina (Mex.) vi 7000.
Palau 108426.

Granados, a Franciscan, was successively Bishop of Sonora and of Durango. *Tarde* XV, pp. 395–441, in this, his major work, has some interesting notes on the arts and sciences in contemporary Mexico.

M.66   GUADALAJARA. Bishop

[Begins:] Sr. Cura de [San José de la Isla]. Parece que Dios allá ... ha resuelto descargar sobre estos paises el poder tremendo de su bengadora justicia [&c.]. 1 l., pp.25.

4to. Guadalajara: J. Fruto Romero. 1813.

Guerra (Icon.) 598.

The name of the parish is inserted in MS.

Juan Cruz Ruiz de Cabañas y Crespo [Bishop 1796–1824] reprints a series of discourses on prevention of the epidemic fevers of 1813, discourses which he says

(p. 1) originally appeared in nos. 8, 9, & 10 of the journal *Amigo de la patria* (*Méx.*), 1812–13, (26 nos.). A similar work or the same work, *Discurso sobre las fumigaciones, útil y provechoso para la salud pública; y un método sencillo de curar la epidemia que [aflige] á los habitantes de la Ciudad de la Puebla y otras poblaciones de Nueva España*, Reimpreso en Guadalaxara á expensas de la Junta de Sanidad, en la oficina de D. José Fruto Romero, año de 1813, is listed by León (1915) 206, and by Iguíniz 167; the major part of the work referred to in these two entries, originally published by order of the Junta de Sanidad of Puebla [see also León (1915) 205], is included in the present edition under a slightly amended title.

This energetic bishop, a supporter of many charitable causes as well as in later years a political supporter of Iturbide, is still remembered for his foundation of the Casa de Misericordia (now the Hospicio Cabañas) of Guadalajara, whose constitution received royal approval in 1803. [See M.68, M.69.].

M.67   **GUADALAJARA. Junta Superior de Sanidad**

Reglamento, que la Junta Superior de Sanidad de Guadalaxara en la celebrada á 28 de Agosto de 1813 ha acordado, para el establecimiento, y gobierno de las Juntas Principales y Subalternas de Sanidad. 4 ll. (last bl.).

4to. Guadalajara: [Junta Superior de Sanidad]. 1813.

Guerra (Icon.) 597.

This brief order provides for the chain of command in matters of public health, and, among other health regulations, enjoins the rigorous separation of the infected from the healthy. Dated 1 September 1813.

M.68   **GUADALAJARA. Junta Superior de Sanidad**

[Begins:] Esta Junta Superior de Sanidad, en desempeño de los objetos de su instituto, ha resuelto circular á toda la Provincia de su cuidado las advertencias, y el método curativo siguientes. Prevenciones económico políticas. 4 ll.

fol. Guadalajara: [J.F. Romero]. 1814.

Guerra (Icon.) 613.

The missing lower 3 to 5 lines of the text are supplied in a full typescript version from a complete copy of the original.

This circular letter dated 14 June 1814 and signed by Juan Cruz, Bishop of

Guadalajara [see M.66, M.69] is concerned with means whereby news of an epidemic may be brought rapidly to the local Junta de Sanidad or Ayuntamiento, with the supply of shelter, food and drugs, with rigorous personal and public cleanliness, and with enforcement of quarantine. The letter goes on to describe the symptoms of the prevailing epidemic fever[s] and prescribes for their treatment.

M.69   GUADALAJARA. Junta Superior de Sanidad

[Begins:] Por encargo de esta Junta Superior de Sanidad han formado sus vocales facultativos los Doctores Don Mariano García de la Torre, y Don Ignacio Otero el metodo curativo siguiente. La fiebre epidémica que reyna [&c.]. 2 ll.

4to. [Guadalajara: s.n.]. 1814.

Guerra (Icon.) 613 *bis*.

This short circular letter dated 17 August and signed by Juan Cruz, Bishop of Guadalajara [see M.66, M.68] notes that the symptoms of the epidemic fever are greatly increased in children with intestinal worms, describes the symptoms marking their presence, and suggests internal and external remedies for evacuation and relief.

M.70   GUTIERREZ CORONEL, Ricardo José

El encanto de los medicos. Idea panagyrica del inclyto medico, e invicto martyr San Pantaleon [&c.]. 12 ll., pp.21.

4to. Mexico: Imprenta nueva de la Bibliotheca Mexicana. 1758.

Beristáin ii p.404, no.1439.
León (Mex.) i 731.
Medina (Mex.) v 4473.

The preliminaries are as follows π^1 ¶4 2 ¶2 ¶¶¶1 *4; C4 [*i.e.* the last leaf] wanting, presumably blank.

A sermon preached in 1757 by the *Catedrático propietario de vísperas de sagrada teología* of the Real Colegio de San Juan y San Pedro of Puebla.

M.71   HERMANOS DE LA CARIDAD DE SAN HIPOLITO

Constituciones de la sagrada religion de la charidad, de S. Hipolyto martyr. Fundada en las Indias occidentales por el venerable padre Bernardino Alvarez. *woodcut on t.p.*, 11 ll., pp. 358.

4to. Mexico: Maria de Ribera. 1749.

Beristáin i p. 132 no. 166.
Guerra (Icon.) 299.
León (Mex.) v 55.
Medina (Mex.) v 3925.
Palau 60022.

Arriving first in New Spain as a soldier, Bernardino Alvarez [1514?–1584] was forced to flee from the City of Mexico after involvement in a murder during a dispute. Having made his fortune in Peru, he returned to the City of Mexico some 30 years later, where he devoted his life and wealth to charity. His first foundation, the Hospital de San Hipólito in the City of Mexico, was founded in 1567, and before the end of his life had become a large institution, caring in particular for the sick and poor of all kinds, especially convalescents, the aged, and the insane, for whom there had been no previous provision.

The Order takes its early foundation from the approval of Gregory XIII [Pope 1572–85] and subsequent Popes, but it was not formally ratified as a regular Order until 1700 when the Bull of Innocent XII [Pope 1691–1700] issued, placing the Order under the Rule of St. Augustine. Before its suppression by the Spanish Cortes in 1820 its hospitals had spread throughout present day Mexico, and had reached Guatemala and Cuba. [See Muriel (1956–60), *1*, pp. 187–231; and see M.143].

M.72   **HERMANOS DE LA CARIDAD DE SAN HIPOLITO**

[Begins:] Fr. [José de Sta. Cruz [&c.]] ... Prior del Convento de Señor San Roque de esta Ciudad de los Ángeles .... Por quanto por parte de [D. José Cadena] con christiano zelo y caritativo afecto se nos ha pedido ... nos dignemos de recibirle, aceptarle, é incorporarle en nuestra Santa Religion por uno de nuestros hermanos [&c.]. *woodcuts & woodcut ornaments.*

broadside. [Puebla: s.n. 17   ].

Rúbrica, two signatures and paper seal on recto.

The names are completed and the document signed in MS; the MS date of 1818 covers the printed date of 17[   ]. The document is the certificate of adoption of José Cadena as a Brother of the Order.

San Roque as one of the saints popularly invoked for protection against pestilence and disease gave his name to the hospital of the Hermanos de la Caridad de San Hipólito of Puebla from its formal foundation in 1592. The importance of the hospital as a mad-house was such that it was enlarged in 1820 under the same Fr. José de Sta. Cruz. Though the Order itself was suppressed in 1821, the hospital continued its work until the present century. [See Muriel (1956–60), *1*, pp. 222–231].

M.73   INSTRUCCION

Instruccion para inocular las viruelas, y método de curarlas con facilidad, y acierto. 1 l., pp. xxxvii.

8vo. Puebla: P. de la Rosa. 1797.

Guerra (Icon.) 502.

Sig. 2 wants 4 leaves, presumably blank.

Though some of the recommendations broadly follow J.I. Bartolache, *Instruccion que puede servir para que se cure á los enfermos de las viruelas epidémicas*, Mexico, 1779, whose second edition is recorded by Medina (Mex.) vii 8680 (following Beristáin, i, p. 226, no. 384) as published in Mexico in 1797, the pamphlet appears to be by another and unidentified hand, and perhaps issued by the health authorites of Puebla. It provides, in the manner of Bartolache, cautious instructions on inoculation, and a moderate mode of treatment for the infected. [See M.13].

M.74   L., *Fray* **S.**

Voz de la naturaleza. 1 l.

fol. Mérida: Jese F. Bates. 1813.

Guerra (Icon.) 599.

The anonymous writer of this address to the public advocates the segregation of lepers, here confused with sufferers from elephantiasis [*elefansis*], citing classical theories of transmission of disease, the laws of Leviticus, of Spain and her colonies, and the practice of the Spanish monarchy in setting up special hospitals for sufferers from skin diseases.

M.75 **LARREATEGUI, José Dionisio [d. 1795/8]**

Descripciones de plantas. Discurso que en la abertura del estudio de botánica de 1 de Junio de 95 pronunció en el Real Jardin de México el Br. D. J.D.L. pp.48.

4to. [Mexico: M. de Zúñiga y Ontiveros. 1798].

Beristáin ii p.104 no.782
Guerra (Icon.) 486.
León (Mex.) vi 102 [?].
Medina (Mex.) vii 8748.
Palau 132166 [probably confused with 132165].

Folding plate supplied in photocopy.

A commentary on the system of Linnaeus, followed by an example fully described in the terms of that system.

Medina refers to the notice in the *Gazeta de Mexico* for 14 December 1798, (i.e. *9*, p.144) which regards this work, available from the press of the Gazette, as an exact summary of the Linnaean system.

M.76 **LEON Y GAMA, Antonio de [1735–1802]**

Instruccion sobre el remedio de las lagartijas nuevamente descubierto para la curacion del cancro, y otras enfermedades. 3 ll., pp.59, 1 l.

4to. Mexico: F. de Zúñiga y Ontiveros. 1782.

Beristáin ii p.332 no.1255.
Guerra (Icon.) 435.
León (Mex.) i 821.
León (1915) 74.
Medina (Mex.) vi 7317.
Palau 135584.

Sig. [J] [i.e. the last leaf] is a singleton; the remaining leaf is presumably blank.

A well-known mathematician and astronomer, León y Gama supports Flores' claim for the newts of Amatitlán as a cure for cancer. His obituary appears in the *Gazeta de Mexico*, 1802–3, *11*, 158–164 (i.e. Supplement to the *Gazeta* of 8 October 1802). [See entry below and M.56].

M.77   **LEON Y GAMA, Antonio de [1735–1802]**

Respuesta satisfactoria a la carta apologetica, que escribieron . . . Manuel Antonio Moreno, y . . . Alejo Ramon Sanchez: y defensa contra la censura . . . de algunas proposiciones contenidas en la Instruccion sobre el remedio de las lagartijas. 5 ll., pp. 32, 1 bl. l.

4to. Mexico: F. de Zúñiga y Ontiveros. 1783.

Beristáin ii p. 332 no. 1255.
Guerra (Icon.) 437.
León (Mex.) ii (2) 196.
León (1915) 76.
Medina (Mex.) vi 7406.
Palau 135585.

The last blank leaf is probably the conjugate second leaf of the singleton sig. E.

León y Gama concedes that information communicated only by ignorant persons should not have been published as a specific remedy. [See entry above and M.56].

M.78   **LIMA Y ESCALADA, Ambrosio de**

Espicilegio de la calidad, y utilidades del trigo que communmente llaman blanquillo. Con repuesta á las razones, que los Protho-Medicos desta Corte alegaron contra él. 4 ll., ff. 22.

4to. Mexico: Heirs of the Widow of B. Calderon. 1692.

Beristáin iii p. 125 no. 1687.
Guerra (Icon.) 169.
León (1915) 32.
Medina (Mex.) iii 1523.
Palau 138398.

·The author took his bachelor's degree in medicine in the University of Mexico in 1658, and later became physician to Gaspar de Sandoval, Conde de Galvi [Viceroy 1688–96] to whom he dedicated this work. His argument, supported by the lean harvest of common wheat of 1691–92, persuaded the Viceroy to encourage the sowing of white wheat and ended the controversy of some 15 years as to whether white wheat was harmful to health.

M.79 LOPEZ, Gregorio [1542–96]

Tesoro de medicinas, para todas enfermedades . . . . Reconocido, é illustrado con algunas notas, por . . . Mathias de Salzedo Mariaca. 6 ll., ff. 56 (= 58).

4to. Mexico: F. Rodriguez Lupercio. 1672.

Andrade 620.
Beristáin iii p. 145 no. 1723.
Guerra (Icon.) 118.
Icazbalceta pp. 237–238.
León (1915) 23.
Medina (Mex.) ii 1063.
Palau 140002.

Andrade copied Beristáin's inaccurate bibliographical statement; and Palau quotes without comment or details of pagination a copy which is given the unlikely date of 1670. Although the imprint on the title-page of the present copy is mutilated, the remainder of the title-page and the dates of the licences leave little doubt that this copy is of the first edition of 1672 whose existence was supposed by Medina.

López, according to the traditional account, was a Spanish hermit of high birth who came to New Spain in 1562 where he continued his wandering life of austerities and prayer. While at the then famous Hospital de la Santa Cruz at Huaxtepec [Oaxtepec] 1580–89 he devoted himself to caring for the sick and to writing the present notes on remedies, annotated and edited for publication some 90 years later by Mathias de Salzedo Mariaca [see Losa (1727)].

It is essentially a compendium of crude and popular vegetable, animal, and mineral receipts arranged in alphabetical order of symptom or necessity. Guerra (1966) has fully covered the history and importance of this work. [See entry below; and WMS. Amer. 101 [LOPEZ].

M.80 LOPEZ, Gregorio [1542–96]

Tesoro de medicinas, para diversas enfermedades . . . . Añadido, corregido, y emmendado en esta segunda impression, con notas de . . . Mathias de Salzedo Mariaca, y Joseph Dias Brizuela. 14 ll., ff. 86 (= 85).

4to. Mexico: F. Rodriguez Lupercio. 1674.

Guerra (Icon.) 123.

León (1915) 26.
Medina (Mex.) ii 1108.
Palau 140003.

The last leaf [Sig. Y[1]] is a singleton.

This 2nd edition adds the notes of José Dias Brizuela [d. 1692]; new entries include a comment on the properties of mandragora under the title *Razon, y sentidos suspensos por tres horas*, which his note regards as highly dangerous.

M.81   **LOPEZ DE BONILLA, Gabriel**

Discurso, y relacion cometographia del repentino aborto de los astros, que sucedió del cometa que apareció por diziembre de 1653. *woodcut diagr. on t.p., & woodcut coat of arms.* 4 ll., ff.12.

4to. Mexico: Widow of B. Calderon. [1654].

Beristáin i p.278 no.484.
Guerra (Icon.) 96.
Medina (Mex.) ii 784.

One section seeks to demonstrate that the air, infected by the comet's passing, could cause illness, choler, unrest, wars, and deaths.

M.82   **LOPEZ DE HINOJOSOS, Alonso [c.1535–1597]**

Summa, y recopilacion de chirugia, con un arte para sa[n]grar muy util y provechosa. [15 ll., ff.201, 8 ll.].

Mexico: A. Ricarco [i.e. Ricardo]. 1578.

Facsimile.

M.83   **LOPEZ DE HINOJOSOS, Alonso [c.1535–1597]**

Summa y recopilacion de cirugia, con un arte para sangrar, y examen de barberos. 2 ed. [8 ll., ff.203, 1 l.].

Mexico: P. Balli. 1595.

Facsimile.

M.84   **MACORP HECAFOC, Narciso [*pseud?*]**

Carta escrita a una señora titulo, sobre el eclypse futuro del dia 13 de Mayo de este presente año de 1752. Y sobre la carta impressa, que escribio el Br. D. Joseph Mariano Medina. 2 ll.

4to. Mexico: Widow of J.B. de Hogal. 1752.

Guerra (Icon.) 304.
Medina (Mex.) v 4085.

Medina comments that the author's name is probably a pseudonym or more probably an anagram. [See M.89].

M.85   **MALPICA DIOSDADO, José Francisco de**

Alexipharmaco de la salud, antidoto de la enfermedad, favorable dietetico instrumento de la vida. Dissertacion medico-moral, que trata del ayuno, y accidentes, que escusan de él, y que hacen licito el uso de las carnes á los enfermos, y valetudinarios. 13 ll., pp. 180.

4to. Mexico: Colegio Real de San Ildefonso. 1751.

Beristáin iii p. 181, no. 1799.
Guerra (Icon.) 302.
León (Mex.) i 852.
León (1915) 50.
Medina (Mex.) v 4047.
Palau 147943.

The ninth leaf of the preliminaries, containing the three sonnets, is a singleton signed ¶ ¶ ¶; the second leaf is presumably blank. The verso of the eighth leaf has a signature of ownership dated 1753.

The author obtained his baccalaureate in medicine from the University of Mexico in 1733 and became physician to the Capuchin sisters of Puebla.

M.86   **MARTINEZ, Enrico [1550/60–1632]**

Reportorio de los tiempos, y historia natural desta Nueva Espana. *woodcut coat of arms on t.p., 1 illus., plate.* 12 ll., pp. 53, 1 l., ff. 55–75, 21 ll., pp. 77–277 (= pp. 371 in all).

4to. Mexico: 'Emp. del mesmo autor.' 1606.

Andrade 22.
Beristáin iii pp. 200 no. 1838.
Guerra (Icon.) 10.
Medina (Mex.) ii 228.
Palau 154297.

The pagination changes to foliation at p. 53 [i.e. G1] and after 21 unnumbered leaves reverts to pagination at the first page numbered 77 [i.e. K1]. There are many errors in numeration, and the total number of pages (excluding the unnumbered leaves of the preliminaries) is in fact 371. The dial plate, which lacks the movable parts, is as usual inserted between pp. 36 and 37 [i.e. after D4]. The presence of signatures I*– I*******✚⁴ suggests that much of the astrological material covering July 1609 to December 1620, and some explanatory material, was added while the book was at press.

Neither the second part, announced on p. 276 [i.e. sig. Pp 3ᵛ], nor two other treatises on agriculture and physiognomy, announced on the last leaf [i.e. sig. Pp 4ʳ], were published. The publisher's device noted by Andrade appears on the verso of the last leaf.

Born in Hamburg, Martínez went early to Seville, and returned to his native city for one and a half years at the age of nineteen. After graduating in mathematics from Paris he travelled to Courland, then part of Poland, and sailed for New Spain in 1589 as *Cosmógrafo del Rey*. In 1599 he was appointed *Intérprete* of the Inquisition. Among his many activities he published books from his own press from 1599 to 1611, some of them his own, and began in 1607 the formidable undertaking of draining the valley of Mexico, a task in which he was partly successful.

Attempting in its 5 books a world picture largely from the astrological viewpoint, the fourth book of the present work deals with the influence of astrology on medical matters. From p. 225 his *Breve relacion del tiempo* attempts an abbreviated history of New Spain from 1520 to 1590. [See Maza (1943)].

M.87   MAYGRIER, Jacques Pierre [1771–1834]

Nuevo metodo para operar en los partos .... Traducido al castellano por Nicolas Molero. 4 ll., pp. 167.

8vo. Mexico: M. Ontiveros. 1821.

Guerra (Icon.) 652.
León (1915) 215.
Medina (Mex.) viii 12080.

A translation, with additions, omissions, and some alterations in the text, of extracts from vol. 1 of J.P. Maygrier, *Nouveaux élémens de la science et de l'art des accouchemens*, 2 ed., 2 vols., Paris, de Pelafol, 1817. In his own *Apendice medico-politico* (pp. 149–167) Molero makes an impassioned plea on physical and moral grounds for the rearing of children by their own mothers. [For another translation by Molero see M.30].

Molero is described on the title-page as *Profesor de medicina y cirugia*.

M.88 MEDINA, Antonio [*fl.* 1750]

Cartilla nueva util y necesaria para instruirse las matronas que vulgarmente se llaman comadres, en el oficio de partear. Mandada hacer por el Real Tribunal del Proto-Medicato. 40 ll.

8vo. Mexico: María Fernández de Jáuregui. 1806.

Guerra (Icon.) 560.
León (1915) 196.
Medina (Mex.) vii 9880.

This primer of midwifery originally appeared under the same title in Madrid in 1750 [see Chinchilla (1841–46), *3*, p. 226] and/or in 1759 [Palau 159368] at the direction of the Protomedicato. According to the present prologue, apparently copied *verbatim* from its original, the Protomedicato had secured the agreement of the King and the Supreme Council of Castile to direct that all midwives should be examined by the Protomedicato in the theory and practice of their craft; the present handbook, in the form of a catechism, was prepared for this purpose.

The title-page describes the author as physician to the royal hospitals, physician to the Queen's household, and *Examinador* to the Protomedicato.

M.89 MEDINA, José Mariano de

Destierro de temores, y sustos vanamente aprehendidos, en el eclypse quasi total futuro del año de 1752. Carta escrita á un amigo. 2 ll.

4to. Mexico: Widow of J.B. de Hogal. 1752.

Guerra (Icon.) 305.

Referred to by Medina (Mex.) v 4085, as a work whose date and place of publication were unrecorded.

The letter and its *Parecer* are dated from Puebla 1751 and the imprint states that the present edition was reprinted in the City of Mexico. The earlier edition, not now traceable, is likely to have been published in Puebla.

The author was domestic chaplain to the Bishop of Puebla. [See M.84].

M.90   MEDINA, José Mariano de

Heliotropio critico racional prognostico computado á el meridiano de la Puebla de los Angeles, para el año bissexto de 1752. *woodcut on t.p.*, 18 ll.

8vo. Puebla: Widow of M. de Ortega. [1752].

Guerra (Icon.) 308.
Medina (Puebla) 548.
Palau 159462.

M.91   METODO

Metodo curativo, que puede contribuir para precaver en mucha parte las desgracias que ocasiona la actual epidemia de viruelas á los pobres que las padecen en los pueblos y campos .... Dispuesto por órden del ... Señor Doctor D. Victoriano Lopez Gonzalo ... Obispo de la Puebla de los Angeles [&c.]. 8 ll.

8vo. Puebla: Oficina del Real y Pontificio Seminario Palafoxiano. 1779.

Guerra (Icon.) 427.
León (1915) 265.
Medina (Puebla) 1035.

Practical instructions for the care of smallpox patients in the successive stages of the disease.

M.92   MEXICO. Archbishop

Franqueada piadosamente á nombre de S.M. por este Real Acuerdo á los Indios y

Naturales de los pueblos epidemiados de esta governacion, la total exempcion de tributos por todo el tiempo que permaneció el contagio en ellos [&c.]. 1 l.

fol. [Mexico: s.n.]. 1738.

Guerra (Icon.) 278.

Signed, with MS annotation on recto in contemporary hand.

A circular dated 18 September 1738 in which Juan Antonio de Vizarrón y Eguiarreta [Archbishop 1731–47, and Viceroy 1734–40] requires his priests to execute the command of the Real Acuerdo [Council of Ministers] to undertake promptly and secretly a re-count of their Indian parishioners. Tax payable by Indian tributaries had been rescinded during the recent epidemic, presumably that of *matlazahuatl* of 1736–37, and was now required to be re-applied.

José Antonio Alzate, in a letter to the Académie Royale des Sciences of Paris, estimated that more than a third of the inhabitants of New Spain died in this epidemic. [The letter is printed in *Anuario de estudios americanos*, 1944, *1*, pp. 766–781].

M.93   MEXICO. Archbishop

[Begins:] Nos el Dr. D. Alonso Nuñez de Haro y Peralta .... Entre las graves obligaciones de nuestro ministerio pastoral, consideramos ser la primera velar cuidadosamente, para que las almas de nuestros subditos consigan la salvacion eterna: y habiendo llegado á nuestra noticia, que se mira comunmente con horror la operacion llamada parto cesareo [&c.].

broadside. Mexico: [s.n.]. 1772.

Guerra (Icon.) 384.

Signed on the recto and dated on the verso in two contemporary hands.

This liberal Archbishop of Mexico [1772–1800], following a *Real Pragmática* issued by Charles III of Spain when King of Naples in 1749, charges his clergy to keep in their houses *un librito pequeño* by José Manuel Rodríguez (i.e. *La caridad del sacerdote*, Mexico, F. de Zúñiga y Ontiveros, 1772) [see M.184, M.185; for the original edition see Medina (Mex.) vi 5523] which explains how they or others in the absence of a surgeon can perform a caesarean section to save the body and soul of the child when the mother is already dead. Rodríguez's work was an adaptation of F.M. Cangiamila,

NOS EL Dr. D. ALONSO NUÑEZ DE HARO Y PERALTA,

por la Gracia de Dios, y de la Santa Sede-Apostólica Arzobispo de esta Santa Iglesia Metropolitana, de México, del Consejo de S. M. &c.

ENTRE LAS GRAVES OBLIGACIONES DE NUESTRO MINISTERIO Pastoral, consideramos ser la primera velar cuidadosamente, para que las Almas de nuestros Subditos consigan la Salvacion eterna: Y habiendo llegado á nuestra noticia, que se mira comunmente con horror la Operacion llamada Parto cesareo por medio de la qual se consigue facilmente extraér del Vientre de las Mugeres Difuntas los Niños, para salvar su vida corporal, como la experiencia ha demostrado muchas veces, ó á lo menos la vida espiritual, y su eterna felicidad, administrandoles el Stô. Sacramento del Bautismo: Teniendo presente una Rl. Pracmatica, publicada en el año de mil setecientos quarenta y nueve, por el Rey Nrô. Sr. D. Carlos Tercero en su Reynado de las dos Sicilias en la qual estableció, y mandó, que se procesase, y castigase como Reo de Homicidio á qualquiera Marido, Pariente, ú otra Persona, que impidiese executar dicha Operacion: Y asimismo las Doctrinas de graves Autores, que resuelven con fundamentos claros, y solidos deducidos de la sana Doctrina de S. Agustin, y Stô. Tomás ser pecado mortal omitir la tal Operacion: Mandamos con precepto formal, á todos los Curas, y Vicarios de nuestro Arzobispado, que siempre que se halle en peligro de muerte alguna Muger embarazada en sus respectivas Feligresias, dispongan que se tenga prevenido, y pronto un Cirujano, que haga dicha Operacion cesarea, luego que se verifique la muerte de la Enferma embarazada, y extraida que sea la Criatura del Vientre materno, le administren el Santo Sacramento del Bautismo. Y porque en muchisimos Pueblos de nuestro Arzobispado estamos informados no haver Cirujanos, ni otras personas instruidas en el modo de hacer la Operacion cesarea, es nuestra voluntad, que todos los Curas, y Vicarios compren, y tengan en su Casa un librito pequeño, que ha dado á la prensa el R.P.Fr. Joseph Manuel Rodriguez de la Regular Observancia del Serafico P.S. Francisco, en el qual explica el modo con que comoda, y facilmente se hace la Operacion, á fin de que los Curas, y Vicarios la hagan por si mismos, quando no haya Persona secular, que pueda hacerla. Y para evitar esta necesidad les encargamos, y mandamos, que cada uno procure en su Parroquia instruir á algunos de sus Feligreses, en una cosa tan facil como la practica de dicha Operacion cesarea. Y siendo este el unico medio para evitar que se sepulten con las Madres Difuntas las Criaturas vivas, y sean socorridas con el Santo Sacramento del Bautismo, y logren la vida eterna, exhortamos á todos los Sacerdotes Seculares, y Regulares, contribuyan con sus particulares persuaciones á desterrar el horror con que comunmente es mirada una Operacion tan util, y necesaria para salvar la vida corporal, y espiritual de los Niños desgraciados que pierden sus Madres antes de nacer. Y para promover por nuestra parte un asunto tan interesante, y de tanta piedad, concedemos ochenta dias de Indulgencia á las Personas que executaren por sí, ó por otros la referida Operacion, ó dieren noticia á los Curas, ó Superiores de sus respectivos Partidos, de alguna Muger preñada moribunda, para el efecto de salvar la Prole despues de Difunta la Madre, mediante la dicha Operacion; y á los que con la brevedad posible Bautizaren la misma Prole. Y para que este nuestro Edicto llegue á noticia de todos, y se guarde puntual, y exactamente: Mandamos que se lea, y fixe en todas las Parroquias de nuestro Arzobispado en el lugar, y sitio acostumbrado. Dado en la Ciudad de México, firmado de Nos, sellado con el Sello de nuestras Armas, y refrendado del Infrascripto nuestro Secretario de Camara, y Govierno, en quatro dias de Diciembre de mil setecientos setenta y dos años.

Alonso Arzobispo de México

Por mandado de S. S. Illmâ. el Arzobispo mi Señor.

Figure 7. MEXICO. Archbishop. *Nos el Dr. D. Alonso Núñez de Haro y Peralta.* Mexico: [s.n.]. 1772. **(M.93)**

Embriologia sacra, Palermo, F. Valenza, 1745. [See M.140 for parallel action by the Viceroy]. Dated 4 December 1772.

Figure 7.

M.94 **MEXICO. Archbishop**

[Begins:] Nos el Doctor Don Alonso Nuñez de Haro y Peralta . . . Arzobispo de México . . . . Por quanto esta N.C. con vivos deseos de socorrer á este público en la presente calamidad de viruelas que le aflixe [&c.].

broadside. Mexico: [s.n.]. 1779.

Rúbrica, signature, and paper seal on the recto.

An edict requiring the provision of special burial-grounds for victims of the small-pox epidemic. Villalba (1802), 2, pp. 241–242, 245–248, points out that the question of place of burial in relation to health had been opened in Spain in 1777. Dated 8 November 1779.

M.95 **MEXICO. Archbishop**

[Begins:] Nos el Dr. D. Alonso Nuñez de Haro y Peralta . . . Arzobispo de México . . . . Por quanto esta N.C. con vivos deseos de socorrer á este público en la presente calamidad de viruelas que le aflixe [&c.]. 4 ll. (1st bl.)

4to. Mexico: [s.n.]. 1779.

Medina (Mex.) vi 7067.
Palau 197263.

MS annotation in contemporary hand on recto of first blank leaf; *rúbrica* and signature on verso of last leaf. A signed copy of the broadside of the same year [see entry above], without the seal. Dated 8 November 1779.

M.96 **MEXICO. Archbishop**

[Begins:] Queriendo desde luego el Exmô. Señor Virrey . . . Marques de Branciforte manifestar su satisfaccion á los cuerpos y personas que han contribuido con sus limosnas para el piadoso fondo de socorros [&c.]. 2 ll. (2nd bl.).

fol. Mexico: [s.n.]. 1797.

Guerra (Icon.) 494.

Rúbrica on recto of the first leaf.

In this circular letter Alonso Núñez de Haro y Peralta [Archbishop 1772–1800, and Viceroy 1787], conveys the Viceroy's thanks to corporate and individual contributors to the fund for assisting victims of smallpox. Although President of the Junta Principal de Caridad, appointed to oversee measures for the relief of patients, this letter is written in his capacity as Archbishop. Dated 11 December 1797.

M.97   MEXICO. Archbishop

[Begins:] Considerando la Junta Principal de Caridad lo agradable que le será á V. tener noticia cierta del número de personas que fueron socorridas en la inmediata epidemia de viruelas [&c.]. 2 ll. (2nd bl.).

fol. Mexico: [s.n.]. 1798.

A circular letter accompanying a statement of numbers of sick and those aided in the smallpox epidemic. The statement is wanting. The Archbishop had probably assumed sole administrative responsibility by this date as the Junta Principal de Caridad had held its final meeting on 20 February 1798. This third estimate (not in the Wellcome Institute Library) which is thought by Cooper [(1965), p. 153 (& footnote)], to be more reliable than either the preceding *Resumen general* of 17 February 1798 issued by the Junta Principal de Caridad or than the *Estado general* of 21 February 1798 issued by the Protomedicato, brings the total to 7,147 deaths. Dated 11 April 1798.

M.98   MEXICO. Archbishop

[Begins:] En Real Cédula de 15 de Mayo de 1804, con referencia á otra de 27 de Marzo de 1789, se sirvió S.M. prevenir el establecimiento de cementarios ventilados [&c.]. 2 ll.

4to. Mexico: [s.n.]. 1809.

Guerra (Icon.) 580.

A circular letter, neither signed nor dated in MS, from Francisco Javier de Lizana y Beaumont [Archbishop 1802–11, Viceroy 1809–10] probably to his parish priests, encouraging interments outside the towns for reasons of health. It accompanied the circular at M.188. Dated December 1809. [See M.41].

M.99 **MEXICO, Ayuntamiento**

Noticia de las proficencias tomadas por esta N.C. acerca de la asistencia de los enfermos, y precaucion del contagio, para su mas puntual execucion. pp. 14, 1 bl. l.

4to. Mexico: [s.n.]. 1779.

Guerra (Icon.) 425.
León (1915) 69; 266.
Medina (Mex.) vi 7052.

Sig. B (of four leaves) begins on the third leaf; Sig. [A] comprises the first, second, seventh, and eighth leaves.

Four Commissioners had been appointed by the Ayuntamiento to issue orders, to prepare lists of the destitute, and to receive information on the progress of the small-pox epidemic. Their plea for financial support is a basic document on the outbreak, which is said to have attacked some 44,000 people, of whom some 9000 to 22,000 are variously estimated to have died. [See Cooper (1965), pp. 67–68]. Dated 31 October 1779.

M.100 **MEXICO, Ayuntamiento**

[Begins:] Noticioso este Ilustre Ayuntamiento de las necesidades que por falta de auxilios, padecen, por la mayor parte, los infelices habitantes de los suburbios de esta Capital, en la epidemia de fiebres [&c.]. 2 ll.

4to. Mexico: [s.n.]. 1813.

Six signatures and *rúbricas* on the verso of the second leaf; completed in MS and dated 29 April 1813.

A brief circular letter, addressed in MS, setting out official recognition of the need to provide shelter, food and drugs for the relief of impoverished victims of the fever epidemic, assigning the addressees' services to one of the *Quarteles menores* into which the city had been divided for purposes of assistance, and tactfully requesting financial contributions for the Ayuntamiento's depleted treasury. During this fever epidemic of 1813, the severest suffered by the city in the nineteenth century, the authorities recorded that 54,119 persons (of those aided by public relief) had contracted the fevers by 31 July, of whom 38,491 had recovered by that date, 7,304 remained sick, and 8,324 had died. Another estimate calculates that more than 20,000 died in the City. [See Cooper (1965), pp. 157–182].

M.101   **MEXICO. Casa de Niños Expósitos**

Constituciones, que para el mejor govierno, y direccion de la Real Casa del Señor S. Joseph de Niños Expósitos de esta Ciudad de México [&c.]. 3 ll., pp. 56, 2 ll.

fol. Mexico: J. de Jáuregui. [1775].

Guerra (Icon.) 402.
León (Mex.) v 437.
Medina (Mex.) vi 5833.
Palau 197258.

Signature and *rúbrica* on verso of last leaf. The final leaf is a singleton; the conjugate second leaf of which is presumably blank. Both León and Palau describe this as a quarto; it is in fact a folio in twos. The title page of this copy is printed in black only, not in red and black as in the copy described by León.

The Casa de Niños Expósitos, or Foundling Hospital, was founded and financed by the well-known Francisco Antonio de Lorenzana y Butrón, Archbishop of Mexico 1766–72. His successor, Alonso Núñez de Haro y Peralta [Archbishop 1772–1800], placed the home on a proper footing with an endowment and a governing body whose constitution was approved by the King in the *Real Cédula* of 19 July 1774 here printed.

M.102   **MEXICO. Hospicio de Pobres**

Ordenanzas para el gobierno del Hospicio de Pobres de la Ciudad de México en sus quatro departamentos. 1 l., pp. 52.

fol. Mexico: M. de Zúñiga y Ontiveros. 1806.

Beristáin i p. 197 no. 327.
Guerra (Icon.) 559.
Medina (Mex.) vii 9863.
Palau 202695.

Sig. 14 [i.e. the last leaf] is a singleton.

The statutes are signed and dated 11 December 1805 by Juan Francisco de Azcárate y Lezama [1767–1831], a noted advocate who filled many senior public appointments in the City of Mexico, including that of Secretary to the Hospicio de Pobres. The hospice was opened in 1774 and at the date of these statutes comprised the *Departamento de la Escuela patriótica, Departamento del Hospicio, Departamento de la*

Corrección de Costumbres, and the *Pequeño Departamento de Partos Reservados*. A fifth department for vaccination was established after the date of these statutes. [See Alfaro (1906); and Flores (1886–88), *2*, pp. 245–250].

A facsimile from another copy is also in the Wellcome Institute Library.

M.103 MEXICO. Hospital Real de Indios

Constituciones, y ordenanzas, para el regimen, y govierno del Hospital Real, y General de los Indios de esta Nueva España, mandadas guardar por S.M. en Real Cédula de 27 de octubre del año de 1776. *engr. coat of arms.* 17 ll., pp.64.

fol. Mexico: F. de Zúñiga y Ontiveros. 1778.

Beristáin iii p.282 no.2060.
Guerra (Icon.) 419.
León (Mex.) i 445.
León (1915) 66.
Medina (Mex.) vi 6091.
Palau 60068.

The first leaf (i.e. the title-page) is a singleton; the remaining leaf is presumably blank.

Known at various times as the Hospital Real de San José, Hospital Real, Hospital Real de San José de los Naturales, the Hospital became commonly known as the Hospital Real de Indios [*or*, de Naturales]. Said to have been founded by the Franciscans *c.* 1531, it was officially founded by *Real Cédula* in 1553 to care for Indian patients. Under royal patronage, it was attached neither to a religious order nor to the Archbishopric until the Hipólitos were given charge between 1701 and 1741.

Following resecularisation and reorganisation it became the site of the Academia de Anatomía Práctica in 1768 whose courses opened in the Real Anfiteatro de Anatomía within the Hospital in 1770. The Hospital was closed in 1822 and its buildings demolished in 1935. [See Howard (1972); Muriel (1956–60), *1*, pp. 115–136; and Venegas Ramírez (1973), pp. 41–65, 175–179].

According to Howard [*op. cit.*, p. 162] it had taken 20 years to produce these and the following constitutions. The detailed historical introduction is also of interest.

Figure 8.

CONSTITUCIONES,
Y
ORDENANZAS,
PARA EL REGIMEN, Y GOVIERNO
DEL HOSPITAL REAL, Y GENERAL
DE LOS INDIOS DE ESTA NUEVA ESPAÑA,

Mandadas guardar por S. M. en Real Cédula de 27
de Octubre del año de 1776.

CON LICENCIA DEL SUPERIOR GOVIERNO
Impresas en México, en la nueva Oficina Madrileña de D. Felipe
de Zúñiga y Ontiveros, calle de la Palma, año de 1778.

Figure 8. MEXICO. Hospital Real de Indios. *Constituciones, y ordenanzas.* Mexico: F. de Zúñiga y Ontiveros.
1778. **(M.103)**

M.104   MEXICO. Hospital Real de Indios

Constituciones, y ordenanzas para el regimen de la botica del Hospital Real, y General de los Indios de esta Nueva España, mandadas observar por S.M. en Cédula de 27 de octubre de 1776. *engr. coat of arms.* 1 l., pp.6.

fol. Mexico: F. de Zúñiga y Ontiveros. 1778.

Beristáin v (Sup.) p.502 no.6092.
Guerra (Icon.) 420.
León (Mex.) i 444.
León (1915) 67.
Medina (Mex.) vi 6092.
Palau 60068.

Bound with the preceding item.

The first leaf (title-page) may have been added from another copy.

M.105   MEXICO. Hospital Real de Indios

[Begins:] D. Joseph del Rincon, Mayordomo Administrador del Hospital Real y General de Naturales del Reyno, sus proprios y rentas; Hace saber á los Facultativos [&c.].

broadside. Mexico: [s.n.]. 1792.

Guerra (Icon.) 477.

A notice dated 17 October 1792 announcing the terms of examination and appointment for the joint posts of anatomist to the anatomical theatre [founded in the Hospital Real in 1768 and opened in 1770] and second surgeon to the same Hospital.

A detailed account of the *oposición*, the candidates, and the aftermath, is provided by Howard (1972), pp. 255–271. The notice was reprinted in the *Gazeta de México*, 1792, 5, (núm. 21), pp. 185–186 (30 October).

M.106   MEXICO. Inquisition

[Begins:] Nos los inquisidores contra la heretica pravedad y apostacia en la ciudad de Mexico .... Hazemos saber ... que muchas y diversas personas ... se dan al estudio de la Astrologia judicaria. 4 ll. (last bl.)

fol. Mexico: [s.n.]. 1616.

Beristáin v (Sup.) p.506 no.300.
Guerra (Icon.) 25.
Medina (Mex.) ii 300.
Palau 193158.

An attempt by the Inquisition to ban astrological and other superstitious practices, and to prevent women taking hallucinatory drugs.

M.107   MEXICO. Junta Principal de Caridad

[Begins:] La caridad y christiano zelo con que mira el Exmo. Señor Marqués de Branciforte, Virrey . . . á este público para socorrerlo y aliviarlo . . . en la presente epidemia de viruelas . . . ha dispuesto, á mas de su Circular de 28 de Febrero último, se forme una Junta principal de Caridad [&c.]. 2 ll. (1st bl.).

fol. Mexico: [s.n. 1797].

In this circular letter, the Junta Principal recites the appointment by Branciforte [Viceroy 1794–98] of its members and its terms of reference and appoints members to the district boards of charity. The contemporary MS note on the recto of the 1st blank leaf records the date and place of the epidemic, and that this unused copy (i.e. not completed in manuscript) belonged to the Archdeaconry of Puebla. Dated 31 October [1797].

M.108   MEXICO. Junta Principal de Caridad

[Begins:] Para socorrer al público en la presente epidemia de viruelas, se ha formado una Junta principal de Caridad [&c.]. 2 ll. (2nd bl.)

fol. Mexico: [s.n.]. 1797.

Rúbrica on verso of first leaf.

In this circular letter, Alonso Núñez de Haro y Peralta [Archbishop 1772–1800], and President of the Junta Principal de Caridad, appoints a priest to each district board of charity, having already empowered those without confessor's licences to hear the confessions of the stricken. This ecclesiastical action parallels the appointment of lay members to the boards in the circular letter of the same date, 31 October 1797. [See entry above].

M.109 **MEXICO. Junta Principal de Caridad**

[Begins:] Para la mejor asistencia de los enfermos contagiados de la actual epidemia de viruelas, y con el fin de evitar á las Sociedades las muchas fatigas que impenden en la solicitud de Facultativos que curen á los infelices á quienes atienden [&c.]. 2 ll. (2nd bl.).

fol. Mexico: [s.n.]. 1797.

In this circular letter addressed to the officers of the *manzanas* (i.e. sub-districts, or blocks, of the eight main quarters of the city), the Junta Principal states that it has allotted a medical man to each quarter, who will assign medical assistance to the *manzanas* under his charge as necessary. The officers of the *manzanas* are ordered to collect contributions from the householders (*vecinos*). Dated 3 November 1797.

M.110 **MEXICO. Junta Principal de Caridad**

[Begins:] La junta principal de Caridad establecida para el socorro de tantos y tan miserables enfermos, victimas de las viruelas, ha tomado varias providencias para su socorro [&c.]. 1 l.

fol. Mexico: [s.n.]. 1797.

Rúbricas of the nine members of the Junta Principal on the verso.

In this circular letter to richer citizens, the Junta Principal announces the division of the city into sub-districts (*manzanas*) and the formation of the district boards of charity (*Sociedades parciales de Caridad*), calls for alms to meet the growing need, and undertakes to return any unused balance, adjusted to the original rate of contribution, after the epidemic. Dated 6 November 1797. [See WMS. Amer. 45 (MEXICO. Junta Principal de Caridad. [1797]).]

M.111 **MEXICO. Junta Principal de Caridad**

[Begins:] La Junta principal de Caridad … llena de ternura y compasion por el síntoma de erupcion de sangre … mandó pasar Oficio al Real Tribunal del Protomedicato, para que examinando la materia, consultase sus preservativos y específicos. pp.7.

4to. Mexico: [s.n.]. 1797.

The Protomedicato, at command of the Junta Principal, suggests remedies for the 'malignant' variety of smallpox, among them Peruvian bark, Huxham's tincture, and oxymel. Dated 11 November 1797.

M.112   **MEXICO. Junta Principal de Caridad**

[Begins:] A fin de dictar la Junta principal de Caridad varias providencias . . . necesita reunir algunas noticias y saber con puntualidad y distincion el número de enfermos que estén curados ó sanos de las actuales viruelas [&c.]. 2 ll. (2nd bl.).

4to. Mexico: [s.n.]. 1797.

Wanting the form originally attached.

A circular letter from the Secretary of the Junta Principal requiring the district boards of charity to return full figures of recoveries and deaths from smallpox on the accompanying form. Dated 13 November 1797.

M.113   **MEXICO. Junta Principal de Caridad**

[Begins:] Razon del número de sugetos que se han contagiado en la actual epidemia de viruelas [&c.]. 1 l.

Mexico: [s.n.]. 1797.

The form circulated to the district boards of charity with the letter of the Junta Principal of 13 November 1797 [see entry above] requesting the return of the figures of recoveries and deaths. This copy is not completed in MS.

M.114   **MEXICO. Junta Principal de Caridad**

[Begins:] El Exmô. Señor Virrey, que con tanta caridad atiende á los pobres contagiados virolentos . . . ha tenido noticia de la inaudita impiedad con que los mismos padres ó allegados les quitan las frezadas, camisas, y otras ropas, y las empeñan ó vendan [&c.]. 2 ll. (2nd bl.).

4to. Mexico: [s.n.]. 1797.

The Secretary of the Junta Principal, Luis Gonzaga de Ibarrola, transmits to the district boards of charity the Viceroy's proclamation [of 16 November] forbidding such pawning or the sale of bed-clothing and clothes. Dated 19 November 1797.

M.115 **MEXICO. Junta Principal de Caridad**

[Begins:] Los socorros de la caridad, y la asistencia gratuita de los médicos, son precisamente para los miserables enfermos virolentos, que por su misma indigencia son socorridos por las Sociedades de Caridad. [&c.]. 2 ll. (2nd bl.).

4to. Mexico: [s.n.]. 1797.

This letter circulated by the Secretary of the Junta Principal, states that attempts by richer citizens to take advantage of medical assistance provided for the poor by the district boards of charity without fee, have been officially noted by the Viceroy and are discouraged by him. Dated 25 November 1797.

M.116 **MEXICO. Junta Principal de Caridad**

[Begins:] Es incomparable el gozo con que los miserables virolentos reciben los socorros de la caridad [&c.]. 2 ll. (2nd bl.).

fol. Mexico: [s.n.]. 1797.

Guerra (Icon.) 498.

A circular letter of thanks for contributions received. This copy is not completed in manuscript. Dated November 1797.

M.117 **MEXICO. Junta Principal de Caridad**

[Begins:] Instruida la Junta Principal de Caridad en que algunos enfermos de viruelas han quedado con varias resultas [&c.]. 2 ll. (2nd bl.).

fol. Mexico: [s.n.]. 1797.

Guerra (Icon.) 497.

In this circular letter the Secretary of the Junta Principal requires the district boards of charity to provide an exact return of numbers of recoveries, current convalescences, and deaths, and an account of funds expended. This copy wants the blank form originally attached. Dated 16 December 1797.

M.118 **MEXICO. Junta Principal de Caridad**

[Begins:] El Exmo. Señor Virrey . . . ha calificado . . . que se tome una razon exacta y puntual del número de enfermos y muertos que ha habido del contagio de viruelas [&c.]. 2 ll. (2nd bl.).

fol. Mexico: [s.n.]. 1797.

The Junta Principal, following the command of the Viceroy Branciforte, orders religious houses and hospitals to return figures of smallpox patients and deaths. This copy of the circular letter wants the blank form originally attached. Dated 30 December 1797.

M.119   MEXICO. Junta Principal de Caridad

[Begins:] Instruido el Exmô. Señor Virrey . . . del estado actual de la epidemia . . . ha calificado del todo necesario que se tome una exacta y puntual razon del número de enfermos y muertos [&c.]. 2 ll. (2nd bl.).

fol. Mexico: [s.n.]. 1797.

In this circular letter to the district boards of charity, the Junta Principal requests complete returns of sick and dead in the epidemic whether they were assisted by the district boards or not, omitting only the patients of religious houses and hospitals to which a separate request has been sent. This copy wants the form originally attached. Dated 30 December 1797.

M.120   MEXICO. Junta Principal de Caridad

Sociedad parcial de Caridad. Manzana núm. [   ] del Quartel mayor núm. [   ] . . . Señor Tesorero.

broadside. Mexico: [s.n.]. 1797.

Contemporary MS note on recto.

A form of request for moneys required by the district boards of charity from the central relief fund organised by the Junta Principal; this copy is neither dated nor completed in MS.

M.121   MEXICO. Junta Principal de Caridad

[Begins:] Razon del numero de personas que se han socorrido por las Sociedades de Caridad . . . en la Manzana Núm. [   ] del Quartel Núm. [   ] que concluida su comision dá cuenta á la Junta Principal [&c.].

broadside. Mexico: [s.n.]. 179[?7].

A form circulated to the district boards of charity. Spaces in the form provide for the return of information on deaths, recoveries, numbers assisted, and expenditure on food, shelter and clothing, and medical assistance etc., full figures for which appeared in the tables whose general summary was dated 17 February 1798 [see M.122]. This copy is neither dated nor completed in MS.

M.122   MEXICO. Junta Principal de Caridad

Estado del Quartel Mayor numero 1 [–8]. En que se manifiestan las Sociedades que contuvo para socorro de los pobres contagiados de viruelas [&c.]. [Followed by:] Resumen general de las Sociedades de Caridad [&c.]. *9 fldg tables.*

Mexico: [s.n.]. 1798.

RESUMEN GENERAL

De las Sociedades de Caridad, que para el socorro de los contagiados de la epidemia de Viruelas del año de 1797, contuvo cada Quartel mayor de los ocho en que se divide México, los Muertos, Sanos, y total de socorridos de cada Quartel, lo erogado en Alimentos, Abrigos, Medicinas, Médicos y Barberos, lo que soportaron las Sociedades, y libraron contra la Caxa de socorros, y el total de lo gastado; cuyo Resumen se ha formado de los ocho Estados parciales de cada Quartel, comprobados con las Cuentas dadas por sus respectivas Sociedades, que manifiestan lo erogado por éstas, y lo que cada una libró y recibió de la Caxa.

Quarteles.	Socieda-des.	Muertos.	Sanos.	Total de so-corridos.	Alimentos. Ps. Rs. Gs.	Abrigos. Ps. Rs. Gs.	Medicinas. Ps. Rs. Gs.	Medicos y Bar-beros. Ps. Rs. Gs.	Gasto de Socie-dades. Ps. Rs. Gs.	Gasto de la Caxa de socorros. Ps. Rs. Gs.	Gasto total. Ps. Rs. Gs.
Núm. 1.	24.	734.	6329.	7063.	5573. 2. 6.	5344. 7. 3.	3936. 2. 6.	3190. 3.	3337. 3.	14707. 7.	18044. 7. 3.
2.	31.	553.	6413.	6966.	6976. 6.	6127. 9.	3729. 1.	3233. 2.	13812. 3.	6253. 1. 3.	20065. 4. 3.
3.	27.	667.	5999.	6666.	7204. 7.	5761. 2. 9.	3039. 4.	3522. 2. 3.	11657. 1. 9.	7870. 6. 3.	19528.
4.	33.	559.	5096.	5655.	6137. 6.	3887. 2.	3041. 3.	3590. 2.	6384. 3.	10271. 4. 6.	16655. 7. 6.
5.	14.	625.	5019.	5644.	3498. 7. 2.	3105. 7.	3015. 6. 6.	2213. 7.	4485. 6. 3.	7348. 5. 6.	11834. 3. 9.
6.	21.	455.	3953.	4408.	6055. 5. 6.	4967. 7. 9.	2686. 7.	2596. 4. 6.	5419. 4. 9.	10887. 4.	16307. 9.
7.	20.	416.	3351.	3767.	5407. 6. 3.	2574. 1.	1931. 2.	2190. 2. 6.	534. 5.	11568. 6. 9.	12103. 3. 9.
8.	11.	442.	3905.	4347.	4081. 1. 3.	4097. 3.	2173. 4.	2106. 7.	7022. 6.	6336. 4.	13358. 4. 6.
	181.	4451.	40065.	44516.	45834. 6. 0.	35865. 4. 9.	23553. 6.	22643. 6. 3.	52653. 6.	75244. 7. 3.	127897. 7. 9.

NOTA 1.   Que segun la Guia de Forasteros que rige en el presente año, fué el total de muertos en el proximo antecedente 12221; y debiendo rebaxarse de estos 5153 que fallecieron de otras enfermedades, resulta haber sido de la de Viruelas 7068, inclusos 21 de los muchos que se inocularon. El exceso que luego se advierte respecto de los 4451 que presentan las Sociedades, dimana de los que fallecieron antes que la Junta principal de Caridad tomase á su cargo los socorros; de los que murieron en los Hospitales, Casas de Comunidad y de gentes pudientes durante la epidemia, y tambien de los que se contagiaron en varios Pueblos de Garitas á fuera, de cuyo número se hicieron cargo las Parroquias de esta Ciudad á quienes reconocen.

2.   En igual epidemia del año de 79 se socorrieron de Garitas á dentro 36865: no se hizo distincion de gastos: murieron mas de 8000 de los socorridos. El gasto de Sociedades, á mas de 6678 ps. 4 rs. 6 gs. que colectaron de limosnas, subió á 65370 ps. El de la Caxa á 37215 ps. 6 rs. 6 gs. y el total á 109264 ps. 3 rs. De manera que el año de 79 murieron casi duplicados que en el de 97, habiendo sido los socorridos como 8000 ménos. Este aumento de socorridos, y minoracion de muertos, ha consistido en que en la última epidemia se dieron las providencias de socorros con mas oportunidad, y que merecieron tal aceptacion general del Público, que se encendió mas la caridad que nunca para la buena asistencia de los contagiados.

México 17 de Febrero de 1798.

Figure 9. MEXICO. Junta Principal de Caridad. *Resumen General de las Sociedades de Caridad.* Mexico: [s.n.]. 1798. **(M.122)**

Guerra (Icon.) 509–517.

The general summary shows that 181 district boards of charity participated in assisting the poor during the epidemic; that 4,451 deaths (adjusted to 7,068) occurred out of 44,516 persons so assisted; and that total expenditure amounted to 127,897 pesos. The figures are further subdivided into amounts spent on food, shelter and clothing, drugs, and medical assistance. The *Resumen general* is dated 17 February 1798; the remaining tables from each of the eight *Quarteles* of the City are undated.

The statements and the summary may have been attached to the letter from the Junta Principal de Caridad, dated 3 March 1798 [see entry below]. The figures do not agree with the short statement issued by the Protomedicato on 21 February 1798 [see M.163], nor with the figures issued by the Archbishop with his letter of 11 April 1798 [see M.97].

Figure 9.

M.123   MEXICO. Junta Principal de Caridad

[Begins:] Los adjuntos estados . . . le manifestarán, que habiendo sido tan crecido el número de los enfermos de viruelas socorridos por las Sociedades [&c.]. 2 ll. (2nd bl.).

fol. Mexico: [s.n.]. 1798.

Two *rúbricas* on verso of first leaf.

A circular letter of thanks from the Junta Principal dated 3 March 1798, originally enclosing statements of the assistance given by the district boards of charity during the smallpox epidemic; these statements were possibly the 9 tables whose *Resumen general* was dated 17 February 1798 [see entry above].

M.124   MEXICO. Junta Principal de Caridad

[Begins:] En virtud de lo resuelto . . . se ha prorateado el sobrante de la Caxa de Socorros entre los mismos contribuyentes que hicieron este fondo [&c.]. 2 ll. (2nd bl.).

4to. Mexico: [s.n.]. 1798.

A circular letter signed by Antonio de Basoco, Treasurer of the Junta Principal, and dated 11 April 1798, returning apportioned amounts of the remaining relief funds to the original contributors. This copy is not completed in MS.

M.125 **MEXICO. Junta de Sanidad**

Instruccion formada para ministrar la vacuna, como único preservativo del contagio de las viruelas, y en defecto de su fluido inocular con el pus de esta; del modo de conocer y distinguir las calidades de las naturales, y el método de curarlas. pp.25.

4to. Mexico: M. Ontiveros. 1814.

Guerra (Icon.) 614.
León (1915) 209.
Medina (Mex.) viii 10910.
Palau 120466.

The last page is a singleton.

Recorded *verbatim* by Medina, and with a minor difference in the title by León, this work in fact prints three official documents. The first, signed by Serrano and dated 28 May 1814, sets out the manner of vaccination, the method of preserving and sending the fluid, and the signs of true and false vaccination. The second, issued by the Junta Municipal de Sanidad on 17 May 1814 and addressed to the public, seeks to allay fear of vaccination by describing the recent experiments successfully carried out on children. The third, issued by the Junta Superior de Sanidad and signed by Serrano and Rafael Sagaz on 28 May 1814, recommends inoculation where no vaccine is available and describes the symptoms of smallpox and methods of treatment. Certain medical terms are described for those without qualifications assisting in the epidemic.

Antonio Serrano Rubio [d. 1833], of Spanish birth, was Director of the Escuela de Cirugía de México at the Hospital Real de los Indios from 1803 to 1827; he was for other periods Surgeon to the Hospital de San Andrés, and *Alcalde examinador* to the Protomedicato; he supported the cause of vaccination from the arrival of the vaccine in the City of Mexico in 1804.

M.126 **MEXICO. Junta de Sanidad**

[Begins:] Aviso importante al publico. La Junta de Sanidad municipal . . . habiendo observado por los estados mensuales . . . que el número de infantes muertos de toces catarales . . . excede en mucho al total de los que han fallecido de otras enfermedades [&c.].

broadside. Mexico: [s.n.]. 1820.

Guerra (Icon.) 643.
León (1915) 282.

This notice, agreed on by the physicians of the Junta and confirmed by the Junta itself on 24 October 1820, recommends remedies and gives advice to the poor for the different stages of the *tos cataral*. The proceedings of the same date [see entry below] record its free issue in 1,000 copies and that its expense was borne by members of the Junta. Dated 24 October 1820, and signed by José María Guridi y Alcocer, Secretary of the Junta.

M.127   MEXICO. Junta de Sanidad

[Begins:] Junta de Sanidad municipal de Mexico: No por captar reconocimiento ó aplausos, sino por satisfacer á la pública espectacion, . . . acordó dicha Junta con aprobacion del Exmo. Ayuntamiento que la nombró, presentar este manifiesto ó reducido extracto de sus actas [&c.]. *table*. pp. 38, 1 bl. l.

4to. [Mexico: s.n. 1821].

Guerra (Icon.) 646.
León (1915) 214.

This document, issued for the benefit of the public, tersely records the proceedings of the weekly meetings of the Junta from 11 July to 29 December 1820, and represents the first co-ordinated attempt to provide a permanent organisation to supervise preventive medicine, social health, and the prompt treatment of epidemics in the City of Mexico. The proposed Constitution of the Junta printed on pp. 6–11 gave it, under the Ayuntamiento, a wide measure of control which superseded to some degree the measures for public cleanliness undertaken by the second Viceroy Revillagigedo [1789–94] recorded in his *Instrucción* to his successor Branciforte [see Instrucciones (1873), paras. 244–247]. The entries include, *inter alia*, the measures taken during an epidemic of fevers among the poor from 24 November and a table on p. 38 showing figures for patients, recoveries, and deaths.

M.128   MEXICO. Real y Pontificia Universidad

Informe, que la Real Universidad, y claustro pleno de ella . . . . Haze a el excellentissimo Señor Virrey de ella en conformidad de orden de su Excelencia de 3 de Julio de este año 1692. Sobre los inconvenientes de la bebida de el pulque. 1 l., ff.17.

fol. [Mexico: s.n.]. 1692.

Andrade 1204.
Beristáin iii p.219 no.1892.
Guerra (Icon.) 170.
León (1915) 31.
Medina (Mex.) iii 1522.
Palau 119394.

This report signed by 28 members of the University and approved by its *claustro pleno* concludes that the suspension of the sale of adulterated pulque should continue; it cites many authorities, legal, theological and medical.

The report is undated but its tenor suggests that it was issued after the pulque riots in the City of Mexico during the same year. The sale of pulque and the number of *pulquerías* had already been restricted by regulations promulgated by the Viceroy in 1672, but with little effect [see Barrios (1971), pp. 20–22].

M.129 **MEXICO. Real y Pontificia Universidad**

Constituciones de la Real y Pontificia Universidad de Mexico. Segunda edicion. 16 ll., pp.238, 11 ll.

fol. Mexico: F. de Zúñiga y Ontiveros. 1775.

Guerra (Icon.) 404.
Medina (Mex.) vi 5836.
Palau 60067.

Sigs. ¶ 6 and [Nn], [i.e. the last leaf, without signature] are singletons; the conjugate second leaves are presumably blank.

The first edition was *Estatutos y constituciones (de la Imperial y Regia Universidad de México) hechas con comission particular de su Magestad*, Mexico, 1668. [British Museum (1959–66), *159*, col. 245]. It also appears as Palau 83577, with a variant title and a phantom edition of 1678.

The prologue describes the buildings, lecture-rooms, and library of the University, the recent activities of outstanding men in each faculty, and generally reveals a new interest in the expansion and modernization of the University. Many details of the University's organisation appear in the main text.

These University Statutes, originally drawn up by Juan de Palafox y Mendoza [Bishop of Puebla 1640–55, and interim Viceroy 1642], the active civil and ecclesiastical reformer, were confirmed by the *Real Cédulas* of 1639 and 1649 printed in the same volume.

M.130 MICHAEL, *M.D., of Milan*

Botica general de remedios experimentados que a beneficio del publico se reimprime por su original en Cadiz. 8 ll.

8vo. Puebla: P. de la Rosa. 1797.

Guerra (Icon.) 505.
Medina (Puebla) 1357.
Palau 33761, 168071.

The dates given by Palau are uncertain.

A copy of this Puebla edition, perhaps the earliest now extant, exists also in the Medina Collection, Biblioteca Nacional de Chile. Two other editions, both attributed to the same author in their colophons, are in the Wellcome Institute Library: *Libro nuevo que contiene varias rezetas utiles, é importantes de la botica general*, Madrid, A. Sancha, [c.1800]; *Libro nuevo que contiene varias recetas utiles e importantes de la botica general*, Seville, Imp. del Setabiense, 1814. Another edition, *Botica general de remedios experimentados*, Valencia, 1807, is in the British Museum. The original [?] edition published in Cadiz seems to be no longer extant. Many editions seem to have been issued. The author remains unidentified.

For a translation and commentary on the text and printing of this badly produced little handbook, whose treatment of its subject is extraordinarily old-fashioned for its period, see Botica (1954).

M.131 MOLINA, Alonso de [1513/14–1585]

Vocabulario en lengua castellana y mexicana. [Followed by:] Vocabulario en lengua mexicana y castellana. *woodcuts (coat of arms and figure on t.ps., and figure on the recto of the last leaf of the first part), & woodcut ornaments.* 2 pts.

fol. Mexico: A. de Spinosa. 1571.

Gallardo iii 3082.
Icazbalceta 68 (60).
Medina (Mex.) i 65.
Valton 13.
Wagner 60.

MS annotations and additions throughout in two hands, and note of ownership of Juan Francisco Manquez dated 1727 on the verso of the last leaf of the second part.

The first edition, containing a shorter Spanish-Náhuatl vocabulary only, was published by Juan Pablos in the City of Mexico in 1555.

The present edition is an invaluable source-book for Náhuatl-Spanish medical, anatomical, and botanical terms.

Molina is said to have arrived in New Spain as a child, where he early learned Náhuatl. He joined the Convent of San Francisco de México and later served as Father Guardian of the Convent of Texcoco, the Colegio de Santa Cruz at Tlatelolco, and the Convent of San Francisco of Puebla. He devoted himself to learning and teaching Náhuatl and preaching to the Indians, and published other works on the language and on Catholic doctrine and practice.

M.132 MONTAÑA, Luis [1755–1820]

Avisos importantes sobre el matlatltzahuatl, o calentura epidemica manchada que pasa a ser peste y que es frequente en esta N.E. con un modo sencillo y facil de socorrer a los enfermos donde no haya medicos que les asistan, y cuya eficacia y seguridad se experimento el año de 1813. 3 ll., pp. 55.

4to. Mexico: M. de Zúñiga y Ontiveros. 1817.

Guerra (Icon.) 628.
León (1915) 212.
Medina (Mex.) viii 11276.
Palau 177531.

The third preliminary leaf is a singleton.

A brisk and detailed discussion of the origins, public control, nature, symptoms, diagnosis and treatment of the fevers of 1813 set out in the scholastic manner. A provisional list of suitable drugs appears on the last two pages.

Luis Montaña, born in Puebla and educated at the Seminario Palafoxiano, afterwards read medicine and took his doctorate at the University of Mexico. He became

Catedrático de vísperas de medicina, Catedrático de clínica at the Hospital de San Andrés and was one of the early teachers of botany in New Spain. His concrete and practical spirit of enquiry made him one of the major influences in establishing the scientific approach to medicine in Mexico [see Izquierdo (1955)].

M.133   MORALES, Joseph

Cartilla de vacunar, con un prólogo para desengaño del público. 1 l., pp.xx, 1 bl. l.

4to. Puebla: P. de la Rosa. 1805.

Guerra (Icon.) 554.
León (1915) 194.
Medina (Puebla) 1512.

Sig. 2 [i.e. pp. xv–xviii] is of two conjugate leaves only; sig. * [i.e. the last leaf, pp. xix–xx] may be a singleton.

The prologue seeks to allay the doubts and fears of the people of Puebla and points out that of the approximately 13,000 people already vaccinated there, it is doubtful whether even one or two have died. The *Cartilla* itself appears to have been independently written for its mission in Puebla by an experienced medical man who deliberately avoids terms of art. According to the title-page the author was a physician of Puebla and a member of the City's *Junta central de vacunación*. A detailed account of the activities of Balmis and the *Real Expedíción Maritima de la Vacuna* in Puebla is given by Smith (1974), pp. 38–40. [See M.156, M157, M.158].

M.134   MORENO, Juan José [d. 1820?]

Fragmentos de la vida, y virtudes [de] ... Vasco de Quiroga primer Obispo de la Santa Iglesia Cathedral de Michoacan .... Con notas criticas, en que se aclaran muchos puntos historicos, y antiguedades Americanas especialmente Michoacan-enses. [Followed by:] Reglas, y ordenanzas para el gobierno de los Hospitales de Santa Fé de Mexico, y Michoacan ... por ... Vasco de Quiroga. *engr. port.* 2 pts.

4to. Mexico: Imprenta del Colegio Real de San Ildefonso. 1766.

Beristáin iii p.282 no.2059.
Guerra (Icon.) 361.
León (Mex.) ii (2) 297.
Medina (Mex.) v 5099.
Palau 181902.

The pagination is as follows: 13 ll., pp. 202, 2 ll., pp. 29. The portrait is inserted after the 13 leaves of preliminaries [i.e. after D1]. Since the two parts of the work together form a perfect quarto it is unlikely that Palau's note is right in believing that there are also copies having 26 ll., pp. 202, 2 ll., pp. 30. Error in counting the 13 leaves as pages may account for the phantom variant.

The author was doctor of theology of the University of Mexico, member of the Colegio Real de San Ildefonso, *Catedrático de filosofía* and Rector of the Colegio de San Nicolás in Valladolid, Michoacán; and *Canónigo magistral*, and *Maestrescuelas* of Guadalajara.

The subject of the present work, Vasco de Quiroga, Bishop of Michoacán from 1538 until his death in 1565, arrived in New Spain as one of four new *Oidores* in 1531. He founded with royal approval the two pueblo-hospitals for Indians referred to in the title in 1532 and 1533.

Warren (1963) regarded this work as the most complete life of Quiroga yet written.

M.135   **MORENO, Manuel Antonio [d. 1803]** *and* **SANCHEZ, Alejo Ramón**

Carta apologética de las reflexiónes sobre el úso de las lagartijas. 2 ll., pp. xxii.

4to. Mexico: J.A. de Hogal. 1782.

Beristáin iii p. 282 no. 2060.
Guerra (Icon.) 436.
León (Mex.) vi 652.
León (1915) 75.
Medina (Mex.) vi 7349.

Sig. G [i.e. the last leaf] is a singleton; the second leaf is presumably blank. Medina records a copy ending on p. xxi, with final page [p. xxii] blank.

A surgeon born and qualified in Spain, and a typical product of the Enlightenment, Moreno was sent to New Spain by Charles III in 1770 to found the Real Escuela de Cirugía in the City of Mexico. In its home in the Hospital Real de Indios he was appointed Professor of Anatomy, and on eventually becoming Director, was responsible for many improvements. He also became surgeon to the same Hospital and to the Hospital de San Andrés.

In this, the second of their three pamphlets on this subject, he and Sánchez refute León y Gama's claim for the therapeutic value of raw newts in the treatment of cancer [see M.76; and M.56 for references to the other publications in the controversy].

M.136   MORENO DE GUZMAN, Bernardo

Descripcion de la epidemia del dia, y medios de librarse de ella y sus recaidas. pp. 20.

4to. [Mexico:] María Fernández Jáuregui. 1813.

Beristáin iii p. 280 no. 2051.
Guerra (Icon.) 606.
León (1915) 208.
Medina (Mex.) viii 10874.
Palau 182190.

The author is said by Beristáin to have been a native of Caracas and to have practiced as a surgeon in the City of Mexico.

M.137   MUÑOZ PAREJO DE ALARAZ, Bartolomé

Theatrum apollineum, triumphales latices medicinae, Hippocratica literaria naumachia phylosofica methodica empirica controversia . . . . moderante cathedram Doctore Bartholomaeo Sanchez Parejo. *woodcut coat of arms.* 2 ll., ff. 56, 2 ll. (2nd bl.).

4to. Puebla: J. de Alcaçar. 1647.

Andrade p. 794.
Beristáin iv p. 104 no. 2315.
Guerra (Icon.) 84.
León (1915) 17.
Medina (Puebla) 17.
Palau 185496, 294058.

An Act, held on 8 and 9 January 1647, in the Convent of St. Augustine, Puebla, at which Dr Bartolomé Sánchez Parejo presided. The thesis, upheld by Bartolomé Muñoz Parejo de Alaraz, claims water as a universal remedy.

Bartolomé Sánchez Parejo is said by Beristáin to have been a native of Lima and to have received his doctorate in medicine from the University of Mexico. He may have been the same B. Sánchez Parejo who arrived in Guatemala from Puebla de los Angeles in 1649 at the invitation of the Ayuntamiento to superintend measures against a severe epidemic [see Martínez Durán (1964), pp. 171–175]. His lack of success and the dislike he encountered there brought him medical disgrace and financial ruin in 1658. The dates of his baccalaureate (1621) and doctorate (1624) from the University of Mexico do not, however, agree with the baccalaureate awarded to [another?] Bartolomé Sánchez Parejo by the same University on 7 March 1641 [see Fernández de Recas (1960), p. 64 (& plate 3); and Guerra (Icon.) 63].

M.138 NEW SPAIN. Laws, statutes, &c.

[Begins:] D. Juan Francisco de Guemes, y Horcasitas, Conde de Rebilla Gigedo . . . . Por quanto en la Real Almoneda, que se celebró en esta Corte el dia nueve de Marzo de este año, se remató el Assiento de la bebida del pulque blanco de esta ciudad [&c.]. pp. 39 (= 37).

fol. Mexico: [s.n.]. 1753.

Guerra (Icon.) 311.
León (Mex.) ii (2) 557.
Medina (Mex.) v 4121.

H2 wanting; the pagination omits pp. 31–32, but the text continues as reprinted in full in León, *loc. cit.*

An attempt by the Conde de Revillagigedo [Viceroy 1746–55], the first Viceroy of that title, to prevent drunkenness and to regulate the sale of pulque, reciting previous laws and opinions of the Protomedicato in similar attempts at regulation since 1671. Dated 9 July 1753.

M.139 NEW SPAIN. Laws, statutes, &c.

[Begins:] Don Carlos Francisco de Croix, Marques de Croix . . . . Hago saber al publico, y especialmente a los sugetos . . . se han dedicado ó dediquen al arte de la cirujía . . . he regulado oportuno hacer entender por este vando las advertencias y prevenciones siguientes.

broadside. [Mexico: s.n.]. 1770.

Guerra (Icon.) 369.

MS signature.

The Marqués de Croix [Viceroy 1766–71] lays down in this *Bando* the regulations for qualification of surgeons graduating from the Escuela de Anatomía Práctica y Operaciones de Cirujía established in the Hospital Real de Indios in 1768. Dated 10 April 1770.

M.140 **NEW SPAIN. Laws, statutes, &c.**

[Begins:] Considerando la importancia ... de que en todos los parages de la governacion de este Virreynato se ponga en práctica la operacion cesarea [&c.]. 1 l.

fol. Mexico: [s.n.]. 1772.

Guerra (Icon.) 381.

Antonio María Bucareli y Ursúa [Viceroy 1771–79], urges the performance of caesarean section, and cites J.M. Rodríguez, *La caridad del sacerdote*, [Mexico, F. de Zúñiga y Ontiveros, 1772]. [See M.184, M.185; for the original edition, see Medina (Mex.), vi, 5523]. Rodríguez's work was an adaptation of F.M. Cangiamila, *Embriologia sacra*, Palermo, F. Valenza, 1745. [See M.93 for parallel action by the Archbishop]. Dated November 1772.

M.141 **NEW SPAIN. Laws, statutes, &c.**

Reglamento formado para el cuerpo de invalidos de Nueva España por . . . Antonio Maria Bucareli y Ursua . . . aprobado . . . por S.M. en Real Orden de trece de Junio de 1773. 1 l., pp.19, 1 bl. l.

fol. Mexico: J.A. de Hogal. 1774.

Beristáin (Mex.) p.294 no.516.
León (Mex.) v 231.
Medina (Mex.) vi 5675.

The Viceroy sets up a corps of army pensioners, following the establishment in Spain of a similar *Cuerpo de Inválidos* in 1761. Approved by *Real Orden* of 13 June 1773, and dated 30 December 1773.

M.142 **NEW SPAIN. Laws, statutes, &c.**

Instruccion y metodo con que se ha de establecer el Hospital para la tropa de la guarnicion del Presidio de Nuestra Señora del Carmen [&c.]. pp.15.

fol. [Mexico: F. de Zúñiga y Ontiveros]. 1774.

Beristáin i p.294 no.516.
León (Mex.) i 272.
Medina (Mex.) vi 5674.
Palau 36497.

Rúbrica on p.15.

This is Pt. 3 only of *Reglamento provisional para el prest, vestuario, gratificaciones . . . y total govierno de la tropa que debe guarnecer el Presidio de Nuestra Señora del Carmen de la Isla de Trís* [&c.], Mexico, F. de Zúñiga y Ontiveros, 1774, quoted by Beristáin, León, Medina, and Palau.

The presidio was situated on the Isla de Trís, Laguna de Términos, Campeche. The present orders issued by Bucareli, following reconstruction plans for the fort, provide minute details of the organisation of a military hospital, including the rations for the patients. Bucareli was particularly concerned in defending and expanding the territory of New Spain, and had issued an instrument for the general regulation of the presidios in 1772. Dated 13 October 1774.

M.143   NEW SPAIN. Laws, statutes, &c.

[Begins:] El Rey. Virrey, Governador y Capitan General de las Provincias de la Nueva-España .... acompañásteis el respectivo al expediente suscitado por el General de la Orden de San Hipólito Mártir . . . sobre reedificar el Hospital en que á su cuidado se curan los dementes [&c.]. 2 ll.

fol. Mexico: [s.n.]. 1776.

Guerra (Icon.) 407.
Medina (Mex.) vi 5906.

Signature and *rúbrica* of certification on the verso of the second leaf. This certified copy is dated 10 July 1776.

The *Cédula*, dated 29 June 1775, refers to the attempts of the General of the Orden de San Hipólito (or, Hermanos de la Caridad de San Hipólito) to raise funds for the rebuilding of the Order's Hospital for the insane, and for the maintenance of the patients. The Hospital de San Hipólito in Mexico City was founded by Bernardino Álvarez in 1567. [See M.71].

M.144   NEW SPAIN. Laws, statutes, &c.

[Begins:] El Bailio Frey Don Antonio María Bucareli y Ursúa ... Virrey, Gobernador y Capitan General ... Siendo continuos los ocursos que se hacen á mi Superior Gobierno, ya por los Indios ... y ya por los asentistas del pulque, sobre que éstos no se arreglan á las condiciones de sus remates [&c.]. 1 l.

fol. Mexico: [s.n.]. 1776.

This order issued by virtue of the Viceregal decrees of 9 August and 7 October 1776, and directed to local administrators for proclamation, seeks to remedy abuses in the controlled sale of pulque and unfermented pulque [*tlachique*] and lays down duties of 1/6 of sale value payable by Indian vendors and 1/4 payable by vendors of other castes. Further conditions are laid down and penalties provided. Dated 22 November 1776.

M.145   NEW SPAIN. Laws, statutes, &c.

Reglamento que se deduce del expediente formado por mí, sobre establecer una Casa, ú Hospital de Convalecencia para la tropa, extramuras de Veracruz [&c.]. pp. 7.

fol. Mexico: [s.n.]. 1781.

Beristáin ii p.164 no.912.
Guerra (Icon.) 429.
León (Mex.) vi 139.
León (1915) 71.
Medina (Mex.) vi 7194.

These orders were issued by virtue of a *Superior Decreto* of Martín de Mayorga [Viceroy 1779–83], promulgated in the same year. Pedro Antonio de Cossio, over whose name these orders were issued, was (according to Beristáin) one of the senior officials of New Spain, becoming *Ministro principal de marina* of the port of Veracruz, *Intendente* of the army, and Secretary of the Viceroyalty. Dated 16 March 1781.

M.146   NEW SPAIN. Laws, statutes, &c.

[Begins:] Desde que dictó sus primeras providencias el Exmo. Señor Virey Conde de Galvez [&c.]. 1 l.

fol. Mexico: [s.n.]. 1786.

Medina (Mex.) vi 7667.

Medina records a copy with a second (blank) leaf;

Three *rúbricas* and addressee in MS on verso.

A circular signed by three *Oidores* of the *Real Audiencia Gobernadora* communicating the King's approval of the local action taken on behalf of the poor during the poor harvest and fever epidemic of 1785. Dated 13 December 1786.

M.147   NEW SPAIN. Laws, statutes, &c.

[Begins:] D. Manuel Antonio Florez . . . . Con el fin de evitar las dudas que pudieran ocurrir en quanto á los negocios que no se expresan en el Real Decreto de 8 de Julio del año próximo pasado . . . acerca de la division del Ministerio de Indias en dos distintas Secretarías, se ha servido S.M. hacer las declaraciones que contiene la Real Orden del tenor siguiente.

broadside. Mexico: [s.n.]. 1788.

Guerra (Icon.) 454.

The *Real Decreto* of 8 July 1787, which divided the Ministerio de Indias into two separate Offices, is further clarified by this proclamation of Manuel Antonio Flores [Viceroy 1787–89] which gives, *inter alia*, scientific affairs including botanical expeditions, education, history, medicine and surgery to the Secretario de Gracia y Justicia. The proclamation is dated 8 April 1788.

M.148   NEW SPAIN. Laws, statutes, &c.

[Begins:] Don Juan Vicente de Güemes Pacheco de Padilla Horcasitas y Aguayo, Conde de Revilla Gigedo . . . . La particular atencion que desde los principios de mi mando me han merecido todos los objetos de policía de esta Capital, me han obligado á mejorar los pocos que habia . . . . Fue uno de mis principales cuidados el arreglo de baños temascales y lavaderos [&c.].

broadside. Mexico: [s.n.]. 1793.

Guerra (Icon.) 479.

Rúbrica on recto.

A *Bando* issued by the Conde de Revillagigedo [Viceroy 1789–94], the second Viceroy of that title, which regulates the use of traditional public steam baths (*temascales*) of the Indians and public washing-places, and seeks to prevent their abuse. Dated 21 August 1793.

M.149   NEW SPAIN. Laws, statutes, &c.

[Begins:] Don Juan Vicente de Güemes Pacheco de Padilla Horcasitas y Aguayo, Conde de Revilla Gigedo . . . . Antonio Maria Bucareli y Ursúa, mi predecesor, deseoso de disipar la preocupacion de los Facultativos de Cirugia de no querer curar á los heridos sin precedente órden de la Justicia, mandó publicar en 14 de Mayo de 1777 el Bando del tenor siguiente: [&c.].

broadside. Mexico: [s.n.]. 1794.

Rúbrica and signature on recto; certificates, *rúbricas* and signatures of receipt and proclamation on the verso.

A *Bando* which recites an earlier proclamation of 14 May 1777 by Bucareli [Viceroy 1771–79] and another by Revillagigedo dated 26 May 1793, which together enjoin surgeons, physicians, apothecaries and midwives to treat those wounded in brawls without the necessity of first obtaining a justice's order to do so. Penalties are confirmed for failure to treat the wounded and to report the case to a justice within eight hours. Dated 23 April 1794.

M.150   **NEW SPAIN. Laws, statutes, &c.**

[Begins:] A esfuerzos de mis estrechas providencias para que se cortara y extinguiera, ó quando ménos se evitase la propagacion de la terrible enfermedad de viruelas [&c.]. 3 ll.

fol. Mexico: [s.n.]. 1797.

Guerra (Icon.) 495.

Wanting the last blank leaf.

As the smallpox epidemic approached Mexico City, stringent regulations issued by Miguel de la Grua Talamanca y Branciforte, Marqués de Branciforte [Viceroy 1794–98] provided for isolation of cases, general quarantine, fumigation, organisation of district officers and Societies of Charity, separate burial of victims of the epidemic, and the raising of relief funds. The advantages of voluntary inoculation are suggested. A full translation from a transcript was published by Cook (1939). Headed *Reservada*, and dated Mexico 28 February 1797.

M.151   **NEW SPAIN. Laws, statutes, &c.**

[Begins:] A esfuerzos de mis estrechas providencias para que se cortara y extinguiera, ó quando ménos se evitase la propagacion de la terrible enfermedad de viruelas [&c.]. 4 ll. (last bl.).

fol. Mexico & Orizaba: [s.n.]. 1797.

Guerra (Icon.) 495.

A variant of the above and issued as a copy of it; headed *Reservada*, and dated Mexico 28 February 1797, and Orizaba (the Viceroy's residence during the epidemic) September 1797; the name of the Viceroy Branciforte appears at the end of the main text.

M.152 NEW SPAIN. Laws, statutes, &c.

[Begins:] Miguel La Grua Talama[nca] y Branciforte . . . . El Rey . . . dignándose comunicarme . . . la Real Orden siguiente: . . . En la Ciudad de Cuba se ha descubierto un específico preservativo del mal de siete dias [&c.].

broadside. Orizaba: [s.n.]. 1797.

Rúbricas and signature on recto, and two MS certificates of proclamation and an endorsement on the verso.

The proclamation of the *Real Orden* recommending the use of compresses soaked in balsam of copaiba on the cut umbilical cord of newborn infants for the prevention of fatal convulsions. Dated 25 March 1797.

M.153 NEW SPAIN. Laws, statutes, &c.

[Begins:] Don Miguel Joseph de Azanza . . . . Por quanto se ha dudado si los Barberos están sujetos á sufrir exámen y obtener licencia del Real Tribunal del Protomedicato [&c.].

broadside. Mexico: [s.n.]. 1799.

Guerra (Icon.) 523.

Rúbricas and signature on recto.

Miguel José de Azanza [Viceroy 1798–1800] rules that barbers require no licence from the Protomedicato provided that they refrain from letting blood, pulling teeth, applying leeches or cupping-glasses, activities which rightly belong to the phlebotomists. The two trades are to distinguish themselves by certain exterior tokens. Dated 29 March 1799.

M.154 NEW SPAIN. Laws, statutes, &c.

[Begins:] Por algunos documentos que existen en la Secretaría del Virreynato concernientes á la última epidemia de viruelas [&c.].

broadside. Mexico: [s.n.]. 1799.

Guerra (Icon.) 524.

Rúbrica, and addressed and dated in MS.

The Viceroy calls for returns of inoculated and uninoculated persons and deaths in each cateory during the recent smallpox epidemic, with the intention of demonstrating the advantages of inoculation. The form of return, originally attached to the letter, is wanting. Dated 14 November 1799.

M.155   NEW SPAIN. Laws, statutes, &c.

[Begins:] Don Miguel Joseph de Azanza . . . . Por quanto seguida causa en el Real Proto-Medicato de México contra D. Narciso Aleman por curandero intruso [&c.].

broadside. Mexico: [s.n.]. 1800.

Guerra (Icon.) 531.

Rúbricas and signature on recto.

The Viceroy proclaims the *Real Cédula* of 27 October 1798 which laid down the course of legal action in all cases concerning the Protomedicatos of the Indies. Dated 21 March 1800.

M.156   NEW SPAIN. Laws, statutes, &c.

Reglamento de Orden de S.M. para que se propague y perpetúe la vacuna en Nueva España. pp.6.

fol. Mexico: [s.n.]. 1810.

Guerra (Icon.) 584.
León (1915) 201.

Appearing over the name of Balmis, presumably as Director of the *Real Expedición Marítima de la Vacuna*, the *Reglamento* provides for the oversight of public vaccination by two medical men under each Intendant or Governor and makes methods and certain warnings in the process clear. [see M.133, M.157, M.158]. Dated 10 October 1810.

M.157 NEW SPAIN. Laws, statutes, &c.

[Begins:] Con esta fecha dirijo al Señor Intendente Corregidor de esta Capital la Orden que sigue: "Vuelto á este Reyno en cumplimiento de Real Orden, el Señor Director de la Expedicion marítima de la vacuna Don Francisco Xavier de Balmis ... formó con aprobacion mia el Reglamento de que incluyo á V.S. cincuenta y cinco exemplares" [&c.].

broadside. Mexico: [s.n.]. 1810.

Guerra (Icon.) 588.
León (1915) 202.

Rúbrica, annotation and addressee in MS on verso.

A circular, quoting an *Orden* to the Intendant of Mexico, probably sent to Intendants and administrative heads throughout New Spain, enjoining methods of raising money in the dioceses and provinces to meet the expenses of the two medical men and the clerks required for general vaccination in each area. With this copy of the circular Francisco Xavier Venegas de Saavedra [Viceroy 1810–13] enclosed 6 copies of the *Reglamento* of 10 October 1810 which appeared over the name of Balmis. [See M.133, M.156, M.158]. Dated 12 December 1810.

M.158 NEW SPAIN. Laws, statutes, &c.

Origen de la vacuna, y medios de encontrarla en el Reyno de Nueva España. 2 ll.

4to. [Mexico: s.n. 1810/11].

Guerra (Icon.) 553.
León (1915) 195.

A circular, neither signed nor dated, apparently issued for information to local administrators in New Spain. It refers to the discovery in certain areas of indigenous cowpox during the earlier *Real Expedición Maritima de la Vacuna* [1803–1806], and to the intention of its Director, Francisco Xavier de Balmis [1753–1819], to re-explore those areas and others where cowpox was believed to exist.

Stewards of haciendas are to be requested to pass information of cowpox among their herds to the head of their province for forwarding to the Director of the Expedition.

A detailed account of Balmis and the Expedition is provided by Smith (1974). [See

M.133, M.156, M.157]. Balmis had returned to New Spain in June 1810, but his work was disrupted by the insurrection of Hidalgo in mid-September and he left for Spain in August 1811.

M.159   NEW SPAIN. Laws, statutes, &c.

[Begins:] Don Felix Maria Calleja del Rey . . . . Siendo muy frequentes los partes que se me dan de que algunos Médicos de esta Capital, se niegan á asistir á los enfermos quando son llamados en horas extraordinarias de la noche [&c.].

broadside. Mexico: [s.n.]. 1815.

Guerra (Icon.) 621.
Medina (Mex.) viii 11040.

Rúbrica and signature on recto.

A *Bando* of Félix María Calleja del Rey, Conde de Calderón [Viceroy 1813–16] confirming that the stringent penalties laid down by Bucareli [Viceroy 1771–79] in his proclamation of 14 May 1777 for failure of surgeons to attend victims of street brawls at night, extend also to a similar neglect by physicians to attend their patients. Officers of the *Alumbrado* are advised not to entertain suspicious requests by servants for fetching medical assistance unless they have had previous notification from the master of the house or some other trustworthy person that the call, restricted to one neighbouring physician, is necessary and urgent. Dated 4 April 1815.

M.160   NEW SPAIN. Protomedicato

Publicas demostraciones . . . que este Real Tribunal del Protomedicato de N.E. hace en la gloriosa proclamacion . . . de . . . Carlos Quarto y . . . Maria Luisa de Borbon. 2 pts.

4to. Mexico: F. de Zúñiga y Ontiveros. [1793].

Beristáin iii p.282 no.2060; iv p.146 no.2413.
Guerra (Icon.) 472.
León (Mex.) vi 653.
León (1915) 134.
Medina (Mex.) vi 8127.
Palau 240058.

Sig. G is a singleton; the last 3 leaves of the gathering are presumably blank.

These are the two winning dissertations on inflammatory obstructions of the liver by Joaquín Pío Eguía y Muro and Manuel Antonio Moreno [d. 1803], published by the Protomedicato to celebrate the accession of Charles IV in 1788.

Eguía received his doctorate in medicine from the University of Mexico in 1784, and later became *Catedrático regente de vísperas de medicina* in the same University, physician to the Hospital de San Andrés and *Protofiscal* of the Protomedicato. Moreno was the surgeon who with Alejo Ramón Sánchez refuted León y Gama's extravagant claim for the therapeutic value of raw newts for cancer [see M.135].

This work is usually given the publication date of 1791. Though the competition was announced in the *Gazeta de Mexico*, 1790–91, *4*, 89–91 (18 May 1790), when scripts were required to be delivered by the end of July, it was only the lengthy personal effort of the Viceroy, the second Revillagigedo [1789–94], that ensured their eventual publication in 1793 [see Instrucciones (1873), paras. 241–243; and Flores (1886–88), *2*, pp. 99–100].

M.161 NEW SPAIN. Protomedicato

Método claro, sencillo y fácil que para practicar la inoculacion de viruelas presenta al público el Real Tribunal del Protomedicato [&c.]. pp.7.

4to. [Mexico: s.n. 1797?].

Guerra (Icon.) 500.
León (1915) 167.

Simplified instructions for communities without medical aid, offered to the public by the Protomedicato at the order of the Viceroy.

M.162 NEW SPAIN. [Protomedicato]

[Begins:] Razon general del número de personas de todas clases que han tenido el contagio de viruelas en la epidemia del año de 1797, con la distincion de sanos, convalecientes y muertos. [&c.].

broadside. Mexico: [s.n.]. 179[8].

This form, probably sent by the Protomedicato to both the 181 special districts (*manzanas*), and to convents, communities, and hospitals, sought final figures of deaths, recoveries and current convalescences. This copy is neither dated nor completed in MS.

The results of this enquiry were published in the *Estado general* dated 21 February 1798 [see entry below].

M.163   NEW SPAIN. [Protomedicato]

[Begins:] Estado general, que comprehende el número de personas de todas clases que han tenido el contagio de viruelas ... con la distincion siguiente. *table.*

broadside. Mexico: [s.n.]. 1798.

Guerra (Icon.) 518.

These figures of deaths and recoveries separated for the convents, communities, hospitals &c., and for the 181 *manzanas* of the city, show that 5,951 deaths occurred out of a total of 56,169 cases. The figures do not agree with the *Resumen general* of 17 February 1798 [see M.122] issued by the Junta Principal de Caridad, nor with the estimate issued by the Archbishop, probably with his letter dated 11 April 1798 [see M.97; and Cooper (1965), pp. 152–153 and footnote]. Dated 21 February 1798.

M.164   NEW SPAIN. Protomedicato

Régimen curativo del sarampion. Formado del órden del Superior Gobierno por el Real Tribunal del Protomedicato para la gente del pueblo pobre y sin proporciones de médico que les asista. 2 ll.

4to. Mexico: M.J. de Zúñiga y Ontiveros. 1804.

Guerra (Icon.) 546.
León (1915) 187.

This brief guide, which is reprinted in the *Gazeta de Mexico*, 1804–05, *12*, 54–56 (29 February 1804), describes the clinical signs and course of measles; recommends such remedies as barley water infused with elder flowers, borage or poppy for minor cases; and advises bleeding for serious cases.

M.165   NUÑEZ de GODOY, Miguel

Glorias del sepulcro de Santo Thomas de Villa-Nueva ... en la translacion de el incorrupto cuerpo de ... Francisco Gomes de Mendiola. *woodcut coat of arms.* 6 ll., pp. 16.

4to. Mexico: María de Benavides, Widow of J. de Ribera. 1700.

Andrade 1138.
Beristáin ii p.362 no.1318.
Medina (Mex.) iii 1773.
Palau 197237.

A sermon on the text *Euge serve bone, et fidelis* [&c.], Matt. 25.

The author was, according to Beristáin, a Doctor of the University of Mexico, and Canon of the Cathedral of Guadalajara; on the title-page of the present work he is described as Prebendary and *Examinador synodal* of the diocese. Andrade adds that he became Dean.

The subject of his discourse, Francisco Gómez de Mendiola [1519–76], had been *Oidor* of Guadalajara [1566–71] and as Bishop of the diocese of the same name from 1571 had lived an exemplary life of poverty and charity. His body, according to Beristáin, was still uncorrupted 23 years after his death.

M.166   **OSASUNASCO, Desiderio de**

Observaciones sobre la preparacion y usos del chocolate. 8 ll.

8vo. Mexico: F. de Zúñiga y Ontiveros. 1789.

Beristáin iv p.66 no.2243.
Guerra (Icon.) 464.
Medina (Mex.) vi 7895.
Palau 206352.

The author notes that the diverse effects of chocolate as of coffee depend on the method of preparation, on the amount used, and on the temperaments of those drinking it. He comments on the varieties obtainable, the ways of making it, and suggests its use as a corrective to purgatives. Notwithstanding its reasonable tone the pamphlet was vigorously attacked in J.A. Alzate's *Gazeta de literatura* of 19 November 1789, the first paragraph of which is quoted by Medina; the article is reprinted in full in the Puebla (1831) edition of this journal, vol. 1, pp. 234–241 [see Per. 6].

M.167   **OSORIO Y PERALTA, Diego**

Principia medicinae, epitome, et totius humani corporis fabrica seu ex microcosmi armonia divinum, germen. *woodcut.* 6 ll., ff. 104 (=105).

4to. Mexico: Heirs of the Widow of B. Calderón. 1685.

Andrade 845.

Beristáin iv p.69 no.2251.

Guerra (Icon.) 146.

León (1915) 30.

Medina (Mex.) iii 1354.

Palau 206757.

The last leaf [Sig. C[c]1] is a singleton. The crude woodcut of Our Lady of Guadalupe [π 2ʳ] in this copy is not noticed elsewhere.

The author obtained his doctorate in medicine in 1662 at the University of Mexico and became *Catedrático de anatomía y cirugía*, and later, *Catedrático de vísperas de medicina*. He held, among other appointments, that of *Protomédico*. Becoming a widower in 1670, he was ordained priest.

Generally claimed as the first work on anatomy printed in New Spain, this scholastic textbook for beginners in medicine is based largely on Hippocrates and Galen. He includes the Latin translation of the Hippocratic *Aphorisms* by Niccolò Leoniceno [1428–1524].

M.168   PAEZ DE LA CADENA, Miguel

[Begins:] Sin embargo de que ahora dos años procuré reunir de todo el Reyno varias noticias relativas á las bebidas, que ya naturales, ó ya artificiales . . . se cosechan [&c.]. 1 l., 2 bl. ll., 5 ll.

fol. Mexico: [s.n.]. 1778.

Guerra (Icon.) 422.

Miguel Paez was the active *Juez Superintendente* of the Real Aduana and of the Ramo de Pulques of the City of Mexico and New Spain [see Medina (Mex.), vi, 6040]. This is an unused copy, not completed in MS, of a document dated 31 December 1778, apparently circulated to the customs officers throughout New Spain, asking for a return of information on wines and spirits against the list of alcoholic liquors in the last 5 leaves of the document.

M.169   PUEBLA. Hospital Provisional de San Francisco Xavier

Resultado del Hospital provisional de San Francisco Xavier de ésta Ciudad de la Puebla de los Angeles, desde el siete de Diciembre, primero de su establecimiento, hasta el treinta y uno del mismo de este año de 1812.

broadside. [Puebla: s.n.]. 1813.

Guerra (Icon.) 609.

The broadside is of 2 sheets joined horizontally.

According to the brief account signed by its Rector, José Ortiz de León, the temporary hospital was established in the Colegio de San Francisco Xavier for the reception of patients suffering from the epidemic of fevers. In spite of some reluctance to use the hospital, for which reason the report is issued, the figures demonstrate that of the 1,396 patients received during the first 24 days of its existence, 877 had been discharged cured, 153 had died, and 366 remained in its care. The report lists the governing body, the medical staff and servants and their pay, as well as contributions by subscribers; among the last are included the well-known brothers Patricio and José Sebastián Furlong. The same fevers struck the region of the City of Mexico in late January 1813 and attained epidemic proportions there during the following April [see Cooper (1965), p. 158].

M.170 PUEBLA. Hospital Real de San Pedro

Fondo piadoso del Hospital Real y General de Puebla.

broadsides. [Puebla: s.n. 1796].

Guerra (Icon.) 493.

MS annotations on verso of the first certificate.

Three certificates of contribution for 2, 3, and 4 reales, each signed by Ignacio Domenech, Prebendary of the Cathedral, and Rector of the Hospital, who instituted sweeping reforms in 1796 and established the *fondo piadoso* to make new funds available. The Hospital, founded *c.* 1545, and closed in 1917, was the centre of medical activity in Puebla from the seventeenth century to the nineteenth century. [See Muriel (1956–60), *1*, pp. 161–174].

M.171 PUEBLA. Hospital Real de San Pedro

Resumen de los enfermos, que han entrado á curarse en el Hospital Real y General de S. Pedro Apóstol de la Ciudad de la Puebla de los Angeles desde el último de diciembre de 1795 hasta igual dia de 1796.

broadside. [Puebla: s.n.]. 1797.

Guerra (Icon.) 504.

The summary includes figures for hospital entries, cures and deaths. It also notes general hospital expenditure during the period, as well as special expenditure for assistance to children whose fathers became patients in the hospital, from the *fondo piadoso* established in 1796. Signed by the treasurer, Miguel López Jurado, and dated 2 January 1797.

M.172   PUEBLA. Junta Principal de Caridad

[Begins:] Muy Sr. mio: Enterada esta Junta Principal de Caridad, de la mucha que tuvo V. con los enfermos virolentos que puso á su cuidado [&c.].

broadside. Puebla: [s.n.]. 1798.

A circular letter of thanks to those who assisted during the smallpox epidemic from Salvador Biempica y Sotomayor [Bishop of Puebla 1790–1802] and his seven fellow-members of the Junta Principal de Caridad of Puebla. Dated 26 January 1798.

M.173   PUEBLA. Junta de Sanidad

Cartilla, ó sea metodo sencillo de curar á los pobres de la epidémia, que en el presente año aflige á los habitantes de esta Ciudad. Dirigida a los socios de las Juntas subalternas. 1 l., pp. 12, 1 l.

8vo. Puebla: P. de la Rosa. 1813.

Guerra (Icon.) 608.
León (1915) 205.
Medina (Puebla) 1597.

The anonymous writer divides his description of the symptoms and their cure into two categories, and matches the numbered prescriptions listed in the *Formulario* (in the last unnumbered leaf) to the symptoms he describes. The introduction records local fears of the epidemic and the reassuring measures taken by the city for its relief, including the establishment of the Hospital Provisional de San Francisco Xavier and its successful collection of funds, and the establishment of the Junta de Sanidad and its *Juntas subalternas* for the assistance of the *manzanas* into which the *Quarteles* of the city had been divided; it refers also to the local shortage of physicians, which the present pamphlet was designed to remedy.

M.174   RAMIREZ, Pedro

[Begins:] Medicina. Quae recentiorum industria [&c.]. [Thesis]. *engr. dedication plate.* 2 ll., pp.xi.

4to. Guadalajara: M. Valdés Téllez Girón. 1805.

Guerra (Icon.) 549.
León (1915) 193.

M.175   RAMOS DE VILCHES, Rafael

Receta que de Órden del Rey N.S. ha remitido al Exmô. Sr. Virey de este Reyno, el Exmô. Sr. Conde de Campo de Alange, para curacion de dolores reumaticos venereos y escorbuticos, que con conocida ventaja de la salud pública se ha practicado en varios lugares. 4 ll.

4to. [Puebla:] Pedro de la Rosa. 1794.

Guerra (Icon.) 483.
León (1915) 149.

Receipts composed of sarsaparilla, lignum vitae, sassafras, senna, tartar emetic, pineshoots etc., and directions for administering them, reprinted from the *Gazeta de Mexico*, 1794, 6, 7–8, 14–15, 22–23, (7 January, 21 January, & 10 February).

The author practised at the royal residences at the Escorial, Aranjuez, and Madrid.

M.176   RECETA

Rezeta muy util, para sanar de todo genero de tercianas o quartanas, aunque sean embejecidas, guardando el metodo siguiente . . . . Esta medicina se hace en la botica de Don Joseph Galiano. 1 l.

broadside. [Mexico: s.n. *c.*1780].

Guerra (Icon.) 428.

The advertisement recommends a mixture of powdered cinchona, salt of gentian, salt of *algenjos* [?ajenjo, wormwood, i.e. *Artemisia absinthium*] and sal ammoniac to be taken three times fasting.

M.177 RECETA

Receta especialisima contra calenturas, tercianas dobles, ó sencillas, aunque sean muy envejecidas.

broadside. [?Mexico: s.n. *c.*1800].

Guerra (Icon.) 467.

The receipt recommends a mixture of juice of sour oranges, and well ground cinchona and sugar, taken on three successive mornings.

M.178 RELACION

Relacion de la prodigiosa restauracion á la vida de un niño tenido por defuncto, executada al contacto de una reliquia del Apostol de las Indias San Francisco Xavier, de la Compañia de Jesus, en la ciudad de Xerez. Año de 1740. 4 ll.

4to. Mexico: Colegio Real de San Ildefonso. 1748.

Guerra (Icon.) 298.

M.179 RELACION

Relacion de una sanidad repentina, que en circunstancias de invocar á San Francisco de Borja alcanzó una religiosa del Convento de Stá. Rosa de la Puebla de los Angeles. 2 ll.

4to. [Mexico: Imprenta del Colegio Seminario. 1758].

Guerra (Icon.) 330.

Internal evidence from the licences printed at the end provide the date and place of publication. The Colegio Seminario was probably the Jesuit Colegio Real de San Ildefonso, whose printing press was active at this time.

M.180 REYES ANGEL, Gaspar de los

Sermon del gran privado de Christo . . . San Juan en la titular fiesta, que patente el S.S. Sacramento celebra la Compañia de Bethlem en su Hospital de Convalecientes de Mexico. 5 ll., ff. 15.

4to. Mexico: Heirs of the Widow of B. Calderón. 1689.

Andrade 906.
Beristáin iv p.208 no.2590.
Guerra (Icon.) 158.
Medina (Mex.) iii 1454.
Palau 265549.

With autograph of Francisco Antonio de la Cruz on the last blank page.

The title-page is a singleton; the second leaf of the gathering is presumably blank. The last leaf [D4] of the last gathering is wanting, also presumably blank.

Beristáin recounts the story of this Jesuit's miraculous restoration to life when a boy. The author is principally known for his printed sermons.

M.181 RINCON Y MENDOZA, José Jacinto del

Defensa juridica ... de ... Antonio Sanchez de Figueroa, en causa criminal, que contra él se sigue por la muerte executada en Juan Joseph de Almanza, Maestro de Boticario, que fue, en esta ciudad. 1 l., pp.21.

fol. Mexico: J.F. de Ortega Bonilla. 1722.

Beristáin iv p.231 no.2635.
Guerra (Icon.) 216.
Medina (Mex.) iv 2690.

M.182 RIO-FRIO, Bernardo de [d. 1700]

Por el venerable Dean, y Cavildo de la Santa Inglesia de Mechoacan, como Patron de los dos Hospitales, intitulados de Santa Fee ... cerca de que se declare, no dever pagar el real tributo los naturales de ellos en virtud de privilegio. 1 l., ff.11.

fol. Mexico: [s.n.]. 1688.

Andrade 900.
Beristáin iv p.234 no.2645.
Guerra (Icon.) 157.
Medina (Mex.) iii 1423.
Palau 268389.

Rio-Frio was *licenciado* in canon law of the University of Mexico, advocate to the *Audiencia*, and canon and treasurer of the Cathedral of Valladolid, Michoacán.

The legal action concerned the two Hospitales de Santa Fe, the one near the City of Mexico, and the other in the diocese of Michoacán, founded by Vasco de Quiroga, Bishop of Michoacán [1538–65], for whose life see M.134.

M.183   **RIVILLA BARRIENTOS, Juan Antonio de**

Lunario octavo regulado, y prognosticado al meridiano de la Puebla, Ciudad de los Angeles .... Con las elecciones de medicina, nautica, y agricultura .... de 1760. Bissexto. *sep. engr. t.p.*, 20 ll.

8vo. Puebla: C.T. de Ortega Bonilla. [1760].

Beristáin iv p.238 no.2656.
Guerra (Icon.) 339.
Medina (Puebla) 661.

M.184   **RODRIGUEZ, José Manuel**

La caridad del sacerdote para con los niños encerrados en el vientre de sus madres difuntas, y documentos de la utilidad, y necesidad de su práctica. Traducidos del idioma italiano ... por ... J.M.R. 21 ll., pp.45.

8vo. Mexico: F. de Zúñiga [y Ontiveros]. 1773.

Beristáin iv p.247 no.2682 [1772 ed.].
Guerra (Icon.) 388.
León (Mex.) ii(2) 624.
León (1915) 62.
Medina (Mex.) vi 5610.
Palau 272985.

This adaptation, adjusted to American conditions, of part of F.E. Cangiamila, *Embriologia sacra*, was produced to provide practical instruction to clergy and laity in caesarean section, following the recommendation of the Viceroy [see M.140] and the pastoral instruction of the Archbishop of Mexico in 1772 [see M.93]. The first edition of this adaptation appeared in 1772, the same year as the instruction [see Medina (Mex.), vi, 5523]; further editions appeared in the City of Mexico in 1799 [see entry below] and in 1818, and another version, by Ignacio Segura, in 1775 [see M.193].

The whole of Cangiamila's work, originally published in Italian in Palermo, F. Valenza, 1745, was translated into Spanish from the French by J. Castellot and published in Madrid in 2 vols. in 1774; 2nd ed., Madrid 1785 [see Palau 42255]. Many other editions were published in Milan, Paris, Munich and Augsburg; the last was published in Lisbon in 1791. A version also appeared in Lima [see P.13]. Copies of most of these versions exist in the Wellcome Institute Library.

Beristáin regarded Rodríguez as one of the outstanding figures of his time. Born in Cuba, Rodríguez took the Franciscan habit, became private adviser to the Archbishop of Mexico and theologian to the Fourth Council of the Province of Mexico. A man of wide interests, he wrote prolifically on religious and moral issues.

Cangiamila [1702–63], after practising as a lawyer, took holy orders, and became a canon of Palermo, and Inquisitor of Sicily. A biography appears in the Madrid translation of 1774 cited above, and his life and work are covered by Pundel (1969), pp. 85–92, 101.

M.185 RODRIGUEZ, José Manuel

La caridad del sacerdote para con los niños encerrados en el vientre de sus madres difuntas, y documentos de la utilidad, y necesidad de su práctica. Traducidos del idioma italiano ... por ... J.M.R. 18 ll., pp.45.

8vo. Mexico: F. de Zúñiga [y Ontiveros]. 1799.

Guerra (Icon.) 529.
León (Mex.) ii(2) 626.
Medina (Mex.) vii 8901.
Palau 272985.

Sig.* [i.e. the last leaf] is a singleton; the remaining leaves of the gathering are presumably blank.

The third edition.

M.186 RODRIGUEZ ARGÜELLES, Anacleto

Tratado de la calentura amarilla, ó vomito negro. *engr. coat of arms.* 4 ll., pp.33.

4to. Mexico: M.J. de Zúñiga y Ontiveros. 1804.

Guerra (Icon.) 548.
León (1915) 184.
Medina (Mex.) vii 9727.
Palau 273522.

The last leaf, sig. [E1], is a singleton, the conjugate leaf presumably blank.

The copy from the library of Nicolas León.

A brisk and practical account drawn largely from the author's own experience both as a medical officer and as a victim during the disastrous epidemic suffered by the Spanish fleet at Havana in 1794. He describes the incidence and symptoms of yellow fever, its immediate and remote causes, and the prognosis; he recommends for the most part a conservative and moderate treatment. He notes, *inter alia*, the place of a warm climate, stagnant water, and marshy areas in the aetiology of the disease; and he acknowledges his debt to Hippocrates and to W. Cullen for some of his observations.

According to the title-page, the author was *Primer profesor medico-cirujano jubilado* of the Royal Fleet, and became also, according to his prologue, *Médico de cámara* to Félix Berenguer de Marquina [Viceroy 1800–03] and *Cirujano mayor* to the military district of Jalapa.

M.187 RODRIGUEZ ARGÜELLES, Anacleto

Tratado de la fiebre epidémica ó endémica, remitente pútrida, petequial y contagiosa observada en esta capital. *engr. coat of arms.* 5 ll., pp. 12.

4to. México: M.J. de Zúñiga y Ontiveros. 1811.

Beristáin iv p. 245 no. 2674.
Guerra (Icon.) 590.
León (1915) 203.
Medina (Mex.) vii 10665

Incomplete: the conjugate leaves π3 and π10 [i.e. pp. 9–10] are wanting; the conjugate leaves π4 and π9 may be from another copy; and the title-page lacks its conjugate blank leaf. The quires, sewn in one gathering, lack signatures except for sig. 3 which appears on the fifth leaf of the gathering.

The author regards the fever, probably typhoid, as a variety of the *calentura amarilla* or *vómito negro* described by him in 1804 [see entry above]. He describes the clinical signs (not omitting the Hippocratic critical days), the proximate and remote causes, and the method of treatment, relying largely, as he admits, on the practice of William Cullen. His simply written tract was intended for use by parish priests and others, in places where no medical assistance was available.

M.188 SAINZ DE ALFARO Y BEAUMONT, Isidoro

Circular, que dirige el Señor Gobernador de la Sagrada Mitra á los parrocos, eclesiasticos, y fieles cristianos del Arzobispado de Mexico, sobre ereccion de cementerios fuera de las poblaciones. 1 l., pp. 36, 1 bl. l.

4to. Mexico: María Fernández de Jáuregui. 1809.

Beristáin i p. 120 no. 139.
Guerra (Icon.) 581.
Medina (Mex.) vii 10306.
Palau 285401.

Two *rúbricas* on p. 36.

The *Gobernador* of the archdiocese argues that ancient opinion, good custom and law, as well as public health and plenary indulgences, are in favour of the use of cemeteries at a distance from churches and towns [see M.41, M.98]. Dated 24 October 1809.

M.189 SALDAÑA Y ORTEGA, Antonio de

Sermon en la solemne accion de gracias por la ereccion canonica de la Congregacion Bethlemita en Religion de Hospitalidad definida, y aprobada por la Sante Sede Apostolica. 4 ll., ff. [13].

4to. Mexico: María de Benavides, widow of J. de Ribera. [1697].

Beristáin iv p. 291 no. 2792.
Guerra (Icon.) 179.
Medina (Mex.) iii 1678.
Palau 287158.

The last leaf [i.e. D 1] is a singleton; the conjugate second leaf is presumably blank.

A sermon on the text *Ego sum ostium ovium*, John 10. Among his ecclesiastical appointments, the preacher was *Catedrático de vísperas de teología* in the Seminario Real de Santa Cruz in the diocese of Antequera (now Oaxaca), and Rector of the Colegio de San Bartolomé in the same city. Many of his sermons were published in the City of Mexico and in Puebla.

M.190 SALGADO, Marcos José [1671–1740]

Cursus medicus mexicanus juxtá sanguinis circulationem, & alia recentiorum
inventa ad usum studentium in hác regali, pontificiá, mexicaná academia . . . . Pars
prima physiologica. 12 ll., pp. 344.

4to. Mexico: Heirs of the Widow of M. de Ribera. 1727.

Beristáin iv p. 293 no. 2797.
Guerra (Icon.) 238.
León (Mex.) iii 382.
León (1915) 37.
Medina (Mex.) iv 2965.
Palau 287390.

Salgado was born in Puebla, studied medicine at the University of Mexico, and
received his doctorate in 1694; he occupied the *Catedra de prima de medicina* from
1722 until his death, and was President of the Protomedicato. His contemporaries
held his knowledge and skill in high regard.

The present work, of which only this first part was apparently published, describes
contemporary physiology for students; it is the first monograph to have been
published in New Spain on this subject, and the first to describe, however
imprecisely, the circulation of the blood. According to Izquierdo (1934) pp. 57–116,
and *ibid.* (1937), it is unlikely that Salgado had read Harvey.

For the possible existence of a pre-publication printed version of the second part see
WMS. Amer. 35 (SALGADO), where a manuscript copy of it, probably the only
one in existence, is described.

M.191 SAN BUENAVENTURA, Francisco de [d. 1738]

Instruccion para novicios de la religion bethlemetica. *engravings (1 on t.p.).* 10 ll.,
pp. 264, 2 ll.

4to. Mexico: J.B. de Hogal. 1734.

Beristáin i p. 295 no. 518.
Guerra (Icon.) 268.
Léon (Mex.) i 275.
Medina (Mex.) iv 3343.
Palau 290359.

Sigs ¶ ¶ and Mm are of two leaves only; the remaining two leaves of each signature are presumably blank.

The author, himself a Bethlehemite [see M.18, M.19, M.20], wrote many works on Catholic practice, and became Prefect of the Convent Hospital of Puebla. The last chapter briefly and crudely describes the parts of the body to which ointments should be applied.

M.192 SANZ, José

Observacion chirurgico-medica de un hidro-sarcocele, ó tumor scirroso en un testiculo con kiste, ó saco, lleno de pus en el escroto. pp. 39.

8vo. [Mexico:] María Fernández de Jáuregui. 1814.

Guerra (Icon.) 619.
León (1915) 210.
Medina (Mex.) viii 10967.

A day by day case report of the lengthy but successful drainage of a hydrosarcocele following the method of the well-known Spanish surgeon Antonio de Gimbernat y Arbós [1734–1816]; it includes an account of the preliminary attempts at a medical cure, and the conferences of physicians headed by Rafael Sagáz. Verses by the grateful and rejuvenated patient, José Florencio de Mora Palacios, a householder and merchant, close the account.

The author, who took daily responsibility for the treatment, is described on the title-page as *Físico honorario de Cámara de S.M.* and *Consultor y mayor de los exércitos nacionales.*

M.193 SEGURA, Ignacio [b. 1729]

Avisos saludables a las parteras para el cumplimiento de su obligacion. Sacados de la *Embriologia sacra* del Sr. Dr. D. Francisco Manuel Cangiamila, y puestos en castellano por el Dr. D. Ignacio Segura. 2 ll., pp. 25.

Mexico: F. de Zúñiga y Ontiveros. 1775.

Guerra (Icon.) 405.
León (Mex.) ii(2) 724.
León (1915) 65.

Format uncertain. A single gathering, signed B on the fourth leaf. The last leaf is a singleton, wanting the blank leaf before the title-page.

An adaptation of a part of Cangiamila's *Embriologia sacra*, by a physician who received his doctorate at the University of Mexico in 1759. It deals largely with the baptismal duties of midwives. [See M.184].

M.194   SPAIN. Laws, statutes, &c.

Compendio de las noticias que S.M. por su Real Orden de 20 de Octubre proximo pasado ordena que se puntualizen para el completo conocimiento de la geografia, fisica, antiguedades, mineralogia y metalurgia de este Reyno de Nueva España [&c.]. 1 bl. l., pp.8, 1 bl. l.

fol. Mexico: F. de Zúñiga y Ontiveros. 1777.

Medina (Mex.) vi 6051.

This collection of *Noticias* approved by *Real Orden* on 20 October 1776 was dated and signed by Antonio de Ulloa at Veracruz on 22 January 1777 and published on 22 February 1777. The present copy bears a *rúbrica* of authentication on p. 8.

Antonio de Ulloa [1716–95] and Jorge Juan y Santacilla [1713–73] joined the French Earth-Measuring Expedition of 1735–44, usually known as the Condamine expedition; they later published their *Relacion historica del viage a la America meridional*, 5 vols., Madrid, A. Marin, 1748 (the first 4 vols. by Ulloa, and the last by Juan). Ulloa was well-known as explorer and scientist, and became governor of Louisiana. During his return to Europe his ship was captured by the British, and he was taken to England where he was treated as a distinguished visitor and elected F.R.S. in 1746.

The present directions for furthering scientific knowledge in New Spain were brought by him to Veracruz during his last voyage to the Americas with the Spanish silver fleet.

M.195   SPAIN. Laws, statutes, &c.

Real establecimiento de un Monte Pio á favor de las viudas, hijos y madres de los cirujanos del exército, y catedráticos de los Reales Colegios de Cirugía. 2 ll.

fol. Mexico: [s.n.]. 1803.

Guerra (Icon.) 541.

An uncertified copy of the *Reglamento* originally issued from the Escorial on 15 November 1798, creating a contributory pension fund for dependents of army surgeons and teachers of surgery in both Spain and the Indies.

M.196   SPAIN. Laws, statutes, &c.

Real Instruccion para el mejor régimen en la recaudacion de los fondos y pago de pensiones del nuevo Monte Pio establecido por S.M. á favor de las viudas, huérfanos y madres de los cirujanos del exército, y catedráticos de los Reales Colegios de Cirugía [&c.]. 4 ll.

fol. Mexico: M.J. de Zúñiga y Ontiveros. 1803.

González de Cossio 84.
Guerra (Icon.) 542.
Palau 251348.

An uncertified copy of the *Real Instrucción* dated Aranjuez 28 May 1799.

M.197   SPAIN. Laws, statutes, &c.

[Begins:] Emmo. Señor: Con esta fecha comunico al Señor Ministro de Gracia y Justicia la Real Orden siguiente: "Exmô. Señor: Sin embargo de que por la Real Orden de 31 de Octubre de 1781 están decididas expresamente todas las dudas que puedan ocurrir sobre los derechos parroquiales que competen á los Capellanes de los Buques de la Real Armada" [&c.]. 6 ll. (1st bl.)

fol. Mexico: [s.n.]. 1804.

Rúbrica of authentication on recto of final leaf.

A series of *Reales Ordenes* of the years 1798 to 1804 addressed to the Viceroy and to the Intendants for the most part settling the limits of duty of naval chaplains. The orders are followed by the *Real Cédula* of 13th April 1804 enjoining the practice of caesarean section after the death of the mother according to the method agreed on by the *Junta de Catedráticos* of the Real Colegio de Cirugía de San Carlos of Madrid. Their instructions are printed after the *Cédula*.

M.198   SPAIN. Laws, statutes, &c.

Nuevo Real establecimiento para gobierno del Monte Pio de los cirujanos del exército y catedráticos de los Reales Colegios de Cirugía. pp.25.

4to. Mexico: M. de Zúñiga y Ontiveros. 1804.

González de Cossio 85.
Guerra (Icon.) 547.
Palau 196622.

The last leaf is a singleton.

Finding that payments from the fund exceeded dues, new and stringent rules were issued to supersede the *Reglamento* of 15 November 1798 and the *Real Instrucción* of 28 May 1799. This is an uncertified copy of the original *Reglamento* issued from the Escorial on 31 October 1803.

M.199   **TORRES, Ignacio de**

Lugar revelado del séláh mystico de la Iglesia .... San Pedro, su venerable ecclesiastica congregacion, sita en el Real Hospital de la Puebla. 10 ll., ff. 10.

4to. Puebla: Heirs of J. de Villa-Real. [1697].

Andrade p.802.
Medina (Puebla) 194.
Palau 336485.

A sermon on the text *Tu es Petrus, et super hanc Petram aedificabo Ecclesiam meam*, Matt. 16. The author held a benefice in the City of Puebla, and was a Censor of the Holy Office in New Spain.

M.200   **TORRES, Nicolás José de [b. 1687]** *and* **DUMONT, José**

Virtudes de las aguas del Peñol, reconocidas, y examinadas de orden de la Real Audiencia, por el Real Tribunal del Protho-Medicato [&c.]. 1 l., pp.21.

4to. Mexico: Imprenta de la Bibliotheca Mexicana. 1762.

Beristáin ii p.209 no.1012 [Dumont]; *ibid.* v p.49 no.3069 [Torres].
Guerra (Icon.) 344.
León (Mex.) v 325 [Dumont].
León (1915) 56.
Medina (Mex.) v 4799.
Palau 336653.

Includes the opinion of Nicolás José de Torres dated 22 February 1752, and another by José Dumont dated 28 December 1752 on the therapeutic value of the waters of Peñol (now Peñón).

Torres received his doctorate in 1719 [see Fernández de Recas (1960), p. 72] and according to Flores (1886-88), *2*, p. 90 *et passim*, passed via the chairs of *Método* [1723-31], *Vísperas*, and *Prima de medicina* to become President of the Protomedicato [see Medina (Mex.) v 3884]. [For Dumont see M.7].

M.201   TORRICO LIAÑO, José de

Sagrada conjuncion de luces en la concurrencia de Sta. Rita, y Sta. Quiteria opuesta á las influencias de el Can Mayor, y la Canicula. *woodcut coat of arms.* 9 ll., ff. 13.

4to. Mexico: F. de Ribera Calderón. 1709.

Beristáin v p. 49 no. 3071.
Guerra (Icon.) 198.
Medina (Mex.) iii 2230.

The first and last leaves (title-page and sig. D) are singletons; the remaining three leaves of each signature are presumably blank.

A sermon in praise of the saints who miraculously freed Mexico from an epidemic of rabies.

M.202   VENEGAS, Juan Manuel [d. *c.*1785]

Compendio de la medicina: ó medicina practica, en que se declara laconicamente lo mas util de ella, que el autor tiene observado en estas regiones de Nueva España, para casi todas las enfermedades que acometen al cuerpo humano: dispuesto en forma alfabetica. 18 ll., pp. 377.

4to. Mexico: F. de Zúñiga y Ontiveros. 1788.

Beristáin v p. 119 no. 3271.
Guerra (Icon.) 458.
León (1915) 105.
Medina (Mex.) vi 7834.
Palau 358378.

Contemporary MS annotations in the index, and a few annotations in the margins of the text.

An encyclopaedia of contemporary knowledge and practice by a physician who is described on the title-page as *Profesor de medicina*; a work of particular use to contemporaries for its symptomatic approach and its many prescriptions.

It was issued at least four times during the nineteenth century in Mexico, in 1827 (imprint 'Filadelfia' but sold in Mexico), in 1841, in 1853, and in 1854. The last is a re-issue of the 1853 edition. The author's son, Luis Venegas, issued the *Continuación ó suplemento a la materia medica* [&c.], Mexico, Imprenta de Galvan, 1837, which was included in the subsequent editions. Copies of all these are in the Wellcome Institute Library.

M.203   VERACRUZ, Alonso de la [1507?–1584]

Phisica, speculatio .... Accessit compendium spherae Campani ad complementum tractatus de coelo. *woodcut on t.p.* 2 pts.

fol. Mexico: J. Pablos. 1557.

Beristáin i p.320.
Guerra (Icon.) 1.
Icazbalceta 31 (30).
Medina (Mex.) i 33.
Palau 359154.
Valton 5.
Wagner 30.

The *De Sphera* occupies 12 ll. (the last leaf blank?), of which ✠ 7 is a cancel leaf. The blank leaf between ff. 6 and 7 of this second part noted in other copies may be the conjugate leaf of the cancel. The last blank leaf of the gathering is missing.

Veracruz, formerly Alonso Gutiérrez, began his career as lecturer in liberal arts and theology in the University of Salamanca, of which University he was also a graduate. Attracted to teach in the New World *c.* 1535, he there became an Augustinian, and enjoyed a rapid advancement in that Order in New Spain. In spite of many official duties, he found time to produce this and two other textbooks, the *Recognitio summularum* (1554), the *Dialectica resolutio* (1554), as well as the first legal treatise printed in the Americas, the *Speculum coniugiorum* (1556); all of these were published in Mexico by Juan Pablos, generally agreed to be the first printer in New Spain whose work can be identified with certainty. [See Bolaño e Isla (1947), and Burrus (1968)].

The *Phisica, speculatio* is generally claimed to be the first work on natural philosophy printed in the New World, some 17 years after the arrival of the printing presses in

Figure 10. VERACRUZ, Alonso de la. *Phisica, speculatio*. Mexico: J. Pablos. 1557. **(M.203)**

Mexico and 4 years after the inauguration of the Real y Pontificia Universidad de México. Though cast in the conventional form of proposition and proof, Veracruz illustrated his material with references to contemporary New Spain; little however, relates directly to medicine.

Figure 10.

M.204   VIRTUDES

Virtudes experimentadas en la piedra imán de venenos, aliás cobra, serpentina, ó de la culebra, que es una cosa misma. 2 ll.

4to. [?Mexico: s.n. *c.*1750].

Palau 370696.

The lodestone is claimed to cure a variety of conditions arising from poisonous animals and plants, as well as cancers of several kinds.

M.205   VIRTUDES

Virtudes del agua de melisa compuesta, (vulgarmente dicha) Agua del Carmen. [pp.4].

Mexico: Reprinted by the Heirs of J. de Jáuregui. 1787.

Facsimile.

M.206   VIRTUDES

Virtudes del palo nombrado del muerto.

sm. broadside. Mexico: J.M. Benavente y Sócios. 1820.

Guerra (Icon.) 639.

The writer extols the efficacy of *palo del muerto* in strengthening the nervous system and in treating all types of nervous disease. He describes methods of making infusions of the wood and the leaves; in the *Nueva farmacopea mexicana* (1874, 1884, 1896, 1904 eds) the plant is identified as *Ipomoea murucoides* (*Convolvulaceae*).

M.207   XIMENEZ, Francisco

Quatro libros de la naturaleza, y virtudes de las plantas, y animales que estan recevidos en el uso de medicina en la Nueva España . . . . Traduzido, y aumentados muchos simples, y compuestos y otros muchos secretos curativos. *woodcut illus., woodcut ornaments (1 on t.p.).* 5 ll., ff.203 (=194), 7 ll.

4to. Mexico: Widow of D. López Dávalos. 1615.

Andrade 60.

Beristáin iii p. 19 no. 1473; *ibid.* v pp. 175–178, nos. 3381, 134.

Gallardo iii 2589.

Guerra (Icon.) 22.

Hernández (1960) pp. 405–407.

Icazbalceta p. 233.

León (1915) 15.

Medina (Mex.) ii 297.

Palau 113531.

Imperfect. Wanting ff. 80–81 (X2–3); ff. 116–118 (Gg2–4) are from another copy.

This is the first separate appearance in print of a significant part of Francisco Hernández's great work on the medicinal plants of New Spain. In his address to the reader, the translator and editor Francisco Ximénez relates how he came to make his translation from a copy of Francisco Vallés' signed and revised version of Nardo Antonio Recchi's abbreviated version of Hernández's work which had come into his possession *por extraordinarios caminos*. The first three books cover the plants, and the fourth deals with animals and minerals. Part of the translator's purpose was to provide information for those living in remote places without physicians or drugs. He adds many useful asides to his original text from his personal knowledge and experience.

Francisco Hernández [1517/18–1587], physician and naturalist, became *Médico de cámara* to Philip II in 1567 and was sent by him in 1570 to New Spain as *Protomédico* to study local products of medicinal value. The final draft of his studies in 16 MS volumes remained a virtually unused quarry until it was destroyed in the Escorial fire of 1671. Philip II had, however, ordered Recchi to make a summary of Hernández's work, and this version, entitled *Rerum Medicarum Novae Hispaniae Thesaurus*, was eventually printed in Rome under the auspices of the Accademia dei Lincei between 1628 and 1651. The fullest account of our present knowledge of Hernández and his achievement is the preliminary essay by Germán Somolinos D'Ardois in the magnificent F. Hernández, *Obras completas*, tom. 1, Universidad Nacional de México, 1960.

Francisco Ximénez was born in Aragón, and after travelling to Florida arrived in New Spain in 1605 where he served in the Hospital de Santa Cruz of the Hermanos de la Caridad de San Hipólito founded by Bernardino Álvarez in 1569 at Huaxtepec (Oaxtepec) where one of Moctezuma's botanical gardens had been located. There he observed the efficacy of local herbs and medicines. In 1612 he joined the Dominican order in the City of Mexico. [See Ximénez, ed. León (1888), p. viii].

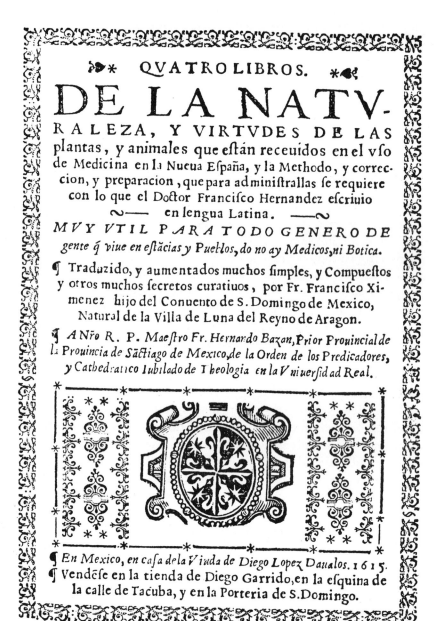

>>* QVATRO LIBROS. *<<

DE LA NATV-

RALEZA, Y VIRTVDES DE LAS
plantas, y animales que están receuídos en el vso
de Medicina en la Nueua España, y la Methodo, y correc-
cion, y preparacion , que para adminiftrallas se requiere
con lo que el Doctor Francifco Hernandez efcriuio
∾—— en lengua Latina. ——∾
MVY VTIL PARA TODO GENERO DE
gente ṹ viue en eftãcias y Pueblos, do no ay Medicos,ni Botica.

¶ Traduzido, y aumentados muchos fimples, y Compueftos
y otros muchos fecretos curatiuos , por Fr. Francifco Ximenez hijo del Conuento de S. Domingo de Mexico,
Natural de la Villa de Luna del Reyno de Aragon.

¶ A Nṙo R. P. *Maeſtro Fr. Hernardo Bazan,*Prior Prouincial de
la Prouincia de Sãctiago de Mexico,de la Orden de los Predicadores,
y Cathedratico Iubilado de Theologia en la Vniuerfidad Real.

¶ *En Mexico, en cafa de la Viuda de Diego Lopez Daualos.* 1615.
¶ Vendẽfe en la tienda de Diego Garrido,en la efquina de
la calle de Tacuba, y en la Porteria de S.Domingo.

Figure 11. XIMENEZ, Francisco. *Quatro libros de la naturaleza.* Mexico: Widow of D. López Dávalos. 1615.
    (M. 207)

Two editions were published in Mexico in the last century; one edited by Antonio Peñafiel, published by the Secretaría de Fomento in 1888; and the other, edited by Nicolás León, published (in Morelia) in the same year. Copies of both are in the Wellcome Institute Library.

Figure 11.

M.208 ZUÑIGA Y ONTIVEROS, Felipe de [*c.* 1717–1793]

Calendario manual y guia de forasteros de Mexico, para el año de 1790. *engr. front., tables.* 1 l., pp.158, 4 ll.

12mo. [Mexico: F. de Zúñiga y Ontiveros. 1790].

This copy wants sigs. O3 and O4 [i.e. the 1st two leaves of the index].

Felipe Zúñiga, an energetic entrepreneur, began publishing in the City of Mexico in 1752, where he came to own the best equipped printing house. He printed the *Gazeta de México* from 1784 and was the first to use type cast in Mexico.

The *Guía de forasteros*, developed from his original brief *Guía*, began its annual publication in 1775; its lists of public appointments, which include the Protomedicato, are valuable.

M.209 ZUÑIGA Y ONTIVEROS, Felipe de [*c.* 1717–1793]

Calendario manual y guia de forasteros en México, para el año de 1792 bisexto. *tables, fldg. map at end.* 1 l., pp.182, 3 ll.

12mo. [Mexico: F. de Zúñiga y Ontiveros. 1792].

Guerra (Icon.) 851.
Medina (Mex.) vi 8234.

M.210 ZUÑIGA Y ONTIVEROS, Felipe de [*c.* 1717–1793]

Calendario manual y guia de forasteros en México, para el año de 1793. *engr. front., tables.* 1 l., pp.186, 2 ll.

12mo. [Mexico: F. de Zúñiga y Ontiveros. 1793].

Medina (Mex.) vi 8314.

This copy wants the 2 engraved maps noted by Medina.

M.211   ZUÑIGA Y ONTIVEROS, Mariano José de [d. 1825]

Calendario manual y guia de forasteros en México, para el año de 1794. *engr. front.,
tables.* 1 l., pp. 192, 2 ll.

12mo. Mexico: Heirs of F. de Zúñiga y Ontiveros. [1794].

Medina (Mex.) vi 8431.

The frontispiece is not noted by Medina.

On succeeding his father, Mariano José Zúñiga continued printing the *Guía de
forasteros* for which Felipe had obtained the privilege, as well as the *Gazeta de México.*
He also printed and published the *Diario de México* from 1809 to 1812.

M.212   ZUÑIGA Y ONTIVEROS, Mariano José de [d. 1825]

Calendario manual y guia de forasteros en México, para el año de 1797. *tables.* 1 l.,
pp. 198, 2 ll.

12mo. [Mexico: M.J. de Zúñiga y Ontiveros. 1797].

Medina (Mex.) vii 8727.
Palau 381678.

M.213   ZUÑIGA Y ONTIVEROS, Mariano José de [d. 1825]

Calendario manual y guia de forasteros en México, para el año de 1803. *engr. front.,
tables.* 1 l., pp. 198, 2 ll.

12mo. [Mexico: M.J. de Zúñiga y Ontiveros. 1803].

Medina (Mex.) vii 9639.
Palau 381682.

This copy wants the map at the end noted by Palau.

M.214   ZUÑIGA Y ONTIVEROS, Mariano José de [d. 1825]

Calendario manual y guia de forasteros en México, para el ano de 1804. *tables.* 1 l.,
pp. 198, 2 ll.

12mo. [Mexico: M.J. de Zúñiga y Ontiveros. 1804].

Medina (Mex.) vii 9746.
Palau 381683.

This copy wants the engraved frontispiece and folding map noted by Medina and Palau.

M.215   ZUÑIGA Y ONTIVEROS, Mariano José de [d. 1825]

Calendario manual y guia de forasteros en México, para el año de 1809. *tables.* 1 l., pp. 216, 2 ll.

12mo. [Mexico: M.J. de Zúñiga y Ontiveros. 1809].

Medina (Mex.) vii 10325.

This copy wants the engraved frontispiece and the two maps noted by Medina.

M.216   ZUÑIGA Y ONTIVEROS, Mariano José de [d. 1825]

Calendario manual y guia de forasteros en México, para el año de 1810. *engr. front., tables, fldg. map.* 1 l., pp. 220, 3 ll. (last bl.).

12mo. [Mexico: M.J. de Zúñiga y Ontiveros. 1810].

Medina (Mex.) vii 10542.
Palau 381686.

Most of the map, not noted by Medina, has been removed; and the plan, noted by Palau, is wanting.

M.217   [ZUÑIGA Y ONTIVEROS, Mariano José de] [d. 1825]

[Calendario manual y guia de forasteros en México, para el año de 1811.]. *tables.* 1 l., pp. 220.

12mo. [Mexico: M.J. de Zúñiga y Ontiveros. 1811].

Medina (Mex.) vii 10689.
Palau 381687.

This copy wants the title-page, the engraved frontispiece, the two maps, pp. 213–220, the three unpaginated leaves of the index and the final blank leaf, as noted by Medina.

M.218   **ZUÑIGA Y ONTIVEROS, Mariano José de [d. 1825]**

Calendario manual y guia de forasteros en México, para el año de 1818. *engr. front.,*
tables. 1 l., pp.232, 2 ll.

12mo. [Mexico: M.J. de Zúñiga y Ontiveros. 1818].

Medina (Mex.) viii 11420.
Palau 381691.

This copy wants the 2 plates with portraits of Ferdinand VII and Maria Isabel as
noted by Medina; it also wants sig. V1 [i.e. pp. 227–228]. The engraved frontispiece
is not noted by Medina.

M.219   **ZUÑIGA Y ONTIVEROS, Mariano José de [d. 1825]**

Calendario manual para el año ... de 1820. Bisiesto. *tables.* 16 ll.

16mo. [Mexico: M.J. de Zúñiga y Ontiveros. 1820].

Medina (Mex.) viii 11962.

M.220   **ZUÑIGA Y ONTIVEROS, Mariano José de [d. 1825]**

Calendario manual para el año ... de 1821. *tables.* 16 ll.

16mo. [Mexico: M.J. de Zúñiga y Ontiveros. 1821].

Medina (Mex.) viii 12103.

M.221   **ZUÑIGA Y ONTIVEROS, Mariano José de [d. 1825]**

Calendario manual y guia de forasteros en Méjico, para el año de 1821. *engr. front.,*
tables. 1 l., pp.244, 2 ll.

12mo. [Mexico: M.J. de Zúñiga y Ontiveros. 1821].

Medina (Mex.) viii 12104.

This copy lacks the engraved frontispiece, not noted by Medina.

PERU
1607–1820

BOTTONI, Federico

Evidencia de la circulación de la sangre. 47 ll.

4to. Lima: I. de Luna, Imprenta de la Calle de Palacio. 1723.

Lastres (1951) ii pp. 195–197.
Medina (Lima) ii 793.
Palau 33785.
Valdizán (1927–29) i pp. 147–150.
Valdizán (1928) 27.

All copies apparently lack one leaf of sig. G. The text is unaffected.

With its abrupt style and discursive approach this remarkable tract is essentially a brief and popularised survey of contemporary ideas about the blood and its composition. The last 16 leaves outline contemporary proofs of the circulation, where the work of Harvey, among many others, is cited with particular distinction. In Bottoni's view, only America resisted the discovery; and he is likely to have been the first to transplant it to Peru. After a wary approach he cites as additional proof of circulation the transfusion attempts of Richard Lower and quotes with enthusiasm the experiments by 'Fabricio medico de Dantzic' on the injection of medicated liquors into the blood [see *Phil. Trans.*, 1667, 2, 564–565].

Bottoni's discursiveness leads him to refer, *inter alia*, to the necessity for restraint in bloodletting, the chewing of coca by the Indians, the use of such indigenous specifics as cinchona [*cascarilla de Loxa*] and ipecacuanha, the existence of chyle, certain therapeutics, and some recent S. American epidemics. He quotes occasionally from his own experience.

The earlier part of the tract is more safely traditional and covers the nature of movement, the four humours, the composition of the blood according to Paracelsian theory, and the three parts of the blood, i.e. the red part (he notes the observation of red corpuscles by Leeuwenhoek and Hooke), the white and fibrous part, and the transparent serum or lymph. He distinguishes throughout between venous and arterial blood, and describes the valves, chambers and movement of the heart.

Little is known of Bottoni, who must have been a man of wide interests. According to the title-page he was of noble Messina lineage, held appointment as *Médico de exercizio* in the Queen's household, and was *Revisor de libros* and *Intérprete de lenguas* to the Inquisition. A contemporary reference cites him as graduate of Salerno, and he refers to his yet untraced *Tractado de la medicina limense* written in Naples and dedicated in 1702.

His tract was given official approval by Juan de Avendaño y Campoverde, *Catedrático de vísperas de medicina* in the University of San Marcos; and the fuller official clearance by the eminent poet and polymath Pedro José de Peralta Barnuevo Rocha y Benavides, *Catedrático de prima de matemáticas*, indicates that he was highly regarded by contemporaries.

P.2   BRAVO DE LAGUNAS Y CASTILLA, Pedro José

Discurso historico-juridico del origen, fundacion, re-edificacion, derechos, y exenciones del Hospital de San Lazaro de Lima. 17 ll., pp.272 (= 276).

4to. Lima: Oficina de los Huerphanos. 1761.

Medina (Lima) ii 1169.
Palau 34802.

The discourse, written in 1757, is primarily concerned with the legal history and rights of hospitals and lazarettos in general, and with the legal questions arising from the re-erection and funding of the Lima hospital (for which Bravo had been largely responsible) after its destruction in the earthquake of 1746. The erudition, clarity and concision of the discourse were greatly admired by the writers of the contemporary *aprobaciones*. According to the text the hospital had been originally endowed by Antón Sánchez in 1563 and its existence confirmed by a *Real Cédula* of 1567.

Among his many governmental appointments Bravo held the offices of *Consejero real* of the Council of the Indies, *Oidor* of the Audiencia of Lima, and *Catedrático de prima de leyes* before retiring from the world as a priest of the Oratory of St. Philip Neri.

P.3   BUENO, Cosme [1711–98]

El conocimiento de los tiempos; efemeride del año de 1780. Bisiesto; en que van

✠

EL CONOCIMIENTO

DE LOS TIEMPOS;
EFEMERIDE DEL AñO DE 1780.
Bisiesto;

EN QUE VAN PUESTOS LOS PRIN-
cipales Afpectos de la Luna con el Sol, y
demas Planetas. Calculados para el Meridiano de efta muy Noble, y muy Leal
Ciudad de Lima, Capital, y Emporio
de efta América Meridional.
CON CALENDARIO DE LAS FIES-
tas, y Santos; en que van notados los dias
Feriados con efta letra F. Los de trabajo
con obligacion de Mifa con efta feñal (*).
Los de Fiefta con efta ✠. Y los de precepto para los Indios con efta ✠✠. Las Sali-
das de los Correos, en que la Letra (A)
defigna el de Arequipa: La (C·) el del
Cuzco: La (V) el de Valles; y la (P)
el de Pafco.
VA AL FIN UNA GUIA DE FORAS-
teros para efta Ciudad.
POR EL DOCT. D COSME BUENO CATE-
dràtico de Prima de Matemàticas, Cofmógrafo
mayor del Reyno, y Socio de la Real
Academia Médica-Matritenfe.
Con licencia: en la Imprenta de los Niños
Huérfanos. Se vende en la Libreria
de la Calle de Palacio;

Figure 12. BUENO, Cosme. *El conocimiento de los tiempos; efemeride del año de 1780*. [Lima:] Imprenta de los Niños
Huérfanos. [1780]. **(P.3)**

puesto los principales aspectos de la luna con el sol, y demas planetas. Calculados para el meridiano de . . . Lima [&c.]. *tables.* 26 ll.

8vo. [Lima:] Imprenta de los Niños Huérfanos. [1780].

Medina (Lima) iii 1482.
Palau 59364.
Valdizán (1928) 104.

Bueno came from Aragon to Peru *c.* 1730 and was awarded his doctorate in medicine by the University of San Marcos in 1750; in 1758 he was appointed *Catedrático de matemáticas* and *Cosmógrafo mayor.* As a physician he was strongly influenced by the clinical ideas of Boerhaave. Among his pupils was Gabriel Moreno [1735–1809] (later to become the master of Unanue), whose obituary notice of Bueno appeared as an appendix to the *Almanaque peruano* of 1799; it is quoted in full by Valdizán, *op. cit.,* 67.

He published these almanacks annually from 1757 to 1798; besides official information, they often include original essays of medical interest by Bueno.

Figure 12.

P.4   BUENO, Cosme [1711–98]

El conocimiento de los tiempos: efemeride del año de 1782. Segundo despues del bisiesto: en que van puestos los principales aspectos de la luna con el sol, y demás planetas. Calculados para el meridiano de . . . Lima [&c.]. *tables.* 28 ll.

8vo. [Lima:] Imprenta Real. [1782].

Medina (Lima) iii 1524.
Palau 59364.
Valdizán (1928) 107.

Marginal annotations in contemporary MS.

P.5   BUENO, Cosme [1711–98]

El conocimiento de los tiempos, efemeride del año de 1794, segundo despues del bisiesto. En que van puestos los principales aspectos de la luna con el sol: calculados para el meridiano de . . . Lima . . . . Va al fin la disertacion sobre los antojos de las mugeres preñadas. *tables.* 32 ll.

8vo. [Lima:] Imprenta Real. [1794].

Medina (Lima) iii 1782.
Palau 59364.
Valdizán (1928) 315.

The dissertation by Cosme Bueno occupies the last 16 leaves.

P.6   **BUENO, Cosme [1711–98]**

El conocimiento de los tiempos, efeméride del año de 1795, tercero despues del bisiesto. En que van puestos los principales aspectos de la luna con el sol: calculados para el meridiano de ... Lima .... Va al fin el catalogo de los Gobernadores, y Virreyes del Perú, con los sucesos memorables de sus tiempos. [&c.]. *tables* 37 ll.

8vo. [Lima:] Imprenta Real. [1795].

Medina (Lima) iii 1795.
Palau 59364.
Valdizán (1928) 342.

The last leaf is a singleton.

The catalogue by Bueno occupies the last 20 leaves.

P.7   **BUENO, Cosme [1711–98]**

El conocimiento de los tiempos, efeméride del año de 1796. Bisiesto. En que van puestos los principales aspectos de la luna con el sol: calculados para el meridiano de ...Lima .... Va al fin una disertacion sobre la naturaleza del ayre y sus propiedades. *tables.* 40 ll.

8vo. Lima: Imprenta Real. [1796].

Medina (Lima) iii 1810.
Palau 59364.
Valdizán (1928) 349.

The dissertation by Cosme Bueno occupies the last 24 leaves.

P.8   **BUENO, Cosme [1711–98]**

El conocimiento de los tiempos, efeméride del año de 1798. Segundo despues del bisiesto. En que van puestos los principales aspectos de la luna con el sol: calculados para el meridiano de . . . Lima . . . . Va al fin un suplemento a la memoria de los . . . Obispos que se publicó el año pasado de 1797. [&c.]. *tables.* 20 ll.

8vo. [Lima:] Imprenta Real. [1798].

Medina (Lima) iii 1858.
Palau 59364.
Valdizán (1928) 357.

The supplement occupies the last 2 leaves.

This is the last of the almanacks published by Bueno.

P.9   COQUETTE, José

Indice de algunas voces usadas en el Peru para designar las substancias fosiles, y servir de interpretacion á la Mineralogía de Kirwan. *tables (4 fldg.).* 1 l., pp. 37.

4to. Lima: Imprenta Real Casa de Niños Expósitos. [1792].

Medina (Lima) iii 1753.
Valdizán (1928) 232.

The first and last leaves were probably originally conjugate. Sig. E is of 2 conjugate leaves only. The folding tables are inserted between B3 and B4.

This reprint of an essay "Indice y suplemento de la Mineralogía de Kirwan", *Mercurio peruano*, 1792, 4 (nos. 127–130), pp. 193–230 (22, 25, 29 March and 1 April) seeks to bring traditional Peruvian mining terminology into line with the new chemical and mineralogical terminology of Europe.

Coquette is said to have been of French origin and to have been closely associated with the Tribunal de Minería since its establishment in Lima in 1786. He was a member of the Sociedad Académica de Amantes de Lima and published other papers in the *Mercurio peruano* on chemistry and electricity. The classic work *Elements of mineralogy* by the many-sided and eccentric chemist Richard Kirwan [1733–1812], first published in London in 1784, was translated into Spanish by Francisco Campuzano and published in Madrid in 1789 [Palau 128076]. Coquette is likely to have used either this edition or the French translation *Élémens de minéralogie* by J. Gibelin, Paris, 1785. Later editions appeared in London in 1794–96 (2 vols.) and in 1810; it was also translated into German and Russian. [See Alcalde Mongrut (1959)].

P.10   FLORES, José Felipe [1751–1824]

Experimentos. Sobre la conservacion de las carnes. pp. xii.

4to. [Lima:] B. Ruiz, Casa de Niños Huérfanos. 1813.

Medina (Lima) iv 2936.
Valdizán (1927–29) iii p. 188.

This is a reprint from the original of the same title first published in Cadiz in 1811 [Palau 92489]. [See M.57; and M.56 for his life].

A note accompanying the original copy of Flores' essay and addressed to the Viceroy of Peru by the Regency at Cadiz on 17 January 1813 is printed at the end. It points out the convenience of export of meat and fish by this method to areas lacking their own supplies, and the advantage of building a productive processing industry.

P.11   GONZALEZ HOLGUIN, Diego [1552–1618]

Vocabulario de la lengua general de todo el Peru llamada lengua Qquichua, o del Inca. Corregido y renovado conforme ala propriedad cortesaua [sic] del Cuzco. Dividido en dos libros. 2 pts.

4to. Ciudad de los Reyes [i.e. Lima]: F. del Canto. 1608.

Gallardo iv 4437.
Medina (Lima) i 42.
Palau 105386.

The author, a native of Cáceres, studied at Madrid and Alcalá and entered the Society of Jesus in 1568. After teaching at the College at Alcalá he was sent to Peru in 1581; he remained in that Viceroyalty in a succession of senior posts of the Order until his death. This and his *Gramática* [see entry below] are his most important works; many words and phrases are of medical interest.

P.12   GONZALEZ HOLGUIN, Diego [1552–1618]

Gramatica y arte nueva de la lengua general de todo el Peru, llamada lengua Qquichua, o lengua del Inca. 4 ll., ff. 143, 1 l.

4to. Ciudad de los Reyes [i.e. Lima]: F. del Canto. 1607.

Bound with his Vocabulario de la lengua general de todo el Peru. 2 pts. 1608.

Medina (Lima) i 38.
Palau 105385.
Palau 105384 [i.e. 1st edition, Seville, 1603].

This grammar and the preceding dictionary were two of several in the Quechua and Aymará languages published following the requirement of the third Provincial Council of Lima (1582–83) that all priests were to catechize in the language of their flock. The work of disseminating the native languages fell largely to the Jesuits; and the first book from the Peruvian press, operated by Antonio Ricardo from Mexico, was in fact the Jesuit production *Doctrina christiana, y catecismo para instruccion de los Indios*, Lima, A. Ricardo, 1584. [See Medina (Lima) i 1.]

P.13   **GONZALEZ LAGUNA, Francisco**

El zelo sacerdotal para con los niños no-nacidos. *plate*(*woodcut*). 17 ll., pp.271, 28 ll.

8vo. Lima: Imprenta de los Niños Expósitos. 1781.

Lastres (1951) ii pp.242–243.
Medina (Lima) iii 1509.
Palau 105409.
Valdizán (1928) 106.

The plate is inserted between sigs. P2 and Q2. This copy lacks, among the last unnumbered leaves, the errata leaf between the *Tabla de los capítulos* and the plate, as well as the final 8 leaves containing the *Bando* issued by the Viceroy Agustín de Jáuregui y Aldecoa [1780–84] dated 1 October 1781, requiring caesarean section on the death of the mother. It is quoted in full by Valdizán who also quotes extensively from the rest of the work.

González, a provincial of the Order of Agonizantes and a member of the Sociedad Académica de Amantes de Lima, is regarded as one of the founders of the Enlightenment in Peru, although his printed works are largely doctrinal. In 1791 he was appointed with Juan Tafalla, on the strength of his botanical knowledge, to oversee the planting of the Lima botanical garden. His broad interests are expressed in his well-known "Necesidad de la historia natural científica", *Mercurio peruano*, 1794, *10*, (nos. 316–319), pp. 25–58 (12, 16, 19, 23 January).

In the present work he traverses the same ground as F.E. Cangiamila and his Mexican follower José Manuel Rodríguez [see M.184], and urges, in accordance with the policy of Charles III first pursued in his Kingdom of Naples (as related in the prologue), the saving of the infant for baptism and the possibility of earthly existence. He emphasizes certain signs indicating the death of the mother, describes the caesarean operation in simple terms, and urges the desirability for mothers to nurse their own offspring. He advocates the proper instruction and licensing of midwives, and baptism by injection into the womb when necessary. An appendix of 15 leaves outlines methods for saving the lives of the drowned, and as a preliminary to more familiar methods, recommends the use of *alkali volatil fluido* in the nostrils and in the mouth.

P.14 LARRINAGA, José Pastor [b. 1763/4]

Cartas historicas á un amigo. Ó apología del pichon palomino que parió una muger, y se vió en esta Ciudad de los Reyes el dia 6 de abril de 1804. 13 ll., pp.215, 1 l.

4to. Lima: B. Ruiz, Imprenta de los Huérfanos. 1812.

Medina (Lima) iv 2826.
Palau 214634.
Valdizán (1927–29) iii pp.186–187.

MS annotation on p.128.

Larrinaga was a successful mulatto surgeon and anatomist, pupil of Francisco Matute (Surgeon to the Real Hospital de San Bartolomé from 1733) and of the well-known physician Cosme Bueno [1711–98] (*Cosmógrafo mayor* and *Catedrático de prima de matemáticas* from 1758). He became *Protocirujano* in 1801, and among his numerous other official appointments included that of Surgeon to the Real Hospital de San Bartolomé. Fairly progressive in his views, he attempted to develop medical education in Peru, and insisted in his pamphlet *Apología de los cirujanos del Perú*, Granada, Imprenta A. de Zea, 1793 [Valdizán (1928), 284] on the equal status of mulatto surgeons. A biography appears in Valdizán (1928), 254; and comments on his relationship with Unanue are to be found in Woodham (1970).

The present characteristically unscientific attempt to justify his belief in an outlandish birth (first reported in the supplement to the *Gazeta de Lima*, 1804, 28 April, núm. 13) does little justice to his practical achievement.

P.15 MARBAN, Pedro [1647–1713]

Arte de la lengua moxa, con su vocabulario, y cathecismo. [Followed by:] Cathecismo menor en lengua española, y moxa. *table.* 2 pts.

8vo. [Lima:] Imprenta Real de J. de Contreras. [1702].

Medina (Lima) ii 712.
Palau 150837–8.

The pagination is as given by Medina except that the 202 pages of the second part in fact total 204. The final leaf containing the *Indice de los capitulos* is a singleton.

Marbán, a Spanish Jesuit, left for the missions of Peru in 1675. The small Moxos tribe which lived around the headwaters of the Madeira river in what is now N. Bolivia first received the missionaries during the seventeenth century. Some words and phrases in the vocabularies are of medical interest.

P.16   NAVARRO, Juan Gerónimo

Sangrar, y purgar en dias de conjuncion. 12 ll., ff.66.

4to. Lima: J. de Contreras. 1645.

Medina (Lima) i 258.
Palau 188268 [?].
Valdizán (1927–29) i pp.85–86.

The second, third and fourth preliminary leaves [π2-4] are supplied in facsimile.

There are some marginal notes in a contemporary hand.

On ff. 39–40 Navarro relates the outstanding success he had enjoyed in the practice of bleeding and purging since he received his doctorate from the University of Valencia in 1615. According to his own statement he reached Panama in 1622 and arrived eventually in Lima by way of Quito and Potosí. He had bled and purged *infinitas vezes a diferentes sujetos en edad, compleccion, y achaques . . . en Hospitales, Communidades, y Conventos, y a mi mismo.*

P.17   PAREDES, José Gregorio [1778–1839]

Almanaque peruano y guia de forasteros para el año de 1810. *tables.* 47 ll.

8vo. [Lima:] Real Casa de Niños Expósitos. [1810].

Medina (Lima) iii 2271.
Palau 212751.

The almanacks by Paredes, of which this is the first, list official appointments, and often carry introductions of medical interest; they were continued, perhaps irregularly, until the year of his death. A biography of his master Gabriel Moreno [1735–1809] occupies A2ʳ–B4ʳ [i.e. ll. 2–8] of this issue.

Paredes, mathematician and physician, filled many public offices and enjoyed many honours in both the colonial and post-colonial period. In 1803 he filled the *Cátedra de prima de matemáticas* by substitution to G. Moreno, whom he also succeeded in 1809 as *Cosmógrafo mayor*; from the same year he taught at the newly founded Real Colegio de Medicina y Cirugía de San Fernando. He obtained his doctorate in medicine from the University of San Marcos in 1815 and was appointed *Protomédico general* in 1824. He became Ministro de Hacienda in the post-revolutionary government. [See Lastres (1951), *3*, 126–127].

P.18   PAREDES, José Gregorio [1778–1839]

Almanaque peruano, y guia de forasteros para el año de 1811. *tables.* 42 ll.

8vo. Lima: Imprenta del Colegio de S. Fernando; [(*colophon:*) Imprenta de los Huérfanos]. 1810.

Medina (Lima) iv 2696.
Palau 212752.

The introductory essay on the dog-days [*canícula*] occupies A2ʳ–B2ᵛ [i.e. ll. 2–6].

P.19   PAREDES, José Gregorio [1778–1839]

Almanaque peruano, y guia de forasteros, para el año de 1817. *tables.* 58 ll. (last bl.).

8vo. Lima: B. Ruiz. 1816.

Palau 212753.

This edition reprints Cosme Bueno's catalogue of the Viceroys &c. at sigs. 1²ʳ–6³ᵛ [i.e. ll. 2–23] which first appeared in 1795 [see P. 6].

P.20   PAREDES, José Gregorio [1778–1839]

Almanaque peruano y guia de forasteros para el año de 1819. *tables.* 49 ll.

8vo. Lima: B. Ruiz. 1818.

Medina (Lima) iv 3376.
Palau 212755.

The last leaf is a singleton.

The introduction, which describes the extent and symptoms of the great epidemic of 1818 (possibly influenza), occupies A2^r–D1^v [i.e. ll. 2–12].

P.21   PAREDES, José Gregorio [1778–1839]

Almanaque peruano y guia de forasteros, para el año de 1821. *tables.* 49 ll.

8vo. Lima: Casa de Niños Expósitos. 1820.

Medina (Lima) iv 3477.

The introduction, a general essay on geology, occupies 1^{2r}–4^{3r} [i.e. ff. 2–15].

P.22   PERU. Laws, statutes, &c.

Arancel general de los derechos de los oficiales de esta Real Audiencia: de los Escribanos mayores de la Governacion, de Rexistros, y de Cavildo: y de los Escribanos Publicos, y Reales, de Provincia, y demas Juzgados, y Tribunales: Receptores, Depocitarios, Alarifes, Medidores, Tasadores, y de las Vicitas, y Examenes de el Protomedicato de este Distrito. 24 ll.

fol. [Lima:] Oficina de los Niños Huerfanos. [1779].

Lastres (1951) ii pp.223–224.
Medina (Lima) iii 1463.
Valdizán (1928) 103.

The *Arancel*, published by proclamation on 10 May 1779 sets out, *inter alia*, the scale of fees due to the *Protomédico* and the officials of the Protomedicato for the examination of physicians, surgeons, apothecaries, oculists, barbers, and for visits of inspection to apothecaries' shops. It was used as a basis for the *Arancel* published in Rio de la Plata in 1787 [see A.8].

P.23   RIVILLA BONET Y PUEYO, José de

Desvios de la naturaleza. O tratado de el origen de los monstros. A que va anadido un compendio de curaciones chyrurgicas en monstruosos accidentes. *plate (engr. coat-of-arms).* 22 ll., ff.116.

4to. Lima: Imprenta Real, J. de Contreras y Alvarado. 1695.

Lastres (1951) ii pp.143–145.
Medina (Lima) ii 675.
Palau 270506.
Valdizán (1928) 20.

The plate is inserted between π1 & π2. This copy lacks the copper engraving of the monster at the end of the preliminaries noted by Medina.

The much discussed question of the authorship of this well-known work has been reviewed by Lastres who opts in favour of Rivilla. The attribution by Unanue and by Medina to the Creole polymath and poet Pedro José de Peralta Barnuevo Rocha y Benavides [1663–1743] has been made largely on the foundation of Peralta's own reference to himself as the author in note 94 to Canto VI of his epic poem *Lima fundada*, Lima, F. Sobrino y Bados, 1732; and Valdizán, accepting the possibility, regards a form of joint authorship as probable. There seems on the other hand no real reason to doubt the testimony of the writers of the *aprobaciones*, *pareceres*, and commendatory sonnets to this work, five of whom clearly refer to Rivilla as the author.

Rivilla was born in Zaragoza and perhaps studied medicine at that University. On the evidence of the title-page and the *aprobaciones* he was qualified in Lima as both physician and surgeon, and held office as *Cirujano de cámara* to the Viceroy, as *Examinador en cirugía* to the Protomedicato, and as surgeon to the Hospital Real de Mujeres de la Caridad.

The work discusses with a wealth of learned references, the question of monsters in general, whether such two-headed phenomena possess one or two rational souls, and the related question of baptism. The appendix (ff. 94–116) discusses cases of general surgical treatment.

The disquisition was initiated by the birth of a xiphopagus monster to Doña Teresa Girón on 30 November 1694, on which the author performed an autopsy (described on ff. 63–65) at the order of the Viceroy in the presence of the physician Francisco Bermejo Roldán, *Médico de cámara* to the Viceroy, *Catedrático de prima de medicina* and *Protomédico general*.

The priest and geographer, Louis Feuillée (1714–25) vol. I, p. 486, in describing his visit of 1709, quotes and illustrates two monsters, the second of which Medina took to be that described by Rivilla. Feuillée describes the monster as having been seen in Lima *depuis peu de jours*; the illustrations however in Feuillée and in the British Museum copy of Rivilla differ in detail and execution from the illustration reproduced in Lastres (1951), *2*, plate XI (2) which is described as examined by Rivilla.

P.24   SARRIA, Remigio

Concertatio medica de febre puerperali, quam pro gradu licentiatus obtinendo, auspice Deo, et praeside D.D. Jos. Hippolyto Unanue Anatomes Professore, sustinebit R.S., baccalaureus medicus, Regi Anatomes Amphiteatri alumnus, in Reg. ac Pontif. Divi Marci Academia [&c.]. [Thesis].

4to. [Lima:] Typis Domus Orphanorum. 1799.

Medina (Lima) iii 1881.
Valdizán (1928) 367.

The last leaf, containing the *corrigenda*, is a singleton.

Sarria argues the thesis *Febris puerperalis, neque est novum febris genus Antiquis ignotum: neque ab una eademque proficiscitur causa*, and adds notes on diet and treatment. A numbered formulary listing the drugs in the new and old styles relates to the text.

P.25   UNANUE, José Hipolito [1755–1833]

Guia política, eclesiástica y militar. Del Virreynato del Perú. Para el año de 1794. Compuesta de órden del Superior Gobierno. *1 fldg. map, tables (5 fldg.).* 4 ll., pp.xii, 1 l., pp.306.

8vo. [Lima:] Imprenta Real de los Niños Huérfanos. [1794].

Medina (Lima) iii 1790.
Palau 344278.
Valdizán (1928) 340.

This copy is wanting the folding tables at pp. 24, 146, 295, as recorded by Medina.

The almanacks published by Unanue are an invaluable source of official information, particularly of public appointments, trade figures, and births, marriages and deaths. [See entries below; and Per.12].

P.26   UNANUE, José Hipolito [1755–1833]

Guia política, eclesiástica y militar. Del Virreynato del Perú. Para el año de 1795. Compuesta de Órden del Superior Gobierno. [*fldg. map, tables (7 fldg.),* 4 ll., pp.xii, 1 l., pp.281, 5 ll.].

[Lima:] Imprenta Real de los Niños Huérfanos. [1795].

Facsimile.

P.27   UNANUE, José Hipolito [1755–1833]

Primer examen de toda la anatomía, que presentan en la Real Universidad de S. Marcos, . . . los alumnos de este: Br. D. Pedro Zarria. Br. D. Remigio Zarria. Br. D. Manuel Seguin. D. Joseph Pezet. D. Miguel Venegas. D. Manuel Rioseco. *woodcut coat-of-arms.* 3 ll., pp. 35, 5 ll.

4to. [Lima:] Imprenta Real de los Niños Huérfanos. 1796.

Medina (Lima) iii 1835.
Palau 344283; 379797 (Zarria).
Valdizán (1927–29) i pp. 175–176.
Valdizán (1928) 350.

The copy examined by Medina appears to lack the dedication occupying the second and third leaves [sig. §] of the second set of unnumbered leaves.

José Hipólito Unanue, the Creole polymath and statesman, became *Catedrático de anatomía* in the University of San Marcos in 1789, and founded the anatomical theatre in the Real Hospital de San Andrés which opened in 1792; he was also responsible for founding the Real Colegio de Medicina y Cirugía de San Fernando which opened in 1809.

This examination represents one practical result of Unanue's labours to improve medical education in Peru. According to a note printed at sig. E2^v [i.e. p. 36] the detailed propositions and questions were to be defended and answered by all the participants, and the three theses in Latin were to be defended by Remigio Zarria [?Sarria, see P.24]. The examination was to be held on 25 January 1796; and the *prelusión*, occupying the final two unnumbered leaves, was delivered by Unanue's master, Gabriel Moreno [1735–1809].

P.28   UNANUE, José Hipólito [1755–1833]

Guia política, eclesiástica y militar del Vireynato del Perú, para el año de 1797. Compuesta de Órden del Superior Gobierno. *1 fldg. map, tables (6 fldg.).* 4 ll., pp. xii, 1 l., pp. 259 (= 275), 7 ll. (last bl.).

8vo. [Lima:] Imprenta Real de los Niños Huérfanos. [1797].

Medina (Lima) iii 1855.
Palau 344280.

P.29   UNANUE, José Hipólito [1755–1833]

Observaciones sobre el clima de Lima, y sus influencias en los seres organizados, en especial el hombre. *tables (2 fldg.)*. 9 ll., pp.9, cxcviii (= 200), 1 l.

4to. Lima: Imprenta Real de los Huérfanos. 1806.

Medina (Lima) iii 2013.
Palau 344286.
Valdizán (1927–29) ii p. 21.

The copy examined by Medina lacked the 9 pp, *Introducción* and index [sigs. [A]4^r–B4^r]. In the same copy the two conjugate leaves of the *Lista de los señores subscriptores* appeared after the single *Fe de erratas* leaf as the final section of the whole work; whereas in the present copy it is inserted after the dedication to Gabriel Moreno [i.e. between sigs. [A]3 and [A]4]. The folding tables are inserted between sigs. I and K.

This wide-ranging classic of environmental medicine, based on the Hippocratic *De aere, locis, et aquis,* is remarkable for its pellucid language, clarity of observation, and poetic vision, and is the work for which Unanue is best remembered. The first section presents the climate of Lima and tabulates the meteorological observations for 1799 and 1800: the second describes the influence of climate on the vegetable kingdom, on man, and on his mind; while the third discusses the influence of climate on diseases of the body and mind and on the means of preventing them. He ends by analysing the medical constitution for 1799. It is fully analysed by Lastres (1955) pp. 63–83.

Unanue, man of letters, physician, and mathematician, became *Protomédico general, Cosmógrafo mayor,* and secretary of the Sociedad Académica de Amantes de Lima, and was among the first to welcome vaccination and to join the revolution against Spain. He filled many senior offices during the first years of the Republic, knew both Bolívar and San Martín, and was without doubt one of the more forward-looking men of his time. Woodham (1970) concludes that his influence on Peruvian medical science was not wholly beneficial.

Figure 13.

OBSERVACIONES
SOBRE EL CLIMA DE LIMA,
Y SUS INFLUENCIAS
EN LOS SERES ORGANIZADOS, EN ESPECIAL
EL HOMBRE.

POR EL Dr. D. HIPÓLITO UNANUE,
Catedrático de Anatomía en la Real
Universidad de San Márcos.

CON LAS LICENCIAS NECESARIAS.

LIMA

EN LA IMPRENTA REAL DE LOS HUÉRFANOS.

MDCCCVI.

Á costa de D. Guillermo del Rio, mercader de libros.

Figure 13. UNANUE, José Hipólito. *Observaciones sobre el clima de Lima.* Lima: Imprenta Real de los Huérfanos. 1806. **(P.29)**

P.30   URRETA, José

Theses pro gradu baccalaureatus in medicina, quas, auspice Deo, et praeside D.D. Jos. Hippolyto Unanue Anatomes P.P. sustinebit J.U., baccalaureus physicus Regii Anatomiae Amphiteatri alumnus, in Reg. ac Pontif. Divi Marci Academia [&c.]. [Thesis]. 5 ll.

4to. Lima: Typis Orphanorum. 1804.

Medina (Lima) iii 1953.
Valdizán (1927–29) iii p.179.

Urreta argues the thesis *Sub torrida zona degentibus, Potio Indica vulgo Chocolate, saluberrima.*

P.31   VARGAS MACHUCA, Francisco de [*c.* 1650–*c.* 1720]

Jesus, Maria, Joseph. Dissertacion canonica, moral, y defensa legal, con que intenta librarse de la irregularidad. . . que se ha intentado imponer a su autor. . . Presbytero, Medico de Profession, Cathedratico Jubilado de Methodo, y actual de Visperas de Medicina, en esta Real Universidad, y Estudio General de San Marcos [&c.]. ff. 15.

fol. [Lima: s.n. 1718].

The author defends his candidature for the *Cátedra de prima de medicina* against the objection of his *Opositor* Dr. Bernabé [Ortiz] de los Rios y Landaeta that a cleric could not in canon law exercise the civil and criminal jurisdiction belonging to membership of the Protomedicato, and could therefore hold neither the office of *Protomédico* nor the *Cátedra de prima de medicina*. Vargas Machuca's defence was evidently found satisfactory since he became *Catedrático de prima* on 14 December 1718 [see Lastres, (1951), *2*, p. 237].

His unsuccessful *Opositor* followed him in the same chair on 14 August 1720.

P.32   VERGARA, José de [d. 1831/3]

Theses pro gradu licentiatus in medicina: quas divino auspicio, et praeside D. Gabriele Moreno, doctore medico, disputatione subjiciet J.V., bacchalaureus medicus in Divi Marci Academia [&c.]. [Thesis]. 4 ll.

4to. [Lima: s.n.]. 1793.

Medina (Lima) iii 1780.
Valdizán (1928) 281.

The date of the disputation *11 Decembris* is substituted in MS for the original printed date [ ] *Novimbris* in the title.

Vergara was one of the group which united around Hipólito Unanue [1755–1833] after the opening of the anatomical theatre in the Hospital of San Andrés in 1792; a date often taken to represent the beginning of a modern attitude to medicine in Peru. Vergara later joined the medical establishment in 1807 as *Alcalde examinador* of the Protomedicato with Miguel Tafur [1766–1833], and as *Catedrático sustituto de vísperas de medicina* of the University of San Marcos, and as *Catedrático de clínica* of the Real Colegio de Medicina y Cirugía de San Fernando founded *c.* 1808. [See Valdizán (1927–29), 2, p. 30; and Valdizán (1928), 233].

The physician and polymath Gabriel Moreno [1735–1809], pupil of Cosme Bueno and master of Unanue, was an important figure of the Enlightenment in Peru. He early became *Fiscal* of the Protomedicato and *Regente* of the *Cátedra de anatomía*, was appointed *Pasante de matemáticas* in 1766 under Cosme Bueno, and became *Catedrático de prima de matemáticas* in 1801 [see Lastres (1951), 2, pp. 295–298; and Valdizán (1928), 197, who reprints the obituary notice by G. Paredes which originally appeared in the *Almanaque peruano* for 1810].

P.33 **VILLALOBOS, Baltasar de**

Método de curar tabardillos, y descripcion de la fiebre epidemica, que por los años de 1796 y 97 afligio varias poblaciones del Partido de Chancay. 10 ll., pp. 143 (= 145).

4to. Lima: Imprenta Real del Telégrafo Peruano. 1800.

Medina (Lima) iii 1891.
Palau 366793.
Valdizán (1927–29) i pp. 188–192.

The title-page may be a singleton.

Villalobos was sent northwards from Lima in 1796 to deal with this severe epidemic, probably not typhus. He here recounts his careful examination of the primary and secondary symptoms and his mode of treatment by bleeding combined with antimony and cinchona. The four sections cover the origin, progress, and nature of the epidemic, its causes, his method of cure and six case reports. He adds a numbered formulary which relates to the main text and to the appendix [p. 105 (i.e. p. 107) to the end] which describes the recognition and cure of all the intermittent fevers for which he regards cinchona and the *opiata febrifuga* of J. de Masdevall (no. 7

in his formulary) as principal remedies. The best brief description is in Lastres (1951), 2, pp. 301–303.

Villalobos, one of Unanue's disciples, was appointed *Médico director* of the Real Hospital de San Lázaro in 1804 on the strength of his supposed successful treatment of leprosy; his cases are, however, likely to have been mis-diagnosed. His remedy is not known.

P.34   **ZEBALLOS, Juan**

Conspectus disputationis medicae de musica quam pro gradu bachalaureatus obtinendo, auspice Deo, et praeside D.D. Josepho Maria Falcon, vespertinae exedrae sub-moderatore, sustinebit D. J.Z., bachalaureus physicus, Regalis Colegii Sancti Ferdinandi pro-rector, anatomesque magister: Limae, in Divi Marci Academia. 2 ll., pp.16.

4to. Lima: B. Ruiz. 1816.

Medina (Lima) iv 3290.
Valdizán (1927–29) iii p.191.

The day [i.e. 27] *Septembris* is inserted in MS.

Zeballos had previously presented a public act on 23 February 1816 under J.M. Falcón and had been passed unanimously. He qualified finally before the Protomedicato as *médico-cirujano* in 1820 [see Lastres (1954), pp. 168–169].

Falcón began teaching in 1812 as *Sustituto de la Cátedra de vísperas de medicina*, and succeeded to the full office in 1825 on the transfer of Miguel Tafur to the *Cátedra de prima de medicina* [see Lastres (1954), pp. 31, 142 n.].

B. Periodicals 1722–1820

Per.1   **ASUNTOS VARIOS SOBRE CIENCIAS**

Asuntos varios sobre ciencias, y artes. Obra periódica. *engraving.* pp.84 (=88).

4to. Mexico: J. de Jáuregui. 1772.

Beristáin i p.135 no.175.
Guerra (Icon.) 376.
León (Mex.) iii 8.
León (1915) 61.
Medina (Mex.) vi 5469.
Palau 10131.

Incomplete. This periodical ran for 13 numbers from 26 October 1772 to 4 January 1773; this set ends with No. 12 (28 December 1772). Each issue is of four leaves except nos. 9 & 12 which are of two. No. 9 has on f. 1 a copper engraving illustrating a hand-operated cotton-ginning machine in action. Some pages of the journal have been left unnumbered.

The editor, José Antonio Alzate y Ramírez [*c.* 1738–1799], graduated as bachelor of theology from the University of Mexico in 1756, but soon returned to his real interests in mathematics, the natural sciences and medicine. He published several scientific and technological journals besides this one, including *Diario literario de México*, 1768; *Observaciones sobre la física, historia natural y artes útiles*, 1787; and *Gazeta de literatura de México*, 1788–95. All four journals are reprinted in the two editions of J. A. Alzate y Ramírez, *Gacetas de literatura de México*, 4 vols., Puebla, Oficina del Hospital de S. Pedro, 1831; and 4 vols., Mexico, Oficina Tipografía de la Secretaría de Fomento, 1893–98; sets of which are in the Wellcome Institute Library. His obituary appears in the *Gazeta de México*, 1798–99, 9, 219–223 (i.e. 4 March 1799).

No. 3 of this periodical [pp. 17–24], dated 9 November 1772, deals with the use of *pipiltzitzintlis* (i.e. *Cannabis sativa*, marijuana) among the Indians; while No. 12 [pp. 81–84], issued as a special supplement to No. 11 of 28 December 1772, discusses the epidemic of *matlazahuatl* prevailing in the suburbs of Mexico City, which the writer suggests might be called the "*vómito prieto*". [i.e. the black vomit, or yellow fever]. Since no epidemic of special importance is known to have occurred in late 1772, and since the symptoms are not fully described, identification remains uncertain.

Per.2   DIARIO DE MEXICO

Diario de Mexico. 26 vols.

4to. Mexico: María Fernández de Jáuregui; J.B. de Arizpe; M.J. de Zúñiga y Ontiveros; J.M. de Benavente. 1805–17.

Beristáin i p.218 no.361.
Guerra (Icon.) 552–587 *passim* (ser. i *only*).
León (1915) 204 (ser. i *only*).
Medina (Mex.) vii 9784 (ser. i *only*); vii 10775 (ser. ii *only*).
Palau 71882; 294800.

The first series of 17 vols. from 1 October 1805 to 19 December 1812 is virtually complete to Vol. XII (30 June 1810) and wants only the final 4 of the 8 preliminary leaves to Vol. I and the title-page to Vol. VIII; thereafter Vols. XIII to XVII are wanting. The second series of 9 vols. from 20 December 1812 to 4 January 1817 is complete only as to Vols. I, V, VI, VIII; the remaining volumes are wanting. All of the volumes in the first series have a rough index and a useful list of subscribers.

The principal editor of this first daily newspaper published in the City of Mexico was the radical lawyer and politician Juan María Wenceslao Sánchez de la Barquera y Morales [1779–1840], editor also of other early Mexican journals [see Per.15, Per.18].

In general, the *Diario*, within its usual limits of 2 daily leaves, prints poetry, belles-lettres, ecclesiastical notices, viceregal proclamations, royal orders, and articles, comments, news and dialogues of philosophical, commercial, mining, academic, scientific and medical interest.

The second series is brisker in tone and purpose; it contains for instance much of interest on the epidemic of fevers of 1813. In both series a limited amount of news from the provinces and Europe is included. The *Diario* is a useful source of information on the changing circumstances and interests of the Capital during this precarious period.

Per.3   **GACETA DE MEXICO**

Gaceta de Mexico, y noticias de Nueva-España; que se imprimirán cada mes, y comiençian desde primero de Henero de 1722. pp.48 [pp.11–14 *only*].

4to. Mexico: Heirs of the Widow of M. de Ribera Calderón. 1722.

Beristáin ii p.84 no.734.
León (Mex.) ii (2) 49 [a reprint].
Medina (Mex.) iv 2675.
Palau 96358.

This, the first periodical published in New Spain, was issued each month during the first half of 1722 and therefore comprises 6 numbers. It is agreed to have been initiated and written by Juan Ignacio María de Castorena y Ursúa [1668–1733], Bishop of Yucatán from 1730. The reprint by León shews that pp. 11–14 are from no. 2 for February 1722.

The journal is primarily concerned with official news from the City of Mexico and the provinces. It was again reprinted, with indexes, and an introduction by Francisco González de Cossio, as the first part of *Gacetas de México*, 3 vols., Mexico, Secretaría de Educación Pública, 1950, a copy of which is in the Wellcome Institute Library.

Per.4 **GAZETA DEL GOBIERNO DE MEXICO**

Gazeta del Gobierno de Mexico. 12 vols. [1st 3 vols. *only*, in 4].

4to. Mexico: J.B. de Arizpe. 1810–12.

Medina (Mex.) vii 10462.
Palau 96361.

The full set ran from 2 January 1810 to 29 September 1821, in 12 vols., and was continued by the *Gazeta Imperial de Mexico*, 2 October 1821 to 31 December 1821, in 2 vols. From 1815 it was issued by a succession of different publishers.

The present incomplete set, with its supplements, runs from 2 January 1810 to 15 December 1812. The periods between 30 June and 14 July 1812 [i.e. nos. 254–258, pp. 693–732] and between 24 September and 20 October 1812 [i.e. nos 293–303, pp. 1101–1102] are wanting.

The journal for this period was published principally on Tuesdays, Thursdays, and Fridays or Saturdays. The 1st vol., for 1810, continues the pattern but not the format of the *Gazeta de México* [see Per.8] which this journal succeeded, and it continues the lists of *donativos*; in the same volume the violence of the times is reflected in the figures (p. 114) for wounded prisoners in the Hospital de San Andrés in the City of Mexico.

Medina prints a letter from the Archbishop Francisco Javier Lizana y Beaumont [Viceroy 1809–10] which justifies the change of title and the change of editor to Francisco Noriega in place of M.A. Valdés.

The remaining volumes of this truncated set are primarily devoted to military news in Europe and New Spain. There are no indexes.

Per.5   GAZETA DE LIMA

Gazeta de Lima. Desde primero de Diciembre de 1743. Hasta 18. de Enero de 1744. [A facsimile of the first issue of the *Gazeta de Lima*. The first South American newspaper; with a description of a file for the years 1744–1763].

4to. Boston: The Merrymount Press for the John Carter Brown Library. 1908.

Facsimile (No. 184 of a limited edition of 200).

Per.6   GAZETA DE LITERATURA DE MEXICO

Gazeta de literatura de Mexico. *engr. plates (some fldg.), tables.* 3 vols.

4to. Mexico: F. de Zúñiga y Ontiveros. 1788–95.

Guerra (Icon.) 453; 466; 473.
León (Mex.) i 87; 88.
Medina (Mex.) vi 7750.
Palau 10139.

This journal with its supplements was published at irregular intervals in nos. generally of 4 leaves by José Antonio Alzate y Ramírez [see Per.1] from 15 January 1788 to 22 October 1795. The present set wants vol. 1; and vol 2 wants the 2 supplements, the ode to the Viceroy, the 5 leaves of the index, 2 plates and nos. 25–47 from 26 July 1791 to 2 October 1792 [i.e. pp. 195–378]. Vol. 3 lacks only the final no. 44 for 22 October 1795 and 1 plate; it includes the 3 hand-coloured plates illustrating the culture of cochineal.

The journal was reprinted with minor omissions in the two editions of J.A. Alzate y Ramírez, *Gacetas de literatura de México*, 4 vols., Puebla, Oficina del Hospital de S. Pedro, 1831; and 4 vols., Mexico, Oficina Tipografía de la Secretaría de Fomento, 1893–98; sets of which are in the Wellcome Institute Library. It contains much of medical and scientific value, and illustrates clearly the breadth of Alzate's interests and his importance in the dissemination of the ideas of the Enlightenment in New Spain.

Per.7   GAZETA DE MEXICO

Gazeta de Mexico. 3 vols.

4to. Mexico: J.B. de Hogal; Heirs of the Widow of M. de Rivera Calderón; María de Rivera. 1728–39.

Beristáin i p.165 no.245.
León (Mex.) ii (1) 20 [a reprint].
Medina (Mex.) iv 2979.
Palau 16038; 96358.

Incomplete. The 141 nos. of this set of the journal cover the period from January 1728 to August 1739; the complete set of the journal reprinted by León includes no. 145 for December 1739. It was then continued in the same numeration (nos. 146–157) as though from January 1740 to December 1742 as the *Mercurio de México*, which León also prints in full. The complete set was again reprinted, with indexes, and an introduction by Francisco González de Cossio, as *Gacetas de México*, 3 vols., Mexico, Secretaría de Educación Pública, 1950, a copy of which is in the Wellcome Institute Library.

In the original bound sets the *Gazeta* has one of two title-pages, *Compendio de noticias mexicanas*, (as in the Wellcome set), or according to León and Medina, *Manual de noticias generales*.

The editor of the journal and its continuation was Juan Francisco Sahagún de Arévalo Ladrón de Guevara [d. 1761], priest and *Primer historiador* and *Chronista general* of the City of Mexico. The 4 leaves allotted to each month print official news in New Spain, Guatemala and Europe; his material was gathered from government and ecclesiastical authorities.

Per.8   GAZETAS DE MEXICO

Gazetas de Mexico, compendio de noticias de Nueva España [y Europa]. *engr. plates & tables (some fldg.).* 16 vols.

4to. Mexico: F. de Zúñiga y Ontiveros [&c.]. 1784–1809.

Beristáin v p.78 no.3146.
Guerra (Icon.) 446–583 *passim*.
León (Mex.) v 338–347.
Medina (Mex.) vi 7526.
Palau 96359.

This set, with its many supplements, runs for the full period of the journal from 14 January 1784 to 30 December 1809, after which it was succeeded by the *Gazeta del Gobierno de México* [see Per.4].

Designed as the vehicle for official news, and issued at varying intervals during its existence, the *Gazeta* remains, with the almanacs, one of the primary printed sources for general information on the last years of New Spain.

GAZETAS
DE MEXICO,
COMPENDIO DE NOTICIAS
DE NUEVA ESPAÑA

Desde principios del año de 1784.

DEDICADAS

AL EXCMÔ. SEÑOR

D. MATIAS DE GALVEZ

Virrey, Gobernador y Capitan general de la
misma &c. &c. &c.

POR D. MANUEL ANTONIO VALDES.

CON LICENCIA Y PRIVILEGIO

MEXICO:

Por D. FELIPE DE ZUÑIGA Y ONTIVEROS,
Calle del Espíritu Santo.

Figure 14. GAZETAS DE MEXICO. Mexico: F. de Zúñiga y Ontiveros. 1784–1809. **(Per.8)**

Apart from the publication of viceregal proclamations and the regular items such as the minting and trade returns which appear in most of the earlier years, special items such as the statement of population for the City of Mexico in 1790 (1792) are often of great interest. News and comment of medical interest includes the occasional statistics of hospitals (e.g. the Hospital Real de San Pedro (1785) and (1787), the four hospitals of the City of Mexico for the years 1790–93 (1794), the Hospital de Pobres in the same city (1795) and a detailed account of its funds and expenditure from its opening in 1774 to 1803 (1806) and those of several provincial hospitals besides), reports on surgical procedures (e.g. Foubert's procedure for treating *fistula in ano* (1795)), medical receipts (e.g. 1802), notices and instructions on vaccination (1804), and some plates representing monsters. There is much else, not always available through the indexes to each volume.

From 1795 the journal is dominated by lists of *donativos*, representing the continual struggle for funds by the Spanish government embroiled in the European war, and, from the beginning of 1806, by the war itself and by European news.

The editor, Manuel Antonio Valdés [1742–1814] began printing for the Jesuit College of San Ildefonso in 1764. After the expulsion of the Jesuits in 1767 he joined the publisher F. de Zúñiga y Ontiveros and remained with his successors until he founded his own successful press in the City of Mexico in 1808. The publication of the *Gazetas* however is regarded as his most important activity. He was assisted by the quarrelsome and uneducated Juan López Cancelada as editor from 1806, whose embittered attitude to eminent government officials, including José de Iturrigaray [Viceroy 1803–08] ended in a heavy fine and banishment to Spain. In Cadiz he continued his attacks in the *Telégrafo americano*, until Ferdinand VII ordered him to seclusion in a religious house.

Figure 14.

Per.9   **GAZETTE DE MEDECINE**

Gazette de médecine pour les colonies. [pp. 50].

Cap-François: Imprimerie Royale. 1778–79.

Facsimile of nos. 1–8.

Includes, between p. 6 and p. 7, *Supplément aux Affiches Américaines*, no. 50 (22 December 1778); and, between p. 34 and p. 35, *ibid.*, nos. 2–4 (12–26 January 1779).

Per.10 JOURNAL DES OFFICIERS DE SANTÉ

Journal des Officiers de Santé de Saint-Domingue. [*table.* pp.244].

Port-au-Prince: Imprimerie du Gouvernement; Cap-Français: P. Roux. [1803].

Facsimile of nos. 1–4.

Per.11 MEMOIRES DU CERCLE DES PHILADELPHES

Mémoires du Cercle des Philadelphes. Tome premier. [pp.264, 4 ll.].

Port-au-Prince: Imprimerie de Mozard. 1788.

Facsimile.

Per.12 MERCURIO PERUANO

Mercurio peruano de historia, literatura y noticias públicas que da á luz la Sociedad Academica de Amantes de Lima. 12 vols. [Vol. 3 *only*.].

4to. Lima: Imprenta Real de los Niños Huérfanos. 1791–95.

Medina (Lima) iii 1744.
Palau 165186.
Valdizán (1928) 140–346 *passim.*

Vol. 3 includes nos. 69–103 from 1 September to 29 December 1791. With its 6 folding tables and 1 folding map it is possibly the most complete copy of this volume recorded. It includes articles on a variety of subjects, literary, economic, scientific, and on the useful arts.

The journal, a vigorous contribution to the intellectual life of Lima, was published from 2 January 1791 under the auspices of the Sociedad Académica de Amantes de Lima of which Hipólito Unanue [1755–1833] was Secretary; its publication ended in 1795. [See Medina (Lima), 3, 1744; and Lastres (1955) pp. 21–22]. The many papers of medical interest are recorded by Valdizán, *loc. cit*; Unanue, responsible for their selection, included papers on anatomy, botany, and natural history, and on many topics of scientific interest [see entry below].

A facsimile reprint in 12 vols. was published by the Biblioteca Nacional del Perú in 1964–66, a set of which is in the Wellcome Institute Library.

Per.13 MERCURIO PERUANO

Mercurio Peruano del dia 10 de marzo de 1793. Núm. 228 [*only*]. pp.167–174.

4to. [Lima: Imprenta Real de Niños Expósitos]. 1793.

This number from vol. 7 of the *Mercurio peruano*, reprints the *Real Orden* dated 17 August 1792 notifying the Viceroy of the shipment from Spain of books requested by the botanist *profesores* of Lima. It also notifies him of the consignment of sets of the three volumes edited by the botanist Casimiro Gómez Ortega which print the newly discovered rough draft of (what was called in the Rome edition of 1628/51) *Rerum medicarum Novae Hispaniae thesaurus* by Francisco Hernández [1517/18-1587], *Protomédico* of the Indies. One set of these was to be reserved for Francisco González Laguna for his services to botany, and twenty-five were to be offered for sale to the public.

Pp. 169–172 describe the loss of the final draft in 17 volumes and recount the discovery of the 6 volumes of the original draft now printed for the first time. The writer describes the complete set of 5 volumes, including the final 2 projected volumes of Hernández's miscellaneous works and commentaries on him which were in fact not published owing to financial difficulties. The first 3 volumes (of which 2 sets are in the Wellcome Institute Library) were printed in Madrid by the heirs of J. Ibarra in 1790 [See Medina (Bib. hisp.-amer.), v, 5397; and G. Somolinos D'Ardois, "Vida y obra de Francisco Hernández" in Hernández (1960), pp. 344–353, 395–397].

Per.14 MERCURIO VOLANTE

Mercurio volante con noticias importante i curiosas sobre varios asuntos de física i medicina. pp. 128.

4to. Mexico: F. de Zúñiga y Ontiveros. 1772–73.

Beristáin i p. 226 no. 384.
Guerra (Icon.) 379.
León (Mex.) i 190.
León (1915) 59.
Medina (Mex.) vi 5491.
Palau 25092.

The set owned by León, and probably the one described by him.

The journal began its appearance on 17 October 1772 and continued for 16 numbers until printing costs forced its editor, José Ignacio Bartolache [see M.10], to cease publication with the issue of 10 February 1773. Each number is of four leaves, and the whole is paginated consecutively throughout. Current medical topics are treated with characteristic trenchancy.

Figure 15.

Nº. 1º.   *Sabado* 17. *de Octubre de* 1772.

MERCURIO VOLANTE

CON NOTICIAS IMPORTANTES I CURIOSAS
SOBRE VARIOS ASUNTOS
DE *FISICA I MEDICINA.*

Por D. JOSEF IGNACIO BARTOLACHE, *Doctor Médico, del Claustro de esta Real Universidad de México.*

PLAN DE ESTE PAPEL PERIÓDICO.

Parva mora est, alas pedibus virgamque potente
Somniferam sumpsisse manu, tegimenque capillis.
Haec ubi disposuit patriâ Iove natus ab arce,
Desilit in terras —————————————

                        Ovid. Metamorph. 1. w. 671. &c.

Se apresta luego, i calza de sus alas
El pie ligero; cubre la cabeza,
I empuñando la vara encantadora,
Deciende en un momento hasta la tierra
El rubio hijo de Jupiter i Maia.

————————————————

NUESTRA América Setentrional, esta gran parte del mundo, tan considerable por sus riquezas; si no lo ha sido igualmente por la florecencia de las letras, esto es, de los estudios i ciencias útiles, cultivadas por sus Habitantes, es porque no podía en solos dos siglos i medio hacer tamaños progresos. El oro i plata de nuestras Minas,
                                                            la

Figure 15. MERCURIO VOLANTE. Mexico: F. de Zúñiga y Ontiveros. 1772–73. **(Per.14)**

Per.15 NOTICIOSO GENERAL

Noticioso General. Num. 454 [*only*]. Del viernes 27 de Noviembre de 1818. pp.4.

fol. Mexico: Imprenta de Arizpe. 1818.

Palau 194287; 294808.

Antonio Serrano Rubio, Director of the Real Academia de Cirugía, announces the start of the course in surgery for 114 students. Of the same number in the previous course 32 students had either failed to satisfy their examiners or had discontinued their course.

The Real Escuela de Cirugía was created in 1768 by Charles III and established in the Hospital Real de Indios, on the model of the schools of surgery in Barcelona and Cadiz. Serrano became its third Director in 1803, and was active in this post until 1827 when he became Director *ad honorem* until his death in 1833. He was also *Cirujano mayor* of the same hospital and of the Hospital de San Andrés, and *Alcalde examinador* of the Protomedicato. [See Valle (1942)].

The periodical *Noticioso General* is generally agreed to have begun publication on 24 July 1815, and at the date of the present number was appearing 3 days a week; authorities do not agree on the date of its last appearance, which was probably during 1824. Palau [294808] evidently regards Barquera y Morales [1779–1840] as the editor between 1817 and 1821 [see Per.2, Per.18].

Per.16 PERIODICO CONSTITUCIONAL

Periodico constitucional del gobierno de Merida de Yucatan sabado 7 de abril de 1821. Núm. 36 [*only*]. pp.4.

fol. Merida: Imprenta P[atriótica Liberal.] 1821.

Guerra (Icon.) 648.
Medina (Mérida) 40 [i.e. three other issues].
Palau 223044.

A brief notice on p. 4 announces Ciprian Blanco's *Estado*, Campeche, 1820 [see M.23] recording the 30,555 vaccinations carried out between 1804 and 1819 [in fact 1820], and that vaccinations are performed every nine days in the council offices.

The *Periódico constitucional* began publication in February 1821 and ended in 1822. Appearing four days a week, it printed royal orders and decrees issued by the Cortes, and other notices of governmental, national, and foreign interest.

Per.17 SEMANARIO DE AGRICULTURA, INDUSTRIA, Y COMERCIO

Semanario de agricultura, industria, y comercio. 5 vols.

4to. Buenos Aires: Real Imprenta de Niños Expósitos. 1802–1807.

Medina (Buenos Aires) 252.
Molinari (1941) p.86.
Palau 307150 [a facsimile].

The first 2 vols. to 29 August 1804 (no. 102) only, of which nos. 1 and 2 of vol. I are wanting.

The journal, concerned with the radical improvement of agriculture, manufacture and trade, was published regularly in 4 leaves on Wednesdays from 1 September 1802 to 11 February 1807, ceasing shortly after the British capture of Montevideo on 3 February 1807. A gap in publication occurred between the issues for 25 June and 24 September 1806 (nos. 197 and 198) following the British capture of Buenos Aires on 27 June 1806. The journal provides instruction and stimulation on a wide variety of the applied arts and sciences including medicine; and it prints royal orders on matters of trade. Medina lists the contents of each issue.

The editor of this enterprising and practical journal was the revolutionary leader Juan Hipólito Vieytes [1762–1815] whose work was later continued by Manuel Belgrano's *Correo de comercio* 1810–11 [see Medina (Buenos Aires), 807]. Gutiérrez (1860), pp. 111–116 prints a brief life of Vieytes.

Per.18 SEMANARIO ECONOMICO

Semanario economico de noticias curiosas y eruditas, sobre agricultura y demás artes, oficios. 2 vols.

4to. Mexico: María Fernández de Jáuregui & J.B. de Arizpe. 1808–10.

Beristáin i p.218 no.361.
Guerra (Icon.) 582.
León (1915) 200.
Medina (Mex.) vii 10311 {vol. 1 only].
Palau 294805; 307180 [vol. 1 only].

The journal, published in issues of 4 leaves every Thursday from 1 December 1808 to 27 December 1810, is lavish with practical advice on a multitude of useful arts from domestic medicine to agriculture and mining. Information, including receipts and formulae of all kinds, is imparted by direct instruction, discussion, or dialogue;

the purpose of the journal was clearly to propagate an experimental view of life. It was edited by Juan Wenceslao Barquera y Morales [1779–1840], also editor of the *Diario de México*. The present journal was continued by him for one year as *El mentor mexicano*, 1811 [Palau 164786]. [See Per.2, Per.15].

Per.19 **SEMANARIO POLITICO Y LITERARIO DE MEJICO**

Semanario politico y literario de Mejico. 5 vols. [1st 2 vols. *only*].

4to. Mexico: M. de Zúñiga y Ontiveros; A. Valdés; C. de la Torre. 1820–22.

Medina (Mex.) viii 11823.
Palau 307244.

Palau notes that this journal, published every Wednesday in 12 leaves, reached 5 volumes. These 2 volumes include nos. 1–32 from 12 July 1820 to 21 February 1821 only, with supplements. At the regular 4 months to the volume as proposed in the prospectus it would have reached May 1822, i.e. the month in which Itúrbide was proclaimed Emperor.

The prospectus and content makes clear its pronounced liberal bias. The present 2 vols. include a miscellany of articles and contributed papers of political, literary, bibliographical and economic interest; and it prints the decrees of the Cortes of 1810–12 and reports the current sessions. Indexes and lists of subscribers are provided.

C. Manuscripts 1575–1927

ADAMS, Edward [*c.* 1824–56]

Notebook containing word-lists in English, Russian, Russian transliterated, and Alaskan Eskimo.

1 l., 28 ll., 1 l.   12 × 17 cm.   [Mikhailovsk, 1850–51].

Bound in original boards.

Holograph, with ink sketches of Arctic birds and a sailing-ship; accompanied by a watercolour signed 'E.A.' showing the interior of a wooden Arctic hut.

Navy Lists and examination records of the Royal College of Surgeons indicate that Adams passed the Royal College of Surgeons examinations in 1847 and became Assistant Surgeon to the Royal Hospital, Haslar, passing to the Plymouth Hospital in the same year. He joined the Franklin Relief Expedition of 1848–49 as Assistant Surgeon to both H.M.S. *Enterprise* and H.M.S. *Investigator*; and held the same appointment in H.M.S. *Enterprise* on the Franklin Relief Expedition of 1850–55 when he wintered in early 1850 and early 1851 at the fortified post of Mikhailovsk (renamed St. Michael['s] after the Alaska Purchase of 1867) in Norton Sound in the Bering Sea. Adams was promoted Surgeon in 1854, gained his Surgeon's certificate in 1855, and died in late 1856. [For a list of the Franklin Relief Expeditions see Sir John Richardson, *Polar Regions*, Edinburgh, A. & C. Black, 1860, pp. 172–174; and for brief references to Adams' activities in Alaska see W.H. Dall, *Alaska and its resources*, London, Sampson Low, Son, & Marston, 1870, pp. 344–345].

Particulars of acquisition not known.

WMS Amer. 108.

ALBARRAN Y DOMINGUEZ, Joaquín María [1860–1912]

Manuscrit de l'Exposé de titres. [Exposé des travaux scientifiques].

536 ll.   31 × 20 cm.   [Paris, 1905].

Unbound.

MS in author's hand with a few leaves in the hands of copyists, in typescript, or taken from Albarrán's printed works; written on the rectos only; printers' notes in the margins.

The MS was published as *Exposé des travaux scientifiques de J. Albarrán*, Paris, Masson et Cie, 1906, on which Albarrán based his important *Médecine opératoire des voies urinaires*, Paris, Masson et Cie, 1909.

Albarrán was born in Cuba and studied in Barcelona from 1872, graduating as physician in 1877. From 1883 he worked in Paris hospitals and became an *interne* in 1884. In 1906 he succeeded Guyon in the Chair of the Clinique des Maladies des Voies Urinaires; and he followed Orfila as the second Hispanic to be appointed lecturer in the Faculty of Medicine in the University of Paris.

Presented by Dr. Julio Sanjurjo d'Arellano, 1935.

WMS. Amer. 102.

ALEMAN, Jesús

Un feto.

2 ll.   27 × 21 cm.   Moroleón, Guanajuato, Mexico, 1893.

Unbound.

Holograph, signed and dated 'Moro León Mayo 20 de 1893'; a tipped-in drawing (presumably by the author) shews the foetus in original size. The MS describes a teratological case and gives exact measurements of the foetus.

Guerra Collection.

WMS. Amer. 99.

AMARILLAS, Joaquín de

[Begins:] Obedeciendo la Superior orden Espedida por el S[eñ]or Intendente Gobernador D[o]n Pedro de Corbalan ... y ciendo la sobre de q[u]e Esponga o de cuenta de los Arboles Frutales, Silbestres, y Yerbas q[u]e en mi Jurisdicion se encuentre q[u]e sean anecsar á Medicamentos Digo: q[u]e las q[u]e en estio de Xiaqui se en cuentran son [&c.].

1 l.   30.5 × 21 cm.   [Mission to the Yaquis, Sonora, Mexico, 1783].

Bound.

Signed, with *rúbrica*; and dated 10 December 1783.

A return on the fruits, trees (economic and medicinal), and medicinal herbs of his area made to the *Justicia mayor* of the Province, Patricio Antonio Gómez de Cossio, by his local deputy [*Theniente*]. [See entries under PABLOS, and TAMAYO, for similar returns from Sonora].

Guerra Collection.

WMS. Amer. 50.

ANDRADE Y PASTOR, Manuel [1809–48]

Papers relating to his professional life.

108 ll.   35 × 22.5 cm.   [Mexico, 1832–48].

Unbound.

The 97 documents include certificates of qualification, licences to carry fire-arms, bills for anatomical equipment and medical books, letters of appointment, an account of a medical case in which Andrade took part and much official correspondence from his later years with other prominent members of the faculty, for example, C. Liceaga, M.F. Jiménez and M. Carpio. Four of the documents are in Andrade's hand.

Andrade qualified as both *cirujano latino* and physician in Mexico 1831–33, and travelled to Paris to further his knowledge 1833–36. On his return he was appointed Director of the Hospital of Jesus; in 1838 he was made Director of the Escuela Nacional de Cirugía, reincorporated the same year into the Establecimiento de Ciencias Médicas (formed 1833) in which he continued to hold the chair of anatomy until his early death. [See Flores (1886–88), *3*, 465–468].

Guerra Collection.

WMS. Amer. 94.

ANDRADE Y PASTOR, Manuel [1809–48]

Datos biográficos del S[eño]r D[o]n Manuel Andrade.

31 ll.   34 × 22 cm.   [Mexico, *c.* 1850].

Unbound.

A series of short biographical drafts on Andrade with copies of documents relating to his life, all in the same unknown hand.

León Collection.

WMS. Amer. 136.

ARECHEDERRETA Y ESCALADA, Juan Bautista [1771–1835]

A formal proposal for the establishment of a resident medical college.

22 ll. (first & last leaves bl.)   21 × 15 cm.   Mexico, [*c.* 1802].

Unbound; in contemporary leather cover in modern slip-case.

Signature, *rúbrica*, and insertions in author's hand.

The proposal, addressed to the Protomedicato, is primarily intended to relieve the poverty of medical students. Chairs (including a chair in surgery), the training of midwives and of nurses for women, are proposed under the direction of the Protomedicato. The College is to be funded by a tax on playing-cards, by a lottery, or by the Minería or Consulados. A seven year course is envisaged for medical students. There is no evidence that this or another copy was in fact received by the Protomedicato. [See M.5].

Guerra Collection.

WMS. Amer. 19.

BARRAGAN, José [d. 1892]

Apuntes para Descripcion de Plantas dados en la E[scuela] N[acional] Preparatoria de México ... Año de 1872.

4 ll., pp. 155, 2 bl. ll.   22 × 15.5 cm.   Mexico, 1872.

Unbound.

A [?holograph] draft, probably prepared for printing, of a students' handbook. It may not in fact have been published.

A respected clinician, botanist, microscopist and member of the Academia de Medicina de México, Barragán was Director of the Hospital de Jesús for the 20 years or so before his death. [See Flores (1886–88), *3*, p. 446; and *La Escuela de Medicina* (*Méx.*), 1892, *11*, pp. 613–614].

León Collection.

WMS. Amer. 124.

BARTRAM, William [1739–1823]

Mr. Bartram on American Birds. Extract from Bartrams travels in N. America [by Edward Sabine].

1 l., pp. 15, 1 l.   6 × 20 cm.   [?Woodbridge, Suffolk, 1813].

Unbound.

Addressed from the War Office to the "Officer Commanding, R.H. Artillery,

Woodbridge, Suffolk" with postmark for 4 Feb. 1813, within contemporary paper covers.

General Sir Edward Sabine [1788–1883], astronomer, meteorologist, ornithologist, researched much into terrestrial magnetism, and in the course of an active service and official career became President of the Royal Society 1861–71.

The holograph list (except minor abbreviations, omissions and alterations) is identical to that in W. Bartram, *Travels through North and South Carolina* [&c.], London, J. Johnson, 1792, pp. 284–294.

Purchased at Stevens 17.3.1931 (83753).

WMS. Amer. 109.

BIANA, Nicolás de

Fly-poster giving notice of the arrival of the *botánico* in the City and of his services to poor patients suffering from any illness.

25.5 × 18 cm.   [Mexico, 1790].

Bound.

Francisco Xavier de Balmis [1753–1819], later Director of the *Real Expedición Marítima de la Vacuna*, derived the use of the roots of the *Agave americana* and the *Begonia balmisiana* from the same Nicolás de Biana, *curandero* of Pátzcuaro, as a remedy for syphilis. [See Balmis (1794), Flores (1886–88), 2, pp. 376–378; and entries under NEW SPAIN, Laws, statutes, &c. (1794), and O'SULLIVAN].

Guerra Collection.

WMS. Amer. 39.

BONANZA, J.M. *and others*

An unsigned undated preliminary *consulta* (a description of the original course of the illness), an undated *respuesta* signed J.M.H., and a second *respuesta* signed J.M. Bonanza and J.M.H. and dated 5 August 1819, on the case of D.ª Maria Montes de Tagle.

6 ll.   31.5 × 22 cm.   [Mexico], 1819.

Bound.

The two responding physicians agree that the preliminary treatment was 'diametrically opposed' to what was required and concern themselves with the aetiology of the condition in constitutional debility, the resultant epilepsy and obstruction, and possible inflammation of the liver. They suggest a suitably nourishing diet with some medication.

Guerra Collection.

WMS. Amer. 70.

BONPLAND, Aimé-Jacques-Alexandre [GOUJAUD], *called* BONPLAND [1773–1858]

Collection of notes written by Bonpland as a student at Montpellier and Paris on materia medica, pharmacy, medicine, geology and zoology.

1. GOUAN (A.) Matière médicale. Par Mr. Gouan à Montpellier: 18 mars–14 avril 1791. 3 sections. I (10 ll.), II (12 ll.), III (12 ll.).

2. [Anon.] Chymie médicale. Montpellier. 1 avril 1791. 1 section. (12 ll.).

3. [Anon.] Thérapeutique. Sections 2–5. [Ends:] 4 juillet 1791. 4 sections. II (16 ll.), III (16 ll.), IV (20 ll.), V (16 ll.).

4. FOUQUET (H.) Semeiologia docente Henrico Fouquet. Monspelii die vigesima prima maii an. 1791. 1 section. (16 ll.).

5. [Anon.] Des pouls. Mont[pellier], 24 /1/1791. 1 section. (6 ll.).

6. [Anon.] [Notes and extracts on medicine]. (Cullen and Boerhaave). I: 19/8/1791; II: 5/3/1792. Montpellier. 4 sections. I (9 ll.), II (6 ll.), III (8 ll.), IV (4 ll.).

7. [Anon.] Mollusques No. 4 and a fragment of another section. An 6 [1797/8]. 2 sections, mutilated. I (12 ll.), II (10 ll.).

8. [Anon.] Galvanisme. Irritation de la fibre nerveuse et musculaire. No. 2, No. 3. 2 sections. II (10 ll.), III (10 ll.).

9. [Anon.]. [Geology], 1 section, mutilated. (10 ll.).

19 pts. [i.e. 215 ll.] 23.5 × 18.5 & 27 × 18.5 cm. Montpellier [and Paris], 1791–1798.

Unbound, in box.

An explorer and botanist with some medical training and experience, Bonpland was the well-known associate of Alexander von Humboldt in the voyage to South and Central America 1799–1804, and his co-author in the voluminous report of the journey and on other topics. After 1816 he resumed an adventurous and unlucky life in S. America, teaching, exploring, botanising and farming until his death.

Purchased 1931 (64697).

WMS. Amer. 103.

BROWN, John [1735–88]

A translation into Spanish of pts. 2, 3, 4 & 5 of Brown's *Elementa medicinae* first published in Edinburgh, 1780.

156ll. (last bl.) 20.5 × 14.5 cm. Mexico, 1808.

Contemporary binding in modern slip-case.

Dated Mexico 2 March 1808, but unsigned.

Although José Mariano Mociño [1757–1820], a member of the Royal Botanical Expedition to New Spain, is known to have translated and adapted the *Elementa*, only Pt. 1 was published [see M.28]. The present MS is either an independent translation (Mociño left for Spain in 1803) or perhaps a fair copy of his draft. [See Rickett (1947) pp. 38, 74].

Guerra Collection.

WMS. Amer. 21.

BUENO, Cosme [1711–98]

[f.1^r:] Descripcion del Obisp[a]do de Buenos Ayres .... [f.5^v:] Provincia de las Misiones de el Uruhay .... [f.9^v:] Descripcion de la Provinzias del Reyno de Chile. Obispado de S[a]ntiago .... [f.21^v:] Descripcion del obispado de la Concepcion [&c.] .... [f.34^v:] Catalogo historico de los Birreyes, y Arzobispos que ha avido en Lima con los succesores mas principales de sus tiempos .... [f.42^r:] Nuevo Virreynato de Buenos Ayres [&c.].

1 bl. l., ff.42, 3 bl. ll. 30 × 20.5 cm. [Spain, *c.*1785].

Bound in full contemporary marbled calf.

Copied in Spain from the revised text completed in Lima *c.* 1785 (i.e. during the Viceregency of the Marqués de Loreto in the Río de la Plata, 1784–89, at f.42^v).

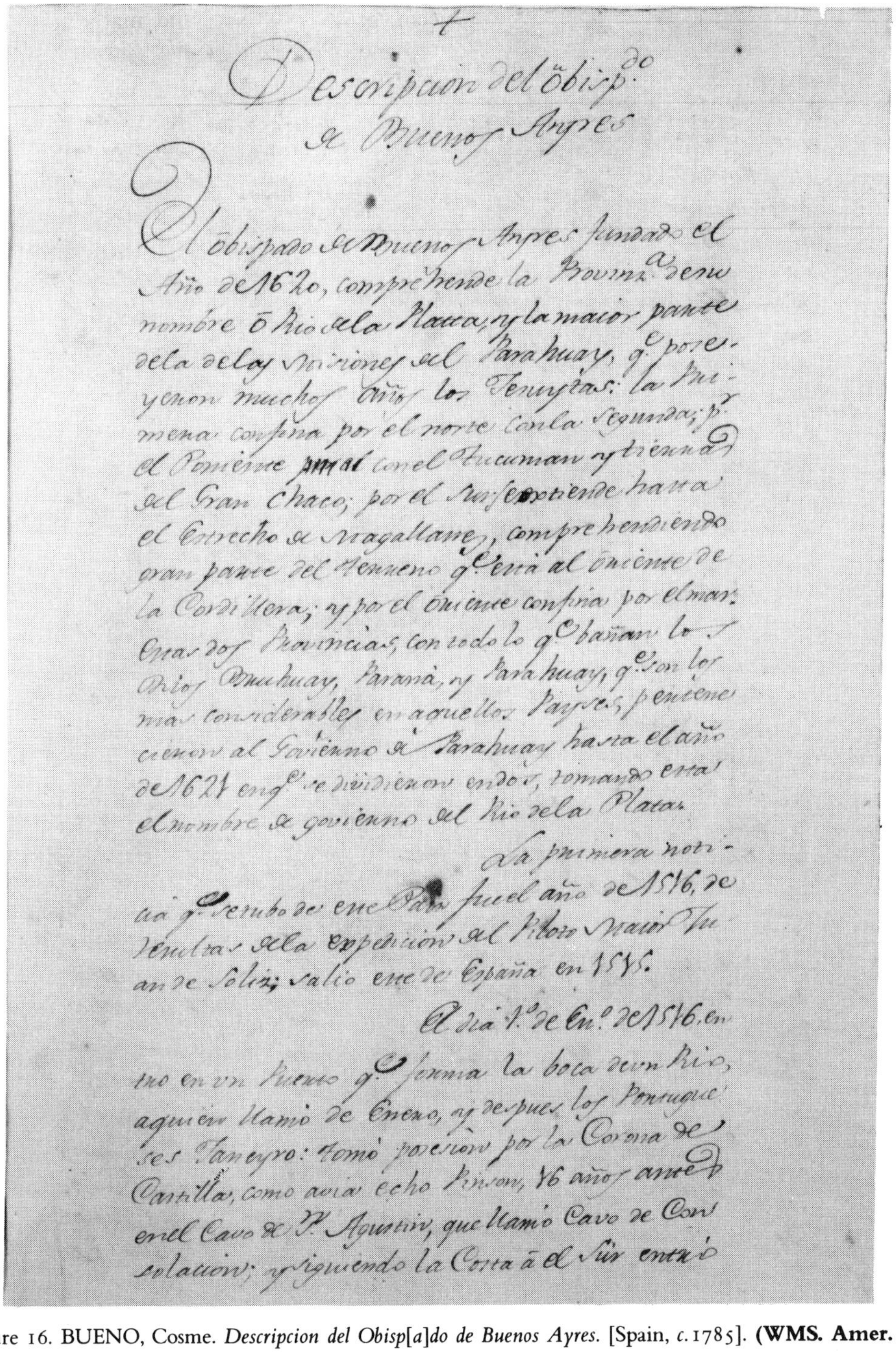

Descripcion del Obisp.do de Buenos Ayres

El obispado de Buenos Ayres fundado el Año de 1620, comprehende la Provinc.a de cuio nombre o Rio dela Plata, y la maior parte dela delos Misiones del Paraguay, q.e poseyeron muchos años los Jesuitas: la primera confina por el norte con la segunda; p.r el Poniente con el Tucuman y tierras del Gran Chaco; por el Sur se extiende hasta el Estrecho de Magallanes, comprehendiendo gran parte del terreno q.e está al Oriente de la Cordillera; y por el Oriente confina por el mar. Estas dos Provincias, con todo lo q.e bañan los Rios Uruguay, Paraná, y Paraguay, q.e son los mas considerables en aquellos Payses, pertenecieron al Govierno de Paraguay hasta el año de 1621 en q.e se dividieron en dos, tomando esta el nombre de govierno del Rio dela Plata.

La primera noticia q.e se tubo de este Pais fue el año de 1516, de resultas dela expedicion del Piloto Maior Juan de Solis; salio este de España en 1515.

El dia 1.o de En.o de 1516 entro en un Puerto q.e forma la boca de un Rio, aquien llamó de Enero, y despues los Portugueses Janeyro: tomó posesion por la Corona de Castilla, como avia echo Pinson, 16 años antes en el Cavo de S.n Agustin, que llamó Cavo de Consolacion; y siguiendo la Costa a el Sur entró

Figure 16. BUENO, Cosme. *Descripcion del Obisp[a]do de Buenos Ayres.* [Spain, *c.*1785]. **(WMS. Amer. 77)**

Bueno, physician, geographer, scientist and mathematician, came to Peru from Aragon in 1730 and became *Catedrático de matemáticas* and *Cosmógrafo mayor* in 1758. His annual almanacks entitled *El conocimiento de los tiempos* published 1757–98 included his historical, geographical, and medical essays and historical lists of viceroys, governors and senior ecclesiastics. The present catalogue of viceroys appeared in the almanacks for 1763 and 1795 (and as a separate in Lima in 1764); the description of Buenos Aires appeared in the almanack for 1776, that of the Bishopric of Santiago in the almanack for 1777, and that of Concepción in 1778. Bueno's essays (except for the list of viceroys and archbishops) were reprinted by Odriozola (1863–76), *3*, pp. 5–10; 207–260.

Some of the present MS material did not appear in the almanacks; the MS is likely to be a copy of Bueno's revised text which was never published as a whole. [See McPheeters (1955) for a valuable note on Bueno and (footnote 8) on the present MS; and see P. 3 *et seq.*].

Said to be from the Archives of the Conde de Revillagigedo, Viceroy of New Spain 1789–94.

Purchased at Sotheby's 1964 (310651).

WMS. Amer. 77.

Figure 16.

BUENOS AIRES. Hospital Bethlemítico de Santa Catalina

Libro XI. de Enfermería da principio en primero de Enero de 1818 . . . y concluye, en Mayo de 1822.

1 l., ff. 399 (=401; some ff. bl. in text & many ff. bl. at end). 30 × 21 cm. Buenos Aires, 1818–22.

Original limp vellum cover with ties.

Wanting: ff.64, 65, 216 (presum. bl.), 337–396 (presum. bl.).

A Patients Register from January 1818 to May 1822 inclusive (forming part of a larger collection), which separately lists within each month military personnel, peasants, prisoners, slaves, and occasionally freed slaves [*morenos libres*] and members of the upper class [*distinguidos*]. Names, designation of case, age, and dates of entry, discharge or death are given.

Figures are drawn up for each month and year for the numbers of sick, those dead, and the cost of drugs and food. A total, cast up for the years 1817–21 inclusive, and signed by Fr. José del Carmen, Prefect of the Hospital, shews that of 5,620 entering the Hospital, 1,238 (i.e. slightly under one quarter) died. The Register contains some 5,000 cases.

Designated in 1580 as the Hospital y Ermita de San Martín, the Hospital passed through several transformations [see Molinari (1937), pp. 73–81] before coming under the direction of the Bethlehemites in 1748. By 1800 it had become a general hospital, and in 1822 it was abolished [see A. Meyer Arana, *La caridad en Buenos Aires*, Buenos Aires, The Author, 1911, 1, pp. 62–65].

Purchased 1982 (337296).

WMS. Amer. 149.

CADENA Y SOTOMAYOR, Melchor Antonio de la [1539–1607]

Two reports by Cadena and accompanying documentation seeking permission from the Council of the Indies for his transfer from Puebla to the City of Mexico on the ground of ill-health. 2 pts.

Ff. 12 (first & last bl. folios not contemporary); ff. 7.   31.5 × 21.5 cm.   Mexico, 1575–1600.

Pt. 1 [WMS. Amer. 90a] bound in marbled paper; pt. 2 [WMS. Amer. 90b] bound in 19th cent. leather wrap.

Signatures and *rúbricas* of Cadena, 8 religious and 6 physicians.

Pt. 1 includes the reports by Cadena [ff. 3 & 4], his letter of presentation by Philip II to a Canonry of the Cathedral of Mexico dated 20 May 1575 at San Lorenzo [f. 5]; and notarial copies of the affirmations of 8 priests and religious of the City of Mexico and Puebla [ff. 6–11].

Pt. 2 includes only the medical evidence of 6 physicians of Mexico and Puebla: Pedro Rengel, Juan de Contreras [d. 1624], Juan de Barrios [see M.9], Pedro de Porras Farfán, Hernando Rangel Ortiz, and Pedro López [1527–1597]; all of whom (1595–99) agree that Cadena's health would benefit by his removal from the cold air of Puebla. His chronic and painful debilitating digestive symptoms are fully described.

Melchor Antonio de la Cadena, an important figure in the ecclesiastical establishment of late 16th cent. Mexico, was Canon and Dean of Tlaxcala (whose

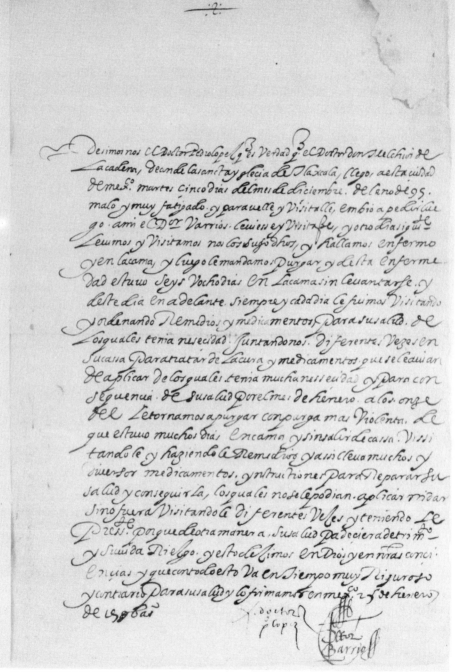

Figure 17. CADENA Y SOTOMAYOR, Melchor Antonio de la. *Two reports by Cadena and accompanying documentation.* Mexico, 1575–1600. (fol. 15ʳ). **(WMS. Amer. 90b)**

Cathedral was at Puebla), *Maestrescuelas* and Dean of Mexico Cathedral, Chancellor of the University of Mexico, and Rector for the term 1573/4, and at his death Bishop-elect of Chiapas. He joined the Colegio de Santa María de Todos Santos in 1590, and founded the *mayorazgo* of his name [See Arechederreta (1796), p. 17; Gibson (1952), pp. 54–61; and Fernández de Recas (1965), pp. [253]–260; Guerra (1949) has commented on these documents and their background, and has transcribed the medical evidence in the second part].

Formerly in the collection of the Mexican bibliographer E. Valton [1880–1963].

Guerra Collection.

WMS. Amer. 90a & 90b.

Figure 17.

CAMARGO, Francisco

Daily prescriptions for unknown patients from 7–13 August, primarily made up by the Botica de Subeldia.

12 ll. (first leaf & last 2 leaves bl.).   20 × 14 cm.   Mexico, c. 1830.

Bound in contemporary folder, in modern slip-case.

Holograph in Latin.

Camargo is listed in the *Guía de forasteros* for 1828 as *Cirujano romancista* and as *Practicante mayor* of the Hospital de Sàn Hipólito for insane men; he also appears as *cirujano* in the *Guía* for 1831 with Juan Subeldia as *Profesor de farmacia* in the Calle de Hospital Real.

Guerra Collection.

WMS. Amer. 28.

CAPITULO

Cap[itu]l[o] para los que no pueden orinar.

6 ll.   20 × 15 cm.   Hispano-America, 18th cent.

Unbound.

Fragment from a receipt book, including remedies for urinary and genital complaints and directions for examining the urine and the pulse.

Guerra Collection.

WMS. Amer. 57.

CARBAJAL, Antonio J. [1847–1914]

La anestesia obstetricial.

16 ll. (last bl.)   34.5 × 25 cm.   [Mexico, *c.*1890].

Unbound and incomplete.

Holograph draft paper on the theory and practice of obstetrical anaesthesia and its development in Europe and Mexico from the time of its "creador" James Young Simpson [1811–70]. Carbajal particularly quotes his teacher, the early proponent of obstetrical anaesthesia in Mexico, A. Ortega de Villar [1825–75], *Profesor de clínica obstétrica* in the Escuela de Medicina, and Ortega's brilliant and prolific successor J. M. Rodríguez Arangoiti [see entry under RODRIGUEZ ARANGOITI] [1828–94], as well as his own experience since beginning practice in 1869. He concludes that there is only value in its proper employment. Carbajal filled minor official appointments in the medical establishment and taught in later years at the Instituto Bacteriológico of Mexico.

An obituary of Carbajal appears in the *Boletín de Ciencias Médicas*, 1914, 5 (2), 49–50.

León Collection.

WMS. Amer. 128.

CARBAJAL, Antonio J. [1847–1914]

Tocologia. Algunas reflexiones sobre el Mecanismo del Parto en las presentaciones occipito-posteriores. Dificultades que presenta y modo de remediarlas.

1 l., ff.6.   32.5 × 21 cm.   Mexico, 1892.

Unbound.

Copyist's MS, signed and dated Mexico 25 November 1892.

Carbajal describes the salient difficulties of occipitoposterior presentation and advises manual version during labour. He describes two cases in which he has taken part, and awards particular praise to Manuel Gutiérrez Zavala [1850–1918] (holder of the chair of obstetrics in the Escuela de Medicina and later Secretary of the same School and member of the Consejo Superior de Salubridad), and to J.M. Rodríguez [see entry under RODRIGUEZ ARANGOITI] for making known their similar experience.

The paper was presented at the First Mexican Medical Congress on 6 December 1892, which was reported in *La Escuela de Medicina (Méx.)*, 1892–93, *12* (1), 95–101.

León Collection.

WMS. Amer. 127.

CARDOSO [fl. 1830–40]

Metodo Preservativo y Curativo de la Colera morbus dado por un facultativo del Pueblo de Amosoque.

Ff. vi–vii (i.e. 2 ll). 21.5 × 15.5 cm. [?Amozoc de Mota, Puebla, Mexico], 1833.

Unbound; stained and faded.

Dated 7 September 1833.

Popular remedies and directions for use during the 1833 cholera epidemic in Mexico.

In the same hand and from the same collection of remedies as WMSS. Amer. 47 [?CARDOSO], 48 [NOMBRE] & 55 [ESCAYOLA], with which it was originally bound; and possibly associated with one leaf of WMS. Amer. 15 [RECETAS]. Perhaps from the remedy book of an *hacienda*.

Guerra Collection.

WMS. Amer. 54.

[?CARDOSO [fl. 1830–40]]

Metodo curativo de las viruellas [*sic*] del año de 1830. Y asegundo para este ano de 1840. Y es como sigue.

Ff. i–v (i.e. 5 ll.). 21.5 × 15.5 cm. [?Amozoc de Mota, Puebla, Mexico], 1840.

Unbound; heavily stained.

Nine simple remedies and a poultice for the 4 stages of early symptoms, eruption, suppuration and drying of the pustules, with notes on general treatment, and brief descriptions of the stages of smallpox.

The text does not follow any known printed source, of which the most characteristic is M. Muñoz, *Método sencillo, claro y facil de asistir a los niños en la actual epidemia de viruelas naturales*, Mexico, T. Uribe y Alcalde, 1830, twice reprinted in San Luis Potosí in the same year.

In the same hand and from the same collection of remedies as WMSS. Amer. 48 NOMBRE, 54 [CARDOSO] and 55 [ESCAYOLA] with which it was originally bound; and possibly also associated with one leaf of WMS. Amer. 15 [RECETAS]. Perhaps from the remedy book of an *hacienda*.

Guerra Collection.

WMS. Amer. 47.

CARTA

Carta de persona fidedigna del Estado de San Luis—observaciones practicas sobre el cholera.

3 ll.   32.5 × 22.5 cm.   San Luis Potosí, Mexico, 1833.

Bound.

Dated 31 July 1833.

An unsigned report on the cholera experience of an *hacienda* whose simple and well-observed management of about 100 cases lost only 4 patients. The author includes a description of his own case.

The main therapeutic agents were manzanilla, chalk, and laudanum administered primarily *per orem* in plentiful liquid, though the administration of laudanum was preferred *per anum*. Reference is made to the case of the local physician Pascual de Aranda [author of *Receta para la colera morbus*, San Luis Potosí [1833]] who recovered from cholera but lost his reason, supposedly from heavy doses of laudanum administered simultaneously by mouth and by clyster.

Having described other successful remedies the writer concludes that there is no single method of treatment suitable for all climates and all patients.

Guerra Collection.

WMS. Amer. 53.

CASTILLERO, Atenógenes

Observaciones medicinales.

Ff.25. 21.5 × 15.5 cm. Puebla, Mexico, *c.* 1850–*c.* 1870.

Folder in slip-case.

Ff. 30–62 of a larger collection (ff. 38–45 wanting).

A collection of miscellaneous medical and surgical receipts, a few of which include Mexican plants.

F.13ᵛ describes a cure for gout undertaken in 1866; f.17 tabulates receipts for powders taken from another source by Castillero, dated Puebla 1850; and ff. 18ʳ–19ʳ describe a *Curación del Colera morvo en Campeche* dated 23 August 1854.

Guerra Collection.

WMS. Amer. 27.

CERVANTES, Vicente [1755–1829]

Ensayo á Materia Medica del Reyno vegetal de Nueva España, ó Discurso sobre las plantas oficinales que crecen en las cercanias de Mexico que ha de servir de inicio en la abertura del curso de Botanica el dia 28 de mayo de 1791.

54 ll. (last 2 bl.). 30 × 20.5 cm. Mexico, 1791.

Modern leather binding in slip-case.

A general introduction occupies ll. 1–5. The remaining leaves describe the indigenous materia medica arranged according to the binomial system of Linnaeus. Mexican names are given in accordance with F. Hernández, *Opera*, ed. C. Gómez Ortega, 3 vols., Madrid, Heirs of Ibarra, 1790; Spanish names where necessary are given in accordance with A. Palau y Verdera's compilation from Linnaeus, i.e. *Parte práctica de botánica*, 8 vols., Madrid, Imprenta Real, 1784–88.

León (1895), no. 161, XIII, lists a manuscript of corresponding title and the same date, as well as the printed version [*ibid.*, IV] published as a monograph by *El Estudio* (*Mex.*), 1879 (i.e. 1889, *1*, (47 pp.)). This printed version differs in detail from the present MS version, and omits some sentences and paragraphs including the note on the verso of the last leaf on the supposed discovery of the nutmeg (*Nueces moscadas*) 60 leagues from Guadalajara.

The *Ensayo para la materia medica mexicana*, Puebla, Oficina del Hospital de S. Pedro, 1832 (also reprinted by *El Estudio* (*Mex.*), 1889, *1*, (54 pp.)), assumed by Rickett (1947), p. 60, footnote 80 (misinterpreting Colmeiro (1858), no. 313) to have been the first publication of Cervantes' lecture, was in fact a totally different report carried out by a commission set up by the Academia Médico-Quirúrgica of Puebla; Cervantes' lecture of 28 May 1791 is only referred to among other lectures by his contemporaries in the introduction (at p. v.)

The list and descriptions are comprehensive and of unusual interest. The botanical courses were first opened by Cervantes in 1788. [See M.33].

Phillipps MSS. Nos. 15994, 16201.

Purchased at Sotheby's 24.6.1919.

WMS. Amer. 81.

CHERVIN, Nicolas [1783–1843]

Certificats de La Guadeloupe.

62 ll. (some bl.).   39.5 × 25.5 cm.   New York, La Guadeloupe, St. Barthélemy, La Martinique, Nevis, Surinam, St. Christopher, and New Orleans, 1817–22.

Bound.

A collection of 32 certified copies of professional opinions and 13 original professional opinions in reply to Chervin's inquiries concerning the non-contagiousness of yellow fever. The opinions are primarily addressed from Guadeloupe. Each document bears the name of the responding practitioner, and the certified copies each bear the official stamp and signature of J. D'Espinville, French Consul in New York, and the date 27 August 1821.

Chervin was born in St. Laurent d'Oingt and died in Bourbonne-les-Bains. He studied medicine at l'Hôtel Dieu, Lyon, and in Paris, where he graduated in 1812. Much of Chervin's career was devoted to proving the non-contagiousness of yellow fever, and for that purpose he travelled across the American continent 1817–22 within the range 37° of latitude from Surinam to Maine. During his journeys he gathered 541 documents from 531 practitioners experienced in yellow fever to support his contention; but in spite of these observations and his own, his opinion was strongly opposed by others. In 1832 he became a member of the Académie

Royale de Médecine. [See Dubois d'Amiens (1846); and Waserman & Mayfield (1971) describe Chervin's yellow fever survey in the United States 1820–22].

Purchased 1933.

WMS. Amer. 113.

CHINCHON, Conde de [1590–1647]

[Begins:] Bien sera s[eño]res que den toda la priesa Posible en enviar al almacen ... todo el acogue [&c.].

2 ll.   29.5 × 21 cm.   Lima, 1632.

Unbound, in folder.

Dated Lima, 5 June 1632.

An order signed by the Viceroy of Peru [1629–39] requesting the prompt supply of mercury by the *Juezes officiales de la R[ea]l [Ha]zienda* of Huancavelica. This fourth Conde de Chinchón and his second wife, Francisca Henríquez de Ribera, have been frequently but mistakenly associated with the introduction of cinchona bark into Europe. [See Haggis (1941); and Jaramillo-Arango (1949)].

Guerra Collection.

WMS. Amer. 92.

CLAH, Arthur Wellington [1831–1916]

Journals, account-books and note-books by a Tsimshian Indian: with reminiscences of his early life; extracts by Sir Henry Wellcome from the journals 1875–1905; and a 'List of journals, account books and other memorandum books of Arthur Wellington Clah', with brief notes by Wellcome on the development of writing and culture.

72 items. var. sizes. Port Simpson, B.C., Vancouver, & Victoria, Canada; New Metlakahtla, Alaska, U.S.A. [&c.], 1859–*c.* 1920.

69 bound and unbound note-books 1859–1910; also typescripts, MS extracts and notes.

Clah, one of the earliest converts made by William Duncan [1832–1918] of the

Clah or Damaks

Number and Count by every years.
and when Clah first born in the May . 1831
first time and all hudsons bay Men Building
New fort . a Nass River . are in that time
and when all the Tsimshens done working
Small fishs about in the Summer . on the same
Month and all the people gone Back a the
Same place . this place Called is name Meddleakhalla
and another time . an all Tsimshens Moving again
in one Day . an in the Same Month . and in the
Same Day about Noon . and my feather an my mother
going Shore thee waited another an in the bay thes
4 miles from medlakhalla
Bay also was Name Kaelleca-Con that place I
was Born . in the Same Day . and in the Same
Month . in May . 1831

and the Same year . Hudsons bay Men builting
New feort a Nass River . in May . 1831
And feort. ~~thing ~~ Stayed a Nass
River about . 3 . years . an Moving again
feort . Simpson . Clquahlahmas .
builting New feort . in July . 1834 .

Figure 18. CLAH, Arthur Wellington. *Journals, account-books and note-books by a Tsimshian Indian.* Port Simpson, B.C., Canada, [&c.], 1859–*c.*1920. (p. 1). **(WMS. Amer. 140(1–72))**

Church Missionary Society after his arrival in 1857 at Port Simpson, became a pupil-teacher, trader and preacher and was closely associated with Duncan whose life he saved from his unconverted fellow tribesmen. He became a prominent member of the Metlakahtla Settlement *c.* 15 miles to the south of Port Simpson set up by Duncan in 1862 and transferred to New Metlakahtla, Alaska, in 1887; and like Sir Henry Wellcome [1853–1936], an outstanding benefactor of the Metlakahtlans, was active in pressing his people's land-claims against the Canadian government.

The journal series was intended to be a history of his people: it includes daily weather-notes, regular pious interjections, and much sporadic material on his life and work, on epidemics, residual potlatch ceremonies, Indian relations with the white man, and on land-claims. [See Arctander (1909), pp. 57, 58 (portrait of Clah facing), 122–123, 133–134; Swanton (1968), pp. 543, 606–607; and Wellcome (1887), pp. 9, 13, 50–51; and entry under WELLINGTON].

Purchased 1911 (300700) from Clah's family after his death.

WMS. Amer. 140(1–72).

Figure 18.

CRAWFORD, John [1746–1813]

To the Right Honourable the Lords Commissioners of his Majesty's Treasury. The Memorial of John Crawford M:D Chief Surgeon of the Colony of Demerary.

3 ll.　38.5 × 24 cm.　London, [1795].

Unbound.

Holograph, unsigned.

A trenchant memorandum proposing, *inter alia*: a better site for the military hospital and barracks at Demerara [Georgetown]; loose, white, light clothing and headgear for the troops; and a physic garden in Essequibo.

Crawford, brother of Adair Crawford, F.R.S. [1748–95] took his medical degrees at St. Andrew's (1791) and at Leyden (1794). In 1790 he was appointed Surgeon-Major to the Colony of Demerara [Guyana] by the Dutch Government, which ill-health forced him to leave in 1794. After a brief period in Europe he arrived in Baltimore in 1796 where he remained as practising physician, reformer, founder of societies, and active Freemason. A man of unusual vigour, originality and learning, he enjoyed a long correspondence with Benjamin Rush, introduced vaccination to Baltimore in 1800, and promoted the unpopular theory of *contagium vivum*. His library is preserved in the Medical Library of the University of Maryland. [*See* Wilson (1942); Doetsch (1964)].

Guerra Collection.

WMS. Amer. 98.

CURSO

Curso teórico y Práctico sobre el arte de la Tintoreria.

4 ll.   27.5 × 23 cm.   [Mexico, *c.* 1850].

Unbound; last leaf damaged.

Brief notes on natural and chemical dyestuffs, of which cochineal was locally the most important.

León Collection.

WMS. Amer. 134.

CURVO SEMMEDO, João [1635–1719]

[Secretos medicos, y chirurgicos, &c.].

8 ll., pp. 269 [i.e. 250].   20 × 15 cm.   [?Mexico, *c.* 1750].

Contemporary leather binding, in modern slip-case.

In the same fine hand throughout, probably by a Religious.

Miscellaneous remedies drawn from printed and other sources. The first 8 leaves provide a subject index to the 573 numbered remedies; pp. 1–45 copy, with omissions and additions, pp. 1–75 of J. Curvo Semmedo, *Secretos medicos*, trans. T. Cortijo Herraiz, Madrid, B. Peralta, 1731 (or perhaps a later edition), giving medical receipts in alphabetical order; the remaining leaves comprise a miscellany of remedies. Pp. 69–74 copy notes on, and a list of, symptoms benefited by the powder of G. Chiaramonte, [*Tratado de la admirable facultad y efectos de los polvos, ó elixir vitae*, Madrid, A. Gonzalez de Reyes, 1706 (originally published in Genoa, 1628)].

Guerra Collection.

WMS. Amer. 22.

DECOCCION

[Begins:] La decoccion, ó cocim[ien]to de el Manungal bebido es contra las picaduras de todos los animales benenosos [&c.].

2 ll.   21 × 16 cm.   [?The Philippines, *c.*1750].

Bound.

Therapeutic uses of Manungal, the vernacular name given in the Philippines to *Samandura* Baill. (*Quassia* L.), (Simaroubaceae).

Guerra Collection.

WMS. Amer. 10.

DIAS, José

Tardes anatomicas Escritas ... en el año de 1800 á 24 de Enero. [Followed by:] Farmacopea Quirurgica de Londres .... Traducida del Ingles por ... Casimiro Gomez Ortega .... Madrid MDCCXCVII. En la Imprenta de la Viuda de D. Joaquin Ibarra, con licencia.

8 ll. (last bl.), 1 l., pp. 2, 157 (= 155).   20.5 × 14.5 cm.   [?Mexico, *c.*1800].

Original leather and paper binding.

Two MSS in different hands.

Ll. 1–8, *Tardes anatómicas*; thereafter, *Pharmacopea quirúrgica*.

The first MS., by an author otherwise unknown, is in catechetical form. The second MS copies the translation by C. Gómez Ortega of *Pharmacopoeia chirurgica* [?by William Houlston (see main Wellcome catalogue of printed books)], 3 ed., London, G.G. & J. Robinson, 1795, published in Madrid in 1797 [Palau 104233]; it adds a translator's preface, a concordance of old and new chemical nomenclature, and an alphabetical list of the remedies described.

Gómez Ortega [1740–1801] was *Alcalde examinador* of the Protofarmaceuticato 1780–99, was appointed *Boticario mayor* and *Médico de cámara*, and belonged to numerous national and foreign learned Societies. He produced more than 40 scientific, literary and translated works, and was largely responsible for organising the Spanish natural history expeditions to the Americas in the late 18th century. [See Roldán y Guerrero (1956)].

León Collection.

WMS. Amer. 85.

DYER, Jairo R.

Alumno S[eño]r Jairo R. Dyer. Curso de 1891, 2° año.

8 ll.   20 × 12.5 cm.   Mexico, 1892.

Unbound.

Signed and dated 7 March 1892.

Detailed holograph case report on a male patient aged 22 admitted to the Hospital Juárez on 21 June 1891 with a stab wound involving the pericardium and pleural cavity. He was discharged cured on 15 February 1892.

León Collection.

WMS. Amer. 129.

EGEA Y GALINDO, Ricardo [d. 1893]

Memoria sobre el Tetános y ensayo crítico de los tratam[iento]s empleados.

1 l., ff. 31.   21 × 13.5 cm.   Mazatlán, Sinaloa, Mexico, 1871.

Unbound.

Signed, with *rúbrica*, and dated 27 April 1871.

The paper, apparently unpublished, describes the types, causes, and symptoms of tetanus, and its duration, prognosis and treatment. In particular it discusses the therapeutic value of opium, chloroform, chloral and alcohol, and concludes that alcohol is the preferred remedy in the contemporary state of medicine.

The author trained in Paris (1869) and in Mexico, and joined the Academia Nacional de Medicina de México in 1872; among his official appointments he was physician to the Hospital Juárez and a Deputy of the Union Congress. He contributed papers to the *Gaceta Médica de México* 1872–91, and published a number of monographs on diverse medical topics. A notice of his death appeared in the *Gaceta Médica de México*, 1893, *29* (6), 201.

León Collection.

WMS. Amer. 123.

EMPIRISMO

Empirismo. Metodo curativo p[ar]a el colera morbo practicado en la micion del Furlon, en la q[ue] comenso dicha enfermedad el 21 de Junio [&c.].

2 ll.   21 × 15.5 cm.   Puebla, Mexico, 1833.

Unbound.

Dated 15 August 1833.

l. 1ʳ: According to a note at the bottom, this page was copied from a reprint made at Leona Vicario from instructions originally printed at Monterrey. Lime-water is the principal ingredient of the internal remedy.

l. 1ᵛ &

l. 2ʳ⁺ᵛ: *Curacion otra de Aguas Cali[en]tes y Zacatecas*. These two remedies were published (in another form) in a reprint of four articles from various journals by *El Reformador*, [Toluca, 1833], [see Guerra (Icon.) 813]; a copy of which is in the Wellcome Institute Library. The reprint was issued free for the benefit of the poor.

Guerra Collection.

WMS. Amer. 56.

ENCINAS, Juan José de

Razon de los Arboles Frutales assi de Castilla como de los Silbestres que produce esta Jurisdición de mi Cargo como de los demas que sirben para la Carpinteria todos por sus nombres como también los que son medisinales como las rayzes q[u]e en d[ic]ha Jurisdición [&c.].

7 ll.   31 × 21 cm.   Mescaltitan, Mexico, 1783.

Bound.

Signed, with *rúbrica*, and dated 2 December 1783.

Official return by the *Theniente de justicia mayor* of the Hacienda of Mescaltitan in response to an enquiry set up by the Intendant; it describes the therapeutic uses of 34 local plants.

Guerra Collection.

WMS. Amer. 66.

ESCAYOLA, Gaspar

Tratamiento del Colera Morbus.

Ff. viii–ix (i.e. 2 ll.).   21.5 × 15.5 cm.   [?Amozoc de Mota, Puebla, Mexico], 1833.
Unbound.

A contemporary copy of the broadside by G. Escayola, *Tratamiento del colera-morbus en Campeche*, Campeche, J.J. Corrales, 1833 [see Guerra (Icon.) 761], a copy of which is in the Wellcome Institute Library. It describes the symptoms of cholera, methods of treatment, and tabulates 4 receipts at the end.

In the same hand and from the same collection of remedies as WMSS. Amer. 47 [?CARDOSO], 48 [NOMBRE], & 54 [CARDOSO] with which it was originally bound; and possibly associated with one leaf of WMS. Amer. 15 [RECETAS]. Perhaps from the remedy book of an *hacienda*.

Guerra Collection.

WMS. Amer. 55.

FERRER ESPEJO Y CIENFUEGOS, José [1800–81]

Lecciones de obstetricia, dadas oralmente para curso de segundo año.

2 ll., ff.183 (last 6 ff. bl.), 1 bl. l.   20.5 × 13.5 cm.   Mexico, 1854.
Disbound.

Portrait of the author inserted.

Inscribed, "Del uso de María Magdelena Caballero" [de Flores], a midwife student in the course taught intermittently by Ferrer Espejo at the Escuela de Medicine of Mexico from 1838.

A much respected figure, Ferrer Espejo filled many temporary chairs in medicine, ending his life as *propietario* of the Chair of Obstetrics; he is said by Porrúa (1964–66) to have translated P. Garnot, *Leçons élémentaires sur l'art des accouchements*, Paris, 1832 (2 ed., 1834). The biography in León (1910) pp. 266–268 confirms that he undertook an obstetrical translation from Garnot, on which this MS may be based. An obituary appears in *La Escuela de Medicina* (*Méx.*), 1880–81, 2, 171.

León Collection.

WMS. Amer. 122.

FLORES, José Felipe [1751–1824]

Relacion del Balsamo, y del Copalchi.

6 ll.   29.5 × 20.5 cm.   Guatemala, 1791.

Signed, with *rúbrica*; and dated 24 September 1791.

A clerk's copy of a detailed return providing a botanical description of Balsam of Peru, [*Myroxylon pereirae* (Leguminosae)], indicating its geographical distribution and climatic preferences, and describing three simple but effective Indian methods of gathering resin from different parts of the tree. Flores recommends the south coasts of Spain for growing both the balsam and *copalchi* trees. He regards the bark of the *copalchi* tree [*Coutarea latiflora*, or *Exostemma caribaeum*, both of the Rubiaceae] as a febrifuge as efficacious as cinchona. Noriega (1902) and Landa (1915) discuss the synonyms of *copalchi* and its therapeutic value. [For biographical references to Flores see M.56].

Guerra Collection.

WMS. Amer. 46.

FREZIER, Amedée François [1682–1773]

Essay d'un traité des bois usuels que produit naturellement L'isle de St. Domingue dans La partie qu'occupe La Colonie francoise par M. Frezier. Le MS m'a ete communiqué par M. Bernard de Jussieu.

2 ll., pp. 65, 8 ll. (last 6 ll. bl., & part of final leaf removed).   23.5 × 18.5 cm. [?Paris, *c.*1755].

Original boards.

The first 2 leaves comprise the index; the first 2 pages, the introduction; pp. 3–65, the text; p. 65v & the following 2 leaves list: (a) plants found in the "Memoire de M. Fauconnier" [probably unpublished] and not referred to in the present text, (b) Frézier's sources, and (c) a list of plants of Saint Domingue cited in J.D. Chevalier [*c.* 1700–1770], *Lettre à De Jean: I. Sur les maladies de St. Domingue. II. Sur les plantes de la même île* [*&c.*], Paris, Durand, 1752, including further plants taken from a manuscript *Livre des simples de l'Amerique* by André Minguet, 1713, referred to in Chevalier's second letter. Nine loose leaves of notes follow, primarily indexes of plants of Saint Domingue taken from diverse sources.

Copy of an attempt by Frézier to correlate material on the economic trees of Saint Domingue. Additional material is appended to each entry from Frézier's original notes and from an unidentified botanist named Fauconnier. Though the MS is primarily concerned with the durability of woods and their suitability for structural use, some plants of medicinal value are described.

Frézier, a French military engineer of British descent, was first sent by Louis XIV on a mission to Peru and Chile 1712–14 to report on navigation; his account of his visit, first published in Paris in 1716, elicited sharp criticism of plagiarism from the priest-scientist Louis Feuillée who had already visited the same area 1707–12, and who published his *Journal des observations physiques*, 2 vols., Paris, in 1714. [See P.23].

Frézier was stationed as chief military engineer in Saint Domingue 1719–25; the present MS, apparently unpublished either by Frézier or by Jussieu, reflects the interest in descriptive and economic botany revealed by his earlier work in S. America. A member of the Académie Royale de la Marine since its first foundation in 1752, Frézier published monographs and papers on a wide variety of topics.

Purchased 1929 (51015).

WMS. Amer. 104.

GALISTEO Y XIORRO, Juan

Conclución Médica. Es peligroso á los Jovenes acostarse con los viejos. [Followed by:] Obserbaciones sobre el hierro que se encuentra en la sangre de la mayor parte de los animales.

6 ll.   20.5 × 16cm.   [?Mexico, *c.* 1757].

Bound.

A note above the title records the source as J. Galisteo, *Diario philosophico, medico, chirurgico* [&c.], [Vol. I, nos. 1–8], Madrid, A. Perez de Soto, 1757, a copy of which is in the Wellcome Institute Library. Both pieces are exactly transcribed from núm. 2 of the journal.

The first extract [ll. 1ʳ–5ʳ] agrees with J.N. Millin de la Couvrealt (who qualified as physician in Paris 1752–54) that though the ancient practice of living and lying with the young will rejuvenate the old through "affinity of bodies", the practice will, by the same token, only undermine the health of the young.

The second extract [ll. 5ʳ–6ᵛ] refers to observations made by J.F. Henkel [1679–1744] and experiments made by others on the presence of iron in the ashes of plants and in the red corpuscles of mammals and man; it notes the beneficial effect of the oral administration of iron compounds.

Juan Galisteo and his relation Felix Galisteo y Xiorro each translated a number of important contemporary French medical treatises into Spanish; his *Diario* stimulated other interest in Mexico. [See M.58].

Guerra Collection.

WMS. Amer. 12.

GARCIA, Crescencio

Cacaloxochitl [&c.].

4 items [i.e. 10 ll.]. 26.5 × 21 cm. & 22 × 17 cm. Cotija, Michoacán, Mexico, 1870–77.

Four signed essays on indigenous materia medica, including botanical descriptions and therapeutic uses, as follows:—

(i) Cacaloxochitl [i.e., *Plumeria rubra* (Apocinaceae), (Frangipani)]. 2 ll., January 1870.

(ii) Zumquez de Mexico [i.e., a species of *Rhus* (Anacardiaceae), (Sumach)]. 1 l., July 1875.

(iii) Araceas Mexicanas [apparently the rhizomes of *Maranta arundinacea*, (Marantaceae), (Arrowroot)]. 1 l., August 1875.

(iv) Cebollin (Veratrum Viride) [i.e., *Veratrum viride* (Liliaceae), (Green hellebore)]. 6 ll. (col. botanical drawing on l.2ʳ.). June 1877.

Leaf 1ᵛ and ll. 5ʳ–6ᵛ of item (iv) constitute a later addition on *Veratrum viride* in another hand taken verbatim from a translation (Paris 1860) of the work by the early U.S. laryngologist H. Green, *Selections from favorite prescriptions of living American practitioners*, New York, Wiley & Halsted, 1858 (at pp. 90–95), a copy of which is in the Wellcome Institute Library. [See the anecdotal but interesting Rhame (1957) on W.C. Norwood [1806–84] and his tincture of *Veratrum viride*, whose name, with those of the U.S. physicians Tully and C.K. Winston, is referred to in both texts].

Though León (1895), no. 292 had little confidence in the botanical work of García, both he (*ibid.*) and Guerra (1950), nos. 131–138, 2380–2394, shew him to have published a remarkable number of monographs and papers in this field. Items (ii) and (iii) of the present MSS were printed in *El Estudio* (*Puebla*), 1875, *1*, 245–248, a copy of which is in the Wellcome Institute Library.

León Collection.

WMS. Amer. 130.

GARCIA JOVE Y CAPELON, José Ignacio [d. 1823]

Formulario de los Medicos ditado p[o]r Dn. Joseph Ignacio García, y Jove Dr. y M[aest]ro y precidente del R[ea]l Tribunal del Proto-medicato de esta Ciudad Mexicana.

Pp.226.   15 × 10.5 cm.   Mexico, *c.*1795[–1838].

Original limp leather binding, in modern slip-case.

Further receipts added in other hands, the last dated 1838. Index of symptoms, pp. 223–226. Primarily receipts drawn from the European pharmocopoeias; a few include indigenous materials, e.g. pulque, aguamiel de maguey.

García Jove was President of the Protomedicato throughout the revolutionary era from 1795 until his death. [See M.59].

Guerra Collection.

WMS. Amer. 34.

GAVILAN, Miguel [Perez]

Recetario del Lazareto de Medicina de Caridad en que se asientan las Medicinas q[ue] ordena su Medico [&c.].

1 l., ff.4, 3 bl. ll.   20 × 14.5 cm.   Mexico, 1813.

Contemporary limp leather.

4 leaves abstracted from the prescription book for 15–30 July 1813; each daily set of entries is signed, with *rúbrica*. A running total of cost of the drugs ends each page. Gavilan was admitted as physician by the Protomedicato on 13 September 1816. [See Protomedicato (1829)].

Purchased from Dr. Francisco Guerra 1967 (314035).

WMS. Amer. 112.

GILIJ, Felipe Salvador [1721–89]

Remedios singulares usado por los Misioneros de tierra firme, q[u]e se allan en el Apendice 1°. de la H[istori]a del Orinoco del Abate Felipe Salvador Gilij. tomo 3° en Roma año 1782.

3 ll.   21.5 × 15.5 cm.   [?Mexico, c.1785].

Bound.

A translation and paraphrase from the Italian of the former Jesuit missionary Gilij (his name is variously spelt), *Saggio di storia americana*, 4 vols., Rome, 1780–84 (vol. 3, pp. 214–217, and paraphrased from vol. 2, pp. 388–389).

The extract describes indigenous vegetable remedies for gangrene, certain skin conditions, burns, measles and smallpox, dysentery, delayed afterbirth, and fevers; it ends by describing antidotes for poisoning by *curare* quoted by Gilij from the *Annual Register for 1769* (Dublin ed., 1773, at p. 522).

Guerra Collection.

WMS. Amer. 8.

GONZALES, Maria [A]polonia

[Begins:] Maria Polonia Gonzales Viuda de Juan Lorenzo, vezina del Puebla de Santiago Molina Puesta a los pies de Vm. [&c.].

2 ll.   30.5 × 21.5 cm.   Santiago Molino, [?Mexico], *c.* 1800.

Bound.

Unsigned.

Accuses Micaela Maria Urbina of witchcraft and of procuring the deaths of some 8 individuals by this and by herbal means.

Guerra Collection.

WMS. Amer. 75.

GONZALEZ MENDOZA, José Eleuterio [1813–88]

Los médicos y las enfermedades de Monterrey.

1 l., ff.25, 52 ll. (bl., exc. l.74^v).   18.5 × 12.5 cm.   Monterrey, Nuevo León, Mexico, 1881.

Original green ¼ leather and boards.

Holograph MS with presentation inscription on first leaf, 'A mi muy querido discípulo y amigo el Dr. Juan de Dios Treviño. Monterey Marzo 8 de 1881'; signed, with *rúbrica*.

F. 2^r–f. 7^r: Los médicos de Monterrey.
F. 8^r–f. 17^r: Las enfermedades de Monterrey.
F.18^r–f. 25^v: [Lists of physicians and pharmacists practising in Monterrey before and after the foundation of the Escuela de Medicina in 1859, and lists of staff and graduates of the School before and after its separation from the Colegio Civil in 1877].

The first two sections provide detailed accounts of major events in the medical life of Monterrey.

The text has been transcribed, with full biographical and bibliographical commentaries by Guerra (1968).

Gonzalitos enjoyed an outstanding medical career in Monterrey as Director (and Professor of anatomy, surgery, and obstetrics) of the combined Colegio Civil and

Escuela de Medicina 1859–77 and thereafter as Director of the separated Escuela de Medicina. His efforts were responsible for the foundation of the Hospital Civil in 1860. As politician, he was elected Deputy to the State Congress of Nuevo León, and twice became its Governor. A man of wide interests and capabilities, he wrote extensively on medicine, medical history, local and national history, statistics and botany. His *Obras completas*, (5 vols. in 7), were published in Monterrey 1885–87.

León Collection.

WMS. Amer. 83.

GONZALEZ URUEÑA, Juan Manuel [1802–54]

Discurso y relación en la que El Catedrático jubilado de Medicina, C. Juan Manuel Gonzalez Urueña dá cuenta del estado que guarda El Establecimiento Médico-quirúrgico de Michoacán y de la instruccion que sus alumnos adquirieron en el curso que concluyó el dia 30 de Noviembre de 1.844.

30 ll.   21.5 × 16cm.   Morelia, Michoacán, Mexico, 1844.

Contemporary gold-tooled leather binding.

A scribal copy of a prize-giving speech at the close of the course for 1842–44. González Urueña expatiates on the value of medicine and physician to society, recounts the history of the School of Medicine, records the numbers of students and the names of the present *cursantes*, and ends by attacking contemporary medical charlatanism.

Born in Michoacán of Spanish parents he became a pupil of Luis Montaña [1755–1820] and Casimiro Liceaga [1792–1855] in Mexico City, where he qualified as physician in 1822. He set up the first school of medicine in Morelia in 1830, abolished by the Union Government in 1852. Several times Deputy to the State Congress of Michoacán, three times Governor of the State, and three times Deputy to the Union Congress, he earned the enmity of Santa-Anna, and died on his way into exile.

His work appeared in both medical and lay periodicals, and his monographs include work on cholera, diabetes, hydropathy, a textbook on anatomy and a manual on the treatment of smallpox, besides further unpublished medical material and translations from the comedies of Mme. de Genlis.

León Collection.

WMS. Amer. 84.

GORMAN, Miguel [1736/49–1819]

Oratio Nuncupatoria Pro Felici Auguratione Tribunalis Proto-Medicatus Habita in Inclytissima Bonaerensi Civitate Anno Domini MDCCCLXXX.

22 ll. (ll. 20 & 21 bl.).   20.5 × 15 cm.   Buenos Aires, 1780.

Bound.

A scribal copy of the Latin oration delivered at the inauguration of the Protomedicato of Buenos Aires on 17 August 1780 of which Gorman had been appointed President. He points out the importance of establishing the institution and indicates the antiquity and honour of the medical profession from remote classical times. [See Canton (1921), *1*, pp. 201–234, on the early history of the Protomedicato in Buenos Aires; and see A.2 for references to Gorman's life].

Guerra Collection.

WMS. Amer. 78.

GRACIDA Y BERNAL, José Timoteo María de [1760?–1815] *and others*

Accounts, and chemical and pharmacological receipts in Spanish and Latin, interspersed with verses in Spanish.

67 ll.   29.5 × 20.5 cm.   Taxco, Guerrero; & City of Mexico, 1782–1821.

The papers are loose, or loosely bound in the original leather wrapper with further annotations on the pasted-down end-papers; some leaves are heavily stained.

In various hands, some in holograph, and several signed by Gracida, with *rúbricas*.

The chemical receipts include those for making colours, dyes, inks, lacquers, and preparations for gilding different surfaces; the pharmacological receipts are copied from a variety of European sources including João Curvo Semmedo [1635–1719]:—

l. 1:   Accounts for 1782 of Gracida's pharmacy in Taxco.

ll. 2–8:   Medical receipts copied from João Curvo Semmedo.

ll. 9–25: "Arcana quedam magna, et maxime uttilia", miscellaneous chemical receipts in Latin and Spanish.

ll. 26–51: "Apuntes de varias medicinas particulares".

ll. 52–53: "Canto funebre" on the death of the son of the Conde de Santiago.

ll. 54–56: Minor accounts for 1816; and accounts for 1807 for the *rancho* of Batansito.

l. 57: Accounts for 1808–14 of fees received by Gracida for examinations conducted in his capacity as a member of the Protomedicato.

ll. 58–67: Miscellaneous accounts and notes for 1782–1815, some relating to the *rancho* of Batansito.

Born in Oaxaca, Gracida received his medical doctorate from the University of Mexico in 1784, and in 1789 won the chair of anatomy and surgery which he held until 1812 when he became *Catedrático de vísperas de medicina*. According to l. 57^r of the present MS he took office as *Protomédico de gracia* in 1808 and as *Protomédico decano* in 1813. [See Flores (1886–88), 2, p. 100; and see entry under NEW SPAIN, Laws, statutes, &c. (1808)].

Guerra Collection.

WMS. Amer. 100.

HERRARTE, Mariano José de

A return describing plants of medicinal value used by the Indians of Guatemala.

12 ll.   30 × 20.5 cm.   Guatemala, 1784.

Bound; signed, with *rúbrica*, and dated 5 February 1784; with counter-rubrication by the President and Captain-General dated 21 February.

Martínez Durán (1964) p. 344 comments that this Recollect friar made the only return from Guatemala in response to the *Real Cédula* of 14 March 1783 requesting samples of useful plants, and information on them.

After making it clear that his private interest in medicinal plants has only been pursued within the capital city, and after confirming that he has there found none of the local flora in José Quer, *Flora española*, 4 vols., Madrid, J. Ibarra, 1762[–64], Herrarte describes some 36 plant and animal remedies used by the Indians, some of them marvellous, and others more matter-of-fact.

Guerra Collection.

WMS. Amer. 40.

HINCAPIE MELENDEZ Y MAYEN, Cristóbal de [1689–1772] *and others*

Chemical, astrological, pharmacological and personal memoranda in Spanish and Latin, with index, some in holograph.

Pp.257 (=264), 8 ll.   15 × 10.5 cm.   Antigua, Guatemala, 1745–73.

Original vellum binding.

The title-page, pp. 165–166, 202–203, and 2 leaves after p. 257 are wanting. The pagination is irregular.

Pp. 138–257 are in holograph.

Pp. 1–35: 'De la definición, divisio, Sugeto, y principio de la chimica.'

Pp. 37–41: 'Signa, quae inveniri solent in regnis animali, minerali, et vegetali.'

Pp. 42–44: blank.

Pp. 45–51: 'Explicacion de las horas Planetarias.'

Pp. 52–54: blank.

Pp. 55–135: 'Nonnullae receptiones ad plura, ut in eis continetur utiles .... Tam
            Chimicae, quam Galenicae.'

Pp. 133 [irreg.]—191: Miscellaneous chemical and pharmacological receipts [pp.
            182–185 on the harvesting of pulque].

Pp. 192–257: Miscellaneous family, local, and ecclesiastical memoranda, most of
            which are dated, including a description of the earthquake of 1751; a
            note on the expulsion of the Jesuits; and diagnostic notes on the pulse.

Hincapié received his medical bacchalaureate from the University de San Carlos de Guatemala in 1723, the third to do so since its inauguration in 1681. He was appointed *Protomédico general* in 1734, and *Protomédico extraordinario* in 1750 with the task of writing a natural history of Guatemala. He ran a printing press 1739–48. According to Martínez Durán (1964) pp. 247–256, Hincapié was both idle and unlucky; the present MS may well be his only surviving work of any length.

Particulars of acquisition not known.

WMS. Amer. 79.

Figure 19.

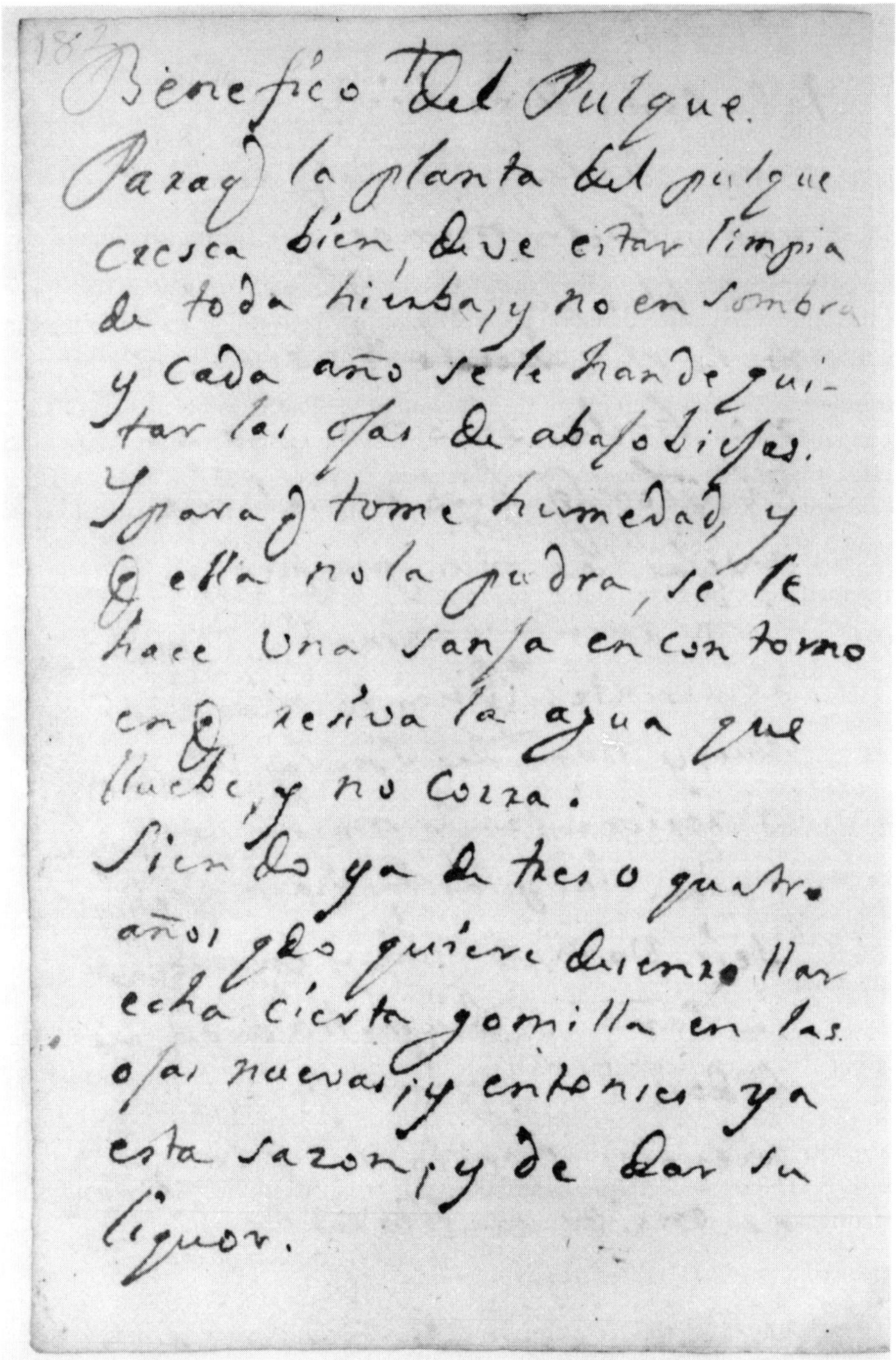

Beneficio del Pulque.

Para q la planta del pulque
cresca bien, deve estar limpia
de toda hierba, y no en sombra
y cada año se le han de qui-
tar las ojas de abajo secas.
Y para q tome humedad, y
q ella no la pierda, se le
hace una sanja en contorno
en q reciva la agua que
llueve, y no corra.
Siendo ya de tres o quatro
años q se quiere desenrollar
echa cierta gomilla en las
ojas nuevas, y entonces ya
esta sazon, y de dar su
liquor.

Figure 19. HINCAPIE MELENDEZ Y MAYEN, Cristóbal de, *and others. Chemical, astrological, pharmacological and personal memoranda.* Antigua, Guatemala, 1745–73. (p. 182). **(WMS. Amer. 79)**

HOLMES, Edward Morell [1843–1930]

Report on the cause of the frosted surface, or, Givre on Vanilla.

Ff. 15; 5 [typescript].   20 × 16.5; 26 × 20.5 cm.   [London], 1914.

Unbound.

Holograph draft (on rectos only) with a typed transcript, apparently unpublished.

The paper regards the presence of the glucoside vanillin as dependent on the ripeness of the pod when gathered and on the treatment to which it is afterwards subjected; contemporary methods of gathering and curing are described.

Holmes was, *inter alia*, Curator of the Museum of the Pharmaceutical Society 1872–1922, and author of many papers on botany and the materia medica. Many of his drafts, pamphlets, and books were purchased in April 1931 (57801–58030) or presented by his widow in 1935 (89200). [For an obituary see *Pharmaceutical Journal*, 1930, 4 ser., *71*, 284–286].

Presented 1935 by Mrs. Holmes (89200).

WMS. Amer. 145.

HOLMES, Edward Morell [1843–1930]

The Botany of the new U[nited] S[tates] P[harmacopoeia].

Ff. 19.   18.5 × 12.5 cm.   [London, 1916].

Unbound.

Holograph draft (on rectos only), wanting f.10 and *c.* 4 leaves at the end, published with little alteration under the above title in *Pharmaceutical Journal*, 1916, 4 ser., *43*, 484–485.

The paper, adding a detailed list of examples, regards the botanical nomenclature of the U.S. Phamacopoeia (presumably 9 ed., 1916) as unnecessarily confusing, pedantic, and on occasion inaccurate.

Presented 1935 by Mrs. Holmes (89200).

WMS. Amer. 146.

HOLMES, Edward Morell [1843–1930]

[Notes for a] Report on Brazilian Drugs [with draft covering letter and rough notes].

Ff.63 (some bl.); 39.   20 × 16; 20 × 12.5 cm.   Sevenoaks, Kent, England, 1917.

Unbound.

A holograph draft report, carried out for Messrs. Coley and Wilbraham, which attempts identification of some 50 items of materia medica forwarded for examination and adds comments from the literature on their method of use and on their medicinal or other commercial value.

Presented 1935 by Mrs. Holmes (89200).

WMS. Amer. 147.

HOLMES, Edward Morell [1843–1930]

Copy [of a] Report on Yagé.

Ff.8.   23 × 15 cm.   [London, 1927].

Unbound.

Holograph draft (on rectos only), published with little alteration as 'Note on Yagé', *Pharmaceutical Journal*, 1927, 4 ser., *65*, 111–112.

The writer refers to a conversation initiated by Sir H. Rider Haggard [1856–1925] on a South American drug 'causing clairvoyant and telepathic effects', to the identification of the drug, and to the writer's attempts at trial with a tincture prepared by W.H. Martindale [1875?–1933] on 'some of our leading scientific Spiritualists . . . including Sir A. Conan Doyle, Professor [Sir] Oliver Lodge, & Sir [W.] F. Barrett.' The author, aware of difficulties of identification and nomenclature, describes indigenous methods of preparation, and refers to a full account of the drug by A. Rouhier in *Bulletin des Sciences Pharmacologiques*, 1926, *33*, 252–261, and to South American work on it. [See Martindale (1977), p. 883 for a succinct account of the alkaloidal relationship of *yagé* (Colombia), with *caapi* (Brazil and Colombia), and with the better known *ayahuasca* (Ecuador, Peru and Bolivia)].

Purchased in April 1931 (57888B).

WMS. Amer. 148.

IBARRA, [?] Manuel

Receta y modo de hacer el Azeyte especifico q[u]e el Dr. Ibarra ha descuvierto, cuyas virtudes son tantas q[u]e parecen increibles, pero la experiencia acredita sus admirables virtudes.

1 l.   29.5 × 20.5 cm.   [?Mexico, *c.* 1785].

Bound.

Part of a receipt (composed of olive oil, Gum Euphorbium [*Euphorbia resinifera*], white wine, onions, rue, saffron, cloves, and black pepper) whose action when applied or rubbed in warm was claimed to counteract cold stomachs, painful joints, obstructions, and related conditions.

A Manuel Ibarra is listed in Protomedicato (1829) as examined and approved as *Profesor de farmacia* on 8 October 1781.

Guerra Collection.

WMS. Amer. 61.

JAMAICA MERCHANT

Trade notes and general memoranda by a merchant captain trading to Jamaica, written on extra fly-leaves and interleavings of a copy of James Bowker, *Kalendarium . . . 1672*, London, A. Clark, 1672.

64 ll.   8vo.   14.5 × 9.5 cm.   Jamaica, 1672.

Original sheep binding with flap and tie.

The two earliest dated entries are for 12th March 1671 [O.S.]. The title-page and text of the Almanack are printed in red and black. The printed text includes a crude woodcut 'The Dominion of the Moon in Mans Body'. The MS notes include a list of the crew, notes on the commodities traded, and notes on relations with the Spanish from whom Jamaica had been seized (1655) and over which British sovereignty had been recently established by the Treaty of Madrid (1670).

The MS is described by K.E.N. Ingram, *A bibliographical survey of the sources of Jamaican history, 1655–1838, with particular reference to manuscript sources*, 2 vols., University of London M. Phil. Thesis (Library), 1970, vol. 2, pp. 899–900.

Particulars of acquisition not known (41767).

WMS. Amer. 107.   *Figure 20.*

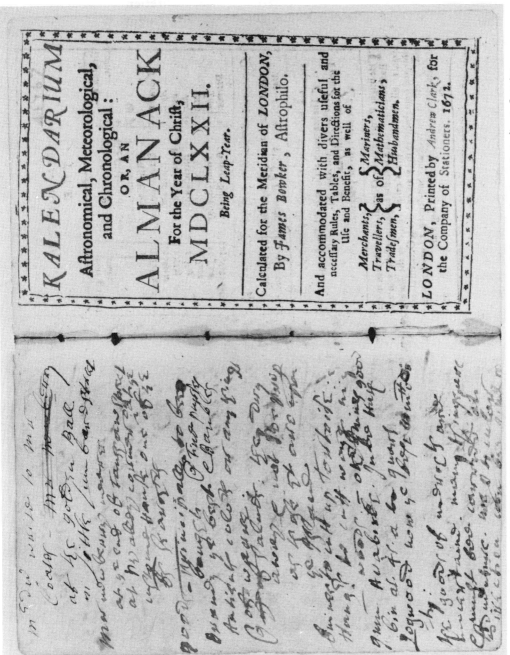

Figure 20. JAMAICA MERCHANT. *Trade notes and general memoranda by a merchant captain trading to Jamaica. Jamaica, 1672.* (**WMS. Amer. 107**)

LAMOIGNON DE MALESHERBES, Chrétien Guillaume de [1721–94] *and* FOUGEROUX DE BONDAROY, Auguste Denis [1732–89]

Extrait d'un Manuscrit de M. De Malesherbes sur les plantes D'amerique avec quelques observations de M. Fougeroux de Bondaroy.

101 ll.   21 × 15.5 cm.   Paris, 1785.

19th cent. ½ morocco; margins slightly cropped.

In several hands; l. 1, ll. 4–23, in the hand of the mineralogist François Pierre Nicolas Gillet de Laumont [1747–1834].

L. 1 records in detail how the original MS by Lamoignon de Malesherbes, *Observations sur quelques arbres et plantes d'Amerique qui meritent d'etre employées en europe, pour des usages plus importans que l'ornement des jardins*, the result of over 30 years work, came to be passed to Gillet de Laumont by the botanist, agronomist, geologist and archaeologist Fougeroux de Bondaroy.

L. 2 comprises the covering letter dated 9th June 1785 in the hand of Fougeroux de Bondaroy allowing Gillet de Laumont to make a copy of the Malesherbes MS.

The plants described are less of medical than of general botanical and economic interest.

Lamoignon de Malesherbes, lawyer, statesman and minister, later acted as counsel for the defence of Louis XVI; all three men associated with the document were members of the Académie des Sciences, with strong interests in botany and agriculture.

Phillipps MS. No. 11799.

Purchased at Sotheby's 24.6.1919 (41879).

WMS. Amer. 125.

LEMOS MARTINEZ, Ignacio Xavier de [1722–77]

A report on the mental condition of Juan José [Mathias] de la Peña y Brizuela.

14 ll.   21 × 15.5 cm.   Mexico, [?1776].

Bound; signed, with *rúbrica*.

The 21 closely-argued paragraphs (possibly a draft), quoting extensively from Paolo Zacchia, *Quaestiones medico-legales*, [9 vols., Rome 1621–61, according to Hirsch

(1935)], argue that Peña y Brizuela should be disqualified by his mental condition from appointment as *Protomédico decano* to which his seniority as member of the faculty would normally have entitled him. Lemos quotes some witnesses by name and clearly describes his condition *como puede testificar todo Mexico.*

Born in Puebla, Lemos was awarded his doctorate in medicine by the University of Mexico in 1764; he was *Catedrático sustituto de prima de medicina* 1769–73, and *Catedrático sustituto de anatomía y cirugía* from 1773 until his death. Peña y Brizuela, born in Mexico, died in 1789; he gained his doctorate in medicine from the same university in 1743 [see Guerra (Icon.) 288, 289, 290], was *Catedrático sustituto de prima de medicina* 1757–60, and held the *Cátedra de vísperas de medicina* from 1776 until his death. Notwithstanding the present report (which bears no sign of receipt by the Protomedicato) Peña y Brizuela died as *Protomédico decano* [see *Gazeta de México,* 1788–89, *3,* p. 225 (20 January 1789)]. Some details of his life are given by Flores (1886–88), *2,* p. 99. Both taught the outstanding clinician, botanist, pharmacologist, and medical reformer Luis José Montaña [1755–1820].

[For commentaries on Zacchia on mental deficiency see Cranefield *and* Federn (1970); and Vallon *and* Genil-Perrin (1912). For Peña y Brizuela see also entry under NEW SPAIN. Real Audiencia (Sala del Crimen)].

Guerra Collection.

WMS. Amer. 9.

LEON, José Eustachio de

Virtudes de la essencia tinturada de el Balsamo Virgen.

2 ll.   31 × 21.5 cm.   Guatemala, *c.* 1770.

Bound.

A copy from a variant of the 2nd printed edition of 1769 whose colophon, evidently an accurate transcript of the printed original, reads 'Reimpresa en Guatemala en la imprenta de Joaquin de Arevalo; impresor de los Tribunales Eclesiasticos, año de 1769' [&c.]. It omits the puff for the apothecary's shop of Francisco Sanches where the tincture could be bought. [See Gt. 15].

Guerra Collection.

WMS. Amer. 63.

LEON, Nicolás [1859–1929]

Scatológica Mexicana.

10ll. [incl. t.p.].   22.5 × 15.5 cm.   [Mexico, *c.*1915].

Bound.

Holograph notes, 17 × 11.5 cm. and smaller, pasted onto the backs of unused coloured plates; rectos only.

Fugitive notes of antiquarian interest on scatalogical remedies drawn from the Badianus MS [Vatican Library, Codex Barberini, Lat. 241] and from 16th and 17th century medical sources printed in Mexico.

The notes were published with a brief introduction by León's contemporary, Demetrio S. García in Mexico (1946), who added a subtitle derived from León's *Escritos varios y publicaciones, 1909–1919, Suplemento Núm. 1*, Mexico, [s.n.], 1919, [item 26B]; copies of both these items are in the Wellcome Institute Library.

Guerra Collection.

WMS. Amer. 1.

LEON, Nicolás [1859–1929]

El eminente clínico internista Dr. Miguel Francisco Jimenez. (Datos para la historia de la medicina en México).

Pp.4.   27.5 × 21 cm.   Mexico, [?1916].

Unbound.

A first draft of preliminary paragraphs, perhaps for his proposed *elogio* on M.F. Jiménez [1813–76], the well-known Mexican clinician and anatomist, which the Academia Nacional de Medicina originally chose León to read on its former President on 24 September 1916. In the event the task was performed by José Terrés using none of the present MS material [see *Gaceta Médica de México*, 1916, *11* (3 ser.), 363–372]. Ramos (1957) has presented a contemporary assessment of Jiménez's achievements as one of a series of papers devoted to the treatment of hepatic abscess.

León Collection.

WMS. Amer. 118.

LIT[I]ASIS

De la litasis.

2 ll.   30 × 21 cm.   [?Mexico, *c*.1820].

Bound.

Method of preparation and administration of potassium bi-carbonate in the treatment of urinary calculi, together with recommendations for diet and general regimen.

Guerra Collection.

WMS. Amer. 60.

LOPEZ, Gregorio [1542–96]

[Tesoro de medicinas, para diversas enfermedades].

Ff. 48.   21 × 15.5 cm.   [Mexico or Spain, *c*.1700].

Original limp vellum cover.

Wanting conjugate ff. 18 & 23.

Further notes on f. 48^v and on the paper lining of lower cover. Note of ownership on the latter "Jph. Alfonzo Pisarr[o] Caballero del Lorden de Santiago", presumably the Viceroy of New Granada [1749–53] of that name.

A copy without title-page, preliminaries, or biographical colophon, of the *Tesoro de medicinas* attributed to the learned hermit Gregorio López and printed in the City of Mexico in 1672 and 1674 [see M.79, M.80], and reprinted in Madrid in 1708 and 1727 [Palau 140004–5]. Though it copies the glosses of Salzedo and Dias Brizuela as printed in the 1674 edition (without quoting their names), it omits many complete entries of that edition. Since it also omits parts of larger entries and adds some independent phraseology in ways which do not tally with the 1672 edition, it is likely to be an individual version, perhaps at one or several removes, of either the full 1674 Mexican edition, or of one of the Madrid editions which copied it.

Principally a compendium of popular remedies arranged in alphabetical order of symptom, the history of this work, the significance of the many MS copies extant, and its place in Mexican medicine have been fully covered by Guerra (1966).

Purchased 1914 (34455).

WMS. Amer. 101.

LUGO-VIÑA Y CARTA, Nicasio [d. 1920]

Curiosidades médicas. Antigua medicina Indo-Americana. Recopilación histórica, con grabados, . . . Trabajo apendiculado con una miscelánea histórica de la antigua medicina européa y otras relíquias.

3 ll., pp. v, 160, 1 bl. l. 22 × 16 cm. Cienfuegos, Cuba, 1909.

Unbound.

Illustrated with drawings and cuttings.

Holograph survey, drawn from printed sources, and written during recovery from an attempt on the author's life in 1908. Dedicated to Sir Henry Wellcome [1853–1936] and sent to him in 1909 for the Burroughs-Wellcome exhibition on the history of medicine.

Pt. I, pp. 1–45: 'El empirismo indígena á través de las edades'.

Pt. II, pp. 46–65: 'Embalsamientos indo-americanos'.

Pt. III, pp. 66–73: 'Teurgía indo-americana'.

[Pt. IV], pp. 74–160: Appendices on miscellaneous topics on medicine and the history of medicine; an extensive bibliography (1890–1909) etc. of the author (pp. 155–158); and index (pp. 159–160).

Author's gift (96000).

WMS. Amer. 131.

LUNARIO

Copia del Livro titulado Lunario Pronostico Perpetuo, Año de 1827. saqüe de lo q[ue] me presiso por no alcansar mas tiempo—Primeramente del año y meses.

9 ll. 21.5 × 15.5 cm. [?Puebla, Mexico, 1827].

Disbound; part of a larger collection, and foliated [73]–81.

Copied from an incomplete, and unidentified, *Lunario*.

Primarily general introductory material, with a section on propitious times for planting (ff. 5^r–6^v), and some medical prognostications (ff. 6^v–9^r).

Guerra Collection.

WMS. Amer. 33.

MACDONAGH, James Armstrong [1820–99]

Journal of a voyage as ship's surgeon on the emigrant ship *Star* sailing from New Ross, Co. Wexford, to Quebec 29 April to 13 June 1853; with observations on subsequent travels in Upper and Lower Canada.

Pp. 112 (= 113). 23 × 19 cm. Canada, 1853.

Original cloth cover.

Both journal and observations include medical detail. The observations include comments on local events, scenes, cities, and Indians; also on national and local government, defences, economics and commerce, land ownership, topography, climate, education, and ecclesiastical organisation.

Macdonagh, elected FRCS in 1873, was educated at Trinity College Dublin and in London, entered the Cunard Company's service as surgeon, served as civil surgeon in the Crimea, and become a well known general practitioner in Hampstead (London) active in local affairs.

Purchased 1931 (79507).

WMS. Amer. 139.

MADDEN, Richard Robert [1798–1886]

The Slave Trade Merchant.

2 ll. 33 × 20.5 cm. Havana, 1838.

Unbound.

Draft poem of 24 stanzas, signed and dated 5 December 1838.

Madden, widely travelled, a prolific author, and active much of his life in the problems of slavery, published this piece, revised and extended, as the prefatory poem (at pp. 9–19) to his *Poems by a slave in the island of Cuba, recently liberated* [&c.], London: T. Ward, 1840, together with much ancillary material on slavery in Cuba and a translation of the autobiography of the slave, Juan Francisco Manzano [1797–1854]. Madden studied medicine in Paris, Naples, and London, practised as a surgeon in London, and was elected FRCS in 1855; he was superintendent of liberated Africans and judge arbitrator in the mixed court of commission at Havana 1836–40.

Manzano, who became a lyric poet and dramatist of Cuban renown, lived some 40 years a slave.

Purchased 1930 (73139).

WMS. Amer. 138.

MAESTRO PHARMACEUTICO

Prontuario o Methodo facil en donde se contienen las más eficaces Medicinas, para curar todo genero de Enfermedades, asi internas, como externas, que pertenecen tanto á la Medicina, como a la Cirugia, trabajadas segun el methodo que hán usado los mas celebres, y modernos Authores; sacado á luz por un curioso Maestro Pharmaceutico natural de esta Ciudad de Mexico.

1 l., pp. 136 (last l. bl.)   20.5 × 14.5 cm.   Mexico, *c.* 1800.

Original gold-tooled leather binding, in modern slip-case.

A finely written list, in red and black, of receipts, doses and uses of 180 numbered remedies drawn primarily from the European tradition (utilising some plants of American origin), which were originally contained in 16 lettered chests to which the list at pp. 1–12 refers. The remedies are indexed (pp. 127–133) by the symptoms for which they are required.

Probably unpublished.

Guerra Collection.

WMS. Amer. 18.

MAGISTERIO

[Begins:] Magisterio rosado.

Pp. 26 (pp. 15–16 bl.).   20.5 × 15 cm.   [Mexico, late 18th cent.].

Unbound.

In 7 hands.

A numbered collection of 76 miscellaneous internal remedies, ointments and plasters, primarily from the European tradition. Receipt 27 is for an ointment based on pulque.

Guerra Collection.

WMS. Amer. 58.

MALDONADO CORRALES, Angel [1890–1955] *and* ESPOSTO, Nicolás

Contribution to the study of Peruvian materia medica [by] Manuel A. Velasquez and Angel Maldonado. Volume I. Lima 1919 . . . . Examen microscópico del Bálsamo de Tolú, bálsamo patológico obtenido del Myroxylon toluifera H.B.K. Por el Dr. Angel Maldonado . . . . Contribución al estudio de la materia médica peruana. Volume II. Lima 1919 [por] Angel Maldonado y Nicolás Esposto. Contribución al estudio del Myroxylon peruiferum Lin. Fil [&c.]. 2 vols. in 1.

228 ll.   25.5 × 20 cm.   Lima, 1919–20.

Bound in the original file covers.

The English versions are corrected for syntax in another hand, probably for publication.

Vol. I (ll. 2–11) is accompanied by an English translation in the same hand on the facing pages; only the English version of Vol. II remains after the introduction. Both vols. were published (with added tables and plates), by Velásquez and Maldonado, as *Contribución al estudio de la materia médica peruana* (3 fascs.), Lima, Universidad Nacional Mayor de San Marcos (Facultad de Medicina), *c.* 1921 (the MS Vol. I in fasc. I, pp. 83–84; Vol. II in fasc. II, pp. 85–133).

Vol. II comprises a general introduction, the history of the use of *Myroxylon peruiferum*, the etymology of its indigenous name *quina-quina* &c., its geographical distribution, a botanical description, a detailed pharmacological study of this and related species, and a bibliography.

After heading the laboratories of Dr. Edmundo Escomel [1880–1959] in Arequipa 1906–15, Maldonado took his D.Sc. in the University of San Marcos and passed to a number of leading governmental and university appointments in pharmacy, the sciences, and archaeology. With H. Valdizán [1885–1929], Manuel A. Velásquez [1863–1923] and others, he published scientific and historical work on medicine, pharmacy, chemistry and archaeology in Peru; with his brother he founded the Laboratorios Maldonado (1923).

Particulars of acquisition not known (96000).

WMS. Amer. 132.

MANJARRES, Andrés

Thesoro Chirugico; y Silva curiosa; Sacada de los más exelentes Authores con todas las cosas más Particulares; Varios Secretos; va Añadido Un Vocabulario De Nombres Arabigos, Griegos, y Latinos, para la Instrucion de los Facultativos. Hecha por D. Andres Manjarres. Año de 1774.

2 ll., pp. 716 (last 2 ll. bl.), 35 ll. [i.e. Index, &c.].   19.5 × 14.5 cm. [Mexico], 1774.

Bound in original ¼ leather, much worn.

Spanish and Latin.

Note of ownership on l. 1ʳ of the well-known physician and surgeon Fra[ncis]co Montes de Oca [1837–85]. A few remedies interspersed in the text, and the last 4 ll. (taken from a formulary of Ignacio García Jove, President of the Protomedicato 1795–1823), are in a later hand, possibly of Montes de Oca.

The miscellany includes:—

Pp. 1–258: 'Thesoro Chirugico' (surgical and medical receipts with brief comments on their use, each section provided with a word-list converting terms of art to the vernacular).

Pp. 259–536: 'De la Apoplegía' (miscellaneous conditions, each with its description, causes, symptoms, prognosis, principles of treatment and pharmacological remedies).

Pp. 537–576: 'Tratado breve de los medicamentos pertenecientes á la Cirugía'.

Pp. 577–676: [Miscellaneous remedies].

It is continued at pp. 677–711 by further miscellaneous receipts and ended by an index to the whole. The remedies are drawn primarily from the European tradition.

León Collection.

WMS. Amer. 86.

MARKHAM, *Sir* Clements Robert [1830–1916]

Travels in Peru in 1853. 2 vols.

Vol. I: 3 ll., pp. 226; Vol. II: 1 l., pp. 227–368 (= 392) (last 2 ll. bl.).   26 × 22 cm. Panama, Peru, London, 1845–1915.

Bound in ½ red morocco.

Holograph with numerous sketches, watercolours, plans, maps and tables also by the author 1845–1860 (some in colour, some loosely inserted); with other printed illustrative material, and some photographs from early 20th cent. Peru.

This fair copy, completed (? for publication) in old age, covers his travels from September 1852 to September 1853 from New Brunswick to Lima and Cuzco, and his return via Lima to Southampton. His detailed account includes archaeological descriptions of Pachacamac, Cuzco, and other Inca sites, and an account of the decisive battle of Ayacucho (1824) from his tour of the battlefield with a participant, as well as lively descriptions of the state of travel in Panama and Peru and of society in Lima and the provinces.

In the first volume is inserted a letter from W.H. Prescott dated 11 September inviting the author to stay at Pepperell, Mass., with an accompanying sketch by Markham of the house dated 15 September 1852. The second volume includes, loosely inserted, a series of 10 letters from Victoria Novoa (and her family) dated Cuzco 1908–15 (who as a child had accompanied Markham on part of the journey), as well as notes on her life and family; other letters concerning the Borda and Ormaza families of Callao, Lima and Iquitos; and notes (with a portrait) on his former travelling companion, Francisco de Paula Taforo [1817–98], one of Chile's best-known liberal clerics, whose appointment to the Archbishopric of Santiago de Chile in 1878 was not ratified by the Vatican.

Though not published *verbatim*, the material is summarised, with some inaccuracy, by Admiral Sir A.H. Markham, *The life of Sir Clements R. Markham, K.C.B., F.R.S.*, London, J. Murray, 1917, pp. 132–163. Some of the material appeared in Markham's *Cuzco, a journey to the ancient capital of Peru; . . . . and Lima*, London, Chapman and Hall, 1856. The journey served as a basis for his cinchona gathering expedition of 1860 recorded in his *Travels in Peru and India while superintending the collection of chinchona* [&c.], London, J. Murray, 1862.

The Dictionary of National Biography 1912–1921, O.U.P., 1927, pp. 367–368, summarises Markham's life; a fuller memoir by Sir. J. Scott Keltie appeared in the *Geographical Journal*, 1916, 47, 165–176.

Purchased from the anthropologist and archaeologist T.A. Joyce [1878–1942], 1932 (65337).

WMS. Amer. 126.

MATIS, Francisco Javier [1763/64–1851]

[Begins:] En Julio de 1818 en la Meza [&c.].

1 l.,   20 × 15 cm.   [?Santa Fe de Bogotá], 1818.

Unbound.

Probably holograph; upper corner missing, affecting the text.

In noting the cure of snake-bite and rabies by applying live chickens to the wound according to local *curandero* practice, Matis recalls the negro practitioner Pío of Mariquita who held the juice of the *guaco* [*Mikania guaco* (Mutis) H. & B. (Compositae)] in his mouth while sucking the author's wound in 1784–85.

Matis, painter, plant collector, and taxonomist to the Mutis botanical expedition 1783–1816 was regarded by A. von Humboldt as a first-rate botanist and botanical artist. Matis is said [Uribe Uribe (1954), p. 103] to have had himself bitten by a snake to test the properties of *guaco*, and Soriano Lleras (1966), p. 129 refers to his paper *Estudio sobre el guaco contra el veneno de las culebras*, as well as to the *curandero* Pío. For identification of the plant see Pérez-Arbeláez (1956), pp. 207–209, 299–300; its properties still apparently await scientific investigation.

Guerra Collection.

WMS. Amer. 65.

MEDICAMENTOS

Medicamentos esperimentados y probechosos para las enfermedades siguientes.

1 l.   21 × 15.5 cm.   [Mexico], 18th cent.

Bound.

Seven miscellaneous home remedies.

Guerra Collection.

WMS. Amer. 7.

MEDICINA

[Medicina microcosmica].

Ff. 3–115, 8 ll. 20 × 14.5 cm. [?Celaya, Mexico, *c*. 1750].

Bound in 18th cent. limp leather in modern slip-case.

Margins cropped, affecting part of the text.

Wanting: ff. 1–2, 83–84; a gathering at the beginning and another at the end of the final index; and perhaps the title-page.

In margin of f. 31^r: "Soi del R.P. D[o]n[?] Lucas Vasquez á 20 de Setiembre de 1778 al estando en Nuestro Com[ven]to de Celalla."

An elaborate work originally in one hand, partly intended for those (f. 28^v, *Prologo al Lector*:) "que havitando entre Barvaras gentes carezcan de medico, y medicina (quales son los misioneros de la Compañia de Jesus)"; the three original parts divided as to:

1. Ff. 30^v–45^r: Extracts from the preliminary lines of a corrupt version of the *Regimen Sanitatis Salernitatum* with paraphrases and commentaries in Spanish.

2. Ff. 45^v–60^r: Remedies drawn from the human body itself.

3. Ff. 61^r–77^r: Simple household remedies.

An additional part [ff. 85^r–115^r] sets out further remedies for specific complaints.

The whole is supplied with indexes, textual figures, pencil sketches of fellow Religious, and additional notes and remedies in other hands primarily on paper spliced into the final index.

Guerra Collection.

WMS. Amer. 26.

MEXICO. [?]Academia Proregia Mariana de Jesús Nazareno

Didactica medica.

Pp. 198 (pp. 185–186 bl.). 20 × 15 cm. Mexico, 1813.

Original limp vellum, in modern box.

Summaries of, and comments on, a series of lectures held 29 April–15 July 1813 as part of an 'Academia' attended by students and presided over by a *Regente*, a body which tallies with that described by Flores (1886–88), *2*, p. 265, as existing in the Hospital de Jesús by 1775.

The series of lectures, brought to an end in part by the epidemics of 1813, examined a miscellany of medical topics, including the use of Latin, the effects of barometric pressure, the mechanics of eating, the diet and the digestion, the nature of muscular movement, and the content of pulque. A model Latin thesis is included at pp. 155–183 for the instruction of students.

Guerra Collection.

WMS. Amer. 24.

MEXICO. Casa de Maternidad

Inventory, accounts, official correspondence and public documents, miscellaneous drafts, medical statistics and a history, relating to the foundation and administration of the Casa de Maternidad, 1867–77.

93 ll. (some bl.).   43.5 × 33 cm. (max.).   Mexico, 1867–1909.

26 documents, some signed and dated, all unbound.

The Casa de Maternidad (officially also the Hospital de Maternidad e Infancia) was founded by the Emperor Maximilian of Hapsburg [1832–67] under the patronage of the Empress Charlotte on 7 June 1865 and inaugurated on 7 June 1866. The documents marked * were printed by León (1910) at pp. 305–360, according to which a similar institution had been set up under Benito Juárez *c.* 1862. The history of the Hospital (no. 26 below) was drafted by Ramón F. Pacheco Rodríguez [1837–1915], Director 1867–70. [See also entry under PACHECO RODRIGUEZ].

1.* 'Inventario de los objetos que ecsisten en la Casa de Maternidad, establecida el dia 6 de Junio de 1866'. Signed by José Ferrer Espejo [1800–81] and by Pacheco on 28 June 1867. Also a copy of the covering letter of the same date forwarding a copy of the inventory to the Republican government. 3 ll.

2. 'Documentos correspondientes a la cuenta del mes de Diciembre de 1867.' The last leaf with receipts signed by Pacheco and 8 members of his staff. 31.12.1867. 4 ll.

3. 'Observaciones generales' [sobre los partos]. January to October 1868. 8 ll.

4. Letter of approbation of the Hospital from the Consejo Superior de Salubridad. Signed by Francisco Montes de Oca [1837–85]. 7.1.1869. 2 ll.

5.* Extracts from the Actas de Cabildo relating to the Hospital. 12.1.1869; 2.2.1869. 2 ll.

6.* Extracts from the same relating to Pacheco's proposed reforms. 2.2.1869. 4 ll.

7. Letter from the Ayuntamiento informing Pacheco of his appointment and salary. 9.2.1869. 2 ll.

8.* Official copy of approval by the Cabildo of the proposals by the Comisión de Hospitales. 9.2.1869. 2 ll.

9.* Certificate of appointment of Pacheco by the Ayuntamiento signed by M. Riva Palacio, Presidente. 10.2.1869. 2 ll.

10. Copy of 'obligaciones y atribuciones de los Directores en Gefe' originally issued by the Ayuntamiento. 12.2.1869. 2 ll.

11*,12. Official copy and another copy of extracts from the Actas de Cabildo of 30.3.1869 relating to Sra. Luciana Arrazola de Baz. 31.3.1869. 2 ll., 1 l.

13.* Draft letter (in pencil) by Pacheco to E. Liceaga [1839–1920] suggesting free daily consultations at the Hospital. 2.4.1869. 2 ll.

14.* Letter by J.M. Vértiz from the Escuela de Medicina to Pacheco, requesting continuance of obstetrical clinics for students at the Hospital. 7.4.1869. 2 ll.

15.* Reply by Liceaga to Pacheco's letter at no. 13 above. 10.4.1869. 2 ll.

16.* Copy of reply by Pacheco (9.4.1869) to no. 14 above, with copy of a covering letter to the Gobernador del Distrito Federal enclosing a copy of no. 14 and the reply. 12.4.1869. 2 ll.

17.* Letter by J.J. Baz to Pacheco. 14.4.1869. 2 ll.

18. 'Noticias estadisticas del Hospital de Maternidad en el año de 1869.' A draft. 6 ll.

19.* 'Reglamento provisional de la Casa de Maternidad y Hospital de Niños.' [A draft by Pacheco, *c*. 1869]. 6 ll.

20. 'Bases para el establecimiento de un hospicio de Maternidad en México.' [*c*. 1869]. 4 ll.

21.* Extract from the Actas de Cabildo of proposals [by Pacheco] describing the poor state of the hospitals in the City and strongly recommending provisional measures. [*c*. 1870]. 5 ll.

22. 'Memoria municipal'. Incomplete draft notes on the health and hospitals of the city. [*c*. 1869]. 8 ll.

23. Official extract from the Actas de Cabildo limiting the length of the Director's appointment and his salary. 5.1.1870. 2 ll.

24. 'Estadistica de la Clinica de Obstetricia'. April, May, August to December 1876; June, July 1877. 8 ll.

25. 'Lista de las medicinas existentes ... en el Botiquín del Departmento de Maternidad.' 19.7.1877. 4 ll.

26. A history of the Hospital signed by Pacheco. 18.10.1909. 6 ll.

León Collection.

WMS. Amer. 121.

MEXICO. Hospicio de Pobres

[Begins:] Una tarde del mes de Mayo de 1760 [&c.].

34 ll. (ll. 1, 15, 32–34 bl.).   31 × 21.5 cm.   Mexico, 1853.

Unbound.

A detailed history of the Hospicio, with tables of its accounts as at 30 April 1852, directed to the *Gobernador del Distrito de Méjico* and dated 14 October 1853. The writer, perhaps Wenceslao Reyes [1807?–1880], the Secretary of the Hospicio, complains of shortage of funds.

Officially opened in 1774, the Hospicio came to provide lodging, medical care, education and occupational training for the indigent. Other services such as the private delivery of unmarried mothers and operation for cataract were added. Its work continued in varying forms until its demolition in the early years of this century. According to the present report an average of 500 cases a day had been assisted. Flores (1886–88), 2, 245–250, and Alfaro (1906) may have used this MS. Fernández del Castillo (1959) has covered the history of the Hospicio from its foundation to the present. [See M.102].

Formerly in the collection of Nicolás León, and probably (if misleadingly) described in his own hand on the first leaf as from the "*Casa de Cuna*" (i.e. *Casa de Niños Expósitos*, whose constitution was approved by *Real Cédula* in 1774).

León Collection.

WMS. Amer. 119.

MEXICO. Hospital Real de Indios

[Begins:] Copia de la representacion, que en 14 de Octubre de 1764, hize al Exmo. S[eñ]or Marqués de Cruillas, Virrey de este Reyno, manifestando el Estado, en q[ue] se hallaba el R[ea]l Hospital de los Indios de esta Nueva Esp[a]ña.

4 ll., & 2 fldg. col. plans [i.e. ff. 92–97]. 30.5 × 21 cm. & 21 × 15.5 cm. (the plans 45.5 × 32.5 cm. & 73.5 × 32 cm.). Mexico, 1764–65.

Unbound; extracted from a larger collection.

The plans are in a scale of *varas*.

Signed by Antonio de Arroyo 'Mayor domo, y Administrador interino' of the Hospital 1761–88, and dated; the financial addendum is dated 31 January 1765.

A covering (but undated) letter by Arroyo (ff. 93–94) establishes that this set of copies, whose originals had been submitted to the Marqués de Cruillas [Viceroy 1760–66] by the Administrador, was passed to Francisco Javier de Gamboa [1717–94], the prominent Mexican advocate who later became *Alcalde del crimen, Oidor, Regente* of the Audiencia, and President of the governing Junta of the Hospital. [See Alcedo (1786–89), *3*, 174; and Osores (1908), *1*, 248–251].

The document points out the many recent additions and improvements to the Hospital carried out under Arroyo's supervision, including the enclosure of waste ground to provide a new *Campo Santo*, accommodation for the nurses and chaplains, for the laundry, for the *temascales*, and for other services, as well as the provision of a large room for a public anatomical theatre. The addendum, listing sources and amounts of income for 1763, draws attention to the serious shortfall in the major item of income from the *medio real* contribution owing to the severe typhus and smallpox epidemics of 1762.

The Hospital is said to have been founded by the Franciscans *c.* 1531; it was officially established by *Real Cédula* of 1553 to care for Indian patients. The Real Escuela de Cirugía was founded within the Hospital by *Real Cédula* in 1768, and opened officially by Viceregal *Bando* in 1770. The Hospital was closed by Iturbide in 1822. As the present report indicates, proposals [printed in Velasco Ceballos (1946) pp. 3–23, with a useful introduction at pp. v–xxxii] for a public anatomical theatre had already been initiated in 1763. [See Howard (1972) for an account of the Hospital and Arroyo's part in its administration; and Flores (1886–88), *2*, pp. 143–165, for an account of the Real Escuela de Cirugía and the Chair of Anatomy based in the Hospital; and M.103].

Another copy of the first plan appears in Venegas Ramírez (1973) at plate II, as well as an historical survey of the hospital at pp. 41–65, 173–179.

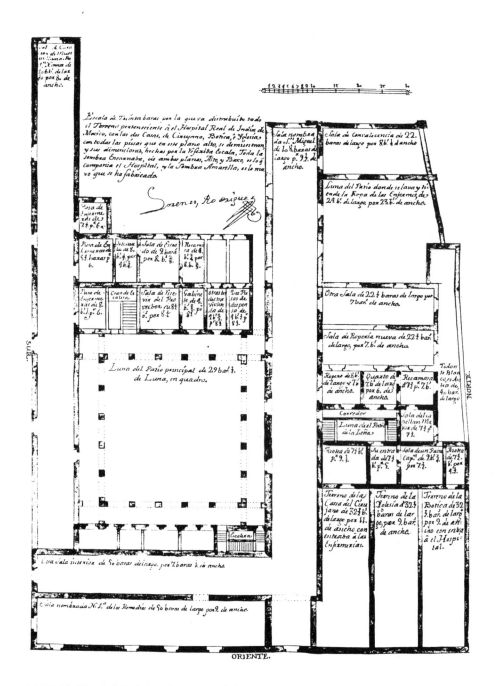

Figure 21. MEXICO. Hospital Real de Indios. *Copia de la representacion* [&c.]. Mexico, 1764–65. ('Mapa de la Obra exterior'). **(WMS. Amer. 135)**

León Collection.

Purchased 1968 (315098).

WMS. Amer. 135.

Figure 21.

MEXICO. Hospital de San Andrés

Ynformes sobre el estado de el Hospital de San Andrés de la Ciudad de Méjico.

26 ll. (last bl.).   20.5 × 15 cm.   Mexico, 1819.

Unbound.

Unsigned; dated 4 September 1819.

A copy of a detailed financial report made by the recently appointed Superintendent (previously at the Hospital Real de San Pedro, Puebla, for 10 years) to the Archbishop of Mexico, arguing that current expenditure may be reduced to meet diminished income without materially reducing services to the 400 daily patients. The Hospital had been largely maintained by Alonso Núñez de Haro y Peralta, Archbishop of Mexico, from its foundation in 1779 to his death in 1800; in the nineteenth century it was the city's most important hospital. [See Muriel (1956–60), 2, pp. 185–203].

León Collection.

WMS. Amer. 80.

[?MEXICO. ?Hospital de San Andrés]

Recetario de Mugeres.

142 ll.   21 × 15.5 cm.   [Mexico?], 1840.

Original limp leather.

In several hands.

Prescription book for the women's section of a large hospital during the period 1 March to 31 July 1840. Most daily sets of entries are completed by the signatures and *rúbricas* of 'Cartami', a few by 'Maldonado', 'A. Carcón', 'Arroyo' and other initials, and by a daily total for the cost of the drugs.

León Collection.

WMS. Amer. 87.

MEXICO. Junta Principal de Caridad

[Begins:] La Junta principal de Caridad establecida para el socorro de tantos y tan miserables enfermos, victimas de las Viruelas, ha tomado varias providencias para su socorro [&c.].

1 l.   30 × 21.5 cm.   Mexico, 1797.

Bound.

Dated 6 November 1797.

Headed 'Pidiendo limosna á sugetos pudientes – y Comunidades', in another hand.

Copy of a circular announcing the division of the City into sub-districts (*manzanas*) and the formation of district boards of charity (*Sociedades parciales de Caridad*), and calling for contributions to meet the growing need. The same text was despatched to recipients in printed form with the *rúbricas* of the 9 members of the Junta Principal [see M.110].

Guerra Collection.

WMS. Amer. 45.

MEXICO. Junta Principal de Caridad

Extracto de las Providencias dictadas por la Junta principal de Caridad, de que fue Presidente El . . . Sr. Dr. D. Alonso Nuñez de Haro y Peralta . . . .. Coleccion de los Oficios . . . .. Estados que manifiestan sus piadosos efectos en la Epidemia de Viruelas que huvo en la Ciudad de Mexico el año de 1797.

9 ll.   30 × 20 cm.   Mexico, 1798.

Contemporary full calf.

Signed, with *rúbrica*, by the Secretary to the Junta Principal, Luis Gonzaga de Ibarrola, also *Escribano mayor* to the Real Tribunal de Consulado of Mexico and its successor from at least 1790 to at least 1821.

This concluding report of the Secretary, dated 28 April 1798, summarises the action undertaken to ameliorate the effects of the great smallpox epidemic of New Spain 1797–98, from the confidential Viceregal circular of 28 February 1797 [see M.150] to the financial report by the Treasurer, Antonio Basoco [used by Cooper (1965),

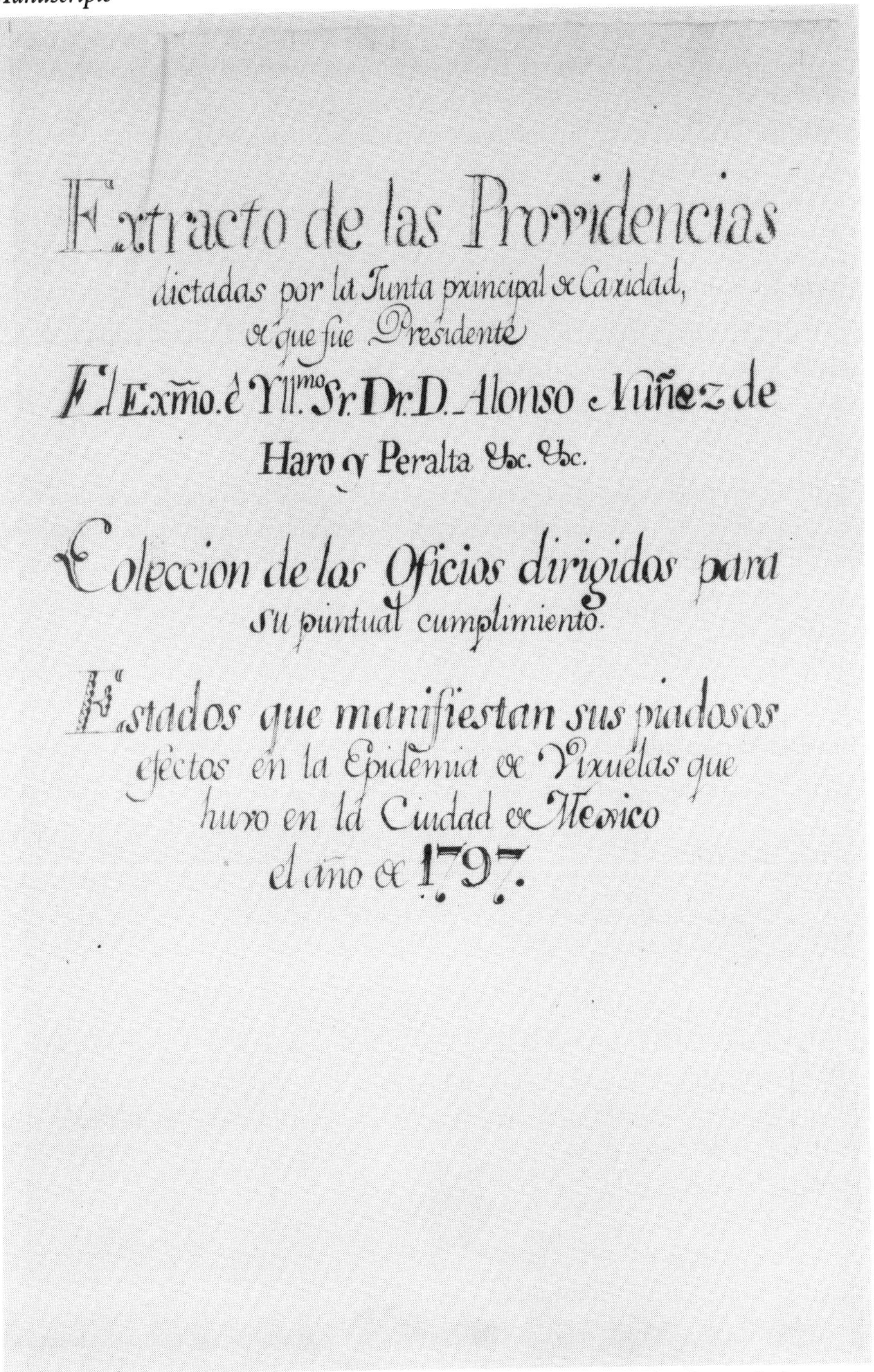

Figure 22. MEXICO. Junta Principal de Caridad. *Extracto de las Providencias dictadas por la Junta principal de Caridad.* Mexico, 1798. **(WMS. Amer. 89)**

pp. 149–152], and the apportioned return of the remaining relief money to the original contributors. The figures for the total number of those infected and the sums disbursed agree with the figures of the *Resumen general* issued by the same Junta Principal [see M.122; and, for the most reliable estimate, M.97].

León Collection.

WMS. Amer. 89.   *Figure 22.*

MEXICO. Junta de Sanidad

[Begins:] Con esta fecha digo a los Cavalleros comisionados de Sanidad publica de las Garitas de S. Lazaro, y la Viga [&c.].

2 ll.   21.5 × 15.5 cm.   Mexico, 1813.

Bound.

Copies of 2 directives dated 27 February & 3 March 1813 to the *Comisionados de sanidad* providing for the quarantine, medical examination, and fumigation of clothing and baggage of the Archbishop-elect and his retinue before allowing them passage to the City.

Guerra Collection.

WMS. Amer. 5.

MEXICO. Junta de Sanidad

Instruccion para oponerse en lo posible a la Introducion del contagio de la Epidemia del Obispado de Puebla, en esta Capital, procurandose establecerla con la mayor economia.

2 ll.   31.5 × 21.5 cm.   [Mexico, 1813].

Bound.

Undated copy of 10 measures (perhaps incomplete) proposed by the impoverished City to maintain quarantine against the spread of infection from Puebla. The principal epidemic of this year of fevers, from which more than 20,000 died in the City alone, was probably typhus. The Junta was composed of 5 members of the Ayuntamiento. [See Cooper (1965), pp. 157–182; and *Diario de Mexico*, 1813, 2 ser., *passim* (from 28 January, p. 157)].

Guerra Collection.

WMS. Amer. 69.

MEXICO. Real y Pontificia Universidad

8 signed certificates, with *rúbricas*, of course-attendance for the three medical students José Joaquín Ruiz, Benito Franco, & Manuel Berganzo.

8 ll.   21.5 × 15.5 cm; 10.5 × 15 cm (approx.).   Mexico, 1833.

The certificates are signed, variously, by [J.]A. Arellano [d. 1861], "Dávila" (probably J.M. Dávila Arrillaga [1798–1870]), [M. de J.] Febles [y Valdés] (the last President of the Protomedicato, 1824–33), by "Franco", by C. Liceaga [1792–1855] (the first director of the Establecimiento de Ciencias Médicas), and by I. Torres [y Padilla] [1810–79]. All are dated before the closure of the University on 19 October 1833 and the subsequent creation of the Establecimiento de Ciencias Médicas on 23 October. [See Flores (1886–88), *3*, p. 65 ff.].

Guerra Collection.

WMS. Amer. 4.

MONTENEGRO, Pedro de [1663–1728]

Noticia de las especies medicinales recogidas en este Departamento de San Miguel de la Rivera Oriental del Uruguay: explicase sus virtudes, uso para los efectos de ellas, y modo de composicion, y demas que contiene a la inteligencia de ello.

12 ll. (first bl.).   30 × 21 cm.   San Miguel, [Paraná, Argentina].   [First quarter of 18th cent.].

Bound in modern vellum.

Authenticating signature and *rúbrica* of J.A. de Arroyo.

A contemporary and fairly accurate copy (with some omissions) of 8 extracts from the work known as *Materia médica misionera* by the outstanding Spanish Jesuit infirmarian, apothecary, herbalist and surgeon who worked in the Guaraní missions from 1702. Furlong (1947) pp. 74–81 conjectures that he was also author of the MS *Tratado de cirugía* of 1725; other modern notices of his life and work appear, with further references, in: Furlong (1933) pp. 52, 62–64; Furlong (1947) pp. 62–63, 66–74, 91–93; Furlong (1948) pp. 92–111, (with 63 of the original 136 plates); the data is well summarised by Molinari (1937) pp. 65–70. A complete copy of the MS now preserved in the Archivo General of Buenos Aires was published by the Biblioteca Nacional [see Montenegro (1945)]. Another copy [see Pérez Fontana (1967), *1*, p. 298] exists in the Osuna Collection in the Biblioteca Nacional in Madrid.

The present MS extracts, without the plates of the original, include Montenegro's comments on the following 8 plants used therapeutically by the Indians (omitting the Guaraní nomenclature of the MSS):– *Arbol de Menjuí (copal)* (pp. 59–63, plate 2 of the 1945 printed version); *Contrayerba del Perú* (pp. 165–169, plates 38, 39); *Canchalagua* (pp. 170–173, plate 40); *Lentisco negro* (pp. 198–201, plate 50); *Pino americano de bálsamo* (pp. 292–296, plate 79); *San Antonino* (pp. 299–301, plate 81);

t

Noticia de las especies medicinales recogidas en este Departamento
de San Miguel de la Rivera oriental del Uruguay: explicase sus virtudes,
uso para los efectos de ellas, y modo de composicion, y demas q.^e contiene
ila inteligencia de ello.

Tratado del Anguay.

El Anguay ô por mejor decir el verdadero Arbol del Menjui
ô Copal calamita hay por todas estas Misiones con abundancia
por todos sus Montes y Bosques es dotado de grandes virtudes para diversas enfermedades, tanto, que los Indios dicen
Ybirapaye, que quiere decir Arbol de ceniceros. es mui pobla-
do de ojas mui lisas y delgadas à seis en rama, las quales
todas miran abiertas ô medio cerradas al Sol desando ta-
pado de él sus ramas y troncos: es la corteza hermosa è
zabaladuras no profundas. hay de este Arbol quatro especies, uno
blanco mui alto, que consta de gruesos y largos troncos, de
fuerte que es Madera peregrina para fabricas de grandes
Yglesias y tirantes, madera incorruptible fuera del agua:
en esta especie hay masculino y femenino, porque el uno fruc-
tifica y el otro no: estos dos arrojan de si el Balsamo del
Brasil, pero mas rubio y mas fuerte en el olor. Las otras
dos especies, que es el negro es mas pequeño de tronco, y
menos alto: hallase en los Montes de Concepcion, el qual,
picado su tronco ô medio cortado espele por la cortadura
ô tallo el perfecto Menjui como yo lo he tenido en mis ma-
nos como una libra que me trajo quando fue à hacer Yerva

N.º 2

Figure 23. MONTENEGRO, Pedro de. *Noticia de las especies medicinales*. San Miguel [Paraná, Argentina], [First quarter of 18th cent.]. **(WMS. Amer. 41)**

Raíz de la China (pp. 323–327, plates 90, 91); *Yerba de la Víbora* (pp. 375–379, plate 110). The Buenos Aires copy and the whole question of the group of materia medica MSS from the Jesuit missions has been studied by Arata (1898–99).

The material has been summarised in part by Furlong (1947) pp. 66–93, Furlong (1948) pp. 92–112, Pérez Fontana (1967) *1*, pp. 252–253, 294–297, 298–310. [See entry under VILLODAS].

Guerra Collection.

WMS. Amer. 41.

Figure 23.

MUÑOZ, Luis [1814?–1876]

Lecture notes.

96 ll. (some bl.).   15 × 9.5 cm.   Paris, 1840.

Original green ¼ leather and boards.

Ll. 6 & 7 removed and replaced by two larger leaves.

French & Spanish; frequently re-written in ink over pencil.

A note by N. León on the lower board reads 'Apuntes autógrafos del Dr. D. Luis Muñoz.'

L. 1. bl.

Ll. 2–34 (l. 8 bl.): Medical therapeutics ([P.] Ricord). 8 April to 13 July 1840.

Ll. 35–39 bl.

Ll. 40–95 (i.e. the vol. in reverse, beginning at l. 95): Anatomy of the nervous system, with ink drawings. ([F.A.] Longet). 24 June to 20 August 1840.

L. 96 bl.

Muñoz, *Catedrático de patología externa* in the Escuela Nacional de Medicina, Director of the women's surgical ward of the Hospital de San Andrés, and Director of Vaccination, was son of the well-known surgeon, J.M. Muñoz González and himself became a leading Mexican surgeon and surgical writer. He visited Europe twice. A brief obituary appears in *Anales de la Asociación Larrey* (*Méx.*), 1876, *2*, 153.

León Collection.

WMS. Amer. 82.

MYERS, Walter [1872–1901]

Clinical and post mortem notes on cases of yellow fever.

4 bl. ll., 70 ll. (& 6 loose inserts), 64 bl. ll.   22.5 × 17.5 cm.   Pará (*now* Belém), Brazil, 1900–1901.

Original ½ cloth, marbled sides.

Holograph notes, some in pencil (the last dated 16 January [1901]), forming part of Myers' work on the aetiology, pathology, and treatment of yellow fever for the Liverpool School of Tropical Medicine. An abstract of the resulting interim report of the expedition by his colleague Herbert E. Durham appeared in *The Lancet*, 1901, i, 572.

A clinical report of Myers' illness with a temperature chart 16–19 January is inserted: he died of yellow fever at the Hospital Domingos Freire, Pará, on 20 January. His publications, primarily on cobra venom, are listed at p. 487 of his obituary notices in the *Journal of Pathology and Bacteriology*, 1901, 7, 481–488; a modern appreciation of this scientist of unusual promise appears in Diepgen (1960), pp. 90–92.

Presented by his sister Stella Churchill [1883–1954], herself a doctor of unusual vigour and attainment (see her obituary in *The Lancet*, 1954, ii, 661), in 1953 (303911).

WMS. Amer. 142.

NEW SPAIN. Laws, statutes. &c.

Copies of the Real Orden of 29 March 1794 and subsequent documentation authorising salary payments in American currency to F.X. de Balmis during his proposed visit to New Spain to collect roots of *Agave americana* and *Begonia balmisiana*.

7 ll.   31 × 21 cm.   Mexico, 1794.

Bound in modern vellum.

Authenticating signature and 7 *rúbricas* of Lic. Pedro Martínez on *papel sellado*.

During his stay in New Spain 1783–92 and his appointment as *Cirujano mayor* from 1790 at the Hospital de San Andrés, Balmis [1753–1819] had satisfied himself and the Faculty of the efficacy of the roots of these plants in the treatment of syphilis. He published his defence (Madrid, 1794) following an attack on his results by the Madrid physician, Bartolomé Piñera y Siles; the defence was republished in translation in Rome (1795) and in Leipzig (1797) [Palau 22740]. [See Balmis (1794), pp. 1–32, and Fernandez del Castillo (1960), pp. 22–25; and entries under BIANA, and O'SULLIVAN]. Balmis is principally remembered as Director of the world-encircling expedition which took vaccination to all parts of the Spanish Empire 1803–06. A detailed account has been published by Smith (1974).

Guerra Collection.

WMS. Amer. 62.

NEW SPAIN. Laws, statutes. &c.

Appointment of José Gracida y Bernal [1760?–1815] as Protomédico de Merced.

4 ll.   30.5 × 21 cm.   Mexico, 1808.

Unbound.

The upper part of the inner margins damaged, affecting the text.

On *papel sellado* for 1808–09.

Signed, with *rúbrica*, by José de Iturrigaray [Viceroy 1803–08], and counter-signed, with *rúbricas*, by others.

The vacancy was caused by the death in 1808 of José Vicente de la Peña, *Catedrático de método* from 1806. The letters of appointment rehearse the submission of three names to the Viceroy, his choice of the first name presented, and the confirmation of the Accountant General that the appropriate dues had been paid by the candidate.

The appointment of the third *Protomédico* [*de Merced*, or *de Gracia*] lay within the prerogative of the Viceroy since the *Real Cédula* of 18 February 1646 [see Flores (1886–88), 2, p. 170; and entry under GRACIDA Y BERNAL].

Guerra Collection.

WMS. Amer. 96.

NEW SPAIN. Laws, statutes. &c.

[Begins:] En oficio de hayer se sirv[e que] decirme el exmo s[eñ]or Virrey, lo que copio. "No debiendo dar ya cuydado las fiebres contagiosas q[u]e aflijen a la ciudad de Puebla y a varios lugares de su Provincia" [&c.].

2 ll. (2nd bl.).   21 × 15 cm.   Mexico, 1813.

Bound.

Official copy (issued by the Intendant at the City of Mexico, Ramón Gutiérrez del Mazo) of an order dated 12 March 1813 requiring suspension of quarantine measures following a favourable report of the Junta de Sanidad.

The outbreak of the fevers of 1813 in fact reached epidemic proportions in the city during April, from which more then 20,000 died in the city alone. [See Cooper (1965), pp. 157–182].

Guerra Collection.

WMS. Amer. 3.

NEW SPAIN. Protomedicato

Certificate of examination and approval in the theory and practice of medicine of the *bachiller* Nicolás Altamirano.

1 l.   31 × 21 cm.   Mexico, 1690.

Bound.

An original copy dated 12 August 1690 on *papel sellado* for 1690–91.

Signed, with *rúbrica*, by Joseph Dias Brisuela, *Catedrático propietario de prima de medicina* from 1687 to his death in 1692.

The certificate describes the candidate's personal appearance, vouches for his *limpieza de sangre*, describes his examination and his oath, and awards him licence to practise.

Guerra Collection.

WMS. Amer. 51.

NEW SPAIN. Protomedicato

A licence and commission to the *bachiller* Pedro Perez, *vecino* of Guadalajara, which also requires those practising medicine in the city to present their qualifications to the local authorities.

2 ll.   27 × 18.5 cm.   Mexico, 1714.

Bound.

Margins and foot are shaved, affecting part of the text.

An incomplete and unsigned copy on *papel sellado* originally for 1710–11 (re-stamped for 1714–15), and dated 22 November 1714 in the text.

Issued by the Protomedicato under the names of Juan de Brizuela [1645–1722], *Catedrático propietario de prima de medicina*, Juan Joseph de Brizuela, *Catedrático propietario de vísperas de medicina*, and Marcos Joseph Salgado [1671–1740], *Catedrático de método*.

The recipient may have been the Pedro Pérez de Vergara who was awarded his bacchalaureate by the University of Mexico in 1702 [see Fernández de Recas (1960), p. 52].

Guerra Collection.

WMS. Amer. 64.

NEW SPAIN. Protomedicato

Certificate of examination and approval in the theory and practice of medicine of the *bachiller* Victorio Gracida.

2 ll.   30.5 × 21.5 cm.   Mexico, [1817–]1839.

Unbound. Dated 9 October 1839, on *papel sellado* for 1838–39.

Authorised copy of the certificate and licence to practice medicine originally issued by the Protomedicato on 20 September 1817 and signed by the President, J.I. García Jove [d. 1823] and the *Protomédicos* M.J. de Flores and the well-known Luis Montaña [1755–1820].

The certificate describes in the usual manner the candidate's personal appearance, vouches for his *limpieza de sangre*, describes his examination and oath, and awards him licence to practise.

Guerra Collection.

WMS. Amer. 97.

NEW SPAIN. Real Audiencia (Sala del Crimen)

Certificamos en la mejor y mas bastante forma, que el derecho Nos permite [&c.].

7 ll.   32 × 22 cm.   Mexico, 1773.

Incomplete.

Dated 9 August to 14 September 1773 on *papel sellado*. 10 signatures, 21 *rúbricas*.

Documents of proceedings brought before the *Alcaldes del crimen* by Juan José [Mathias] de la Peña y Brizuela (physician and member of the Protomedicato, d. 1789) and Manuel García (physician and surgeon to the Real Cárcel and the Recogidas) complaining of the lack of drugs, food and bedcoverings in the infirmary for the prostitutes of the Casa de Recogimiento de Santa Maria Magdalena. The case appeared variously before Domingo de Valcárcel [1700?–1780], Gamboa (perhaps Francisco Javier de Gamboa [1717–94]), Diego de Madrid, and Rojas.

The Audiencia documents include 6 receipts for court compensation against disbursements by Peña and others on behalf of the Recogidas, and make provision for future administration of the Casa and for its financial support from the funds of the expelled Jesuits.

The Casa was founded in 1692 by Francisco Zaraza, *Alcalde del crimen*, and was closed in 1862. [See Porrua (1964–66) under GAMBOA, PEÑA Y BRIZUELA, RECOGIDAS, VALCÁRCEL; and, *Gazeta de Mexico*, 1788–89, *3*, p. 225 (20 January 1789), and entry under LEMOS MARTINEZ, for Peña y Brizuela].

Guerra Collection.

WMS. Amer. 93.

NEW SPAIN. Real Expedición Botánica

[Begins:] Resumen. Habiendo resuelto el Augusto P[adr]e de V.M. que se procediese á una expedicion Botanica en las Provincias de Nueva España [&c.].

2 ll.   20.5 × 15 cm.   [Mexico, 1790–91].

Bound.

A copy of a minute addressed to the Crown summarising the documents concerning the removal of the incompetent and querulous pharmacist Jayme Senseve from the staff of the Expedition, his replacement by the physician José Mociño [1757–1820], and the consequent re-arrangement of salaries. It includes details of other salaries and of the appointment of the surgeon José Maldonado as dissector. Senseve was reinstated by Charles IV in 1791, and the new appointments disallowed. [See Rickett (1947)].

Guerra Collection.

WMS. Amer. 38.

NOMBRE

[Begins:] En el Nonbre [*sic*] de Dios, y Señor nuestro, Para el tabardillo y otras acsidentes [*sic*] sus remedios.

Ff. x–xv, 16–25 (i.e. 16 ll. in all). 21.5 × 15.5 cm. [?Amozoc de Mota, Puebla, Mexico], 1823.

Unbound; the 1st leaf stained and torn.

In two principal hands; highly erratic spelling and syntax throughout.

Ff. x^r–19^r: Popular remedies, principally for *tabardillo*, or exanthematic typhus; also, advice on recognising a good horse, veterinary remedies, and a table listing appropriate days for bleeding, purging, and general activities, according to the position of the moon in the zodiac.

Ff. 19^r–22^v: Copy from an untraced printed source "Brebe istrusio [*sic*] o Cartilla de remedios, Practica para asistir y socorer alos pobres enfermos febrisitantes delos pueblos q. per tenesen ala probinsia depuebla for mada con este objeto de orden de la Junta probinsial de Sanidad; Pueb[l]a 1823."

Ff. 22^v–25^v: Miscellaneous remedies.

Originally bound with the same collection of remedies as Amer. MSS. 47 [?CARDOSO], 54 [CARDOSO], & 55 [ESCAYOLA], but not in the same hand; possibly associated with one leaf of WMS. Amer. 15 [RECETAS]. Perhaps from the remedy book of an *hacienda*.

Guerra Collection.

WMS. Amer. 48.

NORIEGA TELLEZ, F.B.

Apuntes biográficos de mi hermano el Dr. Tomás Noriega, colectados para el Sr. Dr. D. Nicolás Leon.

Ff. 10. 26.5 × 20.5 cm. Guadalajara, Jalisco, Mexico, 1914.

Unbound; dated 2 April 1914.

Notes drawn up for Nicolás León and used by him, with other material, in his paper on Noriega in the *Gaceta Médica de México*, 1915, *10*, 3 ser., pp. 105–111, which also lists his published work.

Tomás Noriega [1854–1910] qualified as pharmacist in Querétaro in 1873. He qualified again at the Escuela Nacional de Medicina, Mexico City, in 1877, and as physician-surgeon in 1879. He served as Deputy Professor of General Pathology from 1887, as Secretary of the Escuela Nacional de Medicina until 1901 when he was appointed to the Chair of the History of Medicine, and as Director of the Hospital de Jesús (1902–10). He was member of many medical societies both national and international, and travelled extensively. His paper, *Importancia de la historia de la medicina* appeared in the *Gaceta Médica de México*, 1903, *3*, 2 ser., pp. 137–143.

León Collection.

WMS. Amer. 117.

NOTICIA

Noticia de varias plantas y sus virtudes.

1 l., ff. 19.   21 × 15 cm.   [Yucatán, *c*. 1815].

Bound in red cloth, initialled J.R. de R. in gold, in slip case.

Brief notes on some 140 remedies, primarily of plant origin, growing in Yucatán.

A closely related MS was printed, with introductory comments, by Nicolás León, "Terapéutica popular de los antiguos Mayas," *Gaceta Médica de México*, 1919–20, *1*, 4 ser., 217–226. The absence of the index of plants, &c. (ff. 17–18) from León's printed version, some textual omissions and variations, and differences of order, spelling and punctuation make it highly probable that León's source (i.e. a MS of the same title from a photographic copy supplied by William E. Gates) was not identical.

Neither MS bears close relation to the MS illustrating 20 Yucatán plants written by a Franciscan friar of Campeche in the early 19th century once in the collection of William E. Gates, and translated and edited by Elizabeth C. Stewart, *Apuntes sobre algunas plantas medicinales de Yucatán* [Maya Society Publication No. 10], Baltimore, 1935.

Guerra Collection.

WMS. Amer. 17.

NUÑEZ DE HARO Y PERALTA, Alonso [1729–1800]

[Begins:] Mui S[eño]r mio: Para poder dar Completa Satisfaczion á una R[ea]l Zedula en orden al Establezimiento … de la Casa Cuna de Expositos [&c.].

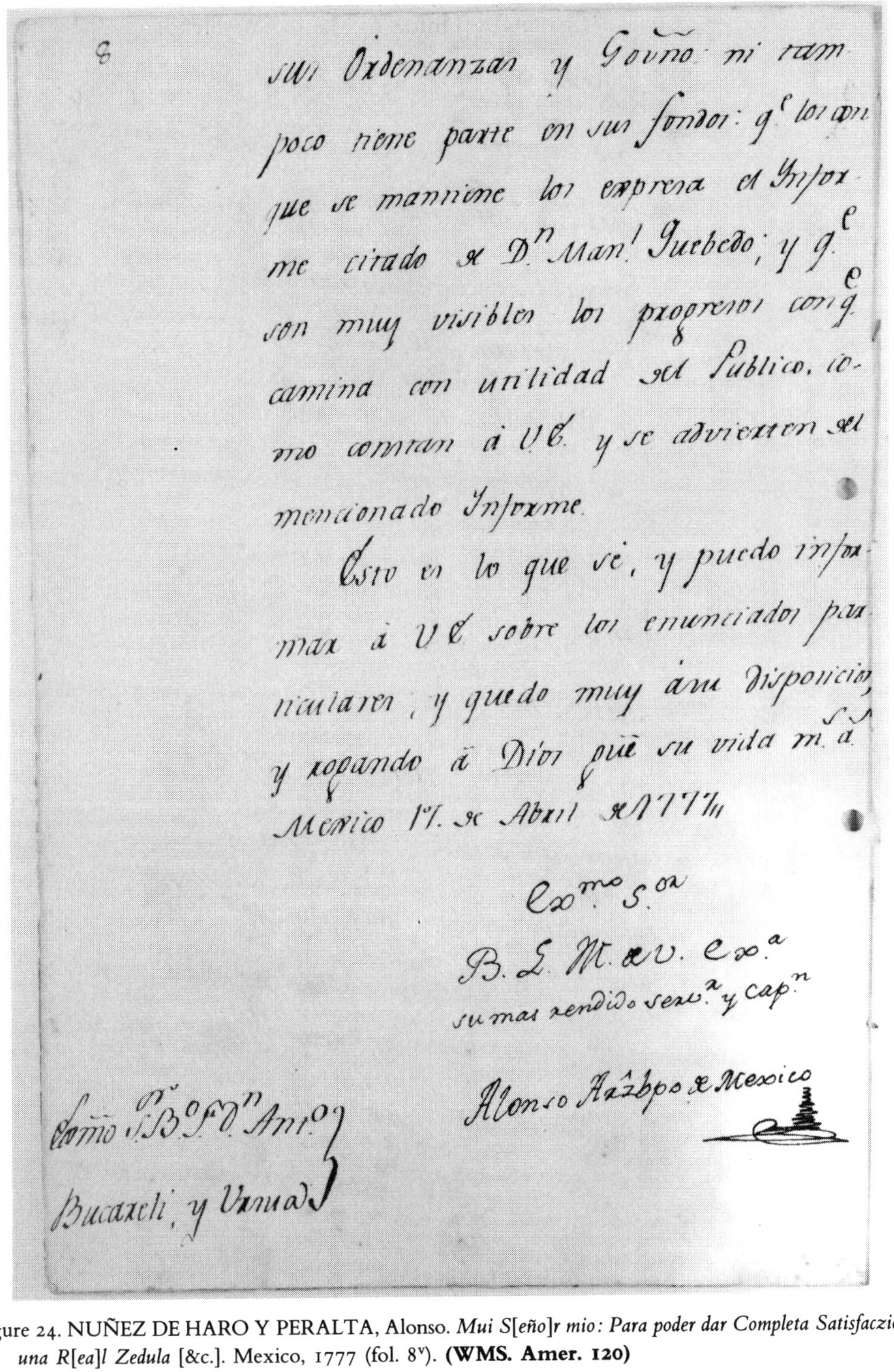

8
sus Ordenanzas y Govno. ni tam-
poco tiene parte en sus fondos: q.e los qn
que se mantiene los expresa el Informe citado de D.n Man.l Quebedo; y q.e
son muy visibles los progresos con q.e
camina con utilidad del Publico, como constan á V.E. y se advierten del
mencionado Informe.
Esto es lo que sé, y puedo infor-
mar á V.E. sobre los enunciados particulares, y quedo muy á su disposicion,
y rogando á Dios gūe su vida m.s a.s
Mexico 17. de Abril de 1777.
Ex.mo S.or
B.L.M. de V. Ex.a
su mas rendido serv.or y Cap.n
Alonso Arzbpo de Mexico
Ex.mo S.r B.o F.r D.n Ant.o
Bucareli, y Ursua

Figure 24. NUÑEZ DE HARO Y PERALTA, Alonso. *Mui S[eño]r mio: Para poder dar Completa Satisfaczion á una R[ea]l Zedula* [&c.]. Mexico, 1777 (fol. 8v). **(WMS. Amer. 120)**

[Followed by:] Informe del Il[ustrisi]mo S[eño]r Arzo[bis]po sobre la casa de niños expósitos.

1 l.; 1 l., ff.8, 1 l.   30.5 × 21 cm.   Mexico, 1777.

Unbound.

2 documents: the first, a copy of a letter from Antonio María Bucareli y Ursúa [Viceroy, 1771–79] dated 20 March 1777; the second signed, with *rúbrica*, and dated 17 April 1777.

A Viceregal request for information on the foundation, siting, funding, and progress of the Casa de Niños Expósitos, followed by a full administrative report by Alonso Núñez de Haro y Peralta [Archbishop of Mexico 1772–1800, Viceroy 1787], who continued support to the Casa founded by his predecessor Francisco Antonio de Lorenzana y Butrón [Archbishop 1766–72] in 1767 [see Flores (1886–88), 2, pp. 250–252]. The Constitution of the Casa had been approved by *Real Cédula* in 1774. [See M.101].

Both documents were printed by León (1910), pp. 616–620.

Among his many other activities Alonso Núñez de Haro y Peralta encouraged post-mortem caesarean section from 1772, and organised relief facilities to meet the major smallpox epidemics of 1779–80 and 1797–98 in the City of Mexico.

León Collection.

WMS. Amer. 120.

Figure 24.

OCHOA Y CADENA, Francisco.

Libro de Medecina y Botanica.

Pp.90 (=92), 112 bl. ll.   21 × 16 cm.   [San Cristóbal de las Casas, Chiapas, Mexico], 1867.

Bound in original limp leather with flap and tie.

Dated 8 December 1867.

A fair copy of a discursive work by a monk and self-taught herbalist of San Cristóbal, evidently well-acquainted with the local flora and its traditional uses. Its 33 chapters include amateur descriptions of 31 herbs, shrubs and trees and their therapeutic uses, as well as shorter descriptions of animal materia medica.

Although arranged for publication the MS has not appeared in print. The well-known bibliophile Canon Agustín Fischer [1825–87] included it in his sale of Mexican books in 1869 (London, Puttick & Simpson, lot 1955).

Acquired by Phillipps (MS no. 21293), it was recorded by León (1895), no. 541.

Particulars of acquisition not known.

WMS. Amer. 115.

O'SULLIVAN, Daniel

Carta Circular. S[eño]r D[o]n.[   ]. [Begins:] Me hallo con el encargo de hacer a la Real Academia Medica de Madrid una relacion exacta de los efectos que aqui se han experimentado del uso de los medicamentos antivenereos que llaman del *Beato* [&c.].

1 l.   20.5 × 14.5 cm.   Mexico, 1792.

Bound.

Dated November [17]92 from the Hospital de Jesús.

Unused file copy of a circular letter inviting comment from members of the Faculty in the City on the efficacy of the remedy for syphilis of "el Beato" [i.e. Nicolás de Biana, the herbalist] for transmittal to the Real Academia de Medicina in Madrid which evidently wished to examine the claims for the remedy. His medicament based on the roots of the *Agave americana* and the *Begonia balmisiana* was enthusiastically adopted and experimented with in Mexico and in Madrid by Francisco Xavier de Balmis [1753–1819], Director of the *Real Expedición marítima de la Vacuna* from 1803. [See Balmis (1794); and Smith (1974) p. 17; and entries under BIANA, and NEW SPAIN, Laws, statutes, &c. (1794)].

O'Sullivan, who signs himself as M.D., qualified as physician before the Protomedicato in early 1790, and in the same year studied under Vicente Cervantes [1755–1829] in the newly founded Real Jardín Botánico of Mexico [see Rickett (1947), p. 63], and established an Academia Pública de Medicina in his private house [see Gortari (1963), p. 249].

Guerra Collection.

WMS. Amer. 37.

PABLOS, Blas Antonio

[Begins:] En cumplimiento del Superior oficio del S[eñ]or Intend[en]te Governador de estas Provincias D[o]n Pedro Corbalán . . . y siendo sobre que esponga y de cuenta de los Arboles frutales, y maderas Para obras de carpinteria, y Yerbas medicinales que hay en esta Jurisdicion de mi cargo que es la del R[ea]l del Rio Chico [&c.].

2 ll.   30.5 × 21 cm.   Río Chico, Sonora, Mexico, 1784.

Bound.

Signed, with *rúbrica*; and dated 6 January 1784.

A return on the fruits, trees (economic and medicinal), and medicinal herbs of his area made to the *Justicia mayor* of the Province, Patricio Antonio Gómez de Cossio, probably by his local deputy. [See entries under AMARILLAS, and TAMAYO, for similar returns from Sonora].

Guerra Collection.

WMS. Amer. 74.

PACHECO RODRIGUEZ, Ramón F. [1837–1915]

En que casos debe practicarse la version y cuando la aplicacion del fórceps. [Followed by:] Modificaciones que presenta en Mexico el cuello del utero de las embarazadas en los dos ultimos meses. Tésis p[ar]a el Concurso á la plaza de adjuntos á la Catedra de Clínica de Obstetricia en la Escuela Nacional de Medicina de Mexico.

6 ll (last bl.); 2 ll., ff.[15], 2 ll. (last bl.).   27 × 21 cm & 33.5 × 22 cm.   Mexico, [1861]; 1869.

Unbound.

The first item, Pacheco's inaugural dissertation presented before the Escuela de Medicina de México, appears as no. 621 in the *Inventario de la ciencia obstétrica mexicana* in León (1910); and the second [*ibid.*, no. 620], was published under the same title in Mexico City in 1869 [see Surgeon-General (1896–1916), 1907, *12*, 392].

Pacheco was the active Director [1867–70] of the Casa de Maternidad in Mexico City [see entry under MEXICO, Casa de Maternidad] who later became head surgeon of the health services of Veracruz [see Porrua (1964–66)].

León Collection.

WMS. Amer. 143.

PERNAMBUCO. Anglican Chaplaincy

Yellow fever. Dec[ember]: 22: 1871 to 1873: May.

3 ll., ff.6. 32.5 × 22 cm. [Pernambuco (or Recife), Brazil, *c.* 1900].

Unbound.

A list, probably taken from the Chaplaincy registers, of the name, age, residence, and year of death of those within the scope of the Chaplaincy who succumbed to the epidemic of 1871–73; prefaced by a commentary and rough analysis by age and residence. Of the 174 deaths listed only 9 were of residents of Pernambuco: the remainder were officers or crew of visiting ships.

The 'Conclusions' suggest that the danger to residents of yellow fever is 'much exaggerated', that those under 30 are particularly at risk, and that young men in certain offices 'need to be specially careful not to give way to any kind of excess.'

Given by the Chaplain to Dr. George Jameson Carr in 1936 and presented by him in the same year (69295).

WMS. Amer. 144.

PHILO VERITAS [*pseud.*]

Carta respuesta de un amigo de los hombres á un Medico recidente en Oaxaca.

6 ll. 31 × 21 cm. [Mexico, ?1797].

Bound.

Signed (pseudonym), with *rúbrica*.

A polemic (possibly intended for printing) defending inoculation against a recent attack in Oaxaca, perhaps engendered by inoculations there against the smallpox outbreak of 1796 [see Cooper, (1965) pp. 96–99, 112–113] which later spread to the Capital in the epidemic of 1797–98. The writer refers to his time as the close of the eighteenth century.

Guerra Collection.

WMS. Amer. 73.

PIÑA, José Joaquín

Tardes Anatomicas, Esplicadas en el Anfiteatro del Hospital R[ea]l de Megico.

104 ll.　21 × 15 cm.　Mexico, [early 19th cent.].

Original vellum binding in modern slip-case.

Ll. 1–84:　　'Tardes anatomicas' (in question and answer form up to and including *Tarde* 16); 30 *Tardes* in all.

Ll. 85–90:　'Tratado de Sindesmología ó Hosteologia reciente'.

Ll. 91–104: 'Tratado de Arterias.'

A note on the fly-leaf reads: 'Estas *Tardes*, fueran escritas por D. José Joaq^n Piña Profesor de Medicina y Cirujia de México.' He is not identifiable with certainty.

The Escuela de Anatomía was established in the Hospital Real de Indios by *Real Cédula* in 1768; the Hospital was closed in 1822. [See Muriel (1956–60), *1*, pp. 131–132, 136); and Howard (1972)].

The MS appears not to have been published.

Guerra Collection.

WMS. Amer. 25.

PROCOPIO COUTO, Juan Bautista and PROCOPIO COUTO, Juan María

Consulta medica.

2 ll., pp. 88.　20 × 14.5 cm.　Mexico, 1771.

Contemporary leather binding with flap.

In several hands; decorative ink drawings on title-page and in early part of text.

224 numbered receipts for miscellaneous symptoms, of which the first 104 and part of no. 105 are in the same hand, probably that of Brother Joseph Rosuela of the Convent of San Diego, Mexico, whose name appears on the title-page. Much of the text up to no. 105 appears to have been taken from an unidentified MS or printed work by J.B. Procopio Couto associated with J.M. Procopio Couto; these are probably related to the well-known literary figure and medical writer Michel Procope-Couteau [*otherwise* Michel Cotelli] [1684–1753].

A few receipts include indigenous materia medica.

Guerra Collection.

WMS. Amer. 23.

RAMIREZ, José Antonio [b. *c.*1760], *and others*

Formularium receptarium, in quo formularium medicum chirurgicum Gadicensis, Formularium medicum ad usum Nosocomi, Pharmacopoeja Classica, et Receptarium Alphabeticum ex varis Auctoribus collectum reperiuntur.

4 ll. (1st & 3rd bl.), pp. 200 (= 192).   20.5 × 15 cm.   Guadalajara, Mexico, 1786–88.

Original full leather binding, gold-tooled.

1 leaf torn; 4 ll. (presumably blank) wanting; some pp. misnumbered.

In one principal hand, presumably that of Ramírez; in the last section additions in other hands.

Note in Spanish on last leaf, of the descent of the MS from Ramírez to his pupil Crisanto de Ocampo and thence to his sons Manuel and Maximo de Ocampo.

I. Pp. 1–50:   'Formularium Medico Chirurgicum in usum Regij Gadicensis Maritimi Nosocomi' [&c.], which follows with some alterations and insertions the text of the formulary of the same title printed in Cadiz in 1752.

II. Pp. 51–72:   'Formularium Medicum Practicum in usum Nosocomi Regalis, Divi Michaelis Guadalaxarensis á Domino Marianno Josepho García de la Torre Medico ejusdem Hospitij.' 1786.

III. Pp. 73–120:   'Pharmacopoeia Classica' [&c.] by Leandro de Vega, *Médico de Cámara* and *Protomédico de la Armada*, who is said to have published a *Farmacopea de la Armada*, Cadiz, 1759 [see Chinchilla (1841–46), *3*, 308].

IV. Pp. 121–199: 'Receptarium alphabeticum ex varis auctoribus collectum.' 1788.

The Hospital Real de San Miguel de Belem of Guadalajara, to which Ramírez was pharmacist after qualifying before the Protomedicato in 1785 [see Protomedicato (1829)], was founded at the instigation of Domingo Arzola, Bishop of Guadalajara, in 1587. After the many vicissitudes recorded in Aguilar (1944), pp. 119–128, in Muriel (1956–60), *1*, 257–262, and in the present catalogue of MSS under

U[RIBE?], the Hospital was transferred to the Escuela de Medicina of Guadalajara in 1888.

Guerra Collection.

WMS. Amer. 29.

RECETA

Receta de las virtudes de las Jojobas.

1 l.   31 × 22 cm.   Mexico, [*c.* 1749].

Bound.

[Coloph:] 'Reimpresa en Mex[i]co con licencia, y aprovacion del R[ea]l Tribunal del Protomedicato. Año de 1749.' The original printed version is unrecorded.

Lists the use and dosage of the seeds of the *Jojoba* (i.e. *Simmondsia* spp.) in urinary conditions, parturition, cancer and flatus.

Guerra Collection.

WMS. Amer. 72.

RECETA

Receta de un especial Balsamo p[ar]a curar toda clase de especie de llagas, tumores, y heridas.

4 ll. (last bl.).   21 × 15.5 cm   [?Mexico, *c.* 1825].

Bound.

Directions for preparing and mixing the olive oil, beeswax, white lead, litharge, terra sigillata, colophony, castile soap, and Balsam of Peru, and directions and indications for use.

Guerra Collection.

WMS. Amer. 14.

[RECETAS]

Miscellaneous receipts.

12 pieces, the largest 21.5 × 15.5 cm.   Amozoc de Mota, Puebla; & elsewhere in Mexico, *c.* 1800–*c.* 1840.

Bound.

Item 10 dated Amozoc, September 1833, but in a different hand from Amer. MSS. 47 [?CARDOSO], 48 [NOMBRE], 54 [CARDOSO] & 55 [ESCAYOLA] which are also from Amozoc at the same period.

Receipts for miscellaneous complaints, a few using indigenous plant remedies. Perhaps from the remedy book of an *hacienda*.

Guerra Collection.

WMS. Amer. 15.

[RECETAS]

A collection of 13 miscellaneous medical receipts.

13 ll., the largest 15.5 × 11 cm.   Guadalajara, Jalisco; San Miguel de Allende, Guanajuato; & elsewhere in Mexico, 1837–74.

Bound.

Signed, with *rúbricas*, by Zamacona, Cevallos, Nava, Paniagua, Rios Landa, and others.

Guerra Collection.

WMS. Amer. 32.

REMEDIOS

Remedios muy Importantes. Esperimentados y saludables para Todo Xenero de personas—Primeram[en]te Para frios y calenturas.

2 ll.   21 × 15 cm.   [Mexico, *c.* 1800].

Bound.

14 domestic remedies listed by symptom using in part the local materia medica. The last 2 remedies are added in another hand.

Guerra Collection.

WMS. Amer. 6.

REMEDIOS

Remedios, y memorial de recetas.

Pp.286–297 (i.e. 6ll.).   20.5 × 15 cm.   [?Mexico, *c.*1825].

Unbound; cropped at base.

Simple domestic remedies (possibly from the remedy book of an *hacienda*) for fevers and for 39 diverse conditions enumerated from head to foot.

Guerra Collection.

WMS. Amer. 59.

REXIMEN

Reximen de las Volas ó Piedras del Puerco Espin.

2ll.   30.5 × 21 cm.   [?Mexico, *c.*1750].

Bound.

Methods of therapeutic use of bezoar stones from the porcupine for a variety of symptoms. The second page translates, with omissions and additions, the entry under *Lapis porcinus* in the first and second eds. of the *Pharmacopoeia matritensis*, Madrid 1739, (pp. 66–67), and 1762, (pp. 61–62).

Guerra Collection.

WMS. Amer. 68.

ROBERTSON, James

Two holograph letters addressed to Dr. James Currie of Liverpool on the use of cold water affusions in fevers in the West Indies.

Pp. 11; 2 ll.   32.5 × 20.5 cm.   Barbados, 1801.

Unbound.

Signed and dated: (1) 16 March 1801, with postscript dated 22 April 1801; (2) 26 March 1801.

The letters, which form part of a larger correspondence, were written following the request of James Currie [1756–1805] for information on cold water affusions in fever. Referring several times to Currie's *Medical Reports, on the effects of water, cold and warm, as a remedy in fever* [&c.], 2 ed., London, for Cadell, Jnr. & Davies, 1798, Robertson commends him (Letter (1), p. 4) for proceeding 'by rational Induction, ... supported by Observation, & Experiment', and demonstrates from cases known to him in the West Indies the importance of exhibiting the remedy not 'during the cold Stage of Fever, or even after the Hot Stage was completely formed and the Sweating Process sometime established', but (Letter (2), l. 2ᵛ), 'in the earlier periods of Fever, and where unquestionably there is less risk from Topical Affections and extreme Debility.' He refers also (Letter (2) l. 2ʳ) to the father of this method of treatment in the West Indies, 'our worthy Friend Doctor [William] Wright [MD, FRS] in 1768–9 in Jamaica,' but mistakenly supposes that 'His Papers on that Subject were not published,' when in fact his observations had appeared in the *London Medical Journal*, 1786, 7, 109–115.

Both letters are quoted in part (with many alterations) in the subsequent edition of Currie's *Medical Reports*, 1804, 4 ed., *2*, pp. 594–600; and Currie quotes (*ibid.*, *1*, pp. 292–294, footnote) an earlier letter by Robertson, described as 'late Surgeon-general of the naval hospital in Barbadoes', dated 4 March 1801 and referred to at the opening of Letter (1).

Purchased 1967 (330344).

WMS. Amer. 137.

RODRIGUEZ ARANGOITI, Juan María [1828–94]

Miscellaneous professional papers.

35 ll.   var. sizes.   Mexico, 1848–92.

Unbound.

29 papers (including a certificate, official correspondence, 3 draft letters to Dr. Antonio Carbajal (1883), sketches of obstetrical forceps and the head of the foetus,

obstetrical notes and a draft *consulta*) by or relating to J.M. Rodríguez, the unusually able and widely read Professor of Clinical Obstetrics in the Escuela Nacional de Medicina, Professor of Chemistry in the Escuela Preparatoria, and President (1884) of the Academia Nacional de Medicina. He published several books on obstetrics, and many papers on this and other topics, many of them in the *Gaceta Médica de México*, 1868–94. [See entries under CARBAJAL].

Guerra Collection.

WMS. Amer. 95.

SABINE, *Sir* **Edward [1788–1883]**

Ornithological notebooks.

Vol.I: 1 l., ff. 100;   Vol.II: 1 l., 41 ll., 18 bl. ll., 28 ll.   22 × 18.5 cm. [Niagara], Canada, 1814–15.

Bound in original red ½ morocco, damaged.

Some leaves excised at end of vol. I, and 20 loose folios inserted.

Text in Vol. II starts at both ends.

Though eventually a General in the Róyal Artillery, and P.R.S. 1861–71, Sabine is best remembered for his work on terrestrial magnetism. His studies in natural history began with his ornithological observations during his service on the Niagara frontier, of which these volumes are a fair copy.

Purchased at Stevens 17.3.1931 (83753).

WMS. Amer. 110.

SABINE, *Sir* **Edward [1788–1883]**

Ornithological memoranda.

44 ll., 6 ll. (loose).   22 × 18 cm., & var. sizes.   [The Arctic], 1818; [H.M.S. *Hecla*], 1819–20.

Unbound.

The same year as his election as FRS in 1818, Sabine was appointed astronomer to the Arctic expedition in search of a north-west passage; in 1819 he was again appointed astronomer to another expedition to the Arctic in H.M.S. *Hecla* under Edward Parry, which set up quarters at Winter Harbour, Melville Island. These observations were made on both expeditions.

Purchased at Stevens 17.3.1931 (83753).

WMS. Amer. 111.

SALAS, José Mariano de

[Begins:] Ex[celentísi]mo S[eñ]or. José Mariano de Salas Cirujano y vec[in]o de esta Ciud[a]d a V.E. con el mayor respeto sup[li]ca. [&c.].

1 l., 31.5 × 21.5 cm.   Mexico, 1823.

Bound.

On *papel sellado* for the reign of Ferdinand VII for 1822–23, and re-stamped for the Mexican Empire.

Salas requests the return of papers documenting his service in the liberation army; he may perhaps be identified with the well-known soldier and politician of the same name, 1797–1867.

Guerra Collection.

WMS. Amer. 67.

SALGADO, Marcos José [1671–1740]

Cursus medicus mexicanus, iuxta sanguinis circulationem, alia que recentiorum inve[n]ta, In compendium redactus. A D.D.D. Antonio Iosepho De Gamboa, et Riaño.

6 ll. (1st bl.), pp. 234, 2 bl. ll.   15 × 10 cm.   [Mexico, *c*. 1730].

Original full calf binding with clasps, gold-tooled; in modern slip-case.

A summary of both the *Pars prima physiologica* of Salgado's well-known textbook for students published in Mexico in 1727 [see M.190] containing the first two tractates, as well as of the second part containing the third and fourth tractates on pathology and fermentation, seemingly unpublished; and, apart from this manuscript, otherwise unknown. However, the sub-headings throughout Gamboa's summary

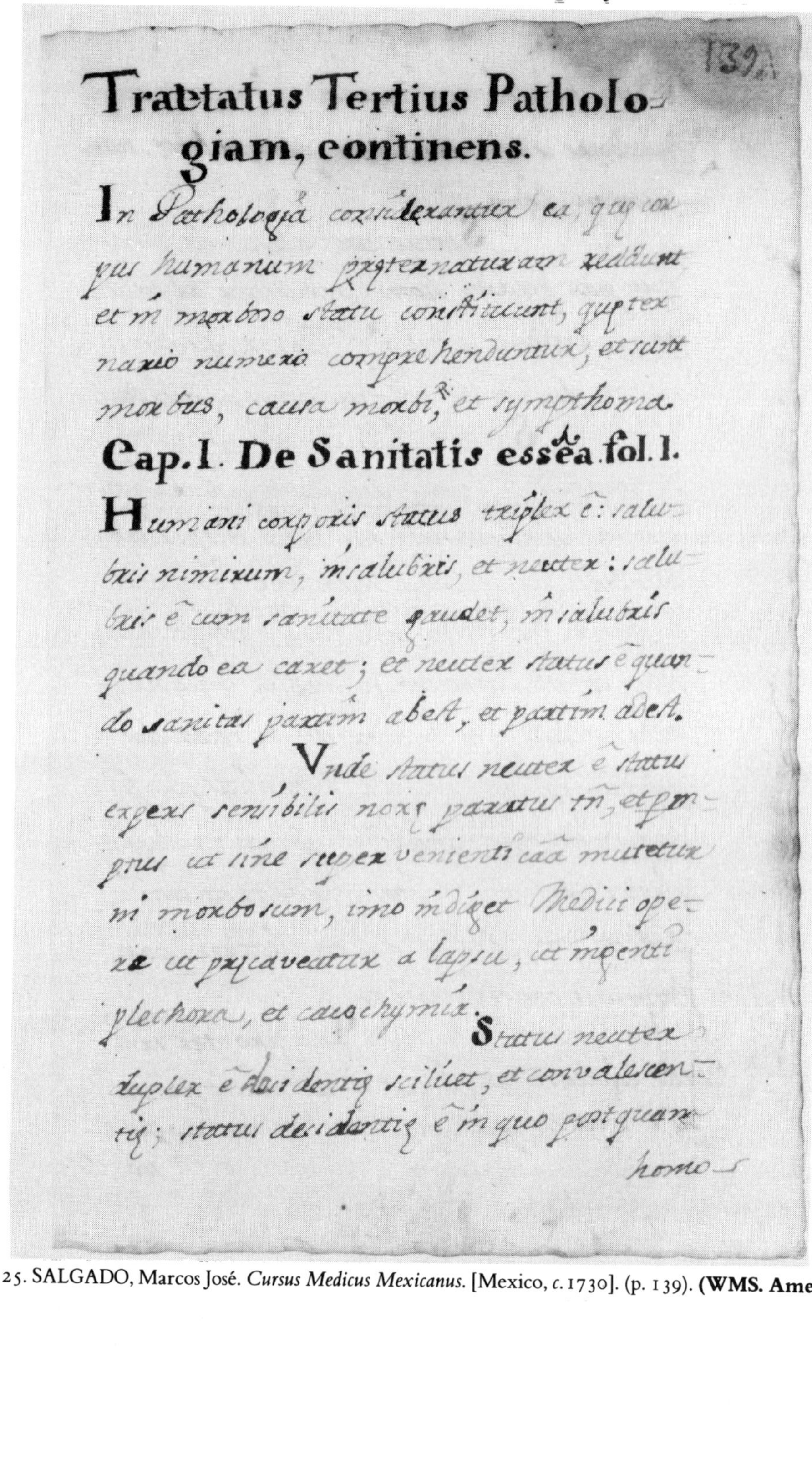

139

Tractatus Tertius Pathologiam, continens.

In Pathologia consideranda ea, quæ corpus humanum præter naturam reddunt, et in morboso statu constituunt, quæ ternario numero comprehenduntur; et sunt morbus, causa morbi, et sympthoma.

Cap. I. De Sanitatis essea. fol. I.

Humani corporis status triplex e: salubris nimirum, insalubris, et neuter: salubris e cum sanitate gaudet, insalubris quando ea caret; et neuter status e quando sanitas partim abest, et partim adest.

Unde status neuter e status expers sensibilis noxæ partus tn, et præ... ... ... venienti causa mutetur in morbosum, imo indiget Medici ope... ... ... præcaveatur a lapsu, ... ingenti plethora, et cacochymia. Status neuter duplex e desidentis scilicet, et convalescentis; status desidentis e in quo postquam homo

Figure 25. SALGADO, Marcos José. *Cursus Medicus Mexicanus.* [Mexico, c. 1730]. (p. 139). **(WMS. Amer. 35)**

refer to folio numbers which in the first two tractates refer accurately to the printed version. Some pre-publication printed version of the third and fourth tractates may therefore have existed, though it is noted in none of the standard bibliographies, nor in Izquierdo (1934, 1937).

Born in 1710 in Cartagena de Indias and receiving his medical doctorate from the University of Mexico in 1740, Gamboa is likely to have been a student of Salgado.

Guerra Collection.

WMS. Amer. 35.

Figure 25.

SAN ALBERTO, José de

Arte de conocer, y de curar las enfermedades por algunas reglas de obserbacion, y esperiencia, p[ar]a algunos de mis hermanos, que se quieran aplicar, a exercer (por Dios) la carida[d] de curar antros[?] Hermanos los relig[ios]os, y tambien los Pobres q[u]e no tienen con que pagar un Medico [&c.].

6 ll., pp. 297 (= 292), 40 ll.   20.5 × 14.5 cm.   Orizaba, Mexico, 1806–14.

Bound in contemporary vellum.

Some pages bl.; pp. 57–60 removed and substituted by 2 contemporary loose bl. leaves; pp. 65–66 removed.

Holograph remedy book by a brother of a convent of Discalced Carmelites at Orizaba:

Ll. 1–6:	Remedies for headache, and title-pages.
Pp. 1–41:	'Distincion primera del conocimiento de las cosas naturales, que componen al cuerpo viviente del Hombre', from an unidentified work by Manuel Martín de la Raga [d. 1771], *Médico de cámara* to Ferdinand VI, President of the Protomedicato, and President of the Real Academia de Medicina from 1759. [See Álvarez-Sierra (1963)].
Pp. 42–55:	'Extracto del invento del Señor Doctor Dn. Franc[is]co Solano de Loque Sobre la predicion de las crisis, buenas o malas Por el pulso.' Solano de Luque [1685–1738], who received his doctorate at Granada, achieved posthumous

European fame for his work on prognosis by means of the pulse.

Pp. 67–297 (= 292): Miscellaneous remedies said by San Alberto to be from the *Palestra farmacéutica* (first published by Félix Palacios y Baya [b. 1678] in Madrid in 1706, and reprinted throughout the century), but drawn also from other sources.

Ll. 1–40:   Index, and miscellaneous remedies.

Guerra Collection.

WMS. Amer. 30.

SAN MIGUEL EL GRANDE. Convento de la Purísima Concepción

Formulario De Compocisiones de barias Resetas particulares, Sacadas de distintos Autores de Medicina; y copiadas en está Villa de S[a]n Miguel el Gr[and]e á 4 de Junio de 1818. Para el uso de la emfermeria de las Mui Reberendas Madres, de Combento de la Puricima Comsepcion de esta Villa.

2 ll., pp. 145. 20.5 × 14.5 cm. San Miguel el Grande (*now* San Miguel de Allende), Guanajuato, Mexico, 1818–[*c.* 1830].

Contemporary black leather binding, in slip-case.

A miscellaneous remedy book in the European tradition, carefully maintained and indexed in one hand to p. 33; thereafter in several hands.

Guerra Collection.

WMS. Amer. 16.

SERRANO, Ignacio

Copia de un Capitulo de la Gazeta de Madrid de 3 de Marso de 1786 num[er]o 18 pagina 149 Para la Curacion de la Vista. [L.4^v:] Prosigue el metodo ... en ... la Gaceta de Madrid numero 19 pag 157.

6 ll.   20.5 × 15.5 cm.   [?Mexico, *c.* 1790].

Bound.

6 cases of amaurosis successfully treated with *Arnica montana*, following the method, suitably modified, of H.J. Collin [1731–84] of Vienna.

Guerra Collection.

WMS. Amer. 20.

[SESSE Y LACASTA, Martín de [1751–1808] *and others*]

[Begins:] Entre los diversos fines á que se dirigió la generosidad de nuestro Soberano en las costosisimas expediciones cientificas ... es el primero y mas importante dar á conocer á sus fieles vasallos el gran tesoro de los Vegetales con que la Naturaleza distinguio este suelo [&c.].

23 ll.   31.5 × 22 cm.   Mexico, 1800.

Bound.

An *expediente* of first drafts and file copies of correspondence and comments and reports following Sessé's request (ll. 1ʳ–2ʳ) to the Director and Administrator (*sede vacante*) of the Hospital General de San Andrés, the *Canónigo doctoral* Juan Francisco Jaravo [d. 1810?], for the use of two small rooms to enable Luis Montaña [1755–1820] and José Mariano Mociño [1757–1820] to carry out clinical tests on indigenous drugs discovered in the course of the Botanical Expedition to New Spain of which Sessé was Director.

Most of the senior staff of the Hospital, including José Ignacio García Jove [d. 1823] (also President of the Protomedicato), and the well-known surgeon and Director of the Real Anfiteatro de Anatomía, Manuel Antonio Moreno [d. 1803], objected strongly to the proposal on grounds of possible danger and delay in the treatment of the poor. The file includes (ll. 9ʳ–21ᵛ) a detailed and energetic rebuttal by Sessé of the objections raised in the individual reports of the *ad hoc* staff committee, and a final letter from the objectors threatening action at the highest official levels.

The proposal however was supported by the Viceroy as Sessé's immediate superior, and the rooms were opened on 5 December 1800, as well as similar accommodation in the Real Hospital de Indios on 11 December. [See Wilson (1962); Arias Divito (1968), pp. 212–223; and Howard (1972), pp. 285–286].

Guerra Collection.

WMS. Amer. 44.

Figure 26.

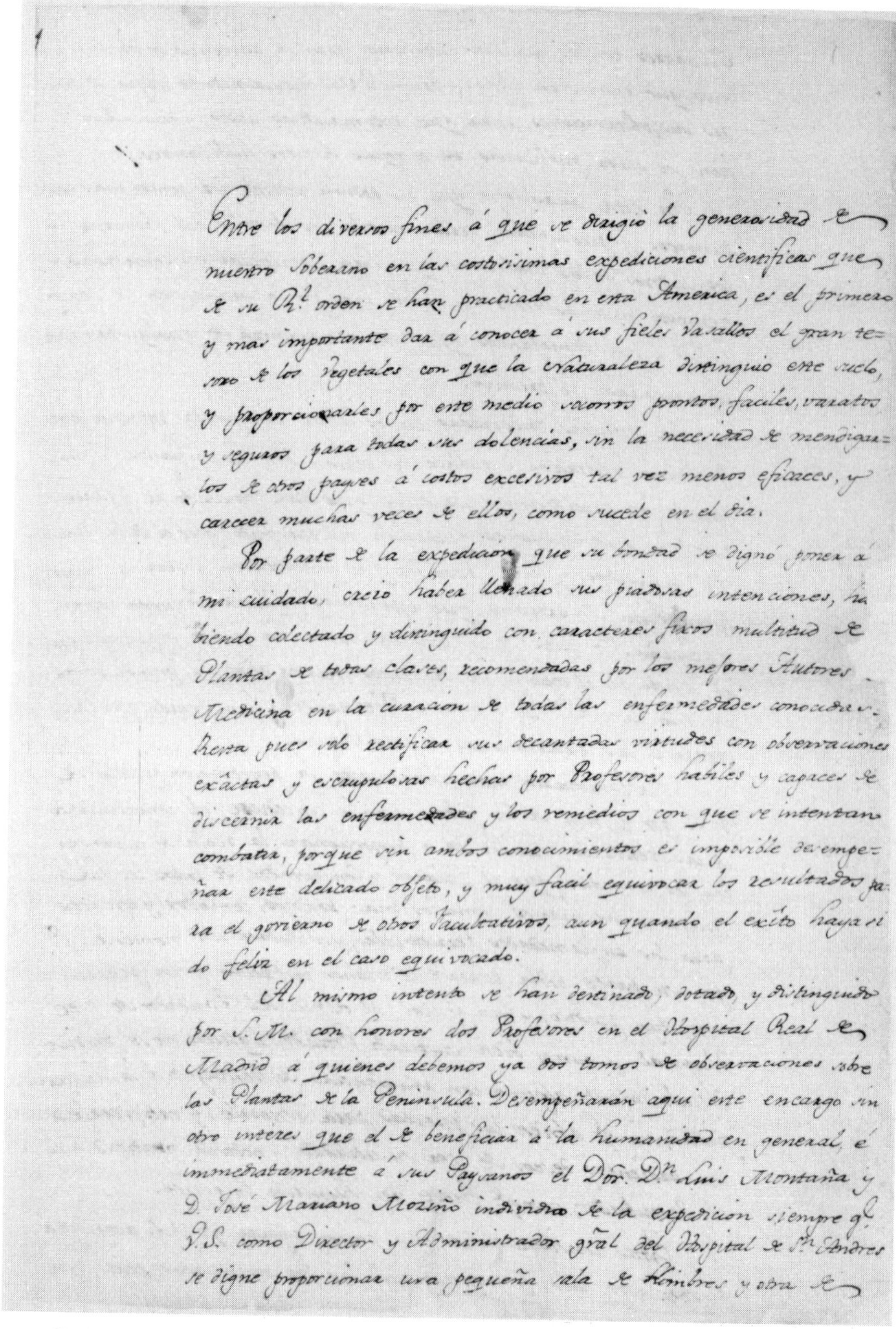

Entre los diversos fines á que se dirigió la generosidad de nuestro Soberano en las costosísimas expediciones científicas que de su R.l orden se han practicado en esta America, es el primero y mas importante dar á conocer á sus fieles Vasallos el gran tesoro de los vegetales con que la naturaleza distinguió este suelo, y proporcionarles por este medio socorros prontos, faciles, varatos y seguros para todas sus dolencias, sin la necesidad de mendigar los de otros payses á costos excesivos tal vez menos eficaces, y carecer muchas veces de ellos, como sucede en el dia.

Por parte de la expedicion que su bondad se dignó poner á mi cuidado, creo haber llenado sus piadosas intenciones, habiendo colectado y distinguido con caracteres fixos multitud de Plantas de todas clases, recomendadas por los mejores Autores de Medicina en la curacion de todas las enfermedades conocidas. Resta pues solo rectificar sus decantadas virtudes con observaciones exactas y escrupulosas hechas por Profesores habiles y capaces de discernir las enfermedades y los remedios con que se intentan combatir, porque sin ambos conocimientos es imposible desempeñar este delicado objeto, y muy facil equivocar los resultados para el govierno de otros facultativos, aun quando el exito haya sido feliz en el caso equivocado.

Al mismo intento se han destinado, dotado, y distinguido por S. M. con honores dos Profesores en el Hospital Real de Madrid á quienes debemos ya dos tomos de observaciones sobre las Plantas de la Peninsula. Desempeñarán aqui este encargo sin otro interes que el de beneficiar á la humanidad en general, é immediatamente á sus Paysanos el D.or D.n Luis Montaña y D. José Mariano Moziño individuo de la expedicion siempre q.e V. S. como Director y Administrador gral del Hospital de S.n Andres se digne proporcionar una pequeña sala de Hombres y otra de

Figure 26. [SESSE Y LACASTA, Martín de, *and others*]. *Entre los diversos fines* [&c.]. Mexico, 1800. **(WMS. Amer. 44)**

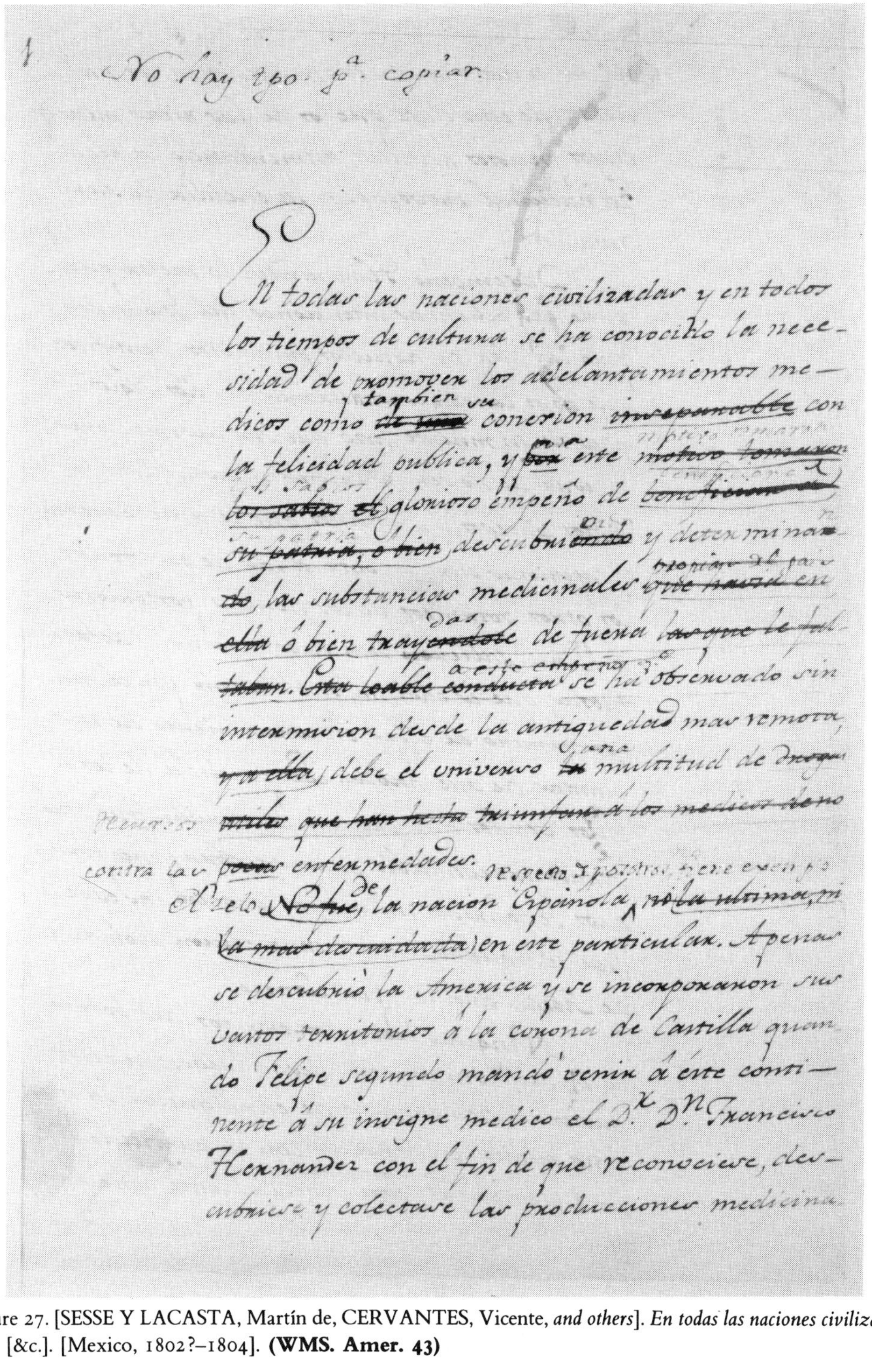

No hay tpo. pa. copiar.

En todas las naciones civilizadas y en todos
los tiempos de cultura se ha conocido la necesidad de promover los adelantamientos medicos como su conexion con
la felicidad publica, y este
el glorioso empeño de
su, o bien, descubrir y determinar
, las substancias medicinales
ó bien trayendolas de fuera
a este . se ha observado sin
intermision desde la antiguedad mas remota,
y debe el universo multitud de
contra las enfermedades.
el de la nacion Española,
en este particular. Apenas
se descubrió la America y se incorporaron sus
vastos territorios á la corona de Castilla quando Felipe segundo mandó venir á éste continente á su insigne medico el Dr. Dn. Francisco
Hernandez con el fin de que reconociese, des-
cubriese y colectase las producciones medicina

Figure 27. [SESSE Y LACASTA, Martín de, CERVANTES, Vicente, *and others*]. *En todas las naciones civilizadas*
[&c.]. [Mexico, 1802?–1804]. **(WMS. Amer. 43)**

[SESSE Y LACASTA, Martín de [1751–1808], CERVANTES, Vicente [1755–1829], *and others*]

[Begins:] En todas las naciones civilizadas y en todos los tiempos de cultura se ha conocido la necesidad de promover los adelantamientos medicos [&c.].

1811.   30 × 21 cm.   [Mexico, 1802?–1804].

Bound.

In several hands.

This file copy of a corrected draft of a report to the Viceroy (probably drawn up at the original direction of Martín de Sessé as Director of the Botanical Expedition and continued by Cervantes after Sessé's return to Spain in 1803) recounts the Expedition's achievement in collecting, identifying, and making known more than 3,000 species. The draft also recalls the extension of the Expedition's work (with Viceregal support) during 1800–04, with the opening of experimental wards in the Real Hospital de Indios and the Hospital General de San Andrés in the teeth of obstruction from the local medical establishment.

Arguing that traditional humoral theories and practice were ill-founded and inefficacious, the report describes a graduated regimen and the use of tincture of opium (in various forms) in carefully graduated doses for treatment of the endemic complaints of diarrhoea, dysentery and diseases of the liver.

Four typical cases from the ward journals for 1800 and 1801 are quoted in detail and the report concludes with a specimen extract from the regular monthly reports on patients treated in the experimental wards.

Guerra Collection.

WMS. Amer. 43.

Figure 27.

SESSE Y LACASTA, Martín de [1751–1808]

[Begins:] Señor. D[o]n Martin de Sessé Cathedratico de Medicina de la R[ea]l y Pontificia Universidad de Mexico . . .. A.L.R.P. de V.M. expone los Meritos que ha contraido en Servicio de V.M. [&c.]. [Followed by:] Relacion de los meritos y servicios de D. Martin de Sesse [&c.].

4 ll., 2 ll.   31 × 21 cm; 29.5 × 21.5 cm.   Aranjuez, Spain, 1804.

Bound.

Ll. 1–4: Official copy on *papel sellado*, signed by Sessé and dated 4 February 1804, of a suit to Charles IV for grant of the title *Médico de cámara* and for financial support and professional recognition for José Mariano Mociño [1757–1820] who had accompanied Sessé to Spain; the suit details Mociño's numerous services on expeditions and in research.

Ll. 5–6: An unsigned copy, not on *papel sellado*, of Sessé's detailed *Relación*, from his service as *Practicante mayor* in the Spanish army at the siege of Gibraltar in 1779 to his appointment as Director of the Botanical Expedition to New Spain [1787], based on the official documents remitted to the Secretaría de Gracia y Justicia de Indias at the order of the Conde de Revillagigedo, second Viceroy of New Spain [1789–94] of that title. [See Arias Divito (1968), and Rickett (1947)].

Guerra Collection.

WMS. Amer. 42.

SILBERIA, Juana

[Begins:] Juana Silberia India Vecina del Pueblo de Santiago de esta Jurisdiccion [&c.].

1 l.   31 × 21 cm.   [Mexico?], 1806–07.

Bound.

Unsigned, on *papel sellado* for 1806–07, restamped for 1808–09, and for the reign of Ferdinand VII.

Official copy of a statement by an Indian woman, describing the practice of sorcery on her son by the herbalist Micaela María and petitioning the legal authorities to prevent her return to Santiago.

Guerra Collection.

WMS. Amer. 76.

SIXTO, José María Luis

[Begins:] Virtudes de la Cabalonga.

Ff. 14, 2 ll. (last bl.).   16 × 11 cm.   Mexico, 1759–88.

Bound.

Inscribed on f.[15]ʳ: 'Para el uso de mi Señora Dª Martina Gonzales. Escrita pⁱ José Maria Luis Sixto', with *rúbrica*.

Medicinal receipts, some using *materia medica* of Mexican origin.

A note on f.9 confines the date of composition to the reign of Charles III of Spain.

Guerra Collection.

WMS. Amer. 36.

TAMAYO, Joseph

Relacion que se me manda dar por mi Alcalde Mayor D[o]n Patricio Antonio Gomez de Cossio y en cumplimiento de mi obligacion la hago segun mi entender y saven.

1 l.   30.5 × 21 cm.   Arivechi, Sonora, Mexico, 1784.

Bound.

Signed, with *rúbrica*; and dated 7 January 1784.

A return on the fruits, trees (economic and medicinal), and medicinal herbs of his area made by the *Theniente de justicia mayor* of the Valle de Tacupeta. [See entries under AMARILLAS, and PABLOS for similar returns from Sonora].

Guerra Collection.

WMS. Amer. 49.

TELLEZ, Guillermo

El mal del pinto. [Followed by:] Terapéutico especial.

Pp. 1–44 [printed text]; pp. 45–115 (i.e. 116) [MS text].   23 × 15 cm.   Mexico, 1889; *c.* 1890.

Unbound.

Signed dedication to Gen. Carlos Pacheco, *Ministro de Fomento*, (whose support the author had received), p. 5.

Téllez, a medical officer in the Mexican army, published his findings on pinta (*mal del pinto, pinto*) after 8 years of officially-sponsored research in the State of Guerrero. The first part constitutes a copy of his only known published work [Palau 329747]; the second part constitutes his MS additions to it, relating particularly to treatment and prophylaxis.

He recognises the syphilitic nature of pinta and advocates treatment with a compound including mercury, iron, arsenic, antimony and bismuth.

León Collection.

WMS. Amer. 133.

TEXCOCO. Hospital de San Juan de Dios

Libro de Elecciones de la Congregacion de N[uestra] S[eñora] de los Dolores fundada en el Co[n]bento y hospital del S[eño]r San Ju[an] de Dios, de esta Ciudad de Tescuco. Año de 1706[.] Unida, y incorporada a la Congreg[acio]n de los Dolores fundada con Authoridad Apostolica en el Colegio Maximo de S[a]n P[edro], y S[a]n Pa[blo], de Mex[ic]o.

18 ll.   30 × 21 cm; 21 × 15 cm.   Texcoco, Mexico, 1706–54.

Original limp vellum cover.

Signed minutes of elections and some associated papers for meetings for the years 1706 to 1748 originally forming part of a larger volume of election records of 100 leaves.

Guerra Collection.

WMS. Amer. 88.

TORRES, Nicolás José de [b. 1687]

Virtudes del Guaiacan, ó Palo S[an]to.

1 l.   20.5 × 14 cm.   [Mexico, *c.* 1750].

Bound.

Signed in aged hand, with *rúbrica*.

Therapeutic uses of bark, wood and gum of guaiacum, *syn.* lignum vitae, lignum sanctum [*Guaiacum officinale*, and *Guaiacum sanctum*].

[For Torres see M.200].

Guerra Collection.

WMS. Amer. 11.

U[RIBE?], J.

Apuntes para la historia del hospital [Real de San Miguel de Belem] de Guadalajara.

1 l., pp.40 (last 3 bl.).   33.5 × 22 cm.   Guadalajara, Jalisco, Mexico, 1888.

Unbound.

Dated and signed.

Fair copy with corrections, some in another hand; probably intended for publication.

A detailed history of the hospital up to the ceremony of transfer to the Escuela de Medicina of Guadalajara on 1 December 1888. Similar material appears in Aguilar (1944), pp. 119–128, and in Muriel (1956–60), *1*, pp. 257–262; but official documents relating to the rebuilding and funding of the hospital by Antonio Alcalde y Barriga [1701–92], Bishop of Guadalajara, and other documents relating to nineteenth-century changes in administration, as well as the speeches of the Governor of Jalisco, General Ramón Corona [1837–89] and the Director of the Escuela de Medicina Dr. Salvador Garciadiego [1842–1901] on its transfer are here quoted *in extenso*, though without reference to source. [See entry under RAMÍREZ].

León Collection.

WMS. Amer. 116.

USSHER, Thomas Neville [d. 1885]

Notebook, letter book and diary.

51 ll., 62 bl. ll., 19 ll.   18 × 11.5 cm.   [Port-au-Prince, Haïti], 1841–56.

Original blue leather binding.

Pen drawing on fly-leaf of physician attending a negro woman, and sketches of three deformed children.

As H.M. Consul formally appointed in 1842 Ussher records negotiations towards an Anglo-Haïtian Treaty, entries and departures of shipping, trade and fiscal matters, and other details of his official and unofficial life in Haïti, including descriptions of the earthquakes of 1842 and their aftermath. Daguerrotype and painting memoranda as well as medical and surgical details are included.

For Ussher's career see Venn (1940–54), *6*, p. 271.

Purchased at Sotheby's 21.10.1918 (43203).

WMS. Amer. 105.

[VASSALLI-EANDI, Antonio Maria]. [1761–1825]

Sull' Arachis Hipogea di Linneo *Mani* de Peruviani, e *tlal-cacahualt* [*sic*] de Messicani.

8 ll. (last bl.). 24 × 17.5 cm. [Turin, Italy, *c.*1806].

Modern paper cover.

The Abàte Vassalli-Eandi lived and died in Turin where he became successively Professor of Physics, permanent Secretary of the Royal Academy of Science, Director of the Observatory, Director of the Museum of Natural History, and Professor of Physics at the Royal Military Academy. From 1784 to his death he researched and published a large number of papers and monographs on aspects of electricity, physiology, meteorology, astronomy, magnetism, and agriculture. The present paper on the botanical description, cultivation, and uses of the peanut [*Arachis hypogaea L.*] is likely to have been the basis for his *Saggio teorico-pratico sopra l'Arachis hypogoea*, Turin, 1807, 47 pp., quoted by Bonino (1824–25), 2, pp. 509–529, and Poggendorf (1863), 2, cols. 1178–1180.

Purchased from Gonelli, Florence, 1931 (64804).

WMS. Amer. 106.

VELAZQUEZ CARDENAS Y LEON, Joaquín [1732–86]

Continuación, de los conocimientos interesantes sobre la Historia natural de las cercanias de la Ciudad de Mexyco. Año de 1790.

45 ll. 30 × 20.5 cm. Mexico, 1790.

Bound in 19th cent. boards.

Regarded by Humboldt as 'the most remarkable geometrician produced by New Spain since the time of Siguenza', and distinguished as astronomer and mathematician, Velázquez was orphaned at an early age and tutored by the remarkable Indian Manuel Asentzio from whom he acquired indigenous history, mythology, and several languages. Educating himself in astronomy, mathematics and scientific method in Mexico City he became an advocate to earn his living, and went with the *Visitador* José de Gálvez to Sonora. Later in California where he corrected cartographical errors, his astronomical observations (including the transit of Venus in 1769) won the admiration of the *abbé* Chappe. His triangulation of the Valley of Mexico corrected locations of sites on the map, and therefore assisted the elaborate drainage works of Cosme de Mier y Trespalacios (d. 1805), *Superintendente del Real Desagüe* and *Regente* elect. He held numerous official and university appointments and ended his life as first Director-General of the Real Tribunal de Minería. [See Humboldt (1811), *1*, 219–222; Arechederreta y Escalada (1796), p. 37, no. 241; *Gazeta de Mexico*, 1786–87, *2* (núm. 5), p. 71 (14 March 1786); and Medina (Mex.), vi, *passim*.].

The present MS., apparently unpublished both as to the earlier part (? now lost) as well as to the present *Continuación*, is copied from a holograph (post 1771) of Velázquez. It includes observations both original and derivative on the fertility, the flora (esp. economic plants) and fauna (esp. birds), the geology, geography, meteorology and atmospheric electricity, of the Valley of Mexico; quotes some observations on terrestrial magnetism by José Ignacio Bartolache [1739–90]; and describes the earthquake of 1768. He refers particularly to the work of the *Protomédico* Francisco Hernández [1517/18–1587] and to its fate, and to the related work of the Dominican Francisco Ximénez. Formerly in the Kingsborough Collection; then Phillipps MSS Nos. 15992, 16202.

Purchased at Sotheby's 24.6.1919. (42991).

WMS. Amer. 114.

VILLODAS, Marcos [d. 1739]

Pojha Ñaña. Materia Medica Misionera o Herbario de las Reducciones Guaranies. Misiones. Año de 1725 por Marcos Villodas, S.J.

1 l., ff.60.   19.5 × 14.5 cm.   Misiones Guaranies, *c.* 1730.

Bound in modern vellum, with modern MS title-page.

In Old Guaraní, with a few words in Spanish.

Irregular gatherings; ff. 39 & 50 are single leaves. At least one final gathering is wanting.

The index of f.1 relates to the titles of the remedies numerated only to f.48^v; many numbers in the sequence 1–205 are omitted.

Amome hecotebe haqueyī eȳramo, ayudaño tetoiporu heçe. Malvaricue
yuquīmiri oguerecobaē rehegua., Cotera aiporami Caāririrehegua
haē Caāuurumorōũ rehegua, haē tacuyeahoçe eȳramo heçebe tomboyī
manziriya. Cotera Eneldo. haē aete ynībiȳracuguaçuramo. mal
varehebe tomboyī vichi chu. haci hamombūu haguāmari,

Teco ñī nbiruā mboyequaā haguā pora rehe, oyeporu Bento
sa huguī eȳbae ūrequīũ haguārehe ocacoũ aiporami yyohīũ tātā
haba oyeporu abeñō.

Conico mohā yyururupi quarama. toipicī naborapocuē, yrun
dīaçepuā rubicharami. amambaimirī. haē lante las peteītēāçepo
nabo. haē amambai toiquīũ. haē guetebo lante la rehebe tomboyīca
tu ȳpīpe mbohapī baso. tomboqua haē ūcuē rehe. tomboyeçea Caquīhai,
rā mbohapī naracāhai ūcuē. haē azucar. Cotera ȳbira ey mboha
pī cucha. haē toūca chupe. mbohapī yebī. Coēup. haē Caāuramo,
Cobaē mohā oipohaño caũpirī mbiruā racī yepi, haē te mbobī āraya
catu rupi yporu yoapīapī ramo; haē bene; =

Mbiruā ypeu ȳmaramo yepe. ndoyecuūi chene, ymombūu bo,
ocuturire yyairacī heguī, tobeque hemimbotarupi tīpiru. haē te ypīū
bōmō toipichū mbeque Caāūcūmohapīpe, yyairireramo rañō,

Co mbiruā racī pohaño vecorami oico abe none mbiruāmirī am
nuaerehe; Serapion ēha Caray ñeē rupi,

Fin de esta prim.ª parte.
Quaria Ymomocoinda   14.
r ũcetiro ambuae pohaño haguā
     ma rehegua
Hacūbae P. H.º Marcos Villodas.
rembiporu tū que aracaē
     Parte Segunda
DJ libro delos Remedios del
     H.º Marcos Villodas.
          &c.
     Libro Seg.do

Libro

Figure 28. VILLODAS, Marcos. *Pojha Ñaña. Materia Medica Misionera o Herbario de las Reducciones Guaranies*. Misiones Guaranies, *c*.1730. (fol. 35ᵛ). **(WMS. Amer. 31)**

A contemporary title to the second part on f.35^v reads: 'Parte Segunda/Del libro de los Remedios del/H? Marcos Villodas.'

The little that is known of this Spanish Jesuit suggests that he was a qualified surgeon who had spent some 20 years exercising his profession at the time of his death; he spent the years *c.* 1724–*c.* 1735 in the Guaraní missions [see Furlong (1947), pp. 62–63, 80–81, 96–97]. Furlong (ibid.), pp. 63, 74–81 rejects the common attribution of the *Tratado de cirugía* to Villodas in favour of Pedro de Montenegro who served with Villodas for a while as the only other qualified medical man in the missions.

This is one of a related group of MSS on indigenous materia medica written by such members of the Jesuit Guaraní missions as Pedro de Montenegro [1663–1728], Segismundo Asperger [1687–1772], and the prolific naturalist José Sánchez Labrador [1717–98]; with the difference that the present MS is written in Guaraní. [See Molinari (1937), pp. 7–70, and Furlong (1947, 1948), for the Jesuit medical missionaries and naturalists serving the Guaraní missions; and see entry under MONTENEGRO].

Guerra Collection.

WMS. Amer. 31.

Figure 28.

VIRTUDES

[Endorsed:] Virtudes de las Pepitas de Cabalonga. [Headed:] Para lo q[ue] sirven las Pepitas q[ue] llaman Ysagur, V[ara] de S[a]n Ygn[acio]. = Y Cabalonga.

1 l.   31 × 22cm.   [Mexico, *c.*1730].

Bound.

A list of 22 therapeutic uses of Cabalonga, probably *Strychnos* spp.

A *Recepta de la Pepita de Covalonga* was published in Mexico in 1730, probably by José Bernardo de Hogal at the same time as his *Virtudes de la piedra quadrada*. [See M.40; and see Medina (Mex.), iv, 3146, 3155, and *Gazeta de Mexico*, 1730, núm. 32, p. 255 (July)].

Guerra Collection.

WMS. Amer. 52.

VIRTUDES

Virtudes del Balsamo Peruano, nombrado de Buda, ó de la Vida.

8 ll. (last 3 bl.); 6 ll. (1st bl.).   21.5 × 15.5 cm.; 22 × 15.5 cm.   [?Mexico, last half 18 cent.].

2 MSS bound separately: WMS. Amer. 13 is a copy of WMS. Amer. 2.

Theory and therapeutic uses of the balsam (regarded as a near-panacea); with the formula of 9 ingredients.

Guerra Collection.

WMS. Amer. 2; WMS. Amer. 13.

WASHINGTON, George [1732–99]

An order for household and plantation supplies.

1 l.   32 × 20 cm.   [Mount Vernon, Va., U.S.A.], 1759.

Unbound.

In the hand of George Washington [President of the United States of America 1789–97]; signed and dated by him 20 September 1759.

One of a series of annual orders sent to England for general supplies; this order including coopers', wheelwrights', and joiners' tools, as well as medicinal, culinary and veterinary items. The medicinal items include such typically 18th cent. drugs as jalap, rhubarb, diascordium, balsam of copaiba, ipecacuanha, spirits of hartshorn, cantharides, tincture of myrrh, laudanum, and sal volatile.

Washington's estates and responsibilities had increased with his marriage to Martha Custis on 6 January of the same year.

Guerra Collection.

WMS. Amer. 91.

Figure 29.

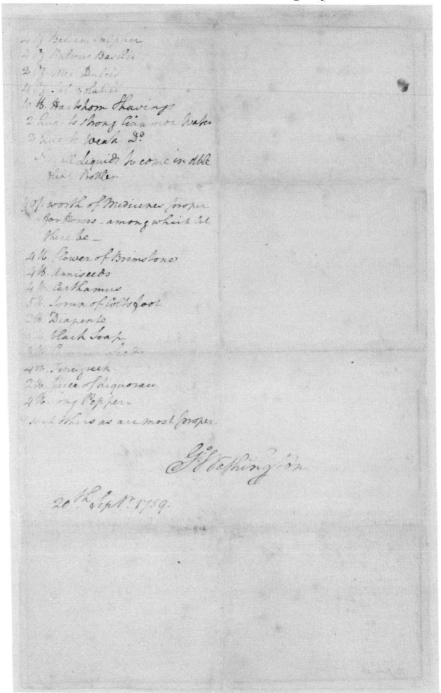

Figure 29. WASHINGTON, George. *An order for household and plantation supplies.* [Mount Vernon, Va., U.S.A.], 1759. (fol. 1ᵛ). **(WMS. Amer. 91)**

WELLINGTON, Albert [1881–1914]

Memorandum and account book.

111 ll.   15 × 9 cm.   Metlakahtla, Port Simpson, Vancouver, & Victoria, B.C., Canada, 1900–1902.

Unbound.

Miscellaneous jottings in a diary for 1900 by a son of Arthur Wellington Clah [see entry under CLAH].

Purchased 1911 (300700) from the Clah family.

WMS. Amer. 141.

ZACATECAS. Hospital de Nuestra Señora de la Veracruz

[Begins:] En la Ciudad de Mexico, en quatro dias, del mes de Diciembre de mil, seiscientos, y ocho años: estando en el Hospital de los desamparados [&c.]. [In margin:] Instrumento de fundación del Hosp[ita]l.

10 ll.   31 × 21 cm.   Guadalajara, Jalisco, Mexico, 1776.

Bound.

Signed, with *rúbrica*.

Notarial copy of the founding documents 1608–21 of the establishment later known as the Hospital de San Juan de Dios; it was run by the Brothers Hospitaller of St. John of God, by whom it was founded, until 1827 when it passed to the City of Zacatecas.

The documents copied include the stringent conditions laid down by the Cabildo of Zacatecas, agreed to by the Order in the provisions dated 23 May 1608, and summarised by Muriel (1956–60), 2, pp. 39–45 (in the informative section on the hospital) at p. 41.

Guerra Collection.

WMS. Amer. 71.

6. REFERENCES

A. Bibliographical references

ANDRADE, V. DE P. (1899). Ensayo bibliográfico mexicano del siglo XVII. 2 ed. Mexico: Imprenta del Museo Nacional.

AUSTIN, R.B. (1961). Early American medical imprints. A guide to works printed in the United States 1668–1820. Washington, D.C.: U.S. Department of Health, Education, and Welfare, Public Health Service (National Library of Medicine).

BERISTAIN DE SOUZA, J.M. (1883). Biblioteca hispano americana septentrional o catálogo y noticias de los literatos ... 1521–1850 [1825]. 6 vols. in 3 [including vol. 5 (Suplemento especial)]. Mexico: Ediciones Fuente Cultural.

BLAKE, A.V. Alves Sacramento. (1883–1902). Diccionario bibliographico brazileiro. 7 vols. Rio de Janeiro: Typographia Nacional [&c.].

BORBA DE MORAES, R. (1958). Bibliographia brasiliana. A bibliographical essay on rare books about Brazil published from 1504 to 1900 and works of Brazilian authors published abroad before the Independence of Brazil in 1822. 2 vols. Amsterdam, Rio de Janeiro: Colibris Editora Ltda.

BRITISH MUSEUM (1959–66). British Museum general catalogue of printed books. 263 vols. London: Trustees of the British Museum.

CUNDALL, F. (1902). Bibliographia jamaicensis. A list of Jamaica books and pamphlets, magazine articles, newspapers, and maps, most of which are in the Library of the Institute of Jamaica. (Facsimile of the New York 1902 ed., reprinted 1971). New York: Burt Franklin.

CUNDALL, F. (1909). Bibliography of the West Indies (excluding Jamaica). Kingston: The Institute of Jamaica.

FACULDADE DE MEDICINA DE LISBOA, Biblioteca. (1942). Catálogo das obras de colecção portuguesa anteriores á fundação das Régias Escolas de Cirurgia (1825). Lisbon: Imprensa Médica.

FURLONG, G. (1953–75). Historia y bibliografía de las primeras imprentas rioplatenses 1700–1850. 4 vols. Buenos Aires: Editorial Guaranía [&c.].

GALLARDO, B.J. (1863–89). Ensayo de una biblioteca española de libros raros y curiosos. 4 vols. Madrid: M. Rivadeneyra; M. Tello.

GONZALEZ DE COSSIO, F. (1947). La imprenta en México 1594–1820. Cien adiciones a la obra de Don José Toribio Medina. Mexico: Antigua Librería Robredo, de José Porrua e Hijos.

GUERRA, F. (1950). Bibliografía de la materia médica mexicana. Mexico: La Prensa Médica Mexicana.

GUERRA, F. (1955). Iconografía médica mexicana. Mexico: Imprenta del Diario Español.

GUERRA, F. (1958). Bibliografia médica brasileira. Período colonial 1808–1821. Yale University School of Medicine.

ICAZBALCETA, J.G. (1954). Bibliografía mexicana del siglo XVI; catálogo razonado de libros impresos en México de 1539 a 1600. [ed. Agustín Millares Carlo]. Mexico: Fondo de Cultura Económica.

IGUINIZ, J.B. (1911). La imprenta en la Nueva Galicia 1793–1821. [*Anales del Museo Nacional de Arqueología, Historia y Etnología, 3* (nos. 4, 5)]. Mexico: Imprenta del Museo Nacional [&c.].

LASTRES, J.B. (1951). Historia de la medicina peruana. 3 vols. Lima: Imprenta Santa María.

LEON, N. (1902–45). Bibliografía mexicana del siglo XVIII. 7 vols. in 8 [including the final index volume by R. Valles]. Mexico: F. Díaz de León & his Widow; J.I. Guerrero; Biblioteca Aportación Histórica.

LEON, N. (1915). Los precursores de la literatura médica mexicana en los siglos XVI, XVII, XVIII y primer tercio del siglo XIX .... Datos biobibliográficos para la historia de la medicina en México. *Gaceta Médica de México, 10,* 3–94.

MEDINA, J.T. (1892). Historia y bibliografía de la imprenta en la América española. Parte II. Vireinato del Río de la Plata, III: Historia y bibliografía de la imprenta en Buenos Aires (1780–1810). [*Anales del Museo de la Plata. Materiales para la historia física y moral del continente sud-americano. Sección de historia americana,* III]. La Plata: Taller de Publicaciones del Museo.

MEDINA, J.T. (1898–1907). Biblioteca hispano-americana (1493–1810). 7 vols. Santiago de Chile: the author.

MEDINA, J.T. (1904). La imprenta en Bogotá (1739–1821). Notas bibliográficas. Santiago de Chile: Imprenta Elzeviriana.

MEDINA, J.T. (1904). La imprenta en Mérida de Yucatán (1813–1821). Notas bibliográficas. Santiago de Chile: Imprenta Elzeviriana.

MEDINA, J.T. (1904–07). La imprenta en Lima. (1584–1824). 4 vols. Santiago de Chile: the author.

MEDINA, J.T. (1908). La imprenta en la Puebla de los Angeles (1640–1821). Santiago de Chile: Imprenta Cervantes.

MEDINA, J.T. (1908–12). La imprenta en México (1539–1821). 8 vols. Santiago de Chile: the author.

MEDINA, J.T. (1910). La imprenta en Guatemala (1660–1821). Santiago de Chile: the author.

MOLINARI, J.L. (1941). Primeros impresos médicos bonaerenses (1780–1810). Buenos Aires: Sebastián de Amorrortu e Hijos.

MOLINARI, J.L. (1943). Algunos impresos médicos menores poco conocidos (1811–1830). *Boletín del Instituto Bonaerense de Numismática y Antigüedades, 1* (¹), 37–47.

MOLINARI, J.L., CARBONE, O.E., URSI, C.G. (1965). Aportaciones al conocimiento de los primeros impresos de la Real Imprenta de Niños Expósitos. *Boletín de la Academia Nacional de la Historia, 37*, 5–45.

PALAU Y DULCET, A. (1923–27). Manual del librero hispano-americano. Vols. 1–7. 1 ed. Barcelona: Librería Anticuaria.

PALAU Y DULCET, A. (1948–77). Manual del librero hispano-americano. Vols. 1–28. 2 ed. Barcelona: Librería Anticuaria de A. Palau.

PENNEY, C.L. (1965). Printed books 1468–1700 in the Hispanic Society of America. New York: Hispanic Society of America.

PIRES DE LIMA. (1910). Catalogo da Bibliotheca da Escola Medico-Cirurgica do Porto. Porto: Encyclopedia Portugueza Illustrada.

RADIN, P. [ed.]. (1940). An annotated bibliography of the poems and pamphlets of J.J. Fernández de Lizardi. The first period (1808–19). The second period (1820–23). [*Occasional Papers (Mexican History Series no. 2, pt. 1)*]. 2 pts. [*Reproduced typescript*]. San Francisco: California State Library.

SILVA, I.F. DA (1858–1911). Diccionario bibliographico portuguez. 20 vols. [including supplementary vols. 8–20, 1867–1911]. Lisbon: Imprensa Nacional.

SURGEON-GENERAL (1896–1916). Index-catalogue of the Library of the Surgeon-General's Office, United States Army, Ser. 2. 21 vols. Washington: Government Printing Office.

TRELLES, C.M. (1918–19). Biblioteca científica cubana. 2 vols. Matanzas: Juan F. Oliver.

VALDIZAN, H. (1927–29). La Facultad de Medicina de Lima. 2 ed. 3 vols. Lima: [s.n.].

VALDIZAN, H. (1928). Apuntes para la bibliografía médica peruana. Lima: Imprenta Americana.

VALTON, E. (1935). Impresos mexicanos del siglo XVI (incunables americanos). Estudio bibliográfico. Mexico: Imprenta Universitaria.

VILLACORTA C., J.A. (1944). Bibliografía guatemalteca. Guatemala, C.A.: Tipografía Nacional.

VINDEL, F. (1930–31). Manual gráfico-descriptivo del bibliófilo hispano-americano (1475–1850). 11 vols. Madrid, [&c.]: F. Vindel [&c.].

WAGNER, E.R. (1940). Nueva bibliografía mexicana del siglo XVI. Suplemento a las bibliografías de ... García Icazbalceta ... Medina y ... León. Traducida por Joaquín García Pimentel y Federico Gómez de Orozco. Mexico: Editorial Polis.

B. General references

AGUILAR, G.F. (1944). Hospitales de antaño. Mexico: Lotería Nacional [&c.].

ALCALDE MONGRUT, A. (1959). La contribución de Joseph Coquette a la bibliografía química peruana en la última decada del siglo XVIII. *Ciencia (Mex.)*, *19*, 141–145.

ALCEDO, A. DE (1786–89). Diccionario geográfico-histórico de las Indias occidentales ó América [&c.]. 5 vols. Madrid: B. Cano; M. González; B. Román.

ALFARO, M.T. (1906). Reseña histórico-descriptiva del antiguo Hospicio de México. Mexico: Imprenta del Gobierno Federal.

ALVAREZ-SIERRA, J. (1963). Diccionario de autoridades médicas. Madrid: Editora Nacional.

ALZATE Y RAMIREZ, J.A. (1831). Gacetas de literatura de México. 4 vols. Puebla: Oficina del Hospital de San Pedro.

ARATA, P.N. (1898–99). Botánica médica americana. Los herbarios de las Misiones del Paraguay. *La Biblioteca (Buenos Aires)*, *7*, 419–448; *8*, 185-192.

ARCTANDER, K.J.L.W.A. (1909). The apostle of Alaska. The story of William Duncan of Metlakahtla. 2 ed. New York, [&c.]: Fleming H. Revell Co.

ARECHEDERRETA Y ESCALADA, J.B. (1796). Catálogo de los colegiales del insigne, viejo y mayor de Santa María de Todos Santos [&c.]. Mexico: M.J. de Zúñiga y Ontiveros.

ARIAS DIVITO, J.C. (1968). Las expediciones científicas españolas durante el siglo XVIII. Expedición botánica de Nueva España. Madrid: Ediciones Cultura Hispánica.

AZNAR LOPEZ, J. (1960). El doctor don José de Flores. Guatemala: Editorial Universitaria.

BALMIS, F.X. DE (1794). Demostración de las eficaces virtudes nuevamente descubiertas en las raices de dos plantas de Nueva-España, especies de ágave y de begónia, para la curación del vicio venéreo y escrofuloso. Madrid: Widow of J. Ibarra.

BARRIOS, V.B. DE (1971). A guide to tequila, mezcal and pulque. Mexico: Editorial Minutiae Mexicana.

BOBB, B.E. (1962). The viceregency of Antonio Maria Bucareli in New Spain. 1771–1779. University of Texas Press.

BOLAÑO E ISLA, A. (1947). Contribución al estudio biobibliográfico de Fray Alonso de la Vera Cruz. [*Biblioteca Histórica Mexicana de Obras Inéditas, 21*]. Mexico: Antigua Librería Robredo, de José Porrua e Hijos.

BONINO, G.G. (1824–25). Biografía mèdica piemontese. 2 vols. Turin: Tipografía Bianco.

BOTICA. (1954). Botica general de los remedios esperimentados, Sonoma, 1838; translation by María López de Lowther, introduction by Viola Lockhart Warren. Los Angeles: The Ward Ritchie Press for the Friends of the U.C.L.A. Library.

BURKE, M.E. (1971). The Royal College of San Carlos. Surgery and Spanish medical reform in the late eighteenth century. [Thesis]. Duke University (University Microfilms, 1975).

BURRUS, E.J. [ed.]. (1968). The writings of Alonso de la Vera Cruz, I. Spanish writings, I. [*Sources and Studies for the History of the Americas, 3*]. Rome: Jesuit Historical Institute.

CANTON, E. (1921). La Facultad de Medicina y sus escuelas. [*Historia de la Universidad de Buenos Aires y de su influencia en la cultura argentina*, dirigida por J.A. García, tomos 5–8]. 4 pts. in 4 vols. Buenos Aires: Imprenta y Casa Editora "Coni".

CARREÑO, A.M. (1961). La Real y Pontificia Universidad de México 1536–1865. Universidad Nacional Autónoma de México.

CATHOLIC ENCYCLOPEDIA (1913–14). 16 vols. New York: Encyclopedia Press.

CHINCHILLA, A. (1841–46). Anales históricos de la medicina en general, y biográfico-bibliográficos de la Española en particular. 8 vols. Valencia: López y Cia; J.M. Cervera.

COLMEIRO, M. (1858). La botánica y los botánicos de la Península hispano-lusitana. Estudios bibliográficos y biográficos. Madrid: M. Rivadeneyra.

COOK, S.F. (1939). Smallpox in Spanish and Mexican California 1770–1845. *Bulletin of the History of Medicine, 7*, 153–191.

COOK, S.F. (1942). Francisco Xavier Balmis and the introduction of vaccine to Latin America, Pt. II. *Bulletin of the History of Medicine, 12*, 70–101.

COOPER, D.B. (1965). Epidemic disease in Mexico City 1761–1813; an administrative, social, and medical study. University of Texas Press, for the Institute of Latin American Studies.

CRANEFIELD, P.F. *and* FEDERN, W. (1970). Paulus Zacchias on mental deficiency and on deafness. *Bulletin of the New York Academy of Medicine, 46*, 3–21.

CUNDALL, F. (1935). A history of printing in Jamaica from 1717 to 1834. [Reprinted from the *Gleaner* (centenary no.) 13 September 1934]. Kingston: Institute of Jamaica.

DICTIONNAIRE DE BIOGRAPHIE FRANÇAISE (1933–). Vols. 1–[in progress]. Paris: Librairie Letouzey et Ané.

DICTIONNAIRE ENCYCLOPEDIQUE DES SCIENCES MEDICALES (1864–89). (Directeurs: A. Dechambre & L. Lereboullet). 5 series in 100 vols. Paris: P. Asselin & V. Masson.

DIEPGEN, P. (1960). Unvollendete. Vom Leben und Wirken frühverstorbener Forscher und Ärzte aus anderthalb Jahrhunderten. Stuttgart: G. Thieme.

DOETSCH, R.N. (1964). John Crawford and his contribution to the doctrine of *contagium vivum*. *Bacteriological Reviews, 28* (1), 87–96.

DONKIN, R.A. (1977). Spanish Red. An ethnogeographical study of cochineal and the Opuntia cactus. *Transactions of the American Philosophical Society, 67*, (N.S.), (5).

DUBOIS D'AMIENS, E.F. (1846). Notice historique sur M. Chervin.... Lu à la séance annuelle de l'Académie royale de Médecine, le 25 novembre 1845. *Mémoires de l'Académie royale de Médecine, 12* (1), xxxvii–lix.

ENCICLOPEDIA UNIVERSAL ILUSTRADA EUROPEO-AMERICANA [1909–30]. 70 vols. Madrid: Espasa-Calpe.

FERNANDEZ DEL CASTILLO, F. [ed.]. (1914). Libros y libreros en el siglo XVI. Mexico: Archivo General de la Nación.

FERNANDEZ DEL CASTILLO, F. (1959). El Hospicio de Pobres, la Escuela Patriótica, y el Internado Infantil. *El Médico (Méx.), 9* (6), 55–60; *9* (7), 67–72; *9* (8), 57–62.

FERNANDEZ DEL CASTILLO, F. (1960). Los viajes de don Francisco Xavier de Balmis. Mexico: Galas de México.

FERNANDEZ DE RECAS, G.S. (1960). Real y Pontificia Universidad de México. Medicina. Nómina de bachilleres, licenciados y doctores 1607–1780 … documentos en el Archivo General de la Nación. Mexico: Biblioteca Nacional, Universidad Nacional Autónoma de México.

FERNANDEZ DE RECAS, G.S. (1965). Mayorazgos de la Nueva España [Biblioteca Nacional de México, Instituto Bibliográfico Mexicano, 10]. Universidad Nacional Autónoma de México.

FEUILLEE, L. (1714–25). Journal des observations physiques. 3 vols. Paris: P. Giffart; J. Mariette.

FLORES, F. DE A. (1886–88). Historia de la medicina en México. 3 vols. Mexico: Oficina Tipográfica de la Secretaría de Fomento.

FURLONG, G. (1933). Los Jesuítas y la cultura ríoplatense. Montevideo: Urta y Curbelo.

FURLONG, G. (1947). Médicos argentinos durante la dominación hispánica. [*Cultura colonial argentina*, 6]. Buenos Aires: Ediciones Huarpes.

FURLONG, G. (1948). Naturalistas argentinos durante la dominación hispánica. [*Cultura colonial argentina*, 7]. Buenos Aires: Editorial Huarpes.

GIBSON, C. (1952). Tlaxcala in the sixteenth century. Yale University Press.

GORTARI, E. DE (1963). La ciencia en la historia de México. Mexico: Fondo de Cultura Económica.

GRANDE ENCICLOPEDIA PORTUGUESA E BRASILEIRA [1936–60]. 40 vols. [including 3 vols. of appendices]. Lisbon & Rio de Janeiro: Editorial Enciclopédia.

GUERRA, F. (1949). La primera historia clínica americana. *La Prensa médica mexicana, 14,* 175–182.

GUERRA, F. (1966). The paradox of *The Treasury of Medicines* by Gregorio Lopez (1542–1596). *Clio medica, 1,* 273–288.

GUERRA, F. [ed.]. (1968). José Eleuterio González [1813–1888]: Los médicos y las enfermedades de Monterrey [1881]. London: Wellcome Historical Medical Museum and Library.

GUTIERREZ, J.M. (1860). Apuntes biográficos de escritores, oradores y hombres de estado de la República Argentina. [*Biblioteca Americana*, 7]. Buenos Aires: Imprenta de Mayo.

HAGGIS, A.W. (1941). Fundamental errors in the early history of cinchona. *Bulletin of the History of Medicine*, *10*, 417–459, 568–92.

HARING, C.H. (1947). The Spanish Empire in America. New York: Oxford University Press.

HENIGE, D.P. (1970). Colonial governors from the fifteenth century to the present. A comprehensive list. University of Wisconsin Press.

HERNANDEZ, F. (1960). Obras completas, tomo I. Vida y obra de Francisco Hernández [por] Germán Somolinos D'Ardois. Mexico: Universidad Nacional de México.

HERRING, H. (1968). A history of Latin America. 3 ed. London: Jonathan Cape.

HIRSCH, A. (1929–34; 1935). Biographisches Lexikon der hervorragenden Ärzte aller Zeiten und Völker. 5 vols. (& Nachträge 1–5, 1935). Berlin & Vienna: Urban & Schwarzenberg.

HOWARD, D.A. (1972). The Royal Indian Hospital of Mexico City. [Thesis]. Duke University (University Microfilms, 1975).

HOYOS SAINZ, L. DE (1949). José Celestino Mutis. Naturalista, médico y sacerdote. Madrid: Editora Nacional.

HUMBOLDT, A. VON (1811). Political essay on the Kingdom of New Spain. [*trans.* J. Black]. 4 vols. London: Longman, Hurst [&c.].

INSTRUCCIONES (1873). Instrucciones que los Vireyes de Nueva España dejaron a sus sucesores, tomo 2. [*Biblioteca Histórica de la Iberia*, 14]. Mexico: I. Escalante.

IZQUIERDO, J.J. (1934). Balance cuatricentenario de la fisiología en México. Mexico: Ediciones Ciencia.

IZQUIERDO, J.J. (1937). The first book on physiology written and printed in the New World. *Bulletin of the Institute of the History of Medicine*, *5* (1), 73–90.

IZQUIERDO, J.J. (1955). Montaña y los orígenes del movimiento social y científico de México. Mexico: Ediciones Ciencia.

JARAMILLO-ARANGO, J. (1949). A critical review of the basic facts in the history of cinchona, *Journal of the Linnean Society* (Botany), *53*, 272–311.

KAY, M. (1974). The fusion of Utoaztecan and European ethnogynecology in the Florilegio Medicinal [in] *Actas del XLI Congreso Internacional de Americanistas, México, 2 al 7 de Septiembre de 1974*. 3 vols. Mexico: Instituto Nacional de Antropología e Historia (1975–76, *3*, 323–330).

LA CONDAMINE, C.M. DE (1759). Mémoire sur l'inoculation de la petite vérole [in] *Histoire de l'Académie Royale des Sciences. Année 1754*, 615–670. Paris: l'Imprimerie Royale.

LA CONDAMINE, C.M. DE (1763). Second mémoire sur l'inoculation de la petite vérole [in] *Histoire de l'Académie Royale des Sciences. Année 1758*, 439–482. Paris: l'Imprimerie Royale.

LANDA, E. (1915). El copalchi. Acción fisiológica y propiedades terapéuticas. Resumen de las observaciones hechas en el Instituto Médico Nacional para averiguar las propiedades medicinales de esta planta. *Gaceta médica de México*, *10*, (3 ser,), 125–132.

LANNING, J.T. (1955). The University in the Kingdom of Guatemala. Cornell University Press.

LANNING, J.T. (1956). The eighteenth-century enlightenment in the University of San Carlos de Guatemala. Cornell University Press.

LASTRES, J.B. (1951). Historia de la medicina peruana. 3 vols. Lima: Imprenta Santa María.

LASTRES, J.B. (1954). La cultura peruana y la obra de los médicos en la emancipación. Lima: Editorial San Marcos.

LASTRES, J.B. (1955). Hipólito Unanue. Lima: [s.n.].

LEON, N. (1895). Biblioteca botánico-mexicana. Catálogo bibliográfico, biográfico y crítico de autores y escritos referentes a vegetales de México y sus aplicaciones, desde la conquista hasta el presente. Mexico: Secretaría de Fomento.

LEON, N. (1910). La obstetricia en México. Mexico: Widow of F. Díaz de León.

LEON, N. (1946). Scatológica mexicana. Materias excrementicias y secretoriales animales usadas por los mexicanos precolombinos y actuales [with introduction by Demetrio S. García]. Mexico: Biblioteca Aportación Histórica, Editor Vargas Rea.

LOSA, F. (1727). Vida del Siervo de Dios Gregorio López, ... A que se añaden los escritos del Apocalypsi, y Tesoro de Medicina, del mismo [&c.]. Madrid: Imprenta de J. de Ariztia.

McPHEETERS, D.W. (1955). The distinguished Peruvian scholar Cosme Bueno 1711–1798. *The Hispanic American Historical Review*, *35*, 484–491.

MARTIN, L. (1968). The intellectual conquest of Peru. The Jesuit College of San Pablo, 1568–1767. New York: Fordham University Press.

MARTINDALE, W. (1977). The extra pharmacopoeia. 27 ed. London: The Pharmaceutical Press.

MARTINEZ DURAN, C. (1964). Las ciencias médicas en Guatemala; origen y evolución. 3 ed. Guatemala: Editorial Universitaria.

MAZA, F. DE LA (1943). Enrico Martínez; cosmógrafo e impresor de Nueva España. Mexico: Sociedad Mexicana de Geografía y Estadística.

MAZA, F. DE LA (1948). Los examenes universitarios de Doctor José Ignacio Bartolache en 1772. Prólogo de F. de la M. Mexico: Imprenta Universitaria.

MOLINARI, J.L. (1937). Historia de la medicina argentina; tres conferencias. Buenos Aires: Imprenta López.

MOLINARI, J.L. (1959). El protomédico Miguel Gorman a través de su correspondencia. *Boletín de la Academia Nacional de la Historia, 30*, 257–287.

MOLL, A.A. (1944). Aesculapius in Latin America. Philadelphia & London: W.B. Saunders.

MONTENEGRO, P. DE (1945). Materia médica misionera. Noticia preliminar de Raúl Quintana. Buenos Aires: Imprenta de la Biblioteca Nacional.

MOREAU DE SAINT-MERY, M.L.E. (1958). Description ... de la partie française de l'isle Saint-Domingue. Nouvelle édition entièrement revue et complétée sur le manuscrit ... par B. Maurel et E. Taillemite. 3 vols. Paris: Société de l'Histoire des Colonies Françaises et Librairie Larose.

MURIEL, J. (1956–60). Hospitales de la Nueva España. 2 vols. Mexico: Instituto de Historia, & Editorial Jus.

NORIEGA, J.M. (1902). Curso de historia de drogas. Mexico: Oficina Tipográfica de la Secretaría de Fomento.

NOUVELLE BIOGRAPHIE GENERALE (1855–66). 46 vols. Paris: Firmin Didot Frères.

NUEVA FARMACOPEA MEXICANA (1904). Nueva farmacopea mexicana de la Sociedad Farmacéutica de México. 4 ed. Mexico: Oficina Tipográfica de la Secretaría de Fomento.

ODRIOZOLA, M. DE (1863–76). Colección de documentos literarios del Perú. 8 vols. Lima: A. Alfaro, Imprenta del Estado.

OSORES, F. (1908). Noticias bio-bibliográficas de alumnos distinguidos del Colegio de San Pedro, San Pablo y San Ildefonso de México. [*Documentos inéditos o muy raros para la historia de México, publicados por G. García, 19 & 21*]. 2 vols. Mexico: Widow of C. Bouret.

PEREZ-ARBELAEZ, E. (1956). Plantas útiles de Colombia. 3 ed. Madrid & Bogotá: Sucesores de Rivadeneyra & Librería Colombiana.

PEREZ FONTANA, V. (1967). Historia de la medicina en el Uruguay con especial referencia a las comarcas del Río de la Plata. 2 vols. Montevideo: Ministerio de Salud Pública.

POGGENDORF, J.C. (1863). Biographisch-Literarisches Handwörterbuch zur Geschichte der exacten Wissenschaften. 2 vols. Leipzig: J.A. Barth.

PORRUA. (1964–66). Diccionario Porrua de historia, biografía y geografía de México; y Suplemento. 2 vols. Mexico: Editorial Porrua.

PRIESTLEY, H.I. (1916). José de Gálvez. Visitor-General of New Spain (1765–1771). [*University of California Publication in History, 5*]. University of California Press.

PROTOMEDICATO (1829). Libro perteneciente al Protomedicato Nacional de Méjico hecho en 10 de marzo de 1829. [Copia fiel del libro original que se conserva en la Biblioteca de la Secretaría de Salubridad y Asistencia Pública. Trabajo mecanográfico que se mando hacer por disposición del Dr. Everardo Landa en el año de 1933]. [*Typescript copy in the Wellcome Institute*].

PUNDEL, J.P. (1969). Histoire de l'opération césarienne. Brussels: Presses Académiques Européennes.

RAMIREZ, J. (1902). Sinonimia vulgar y científica de las plantas mexicanas. Mexico: Secretaría de Fomento.

RAMOS, P. (1957). Perfil biográfico de Miguel Jiménez. *Gaceta médica de México*, 1957, 87, 407–410.

RHAME, J.S. (1957). Doctor W.C. Norwood and Norwood's tincture of veratrum viride. *Journal of the South Carolina Medical Association*, 53, 210–212.

RICKETT, H.W. (1947). The Royal Botanical Expedition to New Spain 1788–1820. [*Chronica Botanica*, 11 (1)]. Waltham, Mass.: Chronica Botanica.

ROLDAN Y GUERRERO, R. (1956). Doctor Casimiro Gómez Ortega. [Paper presented to the 15th International Congress of the History of Medicine, Madrid, 1956]. [*A separate; not included in the official volumes of reports of the Congress.*]

SLOANE, H. (1707–25). A voyage to the islands Madera, Barbados, Nieves, S. Christophers and Jamaica. 2 vols. London: B.M. for the author.

SMITH, M.M. (1974). The "Real Expedición Marítima de la Vacuna" in New Spain and Guatemala. *Transactions of the American Philosophical Society*, 64, (N.S.), (1).

SORIANO LLERAS, A. (1966). La medicina en el Nuevo Reino de Granada, durante la conquista y la colonia. Bogotá: Imprenta Nacional.

STEELE, A.R. (1964). Flowers for the king. The expedition of Ruiz and Pavón and the *Flora of Peru*. Duke University Press.

SUSSMAN, G.D. (1971). Etienne Pariset. *Journal of the History of Medicine*, 26, 52–74.

SWANTON, J.R. (1968). The Indian tribes of North America. [Smithsonian Institution, Bureau of American Ethnology, Bulletin 145]. Washington: Smithsonian Institution Press.

THOMPSON, L.S. (1962). Printing in colonial Spanish America. Hamden, Conn.: The Shoe String Press (Archon Books).

THORNTON, R.D. (1963). James Currie, the entire stranger, & Robert Burns. Edinburgh & London: Oliver Boyd.

URIBE URIBE, L. (1954). Los maestros pintores [cap. XXXI, pp. 102–106, *in* Flora de la Real Expedición Botánica del Nuevo Reino de Granada, tomo 1]. Madrid: Ediciones Cultura Hispánica.

VALDIZAN, H. (1923?–61). Diccionario de medicina peruana. 7 vols. Lima: Talleres Gráficos del Hospital "V.L. Herrera"; Anales de la Facultad de Medicina.

VALDIZAN, H. (1927–29). La Facultad de Medicina de Lima. 2 ed. 3 vols. Lima: [s.n.].

VALLE, R.H. (1942). La cirugía mexicana del siglo XIX. Mexico: Tipográfica Sag.

VALLON, C. *and* GENIL-PERRIN, G. (1912). La psychiatrie médico-légale dans l'oeuvre de Zacchias (1584–1659). Paris: O. Doin et fils.

VAN PATTEN, N. (1930). The medical literature of Mexico and Central America. *Papers of the Bibliographical Society of America*, *24*, (1 & 2), 150–199.

VASCONCELLOS, I. DE (1960). Foi autêntico profeta do urbanismo carioca. *Revista Brasileira de História da Medicina*, *11*, 27–29.

VASCONCELLOS, I. DE (1961). O Doutor José Maria Bomtempo—precursor do urbanismo e da higiene pública na Cidade do Rio de Janeiro. *Revista Brasileira de História da Medicina*, *12*, 171–178.

VELASCO CEBALLOS, R. (1946). La cirugía mexicana en el siglo XVIII. Mexico: Secretaría de Salubridad y Asistencia.

VENEGAS RAMIREZ, C. (1973). Régimen hospitalario para indios en la Nueva España. Mexico: Instituto Nacional de Antropología e Historia, Departmento de Investigaciones Históricas.

VENN, J.A. (1940–54). Alumni Cantabrigienses. Pt. II. 1752–1900. 6 vols. Cambridge University Press.

VILLALBA, J. DE (1802). Epidemiología española: o historia cronológica de las pestes, contagios, epidemias y epizootias que han acaecido en España desde la venida de los Cartagineses hasta el año 1801. 2 vols. Madrid: M. Repullés.

WARREN, F.B. (1963). Vasco de Quiroga and his pueblo-hospitals of Santa Fe. Washington, D.C.: Academy of American Franciscan History.

WASERMAN, M.J. *and* MAYFIELD, V.K. (1971). Nicolas Chervin's yellow fever survey, 1820–1822. *Journal of the History of Medicine*, *26*, 40–51.

WELLCOME, SIR H.S. (1887). The story of Metlakahtla. London & New York: Saxon & Co.

WILSON, I.H. (1962). Scientific aspects of Spanish exploration in New Spain during the late eighteenth century. [Thesis]. University of Southern California (University Microfilms, 1975).

WILSON, J.E. (1942). An early Baltimore physician and his medical library. *Annals of Medical History*, *4*, (3 ser.), 63–80.

WOODHAM, J.E. (1970). The influence of Hipólito Unanue on Peruvian medical science, 1789–1820: a reappraisal. *Hispano-American Historical Review*, *50*, 693–714.

WROTH, L.C. (1945). Some reflections on the book arts in early Mexico. Cambridge, Mass.: Harvard College Library, Department of Printing and the Graphic Arts.

XIMENEZ, F. (1888). Cuatro libros de la naturaleza y virtudes medicinales de las plantas y animales de la Nueva España . . . . [Ed.] Nicolás León. Morelia: Escuela de Artes.

7. INDEX

N.B. Numbers followed by ★ refer to main entries. Other numbers in roman type refer to names occurring in titles (or descriptions) of works or imprints; numbers in italics refer to names occurring in annotations.

Gibson, C., *201*

Gil, Francesco, 80★

Gil de Texada, Vicente, 14★, 15

Gilij, Felipe Salvador, 219★

Gillet de Laumont, François Pierre Nicolas, *230*

Gimbernat y Arbós, Antonio de, *143*

Girón, Teresa, *169*

Gomes, Luiz de Sant'Anna, 10★

Gómez de Cossio, Patricio Antonio, *191, 264, 282*

Gómez de Mendiola, Francisco, *130, 131*

Gomez Moron, Sebastian, 66

Gómez Ortega, Casimiro, *66*, 81★, *185, 205,* 211

Gonzáles, Maria Apolonia (Widow of Juan Lorenzo), 220★

Gonzáles, Martina, *281*

Gonzáles de Batres, Manuel, 26

González Avendaño, Francisco, 60

González de Cossio, Francisco, *179, 181*

González del Campillo, Manuel Ignacio, 81★, *82*

González Holguin, Diego, 163★

González Laguna, Francisco, 164★, *185*

González Mendoza, José Eleuterio, 220★

González Urueña, Juan Manuel, 221★

Gorman, Miguel, 2★, *4,* 222★

Gortari, E. de, *263*

Gouan, A., 195

Gouy, *Comte de,* 30

Gracida, Victorio, 257

Gracida y Bernal, José Timoteo María de, 222★, *223,* 255

Granados y Galvez, José Joaquín, 82★

Green, H., 218

Gregory XIII, *Pope,* 85

Guadalajara, *Bishop,* 82★

 Junta Superior de Sanidad, 83★, 84★

Guadalcázar, Diego Fernandez de Córdoba, *Marqués de,* 68

Guatemala, *Bishop,* 23★

 Junta de Salud, 23★

 Laws, statutes, &c., 24★, 26★

Guerra, Francisco, xi, xiv, xv, xvii, xviii, *9,* 60, *89, 119, 201, 213, 214, 218, 220, 231, 233*

Guillena Carrascoso, J. J., 48

Guillena Carrascoso, J. J., Heirs of, 74

Guillot, 32, 36, 39

Guridi y Alcocer, José María, *112*

Gurpegui, José, *65*

Gutiérrez, Alonso. *See* Vera Cruz, A. de la

Gutiérrez, J. M., *188*

Gutiérrez Coronel, Ricardo José, 84★

Gutiérrez del Mazo, Ramón, *256*

Gutiérrez González y Aragón, Juan Guillermo, *3*

Gutiérrez Zavala, Manuel, *202*

Guyon, Jean Casimir Félix, *190*

Haggard, *Sir* H. Rider, *227*

Haggis, A. W., *207*

Harvey, William, *142, 157*

Havana, Imprenta de la Capitanía General, 18, 19

 Imprenta del Comercio, 19

 Typographia Curiae Episcopalis, 16

Heister, L., *10*

Henige, D. P., xiv

Henkel, J. F., *217*

Henríquez de Ribera, Francisca, *207*

Herbault, Widow, 40

Hermandad de la Sta. Caridad, 2★, 3★, 4★

Hermanos de la Caridad de San Hipolito, 84★, 85★

Hernández, Francisco, *51, 53, 151, 185, 205, 286*

Hernandez, Pedro, 67

Hernández de Gregorio, Manuel, *16*

Herrarte, Mariano José de, 223★

Hidalgo y Costillo, Miguel, *71*

Hincapié Meléndez y Mayen, Cristóbal de, *27,* 224★

Hippocrates, *28, 68, 132, 140, 172*

Hirsch, A., *230*

Hogal, J. A. de, 56, 117, 120

Hogal, José Bernardo de, 65, 69, 73, 142, 180, *288*

Hogal, José Bernardo de, Widow of, 58, 63, 91, 93

Holmes, Edward Morell, 226★, 227★

Picanço, José Correia, *9*
Piña, José Joaquín, 266★
Pineda Ibarra, A. de [?], 23
Pinel, Philippe, *7*
Piñera y Siles, Bartolomé, 254
Pío, *of Mariquita, 240*
Pisarro, José Alfonzo, *233*
Pius, V, *Pope, 61*
Plantation, Catherine [Femme de Pierre Bordes], 31, 37
Plenck, J. J. von, *13*
Poggendorf, J. C., *285*
Polony, Jean Louis, 39★
Ponce de Leon, Juan, *51*
Porras Farfán, Pedro de, *199*
Port-au-Prince, Imprimerie du Gouvernement, 184
Prescott, W. H., *239*
Procope-Couteau, Michel, *266*
Procopio Couto, Juan Bautista, 266★
Procopio Couto, Juan María, 266★
Puebla, *Hospital Provisional de San Francisco Xavier,* 132★, *133*
  Hospital Real de San Pedro, 133★, *134*
  Junta de Sanidad, 134★
  Junta Principal de Caridad, 134★
  Oficina del Real y Pontificio Seminario Palafoxiano, 71, 94
Pundel, J. P., 139
Pyne, *Lieut.* Francis, *41*

Quer, José, *223*
Quiñones, Francisco, 27★
Quiroga, Vasco de, 116, *117, 138*

R., T., *Don* [Tomás Romay?], *18*
Raga, Manuel Martín de la, *275*
Ramírez, J., *27*
Ramírez, José Antonio, 267★
Ramirez, Pedro, 135★
Ramos, P., *232*
Ramos de Vilches, Rafael, 135★

Rangel Ortiz, Hernando, *199*
Rea, *67*
Recchi, Nardo Antonio, *151*
Regalado Tames, Pedro, 66
Reich, Gottfried Christian, 11★
Rengel, Pedro, *199*
Revillagigedo, Juan Francisco de Güemes y Horcasitas, *Conde de, Viceroy of New Spain, 1746–55, 50, 64, 119*
Revillagigedo, Juan Vicente de Güemes Pacheco de Padilla Horcasitas y Aguayo, *Conde de, Viceroy of New Spain, 1789–94, 112, 123, 124, 129, 198, 281*
Reyes, Wenceslao, *244*
Reyes Angel, Gaspar de los, 136★, *137*
Rhame, J. S., *218*
Riaño y Bárcena, Juan Antonio, *62, 63*
Ribera, H. de, 69
Ribera, J. de, Widow of [María de Benavides], 130, 141
Ribera, M. de, Widow of, Heirs of, 142
Ribera, María de, 85, 180
Ribera, María de, Heirs of, 55
Ribera Calderón, F. de, 147
Ribera Calderón, M. de, Widow of, Heirs of, 178, 180
Ricardo, Antonio, 75, 90, *164*
Richard, P., 45, 46
Richardson, *Sir* John, *190*
Richerand, Anthelme Balthasar, *Baron, 10,* 12★
Rickett, H. W., *63, 81, 196, 206, 258, 263, 281*
Ricord, P., *253*
Rincon, Joseph del, 103
Rincon y Mendoza, José Jacinto del, 137★
Rio de Janeiro, Impressão Regia, 7, 9, 10, 11, 12
Rio de la Plata, *Laws, statutes, &c.,* 4★, 6★
Rio-Frio, Bernardo de, 137★
Rios Landa, *269*
Rioseco, Manuel, 171
Riva, Juan Antonio de la, 27★, 28
Riva Palacio, M., *243*
Rivilla Barrientos, Juan Antonio de, 138★
Rivilla Bonet y Pueyo, José de, 168★, *169*